Communications in Computer and Information Science 1208

Commenced Publication in 2007
Founding and Former Series Editors:
Simone Diniz Junqueira Barbosa, Phoebe Chen, Alfredo Cuzzocrea,
Xiaoyong Du, Orhun Kara, Ting Liu, Krishna M. Sivalingam,
Dominik Ślęzak, Takashi Washio, Xiaokang Yang, and Junsong Yuan

More information about this series at http://www.springer.com/series/7899

Sabu M. Thampi · Gregorio Martinez Perez ·
Ryan Ko · Danda B. Rawat (Eds.)

Security in Computing and Communications

7th International Symposium, SSCC 2019
Trivandrum, India, December 18–21, 2019
Revised Selected Papers

Springer

Editors
Sabu M. Thampi
Indian Institute of Information Technology
and Management
Trivandrum, India

Ryan Ko
University of Queensland
Brisbane, QLD, Australia

Gregorio Martinez Perez
University of Murcia
Espinardo, Murcia, Spain

Danda B. Rawat
Howard University
Washington, DC, USA

ISSN 1865-0929   ISSN 1865-0937 (electronic)
Communications in Computer and Information Science
ISBN 978-981-15-4824-6   ISBN 978-981-15-4825-3 (eBook)
https://doi.org/10.1007/978-981-15-4825-3

This Springer imprint is published by the registered company Springer Nature Singapore Pte Ltd.
The registered company address is: 152 Beach Road, #21-01/04 Gateway East, Singapore 189721, Singapore

Preface

These proceedings contain the papers presented at the 7th International Symposium on Security in Computing and Communications (SSCC 2019). SSCC aims to provide the most relevant opportunity to bring together researchers and practitioners from both academia and industry to exchange their knowledge and discuss their research findings. The symposium was held in Trivandrum, Kerala, India, during December 18–21, 2019. SSCC 2019 was hosted by the Indian Institute of Information Technology and Management-Kerala (IIITM-K). The symposium was colocated with the International Conference on Applied soft computing and Communication Networks (ACN 2019).

In response to the call for papers, 61 papers were submitted for presentation and inclusion in the proceedings of the conference. The papers were evaluated and ranked on the basis of their significance, novelty, and technical quality. A double-blind review process was conducted to ensure that the author names and affiliations were unknown to the Technical Program Committee (TPC). Each paper was reviewed by the members of the TPC and finally, 22 regular papers and 7 short papers were selected for presentation at the symposium.

We thank the program chairs for their wise advice and brilliant suggestions in organizing the technical program. We would like to extend our deepest appreciation to the Advisory Committee members. Thanks to all members of the TPC, and the external reviewers, for their hard work in evaluating and discussing papers. We wish to thank all the members of the Organizing Committee, whose work and commitment were invaluable. Our most sincere thanks go to all the keynote speakers who shared with us their expertise and knowledge. We wish to thank all the authors who submitted papers and all participants and contributors of fruitful discussions. The EDAS conference system proved very helpful during the submission, review, and editing phases.

We thank IIITM-K for hosting the conference. Our sincere thanks to Dr. Saji Gopinath, Director at IIITM-K, for his continued support and cooperation. Recognition also goes to the Local Organizing Committee members who all worked extremely hard on every detail of the conference programs and social activities. We appreciate the contributions of all the faculty and staff of IIITM-K and the student volunteers who contributed their time to make the conference a great success.

We wish to express our gratitude to the team at Springer for their help and cooperation.

December 2019

Sabu M. Thampi
Gregorio Martinez Perez
Ryan Ko
Danda B. Rawat

Organization

Chief Patron

Madhavan Nambiar IAS (Rtd.) IIITM-K, India

Patron

Saji Gopinath IIITM-K, India

Honorary General Chair

Ravi Sandhu University of Texas at San Antonio, USA

General Chairs

Mauro Conti University of Padua, Italy
Sabu M. Thampi IIITM-K, India
Gregorio Martinez Perez University of Murcia, Spain

Technical Program Chairs

Ryan Ko The University of Queensland, Australia
Danda B. Rawat Howard University, USA
Jose M. Alcaraz Calero University of the West of Scotland, UK

Workshop Chair

Tony Thomas IIITM-K, India

Advisory Committee

Albert Y. Zomaya The University of Sydney, Australia
Sudip Misra IIT Kharagpur, India
Vijay Varadharajan The University of Newcastle, Australia
Sanjay Madria Missouri University of Science and Technology, USA
Mohan S. Kankanhalli National University of Singapore, Singapore
Kim-Kwang Raymond Choo University Texas at San Antonio, USA
Jiankun Hu The University of New South Wales, Australia
Indrakshi Ray Colorado State University, USA
Guojun Wang Guangzhou University, China

Bharat Bhargava	Purdue University, USA
Chun-I Fan	National Sun Yat-sen University, Taiwan
Xavier Fernando	Ryerson University, Canada
B. M. Mehtre	IDRBT, India
Surya Nepal	CSIRO, Australia

Technical Program Committee

Pradeep Atrey	University at Albany, USA
Mario Goldenbaum	Princeton University, USA
Zbigniew Kalbarczyk	University of Illinois at Urbana Champaign, USA
Donghyun Kim	Kennesaw State University, USA
Seungmo Kim	Georgia Southern University, USA
Sanjeev Kumar	The University of Texas Rio Grande Valley, USA
Suryadipta Majumdar	University at Albany, USA
Kyriakos Manousakis	Applied Communication Sciences, USA
Vishnu Pendyala	Santa Clara University, USA
Sherif Rashad	Morehead State University, USA
Mukesh Singhal	University of California at Merced, USA
Bing Wu	Fayetteville State University, USA
Ping Yang	Binghamton University, USA
Meng Yu	Roosevelt University, USA
Peng Zhang	Stony Brook University, USA
Alberto Huertas Celdrán	University of Pennsylvania, USA
Giuseppe Raffa	Intel Corporation, USA
Zhiyuan Zheng	Texas A&M University, USA
Connie Justice	Purdue School of Engineering and Technology, IUPUI, USA
Thomas Austin	San Jose State University, USA
Sang-Yoon Chang	University of Colorado Colorado Springs, USA
Yang Xiao	The University of Alabama, USA
Ye Zhu	Cleveland State University, USA
Stavros Shiaeles	University of Plymouth, UK
Steven Furnell	University of Plymouth, UK
Mohamad Badra	CNRS, France, and Zayed University, UAE
Youssef Said	Tunisie Telecom, Tunisia
Chin-Chen Chang	Feng Chia University, Taiwan
Young-Long Chen	National Taichung University of Science and Technology, Taiwan
Chin-Laung Lei	National Taiwan University, Taiwan
Chung-Huang Yang	National Kaohsiung Normal University, Taiwan
Chang Wu Yu	Chung Hua University, Taiwan
Rolf Oppliger	eSECURITY Technologies, Switzerland
Martin Hell	Lund University, Sweden
Josep-Lluis Ferrer-Gomila	University of Balearic Islands, Spain
Antonio Ruiz-Martínez	University of Murcia, Spain

Gerardo Pelosi	Politecnico di Milano, Italy
Orazio Tomarchio	University of Catania, Italy
Aneel Rahim	Dublin Institute of Technology, Ireland
Karim Al-Saedi	Mustansiriyah University, Iraq
Abdalhossein Rezai	ACECR, Iran
Salman Abdul Moiz	University of Hyderabad, India
Ashok Kumar Das	IIIT Hyderabad, India
Dhananjoy Dey	DRDO, India
G. R. Gangadharan	IDRBT, India
Angelina Geetha	Hindustan Institute of Technology and Science, India
Shreenivas Jog	Savitribai Phule of Pune University, India
Jenila Livingston	VIT Chennai, India
Jinesh M. Kannimoola	Amrita Vishwa Vidyapeetham, India
Dheerendra Mishra	IIT Kharagpur, India
Purushothama R.	NIT Goa, India
Balaji Rajendran	Centre for Development of Advanced Computing, India
Sushmita Ruj	Indian Statistical Institute Kolkata, India
Navanath Saharia	IIIT Manipur, India
Pritam Shah	Dayananda Sagar University, India
Shina Sheen	PSG College of Technology, India
Tarun Yadav	Ministry of Defence (GOI), India
Dija S.	Centre for Development of Advanced Computing, India
Divya Vidyadharan	College of Engineering Trivandrum, India
Avishek Adhikari	Presidency University, India
Man Ho Au	The Hong Kong Polytechnic University, Hong Kong
Aldar Chun-Fai Chan	Hong Kong R&D Centre for LSCM, Hong Kong
Apostolos Fournaris	University of Patras, Greece
Sophia Petridou	University of Macedonia, Greece
Dimitrios Stratogiannis	National Technical University of Athens, Greece
Nikolaos Bardis	Hellenic Military Academy, Greece
Christos Bouras	University of Patras, CTI&P-Diophantus, Greece
Stefanos Gritzalis	University of the Aegean, Greece
Nicolas Sklavos	University of Patras, Greece
Feng Cheng	University of Potsdam, Germany
Andreas Dewald	ERNW Research GmbH, Germany
Thomas Gamer	ABB AG, Germany
Michael Steinke	Bundeswehr University Munich, Germany
Kira Kastell	Frankfurt University of Applied Sciences, Germany
Wolfgang Hommel	Bundeswehr University Munich, Germany
Andreas Noack	University of Applied Sciences Stralsund, Germany
Karima Boudaoud	University of Nice Sophia Antipolis, France
Mounir Kellil	CEA LIST, France
Turker Yilmaz	EURECOM, France
Badis Hammi	Télécom ParisTech, France

Francine Krief	University of Bordeaux, France
Pascal Lorenz	University of Haute Alsace, France
Mohamed Mosbah	LaBRI, Bordeaux University, France
Farid Nait-Abdesselam	Paris Descartes University, France
Kester Quist-Aphetsi	University of Brest France, France
Weizhi Meng	Technical University of Denmark, Denmark
Michael McGuire	University of Victoria, Canada
Reihaneh Safavi-Naini	University of Calgary, Canada
Omar Abdel Wahab	Concordia University, Canada
Dongxiao Liu	University of Waterloo, Canada
Hanine Tout	École de Technologie Supérieure, Canada
Maicon Stihler	Federal Center for Technological Education (CEFET-MG), Brazil
Paulo de Lira Gondim	Universidade de Brasilia, Brazil
Edward Moreno	Federal University of Sergipe, Brazil
Al-Sakib Khan Pathan	Southeast University, Bangladesh
Sasan Adibi	Deakin University, Australia
Mohiuddin Ahmed	Canberra Institute of Technology, Australia
Zubair Baig	Deakin University, Australia
Sheng Wen	Swinburn University, Australia
Robin Doss	Deakin University, Australia
Mourad Amad	Bouira University, Algeria

Organized by

IIITM-Kerala

Contents

Malware Detection in Android Applications Using Integrated Static Features

A. S. Ajeena Beegom$^{(\boxtimes)}$ and Gayatri Ashok

Department of Computer Science and Engineering,
College of Engineering Trivandrum, Thiruvananathapuram, Kerala, India
ajeena@cet.ac.in, gayu.lalitha@gmail.com

Abstract. Android operating systems based mobile phones are common in nowadays due to its ease of use and openness. Hundreds of Android based mobile applications are uploaded in the internet every day, which can be benign or malicious. The increase in the growth of malicious Android applications is alarming. Hence advanced solutions for the detection of malware is needed. In this paper, a novel malware detection framework is proposed that uses integrated static features and Support Vector Machine (SVM) classifier. The static features considered include permissions, API calls and opcodes. Out of these features, most significant ones are selected using Pearson correlation coefficient and N-grams. Each of these features are then integrated and fed to a classifier. The experimental evaluation of the proposed method and comparison with existing methods shows that the proposed framework is better.

Keywords: Android · Malware detection · Classification · Static features

1   Introduction

Android based devices have become famous in this digital era spanning over millions of users. This makes it the major target of attack through malicious application programs known as malware. The malware available in the market are *Botnets, Rootkits, SMS Trojans, Spyware, Installer, Ransomware, Trojans*, etc.

Botnet is a collection of devices known as *bots* that are connected through internet. Attacks such as distributed denial of service (DDoS) is performed by *Botnets*. *Rootkit* is a group of computer software structured to enforce access to a computer system that is restricted otherwise. *SMS Trojans* send SMS messages stealthily to premium numbers and without the user consent. *Spyware* is a software which is capable of gathering information regarding a person without their consent and communicate those information to another entity without the consumer knowing it. *Ransomware* is a malicious software that demands an amount as ransom for access to user data or it threatens to either publish his

© Springer Nature Singapore Pte Ltd. 2020
S. M. Thampi et al. (Eds.): SSCC 2019, CCIS 1208, pp. 1–10, 2020.
https://doi.org/10.1007/978-981-15-4825-3_1

data or block his data if ransom is not paid. *Trojans* are capable of modifying or deleting data from the device without the user consent infecting personal computers when the device is connected via USB port.

Figure 1 shows the top 10 malware sent out by the MS-ISAC Security Operations Center (SOC) (https://www.cisecurity.org/ms-isac/) showing their percentage shares in January 2018. Each of them belong to any one of the malwares described above. This has motivated us to investigate more on the topic of malware detection techniques for Android applications. In this work, permissions, API calls and source code are analyzed and Android applications are classified as benign or malicious using machine learning techniques.

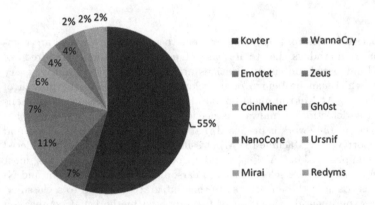

Fig. 1. Malware Seen in January 2018 (https://www.cisecurity.org/ms-isac/)

2   Related Works

Among the static-based approaches for malware detection using permissions, the technique used by Ju [1] and Pehlivan et al. [2] are simple, but corresponds to a bulk feature set that is difficult to process. Wang et al. [3] use three different ranking techniques for identifying the risk-induced permissions from feature set to reduce processing time. Li et al. [4] propose a three-step procedure to identify significant permissions. The steps include permission ranking with negative rate, support based permission ranking and permission mining with association rules. A classifier is then used to classify the application as malicious or benign. Aung et al. [5] suggest a three steps procedure consisting of feature selection, K-means clustering model generation and classification. Kang et al. [6] uses creators information along with permissions, API sequences and system commands for malware detection and classification. SVM based classification is used by Li et al. [7] that uses risky permissions and vulnerable API calls. Machine learning based approaches and multiple classifiers are employed by Milosevic et al. [8] for static analysis.

DroidAPIMiner [9] considers the critical API's capable of distinguishing between malicious and benign applications. Another API based analysis tool is DroidAnalyzer [10] for applications where it decompresses the *apk* files and parses through the assembly codes to come up with keywords and risky API's related to abnormal behavior by assigning suspicion level to each application. Since it uses MD5 hash values in the database, overhead of maintaining a bulky database is avoided, but it is unable to detect code obfuscation. Atici et al. [11] proposed a static feature based technique using control flow graphs. This method is efficient for malware using obfuscation techniques, but it is weak against zero-day attacks. Zhu et al. [12] have proposed a complex method based on deep learning and static analysis that use APIs and the source code of Android applications. Obfuscation-resilient malware detection is proposed in [13].

3 Proposed Approach

The proposed system works in four different phases, namely disassembling, feature extraction, feature selection and classification. Three static features are combined to give the maximum accuracy using appropriate selection techniques. The proposed system architecture is shown in Fig. 2.

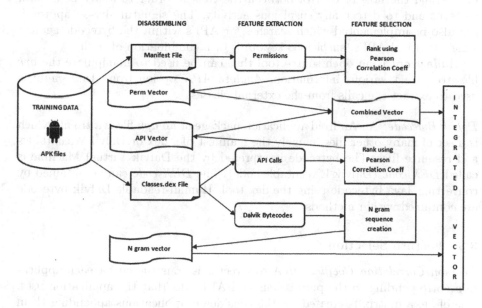

Fig. 2. Proposed framework using integrated static features

3.1 Disassembling

Android Applications contain many prominent files and folders, namely, *META-INF, lib/, res/, Android Manifest.xml, classes.dex* and *resources.arsc*. Among these, the *manifest.xml* and *classes.dex* has the permissions and API calls used by the application respectively. To classify an application as malicious or benign, the Android application package (the *apk* file) needs to be disassembled. This is done using tools such as *apktol, dex2jar, jdgui* etc. Features such as permissions and API calls are extracted from these which is used for building the feature set.

3.2   Feature Extraction

Permissions: Permissions are the basic access rights given to an Android application that helps to control or enforce security against the misuse of sensitive information of users. These permissions can be extracted from the Android *manifest* file from the Android package. Among the permissions considered, significant permissions can be extracted using various techniques. Python libraries are used to extract permissions from the manifest file and to eliminate duplicates.

API Calls: These are a set of procedures and protocols for building an Android application. This information is extracted from the source code and considered as one of the key features. Many malware detection systems are control flow graph (CFG) based or signature-based which uses APIs as features. CFGs are used to understand the flow of control between the calls in order to study behavioral patterns and to detect any suspicious activity. The signature-based approach can also be implemented which searches for API's within the bytecode against a list of critical API's, suspicious keywords or a combination of both.

    Androguard is an open source tool that can be used to manipulate the *apk* files to extract various information. *Analyze APK* option from *Androguard* is used to extract the calls from the external classes.

Dalvik Bytecode: An Android application package or an *apk* file is a zip file which is a set of many other files, namely the manifest file, dex or Dalvik executables and resource files. The bytecode interpreted by the Dalvik Virtual Machine is called *DEX code* (Dalvik EXecutable code). The *DEX code* can be obtained by converting Java bytecode using the dex tool. Human-readable Dalvik bytecode are contained within methods.

3.3   Feature Selection

Pearson Correlation Coefficient: A row vector is constructed for each application corresponding to the permissions and API calls that the application uses. Therefore, a matrix is created for the considered applications appending them with their corresponding class variables as a final column. The class variable signifies to which class the application falls to. A value of 1 is given for a benign class and 0 is given for a malicious class. The pre-processing begins by performing ranking over this constructed matrix using Pearson correlation coefficient [1]. The permission or API variable obtained after disassembling is denoted by X, which is the column vectors of the constructed matrix and the class variable is denoted by C. Column vectors can have a value of 1 which specifies that the corresponding permission is used or 0 specifies that it is not used. The equation (1) can be used to compute the relevance of these variables, using covariance and variance over given data.

$$R(X,C) = \frac{cov(X,C)}{\sqrt{var(X)var(C)}} \tag{1}$$

where cov represents the covariance between two sets of data and var represents the variance over a set of data. Since our case deals with binary classes and Boolean variables, equation (1) is changed to equation (2).

$$R(X,C) = \frac{\sum_{n=1}^{N}(X_n - \overline{X}) * (C_n - \overline{C})}{\sqrt{\sum_{n=1}^{N}(X_n - \overline{X})^2 \sum_{n=1}^{N}(C_n - \overline{C})^2}} \tag{2}$$

Table 1. The 10 most risky permissions and API calls obtained

Rank	Score	Permission	Score	API Calls
1	0.422	READ_EXTERNAL_STORAGE	0.432	abortBroadcast()
2	0.385	RECIEVE_SMS	0.426	chmod()
3	0.380	BIND_GET_INSTALL_PACKAGE	0.401	startService()
4	0.204	BLUETOOTH	0.394	writeTextMessage()
5	0.179	GET_PACKAGE_SIZE	0.382	getrunningTask()
6	0.166	WAKE_LOCK	0.343	sendTextMessage()
7	0.164	CSD_MESSAGE	0.302	setupWindow()
8	0.162	PACKAGE_USAGE_STATS	0.278	setInputstream()
9	0.160	INSTALL_SHORTCUT	0.256	startActivity()
10	0.159	EXPAND_STATUS_BAR	0.224	setVisibility()

The average of all sample values of X is denoted by $\overline{X}$, X_n denotes the total number of samples considered and n can have a value ranging from 1 to N. $R(X,C)$ has a value in the range $[-1,1]$, and if it holds a value 0 then it indicates that X and C are independent, whereas a value of 1 indicates that there is a strong positive correlation between X and C and a value of -1 indicates a strong negative correlation between the variables. In this work we assumed that $R(X,C) = 1$ means that the permission request of X makes applications highly risky whereas $R(X,C) = -1$ means that the permission request of X makes applications less risky. This ranking method is used to consider only the top k features for classification avoiding unnecessary processing. Table 1 shows the scores ($R(X, C)$ value) of the top ten ranked permissions and API calls obtained on our evaluation. Pearson correlation coefficient is used for feature selection over the extracted permission and API vectors.

N-gram: N-gram is a continuous sequence of N items which is extracted from a text sample or a piece of speech. The output of the N-gram opcode extraction is a vector of unique N-gram opcodes from all the classes of the application containing the frequency of each unique N-gram opcode. The opcode sequence generation is shown in Fig. 3.

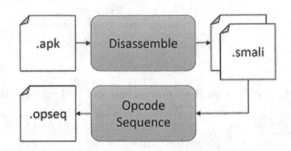

Fig. 3. N-gram opcode generation

An Android application package or *apk* file is a zip file which is a set of many other files, namely, the manifest file, dex or Dalvik Executable and resource files. Disassembling of dex files is done by a process called baksmaling. Set of smali files is extracted from the dex files and each class is represented using a smali file and all the methods are contained within the class. Using N-gram as the feature selection technique a N-gram vector is generated.

3.4 Classification

As shown in Fig. 2, the combined vector of permissions and API calls is integrated with the N-gram vector to give the integrated vector which is then fed to the classifier. The classifier then classifies the test data samples into benign or malicious. Support Vector Machines (SVM), Random Forest or Decision Trees can be used for classification purpose. Depending on the dataset, a cross fold validation is applied for obtaining the training and the test data sets and a corresponding classifier that yields the best results can be selected.

4   Experimental Setup and Evaluation

The analysis is conducted on 500 malicious and 500 benign *apk* samples collected from *Virus share* and *Google Play Store* respectively. The environment is set up on a laptop that runs on *Ubuntu 16.04* and the analysis was conducted using

Python 3.6. Permissions are extracted using the *aapt dump* command provided by *Python* which writes these into text files which is further used for classification. Ranking of permissions are done using Pearson Correlation Coefficient and the top 220 permissions from the extracted 450 are considered for classification. To identify the best classifier, the top 220 permissions identified by the ranking method using Pearson Correlation Coefficient are fed to SVM classifier, KNN classifier and Random Forest classifier by varying the number of top permissions. Figure 4 shows the variation in accuracy levels by each of these classifiers according to the change in the number of top-ranked permissions as features. As seen in this figure, the SVM based classifier gives better results than the other two classifiers for any number of permissions as features.

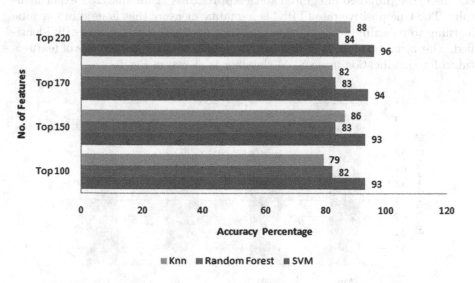

Fig. 4. Classification accuracy versus number of permissions

Androguard is used to extract API calls from the *apk* files and permissions are extracted using Python tools. Baksmaling is executed in order to obtain the N-gram sequences from the sample data. Individually these features are again fed to SVM classifier and Random Forest classifier and the results are analyzed. Table 2 shows the classification results of individual as well as the integrated approach using both SVM and Random Forest classifiers which yield the maximum accuracy using cross validation. The total number of permissions taken for study include 220 with the number of API calls as 460 and the N-grams as 400. The proposed framework achieves a precision of 0.91 and a recall of 0.90 with SVM classifier.

Table 2. Classification results

	Classification accuracy	
Features	SVM	Random forest
Using API calls alone	90%	83%
Using permissions alone	93%	84%
Using Dalvik bytecodes Alone	90%	84%
Integrated static approach	96%	84%

As the SVM based classifier gives better results than Random Forest based classifier, the proposed integrated static approach is again analyzed experimentally. The true positive rate (TPR) is a quality measure that is used in machine learning to measure the proportion of actual positives that are correctly identified. The variation of TPR on malware detection with the percentage of features taken for classification using SVM classifier is shown in Fig. 5.

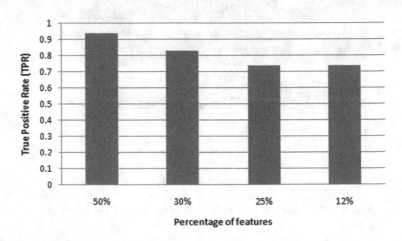

Fig. 5. TPR versus percentage of features

Table 3 shows the comparison of the proposed SVM based integrated static approach with existing systems. SigPID [14] is an Android malware detection system that applies a ranking technique over permissions and does a multi-level pruning process to extract only the significant ones that attains an accuracy of 91%. There are other systems that use sensitive APIs as features [15] which secures an accuracy percentage of 92%. The comparison is also done for existing SVM based systems that uses incremental SVM for classification [16] that has an accuracy of 90.5% whereas the proposed system has an accuracy of 96%.

These studies shows that the proposed framework of integrated static features using SVM classifier for the detection of Android applications as malicious or benign is better than the existing algorithms.

Table 3. Comparison with existing systems

System	Accuracy
Sigpid [4]	91.97%
Detection based on sensitive APIs [15]	92%
Detection based on multi-modal features [17]	94%
Detection based on incremental SVM [16]	90.5%
Proposed integrated system using SVM classifier	**96%**

5 Conclusion and Future Work

Different malware families and their attacks on the current scenario are discussed. To overcome these attacks, an integrated static approach for Android malware detection is proposed. The approach uses various static features in a way to yield the maximum accuracy. From the experimental evaluation and analysis, it is evident that the support vector machine is the best classifier to work with the sample data chosen. The integrated approach attains the maximum accuracy in comparison to the individual static-based methods yielding an accuracy of 96% for the test data. To continue with the work, more dynamic features can be added to enhance the classification efficiency.

References

1. Ju, X.: Android malware detection through permission and package. In: Proceedings of International Conference on Wavelet Analysis and Pattern Recognition, vol. 1, p. 1. IEEE (2014)
2. Pehlivan, U., Baltaci, N., Acartürk, C., Baykal, N.: The analysis of feature selection methods and classification algorithms in permission based android malware detection. In: Proceedings of IEEE Symposium on Computational Intelligence in Cyber Security (CICS), pp. 1–8 (2014)
3. Wang, W., Wang, X., Feng, D., Liu, J., Han, Z., Zhang, X.: Exploring permission-induced risk in android applications for malicious application detection. IEEE Trans. Inf. Forensics Secur. 9(11), 1869–1882 (2014)
4. Li, J., Sun, L., Yan, Q., Li, Z., Srisa-an, W., Ye, H.: Significant permission identification for machine learning based android malware detection. IEEE Trans. Industr. Inf. 14(7), 3216–3225 (2018)
5. Aung, Z., Zaw, W.: Permission based android malware detection. Int. J. Sci. Technol. Res. 2(3), 228–234 (2013)
6. Kang, H., Jang, J., Mohaisen, A., Kim, H.K.: Detecting and classifying android malware using static analysis along with creator information. Int. J. Distrib. Sens. Netw. 11(6), 479174 (2015)
7. Li, W., Ge, J., Dai, G.: Detecting malware for android platform: an SVM-based approach. In: Proceedings of 2nd IEEE International Conference on Cyber Security and Cloud Computing, pp. 464–469 (2015)
8. Milosevic, N., Dehghantanha, A., Choo, K.R.: Machine learning aided android malware classification. Comput. Electr. Eng. 61, 266–274 (2017)

9. Aafer, Y., Du, W., Yin, H.: DroidAPIMiner: mining API-Level features for robust malware detection in android. In: Zia, T., Zomaya, A., Varadharajan, V., Mao, M. (eds.) SecureComm 2013. LNICST, vol. 127, pp. 86–103. Springer, Cham (2013). https://doi.org/10.1007/978-3-319-04283-1_6

10. Seo, S.H., Gupta, A., Sallam, A.M., Bertino, E., Yim, K.: Detecting mobile malware threats to homeland security through static analysis. J. Netw. Comput. Appl. **38**, 43–53 (2014)

11. Atici, M.A., Sagiroglu, S., Dogru, I.A.: Android malware analysis approach based on control flow graphs and machine learning algorithms. In: Proceedings of 4th International Symposium on Digital Forensics and security (ISDFS), pp. 26–31. IEEE (2016)

12. Zhu, R., Li, C., Niu, D., Zhang, H., Ki-nawi, H.: Android Malware Detection Using Large-scale Network Representation Learning, p. 1. Cornell University (2018)

13. Suarez-Tangil, G., Dash, D.K., Ahmadi, M., Kinder, J., Giacinto, G., Cavallaro, L.: DroidSieve: fast and accurate classification of obfuscated android malware. In: Proceedings of Seventh ACM on Conference on Data and Application Security and Privacy, pp. 309–320 (2017)

14. Sun, L., Li, Z., Yan, Q., Srisa-an, W., Pan, Y.: SigPID: significant permission identification for android malware detection. In: Proceedings of 11th International Conference on Malicious and Unwanted Software (MALWARE), pp. 1–8. IEEE (2016)

15. Narayanan, A., Chandramohan, M., Chen, L., Liu, Y.: Context-aware, adaptive, and scalable android malware detection through online learning. IEEE Trans. Emerg. Top. Comput. Intell. **1**(3), 157–1575 (2017)

16. Li, Y., Ma, Y., Chen, M., Dai, Z.: A detecting method for malicious mobile application based on incremental SVM. In: Proceedings of 3rd IEEE International Conference on Computer and Communications (ICCC), pp. 1246–1250. IEEE (2017)

17. Ban, T., Takahashi, T., Guo, S., Inoue, D., Nakao, K.: Integration of multi-modal features for android malware detection using linear SVM. In: Proceedings of 11th Asia Joint Conference on Information Security (AsiaJCIS), pp. 141–146. IEEE (2016)

Intrusion Prediction and Detection with Deep Sequence Modeling

Gaurav Sarraf[(✉)] and M. S. Swetha

Department of Information Science and Engineering,
B. M. S. Institute of Technology, Bangalore, India
sarrafgsarraf@gmail.com, swethams_ise2014@bmsit.in

Abstract. With the wide adoption of the internet and its applications in recent years, many antagonists have been exploiting information exchange for malicious activities. Intrusion detection and prevention systems are widely researched areas, rightly so being an integral part of network security. Adoption of IDSs and IPSs in networks have shown significant results while expanding research from software solutions to hardware-based solutions, promoting such defensive techniques even further. As with all recent computing trends, Machine Learning and Deep Learning techniques have become extremely prevalent in intrusion detection and prediction systems. There have been attempts to improve state of the art, but none is projecting any significant improvement over the current systems. Traditional systems alert the user after an intrusion has occurred, steps can be taken to stop further expansion of the intrusion, but in most cases, it is too late. Hence catering to this issue, this paper proposes system call prediction using a Recurrent Neural Network (RNNs) and Variational Autoencoding modelling techniques to predict sequences of system calls of a modern computer system. The proposed model makes use of ADFA intrusion dataset to learn long term sequences of system-call executed during an attack on a Linux based web server. The model can to effectively predict and classify sequences of system-calls most likely to occur during a known or unknown (zero-day) attacks.

Keywords: Intrusion prediction · Auto-encoding sequence-to-sequence neural-network · Network security · System-call prediction · Cyber-security

1 Introduction

With the vast amounts of data availability and open access to the internet, it has become essential to make it as secure as possible. Securing network infrastructure has become integral because of vast amounts of financial transactions and personal information on stake. Stoneburner et al. [1] discusses important security objectives including availability, integrity, confidentiality, accountability and assurance of data, which is the core ideology of these systems. Almost all intrusions are classified into four classes by popular datasets like KDD Cup

© Springer Nature Singapore Pte Ltd. 2020
S. M. Thampi et al. (Eds.): SSCC 2019, CCIS 1208, pp. 11–25, 2020.
https://doi.org/10.1007/978-981-15-4825-3_2

99 and others, namely probing, denial of service (DoS), user to root (U2R), and remote to user (R2L) attacks. Intrusions can be stopped by static firewalls systems or by deploying more dynamic solutions such as network-based or host-based intrusion detection systems. Both of these options are widely studied and used in enterprise systems.

Intrusion Detection Systems (IDS) are of two types, first, are the network-based IDS analyze all the traffic flowing to and from all the different host on the network they are usually installed on network borders like routers and managed switches. Second, host-based IDS are installed on the user's computer itself, and they are usually installed on all the computers of a network. They can classify peculiar network packets that originate from inside the local network. These systems are further divided as signature-based systems and anomaly-based detection systems. Signature-based detection systems have a database of attack patterns; every packet of network traffic is compared with the saved pattern, detecting abnormal behaviour. These kinds of systems, though easy to use, are useless when the system encounters a zero-day attack. The database of these systems require detailed knowledge of the intrusion and needs frequent updates [2].

On the other hand, Anomaly-based detection systems analyze network behaviour, defined by the network admins or it is learned automatically by the system during its learning phase from datasets. These systems have precise rules of normal and abnormal behaviour. Anomaly-based systems do a better job at detecting unknown attacks [3], but the set of rules defines how well the system performs, which depends on the expertise of network admins. This also means that the system has a high false-positive rate due to strict rules for an 'anomaly' [3].

System-call (SC) analysis for intrusion detection has been discussed by Forrest et al. [4], this idea was less stable did not understand the meaning of the calls made because it analyzed only the frequency of calls. This paper is going to try to solve this problem by learning from SC sequences. A possible solution to the problem stated is to create a system prediction model using end-to-end neural network [5], which can be used to predict SC based on requests made during the attack.

There is a surprising amount of similarity in modern computers, SC and human language. Natural Language processing has an inherent need for languages semantic, meaning understanding for any meaningful results; this, in combination with sequences of words under analysis, has been tried and tested in multiple models before. Industries choice for such kinds of processing is always different variants of RNNs as they are quite efficient in solving sequential problems. Language Processing problems such as Question & Answer, Translation, Word-To-Vector make use of sequence-to-sequence (seq2seq) auto-encoding framework discussed by Chung et al. [6]. The advantage of this method is that it will not only identify malicious sequences in real-time but should also be able to predict a sequence of future SC likely to be executed during an attack.

This paper shows how a language model can be used to predict intrusions of all kinds, including zero-day attacks with the aim of lower false alarm rate compared to other AI-based IDSs [7]. In the follow-up sections of this paper, Sect. 2 discusses Related Work in both deep learning and prediction and detection systems, Sect. 3 explains the system-call model, Sect. 4 describes various models used in the experiment, the results and conclusion.

2   Related Work

2.1   Deep Learning

Recurrent Neural Networks (RNN): While dealing with sequential learning problems, RNNs are an obvious choice [28–30]. They have generated exceptional results in problems such as captioning image, synthesis of speech, and music generation, video analysis, and musical information retrieval. They are suited exceptionally well where the raw underlying features are not individually interpretable like machine perception tasks. RNNs model requires a sequence of input data and the *target* is also a sequence; this makes it seq2seq model. The model though initially designed for temporal sequence structures, works equally well for non-temporal data making it even more powerful. All of these features are due to the introduction of cycles in RNNs computation graph, enabling it to have "memory" to store previous states information.

A statistical model of language proposed by Bengio et al. [8] uses a sequence of sensible sentences to compute the probability of the next word. A sensible sentence should be easily understood and should not have grammatical errors. Models formula is as follows:

$$p(w_1^T) = \prod_{t=1}^{T} p(w_t|w_1^{t-1}) \tag{1}$$

Where w_t stands for the tth word in the sequence, and $T = (w_1, w_2, ..., w_3)$ is the given sentence. The above model, though efficient, is still computationally expensive. The solution to this problem is using the n-gram model, which takes advantage of the fact that temporally closer words in the word sequence are statistically more dependent. Thus the conditional probability of the next word is computed by the formula:

$$p(w_t|w_1^{t-1}) \approx p(w_t|w_{t-n+1}^{t-1}) \tag{2}$$

A traditional RNN theoretically can hold information in memory for infinitely long sequences when trained with Backpropagation through time [9]. The RNN model is incapable of training on long inputs due to problems of gradient explosion or gradient vanishing [10]. This is called the long-term dependency problem which is solved up to an extent by implementing Long Short-Term Memory (LSTM) and Gated Recurrent Unit (GRU) which can remember important information of long sequences of any length. This paper implements the above language model, words and sentences are replaced by the sequence of SC.

Restricted Boltzmann Machine (RBM): In the area of network security RBMs have been a popular choice for IDS because of its ability to solve multiple problems like reduction of dimensionality, collaborative filtering, classification, feature learning and regression making the implementation of these models quite easy. A single algorithm is capable of solving many problems with just minor adjustments to the base model, not to mention the models' models' simple architecture. A simple RBN is a stochastic neural network, where stochastic meaning where every neuron activation has a probabilistic element and neural network, meaning neurons have binary activation based on the neighbours they are connected to. RBM has just two layers and a bias, first is an input layer, second is a hidden layer with latent factors to be learned. This nature of the RBM does not stop it from expanding; the model can easily be made to act like building blocks of a Deep Belief Network (DBNs).

DBNs and RBMs with Classification Layers: Another Deep Learning ideology to be considered is a combination of two or more models which is seen in many variants of RBMs, especially DBNs. Fully connected layer or layers can be added to DBNs as a classification layer to perform classification, which can be trained by applying unsupervised learning as a comprehensive feature extractor instead of using a different technique altogether. These kinds of systems quite useful in acoustic modelling, speech and image recognition. A significant issue explored by Benigo et al. [11,12] with such systems are though the feature extraction is unsupervised, the layers require labelled data.

2.2 Intrusion Prediction and Detection Systems

Intrusion Prediction: There has been a considerable amount of research on prediction system; Hidden Markov Models are the choice for most of the researchers [13,14] to observe previous information and predict the next probable stage of intrusion. Network attack graph based on many attack scenarios was first analyzed by Li et al. [15], the probability of every attack scenario was computed based on the previous location of attack node on the graph. SCl prediction was modelled by Feng et al. [16], in which the author uses a dynamic Bayesian Network to predict the following actions or SC. The idea proposed by Zhang et al. [13] is a combination of intruder classification and anomaly event prediction by developing a hidden Markov model. All of the above-referenced papers use the KDD cup99 dataset.

All of the methodology stated above have a fundamental problem of dependence of limited sequences. The probability computation of the next event is based on only a minimal number of short steps, which should eventually lead to loss of critical information, significantly affecting the prediction result. HMM have the problem of convergence of local optimal point, which makes it challenging to obtain high accuracy [14].

Intrusion Detection: SC modelling introduced by Forrest et al. [4], where a short sequence of SC of a process was to detect intrusions. Recently, neural networks have been the choice forward, showing significant advancements in these systems. LSTM neural network introduced by Staudemeyer et al. [17]. Introduction of the RNN language model by Kim et al. managed to outperform all the other methodology. All of the above-referenced papers use the KDD cup99 dataset and detect intrusions which have already occurred and in no way can warn about an attack which might occur shortly.

3   System-Call Modelling

3.1   Approach Outline

SC modelling is an approach proposed by this paper where we use seq2seq model from machine Question and Answer models to generate SC of a Linux server with previously invoked sequences as questions and generated sequences as answers. This model is divided into two distinct components for the sake of simplicity.

First, is a recurrent auto-encoding seq2seq model, which was first designed with LSTM units and then another model is designed with GRU units, the data from both models are compared in coming sections. The models above are designed to be auto-encoding in nature which helps in denoising the data and also introduces an attention mechanism to improve the models' accuracy. Second, the objective of this component is to improve the performance of multiple classification algorithms by not only giving it information of the invoked SC but also extending the input information by combining the predicted data. Figure 1 shows the above model.

To test the system, the attacks were carried out by a computer locally in the network running Linux Kali. Kali has all the tools installed to carry out similar attacks as the datasets. To test unknown or zero-day attacks, tool exploiting vulnerabilities discovered after 2017 were also used. This was done because the dataset used was released in 2014, thus, simulating a zero-day scenario.

3.2   Prediction Model

Sequence-to-Sequence Model: Question and Answer models are an inspiration towards this approach, we assume the sequence of SC as questions and predicted sequences as answers. These kinds of models deploy an RNN language model; that's what we use here as the generative model. The language model helps us generate semantically correct sequences of SC based on the input sequence. All sequence to one or many models [18] is essentially an elaborate implementation of the encoder-decoder framework. Like any question and answer system, this too is a many-to-many mapping between the input and output.

Just like human conversations, we first understand the input sentence/question 'source', first and then frame an output sentence/answer 'target', by understanding the sequence of input first. The framework does the same, it

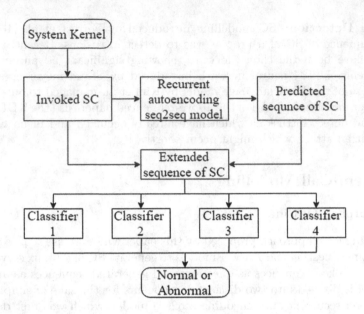

Fig. 1. Prediction model

takes the SC as *source* and generates a *target* SC sequence. It is obvious that we first need to know the words of a language to make sentences; therefore, even our model first needs a vocabulary of SC to generate sequences of calls. Hence we create three sets as shown in Fig. 2, of words/SC where $x_i, y_i \in S, s = \{1, 2, 3, ..., n\}$ where n are all the SC of an OS, $s = \{x_1, x_2, x_3, ..., x_n\}$ represent *source* SC and $s = \{y_1, y_2, y_3, ..., y_m\}$ represents *target* SC. The sets are used by the encoder to generate hidden states at any instance of computation which is given by the formula:

$$y_t = w^{YH} h_t \tag{3}$$

$$h_t = \Sigma(w^{HX} x_t + w^{HH} h_{t-1}) \tag{4}$$

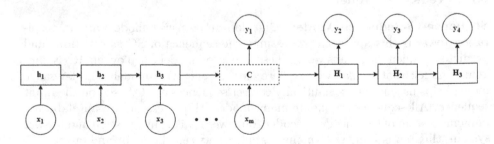

Fig. 2. Sequence-to-sequence prediction model

The decoder is technically a symmetrical copy of the encoder making it an RNN as well, helping it generate a *target* sequence t based on the context c. The generation of each SC requires helps from the hidden states and state at that instance, the probability of which is calculated by:

$$p(y_1, ..., y_{T'}|x_1, ..., x_T) = \Pi_{t=1}^{T'}(y_{T'}|c, y_1, ..., y_{t-1}) \tag{5}$$

The RNN language model was designed to map sequences, but there are still some issues. First is the loss of critical information due to encoding fixed vector in the encoding stage, which is further worsened due to backpropagation learning. Second is the vector c constant, not allowing it to change dynamically based on the decoding process. These issues can be catered to by introducing the attention mechanism, which is explained in the autoencoders section.

LSTM and GRU: LSTM [19,20] and GRU [21] were introduced to solve the vanishing gradient problem in RNNs. These units effectively increase the learning capacity of these models. They help the model remember information about the training sequence for infinitely long sequence. There is no concrete evidence proving the fact that either one, LSTM or GRU is better than the other, hence this paper compares both of the units. Both LSTM and GRU try to replace the simple activation function of an RNN with a unit called cell. These cells generate output at every time-step, but they are usually used as input for the next step. LSTM units consist of three basic gates, input gate (i), output gate (o) and forget gate (f). They perform element-wise multiplication operations. The gates are sigmoid functions, and they help the cell decide how much incoming information should be held and how much information should be forwarded to the next cell. These parameters are set for the first cell, and all the following cell parameters are computed accordingly. On the other hand, GRU has just two gates reset gate (r) and update gate (z). The reset gate operates in between the previous cell and the next cell while the update gate decides how much information should be learned or updated at that time step.

The likelihood of vanishing gradient is reduced by the ability to learn by utilizing Backpropagation through multiple bounded nonlinearities. LSTM exposes only the cell memory to other cells, while GRU exposes the whole-cell state. LSTM has separate input and output gates while GRU does both of these operations with the help of the reset gate.

Variational Autoencoders: As we now have a basic idea of encoder-decoder framework, autoencoders try to recreate input data at the output, after performing encoder-decoder operations. The encoder breaks down the input sequence into a smaller set of data-bits and decoder uses these bits to recreate the input sequence. The critical part of this whole process is the hidden layers, and this represents the same information at a lower density which is well suited for operations such as dimensionality reduction which might reduce the features to be learned by the model.

Autoencoders are popular choices for anomaly detection where the model is trained on normal data, making it easier to detect differences in the data anomalous in nature. Autoencoding network is a boon for this case as we have a significantly lower number of anomaly instances compared to normal instances. To give generative properties to autoencoders by using Variational Autoencoders (VAE) [22]. This model can learn latent variables of the input sequence, so instead of making the model learn some function, we make it learn the probability distribution of the parameters of the training data. The only difference is that instead of modelling data to a single vector, we train it to two vectors, one dealing with the mean of variable distribution μ and standard deviation of variable distribution σ. VAE Fig. 3 produce comparable or even better results than Generative Adversarial Networks (GAN). VAE with LSTM units may sometimes cause it to bypass latent vector (z) due to the bypass-phenomenon, which may lead to encoding no valuable information to z. Hence variational attention mechanism Fig. 4 can be used to solve this problem. We now have sampling in z and a (attention vector) in our computation graph [23]. Variational attention is computer by:

$$c_j = \Sigma_{i=1}^{|x|} \alpha_{ji} h_i^s \quad (6)$$

$$a_j = f(c_j, h_j^t) = tanh(W_c[c_j; h_j^t] \quad (7)$$

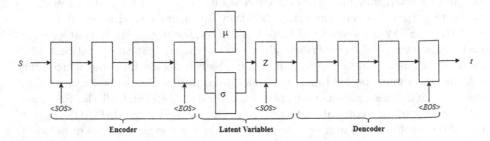

Fig. 3. VAE model

4   System Evaluation

The proposed model was validated on the dataset explained below, this paper uses three different techniques to verify the obtained results. We consider Bilingual Evaluation Understudy Score (BLUE) [24], Term Frequency—Inverse Document Frequency Score (TD-IDF) and Cosine Similarity. This is done to make sure the predicted SC are both syntactic and semantically correct, and also assure that it not just considers the statistical occurrence of SC but are also able to predict SC which makes sense to the Operation Systems. It has been seen that the prediction is usually consistent with attack specific sequences; hence, we deploy multiple anomaly detection classification algorithms to classify the predicted sequences, reassuring that the proposed model does produce sensible results.

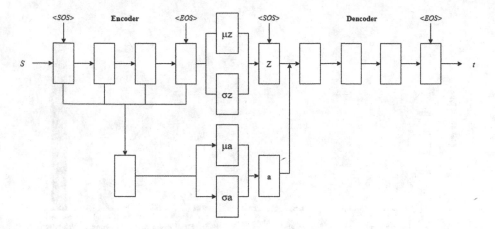

Fig. 4. VAE attention model

4.1 Datasets

Many datasets were considered for this research, some of them being UNM, DARPA, TUIDS, CIDDS and ADFA. ADFA-LD [25] published by National Defense University of Australia was chosen over the other because it is the most in line with the latest attacks and consistent with real-world network scenarios. The dataset is large enough for a neural network training with 6 types of attacks, 833 normal training data and 4372 validation data Fig. 5, gives a summary of the dataset. Creech et al. [26] introduced SC pattern approach to intrusion detection, later [27] they also proposed a host-based anomaly intrusion detection system on the same dataset.

4.2 Learning Process

In training of any neural network, the most important part is the tuning of hyperparameters. These, in many cases, can be the making or breaking factor for any neural network. These are no theoretical guideline for setting the parameters, and it depends on the researcher's experience to determine the right fit or just by trial and error learning.

A good example is determining the learning rate, which can be set to anything between 0 and 1. The lower rate, the model learns better but is very slow and underfitting as a demerit, and the higher the number the model is less accurate but trains faster and has the demerit of overfitting. The hyperparameters include learning rate, dropout of the fitted model, nodes in hidden layers and initialization of training model.

In this experiment, 8 models are trained for prediction. Two types of RNN units were considered LSTM and GRU; each of these units was trained on 4 different variants. The first variant has two hidden layers, and learning rate of 0.1, variants two, three and four, all have three hidden layers and learning rate

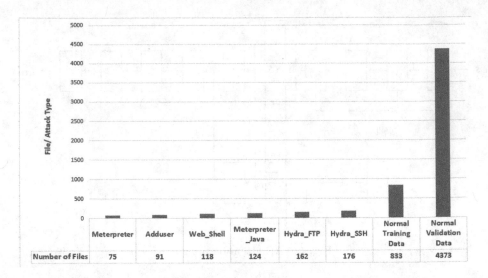

Fig. 5. ADFA-LD summary

of 0.1, 0.01 and 0.001 respectively. The training is stopped and assumed to be completed when the present training loss does not decline any further. The input dimension of the network is the same as output and remains the same due to the auto-encoding property. The model has 256 nodes in its hidden layers with training batch size of 32.

The ADFA dataset is marginally inadequate, for example, if we take sequence length of 30 we have just 4000 input sequences. Any RNN needs to have longer sequences and a relatively large dataset. Hence, to compensate for this, we break the sequences to small bits and create a dataset with a sequence length of 20, 22, 25 and 30. This creates about 21,000 sequences of training data and 4,200 sequences of testing data. The data is now adequate to take advantage of longer sequences of data and extract attack features; this assures a lower number of false alarms by the system.

4.3 Result Analysis

BLUE is considered; first, it is a comparative analysis of phrases generated by a model which counts the number of matching words in a specific position in a weighted fashion. The score is between 0 and 1, the higher the value, the higher the similarity index of the sequence. This technique does provide some advantages over the older techniques has a big disadvantage of not accounting for semantic information of the predicted sequence. Figure 6 shows BLUE score of all 8 different models when the sequence length is 25. It clearly shows that increasing the number of hidden layers (HL) leads to better performance; we can also see that changing the learning rate (LR) does not result in significant improvements. We can hence conclude by saying that we can have a significant

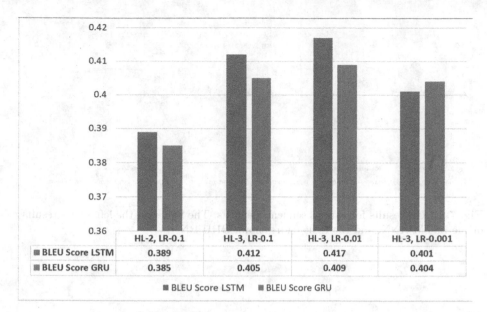

Fig. 6. BLUE results when sequence length is 25

learning rate to speed up the learning process to reduce processing time. Any further increase in HL or LR does not lead to any significant improvement of results when other facts such as processing time are considered. We can also see that LSTM performs better when compared to GRU, this may be due to the more precise movement on data in the units, helping it remember more critical information. It is important to note that GRU performs better with LR as 0.001, but this is not considered as LSTM performs better when LR is set at 0.01.

Figure 7 shows how the models respond to various sequence lengths, it noticed that as the lengths increase the performance improves. This an example of how an RNN improves its performance when the sequence length is increased. This phenomenon is not exhibited for even longer sequences as the models stop improving with any lengths more than 35. The drop in growth may be due to the memory limitation of RNN models; it gets too overwhelmed and forgets critical information causing fall in performance. Therefore it is important to choose the length appropriately for best performance. The sequence length may be increased further if the number of HL is increased, but that comes at the cost of much higher processing time. The TF-IDF scoring system extracts the keywords and compares it with that *target* sequence in a weighted manner. Figure 8 clearly shows that the predicted sequence is very close to the actual *target* sequence syntactically. The score is in between 0 and 1, where 1 states the same sequence. The algorithm is fed with two sequences of data, first is the *target* sequence, and the second is the predicted sequences. TF-IDF is a well-known technique in the fields of data-mining and large scale information retrieval, and this technique assures that the sequence similarities.

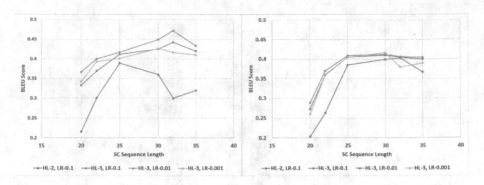

Fig. 7. BLUE results for various sequence lengths. The figure on the left shows results of the LSTM RNN, and the right figure shows GRU RNN.

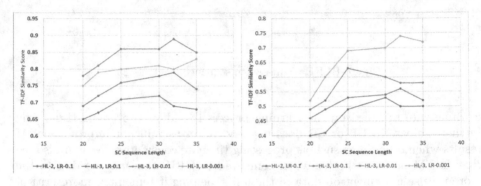

Fig. 8. TF-IDF similarity score between predicted sequence and *target* sequence. The figure on the left shows results of the LSTM RNN, and the figure on the right shows GRU RNN.

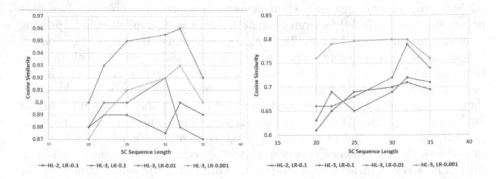

Fig. 9. Cosine similarity score between predicted sequence and *target* sequence. The figure on the left shows results of the LSTM RNN, and the figure on the right shows GRU RNN.

Major demerits of BLEU and TF-IDF systems are its characteristics to score based only on the statistical similarities. This shows that the sequences make sense statistically but might not make sense to the OS. For this, we need to make a correlational analysis of the *target* sequence and predicted sequence this is done by Cosine Similarity score. It is a score between 0 and 1 and takes two encoding vectors, first is the hidden state vector $v1$ of the prediction model, and the second is the *target* sequence encoding vector $v2$. Figure 9 shows cosine similarity between $v1$ and $v2$. It is evident now that the predicted sequence and *target* sequence are syntactically and semantically similar in manner.

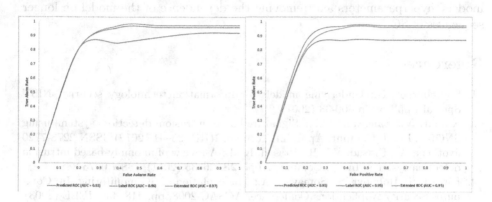

Fig. 10. LSTM model HL-3, LR-0.01. The figure on the left shows the CNN classifier and the figure on the right shows Random Forest classifier.

The predicted sequence should be consistent and should make sense to the operating system. We tested this by using various classifiers which were trained on the training data of ADFA. This method assures that the sequence predicted functional, and the model has learned the critical information correctly. We test the sequences on CNN and Random Forest classifiers. The classifiers were chosen based on their performance when trained on the same dataset, CNN and Random Forest performed the best out of nine different classifiers. The Receiver Operating Characteristic (ROC) curve is used to measure the performance, Area Under Curve (AUC) is used to find the exact precision. A significant advantage of using a predicted sequence can be its ability to improve *target* sequence detection ability by combining the *target* sequence with the predicted one. The amalgam is hugely beneficial when we want to know the exact attack type. The *target* sequence may not have enough information to classify the exact attack type information. Still, with the help of the predicted sequence, we can amplify the characteristic feature of any attack. For this test, only the LSTM model with three HL and LR of 0.01 was considered as it has been outperforming the other models in all the previous tests. In Fig. 10 the labelled ROC, predicted ROC and extended ROC are compared, it is seen that extended ROC performs remarkably better than the *target* sequence, the predicted sequence helps the classifier to make a more precise decision.

4.4 Conclusion

To solve problems faced by other researchers stated above, specifically the inability to predict intrusion on systems, RNN seq2seq language model framework was adopted in this paper. The proposed model can effectively predict SC during an attack in real-time. The results from the model were validated via various techniques, assuring improvements in various anomaly detection techniques. The paper also shows how the classification of attacks can be carried out via various algorithms parallelly with the prediction models' generated SC. Future work will include validation of the proposed model on other datasets, further tuning of the models' hyperparameters and removing the dependence of the model on longer sequences of SC.

References

1. Stoneburner, G.: Underlying models for information technology security. NIST Special Publication 800-33 (2001)
2. Kumar, V., Sangwan, O.P.: Signature-based intrusion detection system using SNORT. Int. J. Comput. Appl. Inf. Technol. **I**(III), 35–41 (2012). ISSN 2278-7720
3. Jyothsna, V., Prasad, V.V.R., Prasad, K.M.: A review of anomaly-based intrusion detection systems. Int. J. Comput. Appl. **28**, 26–35 (2011). ISSN 0975-8887
4. Forrest, S., Hofmeyr, S., Somayaji, A.: The evolution of SC monitoring. In: Computer Security Applications Conference, ACSAC 2008, pp. 418–430. IEEE (2008)
5. Xu, Z., Yu, X., Tari, Z.: A multi-module anomaly detection scheme based on system call prediction. In: 2013 Industrial Electronics and Applications, pp. 1376–1381. IEEE (2013)
6. Chung, Y.-A., Wu, C.-C., Shen, C.-H., Lee, H.-Y., Lee, L.-S.: Audio word2vec: unsupervised learning of audio segment representations using sequence-to-sequence autoencoder. abs/1603.00982 (2016)
7. Lipton, Z.C., Berkowitz, J., Elkan, C.: A critical review of recurrent neural networks for sequence learning (2015). https://arxiv.org/pdf/1506.00019.pdf
8. Bengio, Y., Ducharme, R., Vincent, P., Jauvin, C.: A neural probabilistic language model. J. Mach. Learn. Res. **3**, 1137–1155 (2003)
9. Werbos, P.J.: Backpropagation through time: what it does and how to do it. Proc. IEEE **78**(10), 1550–1560 (1990)
10. Bengio, Y., Frasconi, P., Simard, P.: The problem of learning long-term dependencies in recurrent networks. In: IEEE International Conference on Neural Networks, vol. 3, pp. 1183–1188. IEEE (1993)
11. Fiore, U., Palmieri, F., Castiglione, A., De Santis, A.: Network anomaly detection with the restricted Boltzmann machine. Neurocomputing **122**, 13–23 (2013). https://doi.org/10.1016/j.neucom.2012.11.050
12. Benigo, Y., Lamblin, P., Popovici, D., Larochelle, H.: Greedy layer-wise training of deep networks. In: Advances in Neural Information Processing Systems. MIT Press, Cambridge (2007)
13. Zhengdao, Z., Zhumiao, P., Zhiping, Z.: The study of intrusion prediction based on HsMM. In: Asia-Pacific Services Computing Conference, APSCC 2008, pp. 1358–1363. IEEE (2008)
14. Qiao, Y., Xin, X.W., Bin, Y.: Anomaly intrusion detection method based on HMM. Electron. Lett. **38**(13), 663–664 (2002)

15. Li, Z., Lei, J., Wang, L.: Data mining approach to generating network attack graph for intrusion prediction. In: International Conference on Fuzzy Systems and Knowledge Discovery, pp. 307–311. IEEE (2007)
16. Feng, L., Guan, X., Guo, S.: Predicting the intrusion intentions by observing system call sequences. Comput. Secur. **23**(3), 241–252 (2004)
17. Staudemeyer, Omlin C W.: Evaluating performance of long short-term memory recurrent neural networks on intrusion detection data. South African Institute for Computer Scientists and Information Technologists Conference. 2013:218–224. (2013)
18. Bahdanau, D., Cho, K., Bengio, Y.: Neural machine translation by jointly learning to align and translate (2014). https://arxiv.org/abs/1409.0473
19. Hochreiter, S., Schmidhuber, J.: Long short-term memory. Neural Comput. **9**, 1735–80 (1997). https://doi.org/10.1162/neco.1997.9.8.1735
20. Gers, F.A., Schmidhuber, J., Cummins, F.: Learning to forget: continual prediction with LSTM. In: Ninth International Conference on Artificial Neural Networks ICANN 1999, (Conf. Publ. No. 470), Edinburgh, UK, vol. 2, pp. 850–855 (1999). https://doi.org/10.1049/cp:19991218
21. Cho, K., et al.: Learning phrase representations using RNN encoder-decoder for statistical machine translation (2014). https://arxiv.org/abs/1406.1078
22. Kingma, D.P., Welling, M.: Auto-encoding variational bayes (2013). arxiv.org/abs/1312.6114
23. Bahuleyan, H.: Natural language generation with neural variational models (2018). https://arxiv.org/pdf/1808.09012.pdf
24. Papineni, K., Roukos, S., Ward, T.: BLEU: a method for automatic evaluation of machine translation. In: Meeting on Association for Computational Linguistics. Association for Computational Linguistics, pp. 311–318. (2002)
25. Creech, G., Hu, J.: Generation of a new IDS test dataset: time to retire the KDD collection. In: Wireless Communications and Networking Conference (WCNC), pp. 4487–4492. IEEE (2013)
26. Creech, G., Hu, J.: A semantic approach to host-based intrusion detection systems using contiguous and discontinuous system call patterns. IEEE Trans. Comput. **63**, 807–819 (2013)
27. Creech, G.: Developing a high-accuracy cross-platform host-based intrusion detection system capable of reliably detecting zero-day attacks (2014)
28. Lin, S.-W., Ying, K.-C.: An intelligent algorithm with feature selection and decision rules applied to anomaly intrusion detection (2012). https://doi.org/10.1016/j.asoc.2012.05.004
29. Chung, J., Ahn, S., Bengio, Y.: Hierarchical multiscale recurrent neural networks. arXiv:1609.01704 (2012)
30. Lipton, Z.C., Berkowitz, J., Elkan, C.: A critical review of recurrent neural networks for sequence learning. arXiv:1506.00019 (2012)

Secure Authentication Using One Time Contextual QR Code

Divyans Mahansaria[✉] and Uttam Kumar Roy

Jadavpur University, Kolkata, India
divyansmahansaria@gmail.com, royuttam@gmail.com

Abstract. Traditional methods of authentication are subject to a wide variety of attacks. There is a high demand to deploy necessary mechanisms while authenticating a user to safeguard him/her and the system from the vulnerable attacks. In this paper, a novel one time Quick Response (QR) code based solution has been proposed to counter various types of security breach during the authentication process. The QR code will facilitate context-based authentication. Some information is stored within the QR code which changes for each authentication of the user. Using this information the user needs to derive a one-time password corresponding to his/her actual password. The proposed scheme can be well and easily adapted in various existing and new systems. The experiment and analysis shows that it is more efficient than the existing algorithms in countering security threats.

Keywords: Secure authentication · Contextual QR code · OTP · Secret information · Security attacks

1 Introduction

Authentication is the process of determining whether a person who is requesting access for a system is a legitimate one. Existing authentication mechanisms include the use of login credentials (e.g. username and password), biometrics (e.g. face, voice, fingerprint etc.), digital certificates, combination of ATM Card and PIN, One Time Password (OTP) via Short Message Service (SMS), multifactor authentication products like SecurEnvoy, RSA SecureID etc. Out of these techniques, login credential is the most common and adopted worldwide. Unfortunately, it is subject to a wide variety of attacks such as key-logger and asterisklogger, eavesdropping, shoulder surfing, brute-force, dictionary attack, replay attack, Trojan Horse attack, man in the middle attack, phishing attacks, SQL injection and others.

Virtual keyboard or on-screen keyboard is used in few of the applications to prevent key-logging. Also, extensions to the virtual keyboard have been proposed to make it more secure [9,20]. However, they cannot handle both shoulder surfing and screen capturing.

© Springer Nature Singapore Pte Ltd. 2020
S. M. Thampi et al. (Eds.): SSCC 2019, CCIS 1208, pp. 26–40, 2020.
https://doi.org/10.1007/978-981-15-4825-3_3

As a propitious alternative to traditional alphanumeric passwords, graphical password [22] with challenge-response [7,17,21] based authentication methods have been proposed to make the system stronger. However, they are still susceptible to either of key-logging, mouse-logging, screen capture or shoulder surfing attack [2]. Also, some cases require an additional device [2] like a stylus that limits the usability. When compared to text based password scheme some of the graphical password schemes have less password space and thus reduce the entropy of the system [17].

Biometric-based (e.g. fingerprint, face, voice, iris etc.) authentication are often used in some of the high end applications. Some interesting techniques have also been proposed to carry out authentication that use the characteristics such as haptic, gaze, handwriting, brain waves etc. which are unique to a human body [3,4,11,18]. These systems assure greater security but have limited applicability due to their high installation and maintenance cost and also difficulty in implementation. A compromised biometric system is a major security risk as biometrics of the user does not change.

The usage of one-time password rather than just static password has proved to be useful while carrying out authentication. It is an efficient way to improve the security level of a system. It is not vulnerable to replay attack. However, recently there have been compromises on SMS OTPs sent on mobile phones. Using suitable tools mobile traffic of an end user including SMS could be intercepted by the attacker. Moreover, mobile phone malware, and especially Trojans, are being used by criminals to obtain SMS messages containing OTPs [5].

1.1 Use of Quick Response (QR) Code for Securing Applications

QR code or 2D matrix bar code can hold large amount of data in a small space and in both horizontal and vertical directions. It has error correction capability and a fast response time. QR code is being increasingly used in various applications to easily store and retrieve information. In some of the proposed research work QR code has been used to secure applications [1,6,14,23]. A public QR Code and some user-specific information could be merged together to form contextual QR Code which can provide data related to a particular context. Rouillard [12] combines context-aware QR codes from two parts: Public Part (which is "traditional" QR code info) and Private Part (which is XML-based context data). The private part can represent information like user's profile, user's location, device used by the user, time, and type of environment etc. The combined information is used for computing contextual messages.

In this paper, a novel authentication solution has been proposed to counter various forms of security breach during the authentication process. During each authentication request received from the user of the system, a one-time contextual QR code is generated. Contextual information present in the QR code is a random id which is unique for a particular login. The information present in the QR code is encrypted. During authentication a device which is capable of scanning a QR code, such as a usual smartphone, having the custom software which has been developed for the proposed scheme is required. The custom software will decode and subsequently decrypt the contents of the QR code. After decryption, a piece of information will be shown to the user using which the user needs to derive the OTP corresponding to his/her actual password. The experiment and analysis shows that it is more efficient than the existing algorithms in countering security threats. The proposed scheme can be well and easily adapted in various existing and new systems.

2   Related Works

2.1   Lamport and S/Key One-Time Password System

An OTP based scheme for user authentication was suggested by Lamport [15] in the early 1980s. Based on this idea, a prototype software system, the S/KEY [19] one-time password system was also developed. In this scheme a one-way function is used to generate a finite series of OTPs based on a chosen password. A one-way function is easy to compute but computationally infeasible to invert. It is applied on a chosen password for certain number of times to generate different OTPs.

Let x denote the chosen password. The finite series of OTPs is computed as -

$$F^{n-1}(x).....F(F(F(x))), F(F(x)), F(x), x \tag{1}$$

Initially, the value $F^n(x)$ is stored at the server end. The server does not store the actual password x. In i^{th} authentication client calculates the OTP as -

$$OTP_i(x) = F^{n-i}(x) \tag{2}$$

This OTP is send by client to the server for authentication. The server on receiving the OTP performs a hash of it and compares it with the stored OTP of previous login.

$$F(OTP_i(x)) = F(F^{n-i}(x)) \tag{3}$$

If there is a match then authentication is successful and server updates its stored value to current OTP i.e. $F^{n-i}(x)$. In the subsequent authentication the client increments 'i' by 1 and computes next OTP. Thus, the OTPs used for authentication are $F^{n-1}(x)$ to x. Also, if server and client are out of synchrony the server could send a challenge 'i' corresponding to which the client needs to calculate the OTP. After 'n' authentications a new value of x needs to be generated for further 'n' time authentications.

The generation of a new password after a certain number of authentications makes the scheme constrained. Also, the host could be impersonated as there is no means to verify the authenticity of information send by the host to client. The computational requirements are high during the calculations for the chain's initial values, which make the system unsuitable for devices with limited resources. Moreover, it is very much inconvenient for users to manually type a long OTP.

2.2 Scheme of Bicakci and Baykal

Bicakci and Baykal [13] proposed infinite length hash chains using a public key algorithm. Let 'd' denote the private key, 'e' denote the public key, 's' denote the seed value and $A^N()$ denote public key algorithm 'A' applied 'N' times. The infinite length hash chain originated from the initial seed 's' is –

$$s, A(s, d), A^2(s, d), \cdots A^{N-1}(s, d), A^N(s, d), \cdots$$

The client calculates OTP for i^{th} authentication as –

$$OTP_i(s) = A^i(s, d) \tag{4}$$

This OTP is send to server for authentication. The server on receiving the OTP calculates –

$$s = A^i(OTP_i(s), e) \tag{5}$$

If the shared secret seed matches then the authentication is successful. The drawback of this method is that increasing the number of cascaded exponentiation increases the computational complexity and thus making this algorithm difficult to implement in devices having limited computational capacity. To facilitate faster implementation of the algorithm, during each authentication the previous OTP can be stored at both client and server end. However, if the previous OTP is lost or damaged a large exponentiation might be required to generate or verify the subsequent OTP. Moreover, it is very much inconvenient for users to manually type a long OTP.

2.3 RSA SecurID Authenticator

RSA SecurID [10] is a hardware device that generates time-synchronized token codes every sixty seconds. A token code is computed as a cryptographic function of the current time and a shared secret between the corresponding SecurID and the authentication server. This token code acts as an OTP for the user to authenticate. The same token code is generated at both authentication server and client end and thus when client sends the token code to the authentication server it is able to validate the correctness of the token code.

RSA SecurID is an efficient OTP generation technique. However, the usage of it is limited because of the device procurement cost for each individual user and the need to carry an additional device for authentication. Moreover, there is a lag in setup time as the RSA SecurID device needs to be shipped to the user and the device needs to be replaced with a new one in every few years.

2.4 Scheme of Eldefrawy et al.

Eldefrawy et al. [16] scheme extends Lamport's idea of finite series of hash chain generation for authentication. In this scheme, an infinite length hash chain is generated using two different one-way hash functions, $h_A()$ and $h_B()$, one for the seed updating and other for the OTP generation.

$$OTP(x, y) = h_B^y(h_A^x(seed))|_{x:1->\infty, y:1->\infty} \tag{6}$$

At the time of authentication, at first, the user provides the current status of the OTP to the server. The current status allows the server to synchronize its seed with the client's current seed to get the same seed value on both sides. Next the server challenges the user with new indexes (i.e. x and y values) based on which user computes the OTP. This OTP is then sent to the server for verification and if found correct the server authenticates the user.

In this scheme, the ability to resist predictable attack is not strong enough. Specifically, probability of guessing next challenge is $1/m^2$ where m is the range of x and y coordinates of a challenge. There is an additional risk to securely store the seed at the client end. Here a chain of hash functions are applied depending on the challenge x & y and thereby increasing computational overhead at the time of authentication. Moreover, it is very much inconvenient for users to manually type a long OTP.

Our proposed solution detailed in Sect. 3 of this paper addresses and resolves the issues prevalent in the above related works.

3 Proposed Solution

In this section, the working principle of the solution is described in details. For a better understanding, we divide the solution into three phases: *registration*, *device setup* and *authentication*.

3.1 Registration Phase

The first-time user should register to setup the authentication credentials. The registration process is similar to most of the current systems that use and password to carry out authentication. Hashing algorithm is the common approach to store passwords securel. [24]. The hash values of the chosen username and password are stored in the database to maintain secrecy. It is assumed that registration is carried out in a secure environment and the authentication credentials are not stolen at the time of registration. Alternatively, the registration of new users can be done by the admin of the system as per the organizational policy and the authentication credentials are shared with the users. The registration password can be changed by the user anytime.

Following notations are used:

U_{plain} → plaintext username,
P_{plain} → plaintext password,
$h()$ → one-way hash function,
U_h → hash value of username,
P_h → hash value of password

Thus, $U_h = h(U_{plain})$ *and* $P_h = h(P_{plain})$

The values U_h and P_h are stored against the respective user details in the database.

3.2   Device Setup

At the time of login the user should have a device (such as a smartphone) which is capable of scanning a QR code. Custom software which has been specifically developed for the proposed solution needs to be installed on this device. The software installation on any device is a one-time activity. The custom software contains the public key of public-key encryption algorithm. It is used to decrypt the information received from the authentication server.

3.3   Authentication Phase

In order to gain access to various systems and confidential data, a user needs to be authenticated. Thus, it is of paramount importance to safeguard the authentication phase from the vulnerable security attacks. During authentication process information exchange takes place between the authentication server and the user in order to verify the identity of the user.

Authentication Server—Generate Login Information: The responsibility of the authentication server is to facilitate authentication for a user that attempts to access a secured system. On receiving a login request from the user certain tasks are performed at the server end.

A mapping is generated between the alphanumeric characters and symbols (using which a password can be formed) and a pre-defined set of generic elements. In one of the proposed mapping, each cell of the QWERTY keyboard layout contains a mapping character. The alphabet cells of the QWERTY keyboard layout will contain a random alphabet mapping; the numerical cells of the QWERTY keyboard layout will contain a random numerical mapping and the symbol cells of the QWERTY keyboard layout will contain a random symbol mapping. Thus, all the 26 alphabets (a–z), numerals (0–9) and 14 chosen symbols of QWERTY keyboard layout will contain a mapping element. The 14 chosen symbols are listed in Table 1.

An example of the generated mapping is shown in Fig. 1. Here, the elements in black are the usual keyboard elements of the QWERTY keyboard layout. The elements in red are the mapping elements against each usual element of the QWERTY keyboard layout.

The authentication server also generates a unique random id for the particular authentication request and makes an entry of it into a database with status as active. Also, current timestamp in UTC (Coordinated Universal Time) is stored against the random id.

The concatenated value of generated mapping information and random id is encrypted using private key of the authentication server. The encrypted information is then encoded in a QR code. This QR code is sent to the end user who requested for login.

Table 1. Symbols

Symbol	Name	Symbol	Name
!	Exclamation	*	Asterisk
@	At sign	(	Open parenthesis
#	Hash	)	Close parenthesis
$	Dollar sign	−	Minus
%	Percentage	+	Plus
^	Caret	_	Underscore
&	Ampersand	=	Equal

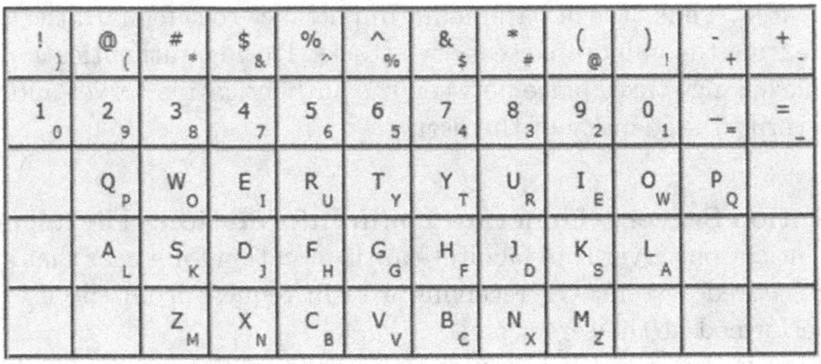

Fig. 1. Randomized QWERTY keyboard layout mapping

Following notations are used:

M $\rightarrow$ mapping information,
R $\rightarrow$ random id,
$K_{PR} \rightarrow$ private key,
$K_{PU} \rightarrow$ public key,
A $\rightarrow$ public-key encryption algorithm,
$E_A() \rightarrow$ encrypted value using A,
$D_A() \rightarrow$ decrypted value using A,
$E_{QR} \rightarrow$ encoded information in QR code,
$D_{QR} \rightarrow$ decoded information from QR code

Thus,

$$E_{QR} = Encode(E_A(K_{PR}, (M\|R))) \tag{7}$$

This information is sent to the end user in the form of QR code.

User—Derive OTP: In case of authentication for applications on devices other than mobile phone, such as a desktop or a laptop, the user scans the QR code using the custom software installed on the QR code scanning device. In case of applications accessed on mobile phones there would be an additional link besides QR code and on clicking the link the custom software will launch. Here, internally the QR code data will be passed to the custom software.

The custom software at first decodes the QR code.

$D_{QR} = Decode(E_{QR})$

$$D_{QR} = E_A(K_{PR}, (M||R)) \quad (Using\ Eq.\ 7) \tag{8}$$

The pre-defined public-key algorithm and the stored public key are used by the custom software to decrypt the decoded information to obtain the mapping information and the random id.

$$D_A(K_{PU}, (D_{QR})) = (M||R) \quad (Using\ Eq.\ 8) \tag{9}$$

The custom software has the required function to separate M and R from the concatenated value of M and R. The user enters the username chosen at the time of registration. The OTP to be entered needs to be derived from the mapping information presented to the user. In case of mapping information shown in Fig. 1, the user needs to find out the corresponding mapping character for each element of the user's actual password. The sequence of the mapped characters is the derived OTP. In case of an uppercase letter present in the actual password, the corresponding mapped letter will be in uppercase. Similarly, for lowercase letter present in the actual password the corresponding mapped letter will be in lowercase.

Example: Suppose the password of a user is "Data@1". The OTP corresponding to "Data@1" from Fig. 1 can be derived as follows – For "D" the mapping character is "J", for "a" the mapping character is "l", for "t" the mapping character is "y", for "a" the mapping character is "l", for "@" the mapping character is "(" and for "1" the mapping character is "0". Thus, the derived OTP as per the mapping is ""Jlyl(0"".

On submitting the authentication information, the username (U_{plain}), OTP and QR code are posted to the authentication server.

3.4 Authentication Server—Verify OTP

The authentication server on receiving the authentication request at first checks whether the user account is locked, and if found locked the authentication request is denied. If user attempts to login using invalid information for a pre-determined number of consecutive times the account will be locked and additional verification needs to be done to unlock the account.

The received QR code is decoded and then decrypted using the public-key algorithm. Mapping information and random id are obtained from the decrypted information. This process is the same as carried out at custom software end to obtain mapping information and random id from QR code. The authentication server checks whether the random id (obtained from QR code) has status as active in the database. If it is active the status is changed to inactive or else the authentication request is rejected. The timestamp stored in the database against the random id is obtained. The difference between this timestamp and current time (in UTC) is calculated. If it is exceeds the set time limit then the authentication request is rejected.

The actual password is derived from the user-entered OTP and the mapping information present in the QR Code. The hash values of the username and the password are matched against the values (from registration phase) present in the server database. If it matches the user is successfully authenticated or else the authentication request is rejected.

4   Security Analysis, Applicability and Discussion

4.1   Security Analysis

Firstly, we compare the proposed scheme with SMS based OTP which is widely used in many of the secure applications. Recently there have been compromises on SMS OTPs sent on mobile phones [5]. Using suitable tools, mobile traffic of an end user including SMS could be intercepted by an attacker. This would reveal the OTP (sent via SMS) at the interception point. Also, mobile phone malware capable of receiving SMS containing OTPs are becoming a rising threat. Upon reception, in the background the SMS could be forwarded to an attacker and deleted from the mobile phone to hide the fact that SMS containing OTP ever arrived at the infected phone. The authentication solution proposed in this paper does not send the OTP over a mobile network so it is resistant to the capture of mobile traffic. Unlike the SMS based OTP system, the one-time password in the proposed scheme is not distributed as plaintext. Mapping information in encrypted QR code is sent to the user using which the user derives the OTP from actual password known only to the user and the authentication server. Thus, malware-infected mobile device used for scanning a QR code does not have the possibility to reveal the authentication credentials.

Phishing attack aims at obtaining sensitive information by masquerading as a trustworthy entity through electronic means. It often directs user to enter details at a fake website which has been developed identical to a legitimate one. The QR code used in the proposed solution can only be generated at the authentication server end which has the private key of the public-key encryption algorithm. Any other form of QR code will not be resolved by the custom scanning software and hence mapping information will not be shown to the user. Also, there is an upper bound on the time within which user should be authenticated after QR code generation. So a QR code captured by an attacker to deceive the user at a later point in time will not be of any significance. Thus, with the proposed scheme, phishing attack on authentication information will be very difficult to achieve.

The usage of one-time password rather than static password has proved to be useful while carrying out authentication. It is an efficient way to improve the security level of a system. In the proposed method of authentication, the password entered by the user is valid only for a particular authentication request. In subsequent logins, the mapping information changes and hence the password to be entered changes as well. The use of OTP makes a system secure against key-logger software that runs in the background to track the keys struck on a keyboard and asterisk logger that has the capability to show the hidden passwords masked behind asterisks. In a compromised system, a password-stealing Trojan could acquire the password cached in browser memory. However, this kind of attack can be prevented with the use of OTP as the actual password is never entered by the user.

In replay or playback attack, a message which was earlier sent by a legitimate user is fraudulently repeated again. In our implementation, the dynamically generated QR code contains a unique random id and a database in the server is used to track whether the random id is active or not. Authentication is allowed only if the random id is active and it is marked as inactive after its usage towards an authentication. So a replay of the already used authentication information will be rejected by the server and thus making the authentication system secure against replay attack.

Shoulder Surfing is using direct observation techniques, such as, looking over someone's shoulder, to get information. It can also be done long distance with the aid of binoculars or other vision-enhancing devices. In the proposed solution, shoulder surfing on the keyboard by directly observing through eyes or by video recording can just reveal a temporary password valid for the particular authentication. The mapping information displayed to the user is on the hand-held device which is close to user's body. So it is nearly impossible to shoulder surf both on the screen of the handheld device and the keyboard of the system simultaneously. Thus it is resilient against shoulder surfing.

Brute-force and dictionary attack on password uses all possible combination of passwords and an exhaustive list of dictionary words respectively to crack the password of a system. In our implementation, any combination of alphabets (both a–z and A–Z), numbers (0–9) and 14 special symbols can form the password.

Total possible passwords of length 'L', $N = (76)^L$
For $L = 3$, $N = (76)^3 = 4.39 * 10^5$
For $L = 4$, $N = (76)^4 = 3.34 * 10^7$

Thus the password space is very large. Also, the system locks out the user account in few invalid attempts. Thus it is nearly impossible to obtain the user's credentials using brute-force and dictionary attack. This is in-line with most of the existing username and password based authentication systems.

In SQL injection, a malicious script is written as the user input and it gets executed against database to compromise the stored information of database. In the proposed scheme, the server processes the received information before executing the database query. The hash values of the username and the derived password from OTP are verified against the database. So SQL injection in the username and password fields will not be of any significance.

In pre-play attack, an attacker prepares for the attack in advance by predicting the next challenge to be used for authentication. In the proposed scheme, the generated QR code is encrypted by private key of authentication server. Any other form of QR code will not be resolved by the custom software and thus making it infeasible to generate next challenge by attacker.

Thus, the above discussion illustrates the usefulness of the proposed scheme in countering different types of security attacks during the authentication process.

4.2 Applicability

At the time of authentication a device capable of scanning a QR code such as a smartphone is required. Smartphones are already in use worldwide by a very large number of mobile phone users and the usage of smartphones show an increasing trend in near future. Additional devices like token generator, chip-based card along with reader, biometric devices etc. are not required. Thus the infrastructure cost and the lag time to setup an authentication system is reduced to a large extent. This increases the applicability of the proposed scheme.

4.3 Discussion

The overall comparison of the proposed system with other OTP based authentication systems is shown in Table 2.

Mobile SMS-based OTP system is being commonly used to authenticate users, especially during transactions. However, it is prone to malicious software installed on a mobile device. Also, there is mobile network dependency to receive the SMS. Lamport & S/Key and Bicakci and Baykal scheme requires system re-initialization after certain number of authentications. They are prone to pre-play attack as well. Lamport & S/Key, Bicakci and Baykal and Eldefrawy schemes perform a high computation at client end and additionally there is an overhead to store secret. RSA SecurID generates token in a dedicated hardware device. Thus, there is no extra resource required at client side to generate the OTP. However, in case of RSA SecurID, the device procurement cost is high and it needs to be replaced after a certain lifetime. There is a lag time to setup the RSA SecurID system for a user as a dedicated hardware device needs to be tagged and shipped to a user. The proposed system of password entry eliminates all the mentioned problems. It has high usability and also it can be easily integrated with existing password entry systems.

Table 2. Comparison with other OTP based authentication systems

Metric↓ System→	SMS-based OTP	Lamport and S/Key	Bicakci and Baykal	Eldefrawy et al.	RSA SecurID	Proposed scheme
Usability	Very high	Low	Low	Low	High	High
Initial setup time	Small	Medium	Medium	Medium	High	Small
Device cost	Low	Low	Low	Low	High	Low
Operational cost	Medium	Low	Low	Low	Low	Low
Number of authentications before re-initialization	Unlimited	Low	Medium	Unlimited	High	Unlimited
Resistance to pre-play attack	High	Low	Medium	Medium	High	Very high
Client computational requirements	Not applicable	High	High	High	Not applicable	Low
Additional overhead to store secret	No	Yes	Yes	Yes	No	No
Mobile network dependency	Yes	No	No	No	No	No
Prone to SMS capture malware installed on mobile device	Yes	No	No	No	No	No
Type of encryption algorithm	Hash function	Hash function	Public key	Hash function	Hash function	Public key

5 Usability Study

A usability study has been conducted to determine the error rate and the time taken by the users to authenticate using the proposed method. The study was performed on 50 participants who are regular users of computer and mobile phone. The participants were given a presentation in which the new authentication method was described in details. Also, the participants had hands-on experience with the new method of authentication. All the participants were given same passwords for the experiment. The passwords varied in length from 3 to 8 elements and each of the passwords had minimum of one number or symbol along with the alphabets (a–z, A–Z).

The average value of entry time of OTP after the appearance of mapping information on user's handheld device is shown in Fig. 2.

It can be seen from the graph that on an average password of length 3 characters was derived and entered in 6 s and password of length 8 characters was derived and entered in 14 s. We believe that the entry time taken by the users will reduce to some extent once they use the new authentication method for considerable number of times.

We found that invalid OTPs were entered in 5% of the total authentication attempts of all the users. This result may be due to the fact that the proposed authentication method is still new for the users. We believe that the authentication failure percentage will reduce as the users become comfortable using the new method of authentication.

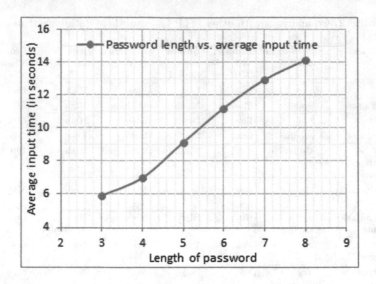

Fig. 2. Password length vs average input time

6   Conclusion and Future Work

The security attacks on different authentication mechanisms, particularly the use of authentication credentials (e.g. username and password), are increasing to an alarming extent. Thus it is very important to deploy necessary mechanisms while authenticating a user to safeguard him/her and the system from the vulnerable attacks. In this paper, we have proposed a novel solution of generating OTPs using a mapping information and context-aware QR code. The discussion in earlier section establishes that it can counter various kinds of security attacks on a system. In the proposed solution there is a trade-off between the time taken to authenticate a user and the security of the system so depending on the need it can be deployed in applications where a greater security is desired. However, the new method is easy to integrate and adapt to existing systems.

As part of future work we will carry out study to make the OTP derivation faster. The increase in number of participants and several iterations of authentication spanning a considerable period of time will provide a holistic result of the usability study. Studies have been carried out to analyze the factors that determine the user's intention to use the QR code [8]. In our future work the plan is to focus on the QR code design to make it more user-oriented. Also, an exhaustive analysis will be carried out on other types of security attacks which have not been addressed in the scope of the proposed solution.

Acknowledgement. This work is partially supported by the project entitled "QR code-based Multi-Factor Authentication Using Mobile OTP and Multi-dimensional Infinite Hash Chains" under RUSA 2.0 (Ref. No. R-11/668/19), Govt. of India.

Compliance with Ethical Standards. All procedures performed in studies involving human participants were in accordance with the ethical standards. Informed consent was obtained from all individual participants included in the study.

References

1. Shah, A.T., Parihar, V.R.: Overview and an approach for QR-code based messaging and file sharing on android platform in view of security. In: International Conference on Computing Methodologies and Communication (ICCMC), Erode, India. IEEE (2017)
2. Kayem, A.V.: Graphical passwords - a discussion. In: 30th International Conference on Advanced Information Networking and Applications Workshops (WAINA), Crans-Montana, Switzerland. IEEE (2016)
3. Malek, B., Orozco, M., Saddik, A.E.: Novel shoulder-surfing resistant haptic-based graphical password. In: Proceedings of the EuroHaptics 2006 Conference, Paris, France (2006)
4. Borkotoky, C., Galgate, S., Nimbekar, S.B.: Human computer interaction harnessing P300 potential brain waves for authentication of individuals. In: Proceedings of the 1st Bangalore Annual Compute Conference (COMPUTE 2008), Bangalore, India. ACM (2008)
5. Mulliner, C., Borgaonkar, R., Stewin, P., Seifert, J.-P.: SMS-based one-time passwords: attacks and defense. In: Rieck, K., Stewin, P., Seifert, J.-P. (eds.) DIMVA 2013. LNCS, vol. 7967, pp. 150–159. Springer, Heidelberg (2013). https://doi.org/10.1007/978-3-642-39235-1_9
6. Conde-Lagoa, D., Costa-Montenegro, E., González-Castaño, F.J., Gil-Castiñeira, F.: Secure eTickets based on QR-codes with user-encrypted content. In: Digest of Technical Papers International Conference on Consumer Electronics (ICCE), Las Vegas, NV, USA. IEEE (2010)
7. Gupta, D.: A new approach of authentication in graphical systems using ASCII submission of values. In: 13th International Wireless Communications and Mobile Computing Conference (IWCMC), Valencia, Spain. IEEE (2017)
8. Shin, D.H., Jung, J., Chang, B.H.: The psychology behind QR codes: user experience perspective. Comput. Hum. Behav. **28**(4), 1417–1426 (2012)
9. Shangfu, G., Jun, L., Yizhen, S.: Design and implementation of anti-screenshot virtual keyboard applied in online banking. In: International Conference on E-Business and E-Government (ICEE), Guangzhou, China, Guangzhou, China. IEEE (2010)
10. Brainard, J., et al.: Fourth-factor authentication: somebody you know. In: 13th ACM Conference on Computer and Communications Security, Virginia, USA. ACM (2006)
11. Xu, W., Tian, J., Cao, Y., Wang, S.: Challenge-response authentication using in-air handwriting style verification. IEEE Trans. Dependable Secure Comput. **17**(1), 51–64 (2020)
12. Rouillard, J.: Contextual QR codes. In: Proceedings of the Third International Multi-Conference on Computing in the Global Information Technology (ICCGI 2008), Athens, Greece. IEEE (2008)
13. Bicakci, K., Baykal, N.: Infinite length hash chains and their applications. In: Eleventh IEEE International Workshops on Enabling Technologies: Infrastructure for Collaborative Enterprises, Pittsburgh, USA. IEEE (2002)

14. Saranya, K., Reminaa, R.S., Subhitsha, S.: Modern applications of QR-code for security. In: 2nd IEEE International Conference on Engineering and Technology (ICETECH), Coimbatore, India. IEEE (2016)

15. Lamport, L.: Password authentication with insecure communication. Commun. ACM **24**(11), 770–772 (1981)

16. Eldefrawy, M., et al.: Mobile one-time passwords: two-factor authentication using mobile phones. J. Secur. Commun. Netw. **5**(5), 508–516 (2012)

17. Potey, M.M., Dhote, C.A., Sharma, D.H.: Secure authentication for data protection in cloud computing using color schemes. In: International Conference on Computational Systems and Information Systems for Sustainable Solutions (CSITSS), Bangalore, India. IEEE (2016)

18. Kumar, M., Garfinkel, T., Boneh, D., Winograd, T.: Reducing shoulder-surfing by using gaze based password entry. In: SOUPS 2007 - Proceedings of the 3rd Symposium on Usable Privacy and Security. ACM, Pittsburgh, Pennsylvania, USA (2007)

19. Haller, N.: The S/KEY one-time password system. In: ISOC Symposium on Network and Distributed System Security, San Diego, CA, USA (1994)

20. Malutan, R., Grosan, C.: Web authentication methods using single sign on method and virtual keyboard. In: Conference Grid, Cloud and High Performance Computing in Science (ROLCG), Cluj-Napoca, Romania. IEEE (2015)

21. Wiedenbeck, S., Waters, J, Sobrado, L, Birget, J.C.: Design and evaluation of a shoulder-surfing resistant graphical password scheme. In: Proceedings of Advanced Visual Interface (AVI 2006), Venezia, Italy. ACM (2006)

22. Suo, X., Zhu, Y, Owen, G.S.: Graphical passwords: a survey. In: Proceedings of the 21st Annual Computer Security Applications Conference, Tucson, AZ, USA. IEEE (2005)

23. Kao, Y.W., et al.: Physical access control based on QR code. In: International Conference on Cyber-Enabled Distributed Computing and Knowledge Discovery, Beijing, China. IEEE (2011)

24. Singh, M., Garg, D.: Choosing best hashing strategies and hash functions. In: International Advance Computing Conference, Patiala, India. IEEE (2009)

A Proximity-Based Measure
for Quantifying the Risk of Vulnerabilities

Ghanshyam S. Bopche[1,2]([✉]), Gopal N. Rai[3], D. R. Denslin Brabin[4],
and B. M. Mehtre[2]

[1] SRM University AP, Amaravati, Andhra Pradesh, India
ghanshyambopche.mca@gmail.com
[2] Centre of Excellence in Cyber Security, IDRBT, Hyderabad, India
mehtre@gmail.com
[3] Collins Aerospace, Hyderabad, India
gopalnrai@gmail.com
[4] Madanapalle Institute of Technology & Science (MITS),
Madanapalle, Andhra Pradesh, India
denscse@gmail.com
https://srmap.edu.in/
http://www.idrbt.ac.in
https://www.rockwellcollins.com/
https://www.mits.ac.in/

Abstract. Identification and remediation of the system vulnerabilities
that pose the highest risk are crucial for maintaining the security posture
of computer networks. In literature a large number of metrics available
for vulnerability risk assessment. However, they fail to consider critical
network risk conditions that affect the success of an adversary. Consequently, evaluation of the vulnerability risk based on current metrics is
misleading, and hence, the derived vulnerability remediation plan often
results in an ineffective application of countermeasures. To overcome this
problem, we have proposed a comprehensive, integrated metric called
Improved Relative Cumulative Risk (IRCR). For a given vulnerability,
IRCR takes into account the CVSS Base Score, vulnerability proximity from the attacker's initial position, and the risk of the neighboring
vulnerabilities. The proposed metric tested on a synthetic network, and
experimental results show that IRCR can be used effectively for assessing the security risk of each of the exploitable vulnerabilities. Based on
the IRCR recommendations, an administrator can accurately determine
top vulnerabilities and prioritize the vulnerability remediation activities
accordingly. To validate the efficacy and applicability of the proposed
method, we have compared the IRCR metric with the state-of-the-art
attack graph-based metrics such as cumulative attack probability, and
cumulative attack resistance. Experimental results demonstrate that the
proposed IRCR metric can be complementary to the current attack
graph-based metrics in measuring the influential levels of exploitable
vulnerabilities.

Keywords: Vulnerability · Exploit · Diversity · Multistage attack ·
Attack graph · Security metric · Network hardening · Proactive defense

© Springer Nature Singapore Pte Ltd. 2020
S. M. Thampi et al. (Eds.): SSCC 2019, CCIS 1208, pp. 41–59, 2020.
https://doi.org/10.1007/978-981-15-4825-3_4

1   Introduction

Purpose of vulnerability analysis and risk assessment techniques is to uncover vulnerabilities in the critical enterprise infrastructure and mitigate them before the security attack becomes a reality. In particular, risk assessment techniques help security administrators in deciding appropriate countermeasures to deter any plausible attack. Traditional information security planning and management process begin with vulnerability scanning, followed by the risk assessment, and finally, network hardening [1]. Estimating the risk of vulnerabilities in today's network environment has become a severe problem, primarily, because Cyber attacks have become more sophisticated wherein adversary combines multiple vulnerabilities to compromise the critical network resources incrementally.

Large number of vulnerability risk assessment methods were developed by security vendors and non-profit organizations such as US-CERT [2], SANS, [3], NVD [4], Vupen Security [5], Secunia [6], and Microsoft [7]. Standardization efforts on security metrics, such as Common Vulnerability Scoring System (CVSS) [8–10] and Common Weakness Scoring System (CWSS) [11] focus on ranking well-known vulnerabilities and software weaknesses, respectively. Such scoring help administrator in measuring the severity and impact of the individual vulnerabilities, and hence in the process of patch management. Although popular, both CVSS and CWSS do not capture the interdependency (here, cause-consequence relationship) between vulnerabilities and hence are deemed insufficient in the context of multistage, multi-host attacks [12,13]. Furthermore, CVSS and CWSS measures the severity of software vulnerability/weakness in isolation and do not capture their impact on the overall security risk of a network [14]. Consequently, the use of such risk scoring systems often results in an imprecise risk prioritization and sub-optimal security countermeasures.

Because of the limitations of CVSS and CWSS as stated above, a vulnerability risk assessment process requires additional steps to evaluate the risk posed by the exploitable vulnerabilities. It can be done by combining the CVSS Base Scores with the various security parameters (or risk conditions) of the underlying network. To evaluate the security risk of the exploitable vulnerabilities, a suitable model that considers various network risk conditions, and which imitates the adversary's choice of vulnerability exploitation, should be utilized. There is a plethora of research work [15–19] on the efficient generation and ranking of the potential attack paths in the network; to model and analyze multistage attack scenarios in order to provide high-level metrics for network risk assessment [20].

Existing attack graph-based security metrics such as cumulative attack probability [21], and cumulative attack resistance [22] consider the interdependency between the exploitable vulnerabilities for assessing the security risk posed by each of the exploitable vulnerability uncovered in a given network. However, they do not consider the vulnerability diversity along the attack path(s). Chen et al. [23] used diversity among network vulnerabilities as an important risk condition to assess the security risk of a network. Whereas, Wang et al. [14,24] used vulnerability diversity along the attack path to measure the robustness of a system against the zero-day attacks. Suh-Lee and Jo [25] used the proximity of the un-trusted network and risk of neighboring hosts as important risk conditions to assess the security risk of each vulnerability (both exploitable and non-exploitable) in a given system. However, they do not consider critical network risk conditions such as the cause-consequence relationship between the exploitable vulnerabilities and the exploit diversity along the attack paths. Mukherjee and Mazumdar [26] proposed metric to compute attack difficulty of an individual exploit e relative to its position in the attack path. However, they do not consider the vulnerability diversity along the attack path(s). Work of Wang et al. [14,21,22,24], Chen et al. [23], Suh-Lee and Jo [25], and Mukherjee and Mazumdar [26] motivated us to consider various network risk conditions (i.e. the conditions which affect the success of an adversary) for the vulnerability risk assessment. Such risk conditions include but are not limited to

– Proximity of the vulnerability from the attacker's initial position (i.e., the minimum resistance posed by the vulnerabilities to the attacker along the available attack paths),
– Vulnerability diversity along the attack paths,
– Risk of the neighboring vulnerabilities from where the target vulnerability under consideration reached directly and exploited.

Such risk conditions affect the success of an adversary and hence, the risks posed by the exploitable vulnerabilities. We have used an exploit-dependency attack graph [27] as a network security model in conjunction with the CVSS Framework [10]. The generated exploit-dependency attack graph for a given network captures the adversary's all possible attacking strategies, and also various risk conditions that affect the risk posed by the exploitable vulnerabilities. Our objective is to dynamically adjust the static risk level of the network vulnerabilities (i.e., CVSS Base Score [10]) with various risk conditions of the underlying network.

In this paper, we propose a new metric called Improved Relative Cumulative Risk (IRCR) for quantifying the security risk of each of the exploitable vulnerability present in the network. IRCR is a comprehensive, integrated measure that considers various factors (network risk conditions) such as (i) CVSS Base Score, (ii) the proximity of the target vulnerability from the attacker's initial position, (iii) vulnerability diversity along the attack path(s), and (iv) the risk of other neighboring (predecessor) vulnerabilities whose exploitation leads to the exposure of the vulnerability under consideration. It is observed that the above-stated risk conditions affect the likelihood of adversary's success significantly [14,22–25]. The more the resistance posed by the vulnerabilities along the attack path(s), the more the time/effort an adversary has to spend in compromising the target. Further, more the different kind of vulnerabilities along the attack path, more the effort (in terms of time, skill, and resources) adversary has to spend. Finally, more the number of ways by which an attacker can reach a targeted vulnerability from the other vulnerabilities (predecessors), more the chances of its exploitation, and hence carving out the attack path to the destination host, therefore increased success probability.

The rest of the paper is organized as follows. Section 2 establishes a basis for using various risk conditions during the process of risk scoring. In Sect. 3, we discuss the method of computing the Improved Relative Cumulative Risk (IRCR) score. The experimental results for the example network presented in Sect. 4 to validate the usefulness of the proposed metric. Finally, Sect. 5 closes with conclusions and directions for future work.

2 Network Specific Risk Conditions

For our purpose of combining the standard CVSS Base Score [10] with the network-specific risk conditions, we make use of an exploit-dependency attack graph [27], which is in general space-efficient and more expressive. Mainly, the attack graph takes into account network configuration details, vulnerability details, security advisory, and succinctly depicts all potential multistage, multi-host attack scenarios. It imitates the adversary's choice of vulnerability exploitation and successfully captures various risk conditions that affect the success of an adversary and hence influence the risk posed by the vulnerability. In this paper, we used MulVAL tool [17] for the generation of an exploit-dependency attack graph. This paper does not explore how to generate the attack graph, but rather how to analyze. Network risk conditions which we have used to augment the static risk level (i.e., CVSS Base Score) of each exploitable vulnerability in the network are as follows:

2.1 Attack Path Resistance

To reach, and exploit vulnerability v in a network, there could be one or more attack paths available to an adversary. According to Wang et al. [22], network security should be measured as the smallest amount of effort required to reach and compromise the target. Phillips and Swiler [28] proposed shortest path metric which signifies the minimum number of hurdles (here, vulnerabilities) along the attack path, an attacker has to exploit to compromise the target. Author's intuition is: farther away the target vulnerability is from the attacker's initial position, the more effort she has to spend to reach and exploit it. The longer distance implies an adversary should have the greater endurance to reach the vulnerability v and hence lower the probability of vulnerability exploitation. However, the idea of the shortest attack path is misleading as it treats each type of vulnerability equally and does not capture attackers effort. Since each type of vulnerability poses a different amount of resistance during exploitation, an attacker has to spend a different amount of effort. Therefore, the vulnerability resistance along the attack paths is the correct measure of attackers effort compared to attack path length. The intuition behind considering the least resistance path is that, given the option of different available attack paths which are reachable from attacker's initial position to the vulnerability, an attacker chooses the path which requires the least amount of effort [29]. Therefore, the minimum resistance path to a targeted vulnerability considered as a necessary risk condition.

Figure 1 shows network risk conditions, which used in our proximity-based vulnerability risk computation. Circle shows vulnerabilities v_1, v_2, v_3, v_4, and respective post-conditions by Diamond shape. Vulnerability v_4 can be reached and exploited from the immediate predecessors v_1, v_2, v_3. Out of three attack paths, there is a repetition of vulnerability v_1 along the third attack path. r_i alongside each vulnerability, v_i represents the individual resistance posed by the vulnerability to an attacker (in terms of time and effort) during successful exploitation. In other words, to say, $r(v)$ represents the effort put by an attacker until the successful exploitation of the vulnerability [30]. Higher the value of $r(v)$, it is harder to exploit the vulnerability v. Such values obtained for each of the well-known, reported vulnerability based on their CVSS Temporal Score [31].

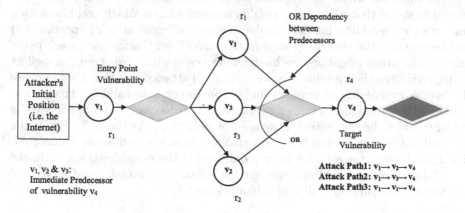

Fig. 1. Sample attack graph.

2.2 Vulnerability (or Exploit) Diversity Along the Attack Path

Exploit diversity along the attack path signifies the number of different kinds of exploits adversary has to successfully execute to reach and exploit the target vulnerability v. Essentially, the attack path with different kinds of exploits indicates that an adversary must possess knowledge about the different exploitation technologies to follow the path. In a sufficiently diversified attack path, an adversary has to spend an individual and independent effort in successfully exploiting each vulnerability coming across the attack path [32].

After getting access to a particular host in a network (pivot point), an adversary performs reconnaissance from that point onward and move on to the next target machine by successfully exploiting vulnerabilities in it. An adversary may encounter one or more vulnerabilities in the next target machine(s) during the reconnaissance. If the next vulnerability is similar to the kind of vulnerabilities already exploited along the path, then the probability of its exploitation is more. Therefore, the number of different kinds of vulnerabilities (exploits) along the attack path(s) also can be considered as an essential risk condition. Such a risk condition indicates the attacker's knowledge. As shown in Fig. 1, along the third attack path, an adversary needs to exploit the vulnerability v_1 twice to reach the target vulnerability v_4.

2.3 Risk of the Neighboring Vulnerabilities

An exploit-dependency attack graph [27] captures the cause-consequence relationship between the exploitable vulnerabilities, and it shows how many ways an adversary can reach and exploit v, a vulnerability under consideration. For each intermediate (non-entry point) vulnerability in an attack graph, there could be one or more neighbors (i.e., immediate predecessors from where the vulnerability directly reached and exploited). Let $PD(v_i)$ signifies the set of such neighboring vulnerabilities on which the exploitation of the vulnerability v_i depends. It is crucial to notice that when many neighbors coexist in an attack graph, reaching the target vulnerability is more feasible (because of more attack opportunities) and hence more the chances of exploitation [22]. Even though the attack paths arising from other neighbors are harder than the original one (here, least effort path), they nevertheless represent possibilities of attacks, and thus they increase the overall probability of exploitation of the target vulnerability. That is the vulnerability with a large number of immediate predecessors is more likely to be exploited than the one with less number of neighbors. As shown in Fig. 1, the vulnerability v_4 can be reached and exploited from three different vulnerabilities. Even though the attacker follows only one of the possible attack path, the availability of many neighbors represents possibilities of attacks, and thus, they increase the overall probability of exploitation of v_4.

2.4 The Conjunctive (AND) and Disjunctive (OR) Dependency Between Predecessors

Mostly, there can be either conjunctive (AND), or disjunctive (OR) dependency relationship between the exploits in an exploit-dependency attack graph [27]. The conjunctive dependency between the predecessor exploits implies that the successor exploit cannot be executed successfully until all of the participating exploits (in an AND dependency) executed successfully. Whereas, the disjunctive dependency between predecessor exploits indicates the successor can be executed successfully if any one of the predecessor vulnerability exploited successfully. Compared to the conjunctive (AND) dependency, disjunctive (OR) dependency between predecessors leads to the higher probability of the successful exploitation of the successor and hence increased risk. As shown in Fig. 1, there is an OR dependency between the immediate predecessors of vulnerability v_4.

3 Measuring Security Risk of Vulnerabilities

In this section, we discuss how to use different network risk conditions for the evaluation of the security risk of each exploitable vulnerability. To calculate the risk value, we define the Diversity-adjusted vulnerability score (DVS), Neighborhood proximity-adjusted vulnerability score (NVS), and finally Improved relative cumulative risk (IRCR) for each exploitable vulnerability v_i in a network $\mathcal{N}$.

3.1 Diversity-Adjusted Vulnerability Score (DVS)

Each vulnerability in a target network is positioned a certain distance apart from the attacker's position (here, un-trusted external network) and can be reachable through one or more attack paths. According to Wang et al. [22], network security should be measured as the smallest effort required to reach the goal. The shortest path metric [28] assumes the same amount of effort is required to exploit each vulnerability along the attack path and counted the number of hurdles (vulnerabilities) along the path as a measure of attackers effort. However, each type of vulnerability poses a different amount of resistance to the adversary. Therefore, we have used vulnerability resistance along the attack path(s) to calculate the risk. For an example attack graph shown in Fig. 1, the resistance of each of the attack path calculated as:

$$PR(AP_i) = \sum_{j=1}^{n} r_j \tag{1}$$

Here r_j signifies the individual resistance posed by the vulnerability to the attacker. As shown in Fig. 1, the resistance posed by the attack paths 1, 2, and 3 simply sums of the individual resistance values of vulnerabilities along the attack paths. However, if there is a repetition of already exploited vulnerability along the attack path (third attack path in Fig. 1), then the attacker can use previously engineered exploits with little or no modification. In such a case, the resistance posed by the repeated vulnerability is much smaller than the posed resistance. For repeated vulnerability v_1 in attack path 3, the resistance value becomes $0.3 * r_1$. Such a reduction in the resistance is due to the attackers acquired skills, tools, and techniques. It is the only subjective parameter used in our risk calculation method. An administrator can choose this value based on the effort required to tweak the already engineered exploit for exploiting the repeated vulnerability in a network. To the best of our knowledge, there is no study on how much reduction in the attacker's work factor (vulnerability resistance) happens when the attacker exploits the same vulnerability repeatedly. Such reduction in work factor (attackers effort) could be different for different classes of vulnerabilities. Based on the above-stated discussion, the path resistance (PR) of attack path 3 in Fig. 1 can be calculated as:

$$PR(AP_3) = r_1 + (0.3 * r_1) + r_4$$

Once we calculate the resistance posed by each of the attack path available to reach the target vulnerability v_i in an attack graph, we focus on the attack path with minimum resistance value. It is because network security should always be measured as the smallest effort required to reach the target [22]. The lower the attack path resistance, closer the vulnerability is, analogically, to the untrusted network, and therefore, higher the risk of target vulnerability exploitation. The problem of finding the distance of vulnerability from the attacker's position is analogous to the single-source shortest path (SSSP) problem. For the vulnerability, v_4 in example attack graph (Fig. 1), the minimum path resistance (MPR) is the minimum of all attack path resistance values. That is:

$$MPR(v_4) = min(PR(AP_1), PR(AP_2), PR(AP_3)) \qquad (2)$$

Here, $MPR(v_i)$ indicates the minimum resistance attacker has to face during the exploitation of v_i. If there are two or more attack paths available to an attacker to reach the vulnerability v_i, then the attack path that poses minimum resistance should be considered for calculating the MPR value [29]. To calculate the security risk posed by an exploitable vulnerability, we define the Diversity-adjusted vulnerability score (DVS) for each vulnerability v_i as follows:

$$DVS(v_i) = CVSS(v_i) \times \frac{1}{MPR(v_i)} \qquad (3)$$

A lower value of DVS is desirable for better network security. Smaller the value of MPR, higher the DVS of vulnerability v_i.

3.2   Neighborhood Proximity-Adjusted Vulnerability Score (NPVS)

In an exploit-dependency attack graph [27] except the entry point vulnerabilities others may have one or more predecessor vulnerabilities. Therefore, the neighborhood $N(v_i)$ of a particular vulnerability v_i consists of the set of vulnerabilities that directly invoke (or trigger) v_i, i.e., $N(v_i) = \{v_j \in V : v_j v_i \in E\}$. Here, V is the set of all exploits present in the attack graph, and E is the set of edges between the exploits. Here, we focus on the vulnerability neighborhood to understand "how many ways an attacker can reach a particular vulnerability?"

First, we define the neighborhood as the predecessor sets $PD_1, PD_2, \ldots PD_n$ for each exploitable vulnerability in an attack graph such that:
$PD_i = \{$ a group of vulnerabilities in an attack graph (immediate predecessors) from where the vulnerability v_i directly reached and exploited$\}$.

By definition, all vulnerabilities in a predecessor set PD_i invokes the vulnerability v_i. The reachability from a group of predecessor vulnerabilities to the target vulnerability v_i is explicitly specified in the network access points, i.e., routers and firewalls. Necessarily, there can be either conjunctive (AND), or disjunctive (OR) dependency relationship between exploits in an exploit-dependency attack graph [27]. The conjunctive dependency between the predecessor exploits implies that the successor exploits not successfully executed until all of the participating exploits (in an AND dependency) executed successfully. Whereas, the disjunctive OR dependency between the predecessor exploits indicates that the successor vulnerability can be executed successfully if any one of the predecessor vulnerability exploited successfully.

It is crucial to notice that when many neighbors coexist in an attack graph, reaching the target vulnerability is far easier. In other words, more attack opportunities mean less security because attackers have a better chance to reach the target. Even though the attack paths arising from other neighbors are harder than the original (least effort) one, they nevertheless represent possibilities for attacks, and thus they increase the overall probability of exploitation of the target vulnerability. Therefore, we have considered the normalized DVS score (i.e., NDVS) of each neighboring vulnerability for computation of the NPVS of vulnerability under consideration. In particular, $NDVS(v_i) = \frac{DVS(v_i)}{10}$.

For a given vulnerability v_i having a predecessor set PD_i, the neighborhood proximity-adjusted vulnerability score (NPVS) is:

$$NPVS(v_i) = \begin{cases} NDVS(v_j) \times NDVS(v_k); \text{ when } v_j \text{ and } v_k \text{ are Conjunctive} \\ NDVS(v_j) + NDVS(v_k) - NDVS(v_j) \times NDVS(v_k) \\ \qquad\qquad ; \text{ when } v_j \text{ and } v_k \text{ are Disjunctive} \\ NDVS(v_j) \qquad ; \text{ when } v_j \text{ is the only neighbor of } v_i \\ 1 \qquad\qquad ; \text{ when } v_i \text{ is the entry point vulnerability} \end{cases}$$
$$(4)$$

For the first two cases in Eq. 4, vulnerability v_i is the immediate successor of the vulnerabilities v_j and v_k. For the entry-point vulnerabilities (whose exploitation does not depend on the exploitation of any other vulnerability), the predecessor set $PD_i = \{\phi\}$. Therefore, the $NPVS$ value for such directly exploitable vulnerabilities is highest, i.e., 1. For the vulnerabilities that are not directly exploitable, higher DVS value with the more significant number of OR-ed invokers (predecessors) results in a higher $NPVS$ value. The magnitude of $NPVS$ for a vulnerability also depends on the AND-OR relationship between predecessor vulnerabilities. Compared to the AND dependency, an OR dependency between predecessor vulnerabilities leads to a higher $NPVS$ score.

3.3   Relative Cumulative Risk

To calculate the cumulative risk of each exploitable vulnerability in the network, we need to take into account the values computed in the previous step (Eqs. 3 and 4) and aggregate them in a way that can express the security risk condition around the vulnerability in question. The improved relative cumulative risk (IRCR) of each exploitable vulnerability v_i in the network is calculated as:

$$IRCR(v_i) = DVS(v_i) \times NPVS(v_i) \qquad (5)$$

As shown in the Eq. 3, $DVS(v_i)$ is the individual $CVSS$ value of a vulnerability v_i, adjusted by the minimum path resistance value (MPR). The security risk because of the neighboring vulnerabilities represented by the $NPVS(v_i)$ value (as shown in the Eq. 4). The higher the DVS of a vulnerability with a large number of invokers, the greater the $NPVS$ becomes. Since $CVSS$ Base Score captures the severity (impact) of the vulnerability and risk conditions capture the likelihood (probability) of vulnerability exploitation, as per the classical definition of risk, $IRCR$ measures the security risk posed by the vulnerability.

The larger the value of $IRCR$, the higher the risk posed by the vulnerability. Therefore, the administrator decides on the patching order of vulnerabilities based on their $IRCR$ value. In practice, patching of all vulnerabilities in the network is mission impossible for the administrator. The vulnerabilities for which no patch is available (or whose patching may hurt the business performance), the goal of the administrator's is to reduce the risk posed by them. Since the lower value of $IRCR$ desired for secure network configuration, the purpose of the administrator's is to decrease the value of $IRCR$. It can be achieved by disabling the initial conditions, patching of entry-point vulnerabilities, and network reconfiguration. Patching of entry-point vulnerabilities remove all the attack paths and hence the $IRCR$ of all the other network vulnerabilities reduce to 0. If patches are not available for the entry-point vulnerabilities, then one needs to disable the initial conditions, which lead to the longer attack sequence and hence the higher value of attack path resistance. Further, through disabling the initial conditions that lead to the removal of most of the attack paths and hence smaller cardinality of predecessor set PD_i of target vulnerability. The larger the value of exploit diversity along the attack path for a particular vulnerability, lower the $IRCR$ score. There are many possible ways to increase the exploit diversity along the attack path for network hardening and have been suggested in [14,24,33].

3.4 Computational Complexity

Among the available attack paths, finding the minimum resistance value path from the attacker's initial position is analogous to the single-source shortest path (SSSP) problem. In particular, the problem is similar to finding the shortest path from a single source in a directed weighted graph. The exploit-dependency attack graph, we generated for our example network is a weighted directed acyclic graph (DAG). We have employed a breadth-first search (BFS) algorithm to compute the minimum effort(resistance) attacker has to spend to reach and exploit the vulnerability under consideration. With BFS, the proximity (minimum path resistance) of a vulnerability from the attacker's position computed in $\mathcal{O}(E)$, where, E is the total number of edges in an exploit-dependency attack graph. Further, finding all predecessor sets $PD_1, PD_2, \ldots, PD_n$ for all n vulnerabilities in an attack graph can also be done in $\mathcal{O}(E)$ using the BFS. The calculation of improved relative cumulative risk (IRCR) value takes $\mathcal{O}(V)$, where V is the total number of exploitable vulnerabilities in the attack graph G. The number of vulnerabilities in the attack graph is a finite constant, $V = \mathcal{O}(n)$. Therefore, the computation time for the whole process of $IRCR$ calculation is $\mathcal{O}(E)$.

4   Experimental Setup and Results

The topology of the Test Network is shown in Fig. 2, which is same as the network topology used in [30], and [34]. There are Four machines located within Two subnets. $Host_3$ is attackers target machine, and $MySQL$ is the critical resource running over it. The attacker is a malicious entity in the external network, and her goal is to obtain root-level privileges on $Host_3$. The job of firewalls is to separate the internal network from the Internet.

Firewall policies that limit connectivity in the network configuration given in Fig. 2. Table 1 shows the system characteristics for the hosts available in the example network. Table 2 shows nine example vulnerabilities and their basic and temporal vectors. Such kind of data is available in public vulnerability databases viz. NVD [4], Bugtraq, OSVDB, etc. Here external firewall allows any external host to only access services running on host $Host_0$. Connections to all other services/ports on other hosts are blocked. The host's within the internal network have authority to connect to only those ports specified by the firewall policies as shown in Fig. 2. The number 1, 2 and 3 represents the open services which refer to the numbers assigned to each host in Table 1; -1 represents source host is prevented from having access to any service on the destination host; 0 means a self-connection. An attack graph generated for the example network is shown in Fig. 3.

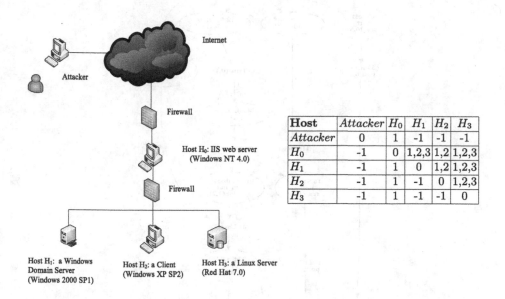

Host	Attacker	H_0	H_1	H_2	H_3
Attacker	0	1	-1	-1	-1
H_0	-1	0	1,2,3	1,2	1,2,3
H_1	-1	1	0	1,2	1,2,3
H_2	-1	1	-1	0	1,2,3
H_3	-1	1	-1	-1	0

Fig. 2. An example network and connectivity-limiting firewall policies.

Table 1. System characteristics for the network configuration [30]

Host	Services	Ports	Vulnerabilities	CVE IDs
$Host_0$	1. IIS_Web_Service	80	IIS buffer-overflow	CVE-2010-2370
$Host_1$	1. ftp	21	ftp-rhost overwrite	CVE-2008-1396
	2. ssh	22	ssh buffer-overflow	CVE-2002-1359
	3. rshd	514	rsh-login	CVE-1999-0180
$Host_2$	1. Netbios-ssn	139	netbios_ssn_nullsession	CVE-2003-0661
	2. rshd	514	rsh-login	CVE-1999-0180
$Host_3$	1. LICQ	5190	LICQ-remote-to-user	CVE-2001-0439
	2. Squid_proxy	80	Squid-port-scan	CVE-2001-1030
	3. MySQL_DB	3306	Local-setuid-buffer-overflow	CVE-2006-3368

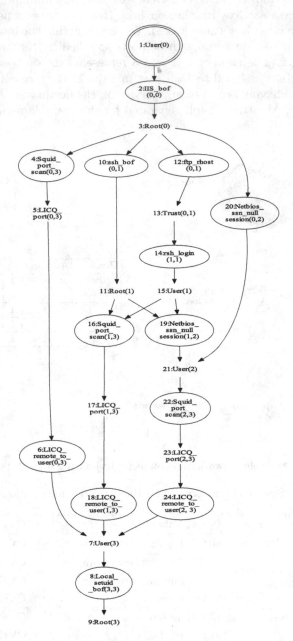

Fig. 3. An exploit-dependency attack graph for the example network. Attacker's initial position is shown by a Double Oval, exploits (vulnerabilities) by an Oval, and respective post-conditions by a plain text.

Table 2. Vulnerability attributes vectors (as per CVSS v3.0 specifications.)

Vulnerability CVE IDs	Basic vector	CVSS base score	Temporal vectors	CVSS temporal score
CVE-2010-2370	AV:N/AC:L/PR:N/UI:N/S:C/C:N/I:L/A:N	5.8	E:F/RL:O/RC:C	5.4
CVE-2008-1396	AV:N/AC:L/PR:N/UI:N/S:U/C:L/I:N/A:N	5.3	E:F/RL:O/RC:C	4.9
CVE-2002-1359	AV:N/AC:L/PR:N/UI:N/S:C/C:H/I:H/A:H	10	E:H/RL:O/RC:C	9.5
CVE-1999-0180	AV:N/AC:L/PR:N/UI:N/S:U/C:L/I:L/A:L	7.3	E:P/RL:O/RC:C	6.6
CVE-2003-0661	AV:N/AC:L/PR:N/UI:N/S:C/C:L/I:N/A:N	5.8	E:F/RL:O/RC:C	5.4
CVE-2001-0439	AV:N/AC:L/PR:N/UI:N/S:U/C:L/I:L/A:L	7.3	E:H/RL:O/RC:C	7
CVE-2001-1030	AV:N/AC:L/PR:N/UI:N/S:U/C:L/I:L/A:L	7.3	E:P/RL:O/RC:C	6.6
CVE-2006-3368	AV:N/AC:L/PR:N/UI:N/S:U/C:L/I:N/A:N	5.3	E:H/RL:O/RC:C	5.1

Table 3. Results of proximity-based vulnerability ranking (for attack graph shown in Fig. 3). Vulnerabilities are sorted in the decreasing order of $IRCR$.

Vulnerability instance	CVE IDs	CVSS base score	CVSS temporal score	p	r	MPR	DVS	NPVS	IRCR	Rank
IIS_buffer_overflow(0,0)	CVE-2010-2370	5.8	5.4	0.54	1.85	1.85	3.14	1.00	3.135	1
SSH_buffer_ overflow(0,1)	CVE-2002-1359	10	9.5	0.95	1.05	2.90	3.44	0.31	1.079	2
Squid_port_ scan(1,3)	CVE-2001-1030	7.3	6.6	0.66	1.52	4.42	1.65	0.43	0.715	3
Squid_port_ scan(0,3)	CVE-2001-1030	7.3	6.6	0.66	1.52	3.37	2.17	0.31	0.680	4
Netbios-ssnnull session(1,2)	CVE-2003-0661	5.8	5.4	0.54	1.85	4.76	1.22	0.43	0.528	5
Netbios-ssnnull session(0,2)	CVE-2003-0661	5.8	5.4	0.54	1.85	3.70	1.57	0.31	0.491	6
ftp_rhost(0,1)	CVE-2008-1396	5.3	4.9	0.49	2.04	3.89	1.36	0.31	0.427	7
Squid_port_scan(2,3)	CVE-2001-1030	7.3	6.6	0.66	1.52	5.22	1.40	0.26	0.363	8
LICQ_remote_ to_user(0,3)	CVE-2001-0439	7.3	7	0.7	1.43	4.80	1.52	0.22	0.330	9
Local-setuid buffer-overflow(3,3)	CVE-2006-3368	5.3	5.1	0.51	1.96	6.76	0.78	0.34	0.266	10
LICQ_remote_ to_user(1,3)	CVE-2001-0439	7.3	7	0.7	1.43	5.85	1.25	0.17	0.206	11
Rsh_login(1,1)	CVE-1999-0180	7.3	6.6	0.66	1.52	5.41	1.35	0.14	0.184	12
LICQ_remote_to_user(2,3)	CVE-2001-0439	7.3	7	0.7	1.43	6.65	1.10	0.14	0.154	13

Table 3 shows 13 vulnerability instances of the example network in Fig. 2. As shown in Table 3, each vulnerability instance has assigned rank depending on their severity levels measured by the $IRCR$ metric (Eq. 5). The vulnerabilities sorted in decreasing order of their $IRCR$ score. Since the lower value of $IRCR$ desired for secure network configuration, vulnerabilities with higher $IRCR$ score need to be patched first with top priority.

Figure 4a shows the $IRCR$ and the $CVSS$ Base Score for each vulnerability instance in the test network. Along the x-axis, there are different vulnerabilities, and along the primary (left) and the secondary (right) y-axis the values of $IRCR$ and $CVSS$, respectively. Figure 4a is a point plot, and the line between two vulnerability instance has no significance other than to indicate the trend. Since the vulnerabilities with the higher $IRCR$ needs to be patched first with the highest priority, we have plotted the vulnerabilities in decreasing order of their $IRCR$ value. As evident from Fig. 4a, the values of $CVSS$ Base Score experience differing fluctuating trend. Taking this fact into account, one can say that exploitable vulnerability with a higher $CVSS$ score need not pose a higher risk and vice versa. For vulnerabilities (or vulnerability instances) having the same CVSS score, there is no way to know in which order they should be patched. It hinders the decision on taking hardening strategies. However, $IRCR$ can reflect the influential level of vulnerability instances more precisely, as the risk estimated by considering various network risk conditions.

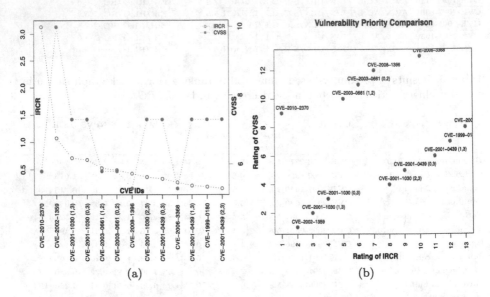

(a)   (b)

Fig. 4. Plot (a) showing vulnerability instances, and their respective values for $CVSS$ and Improved Relative Cumulative Risks ($IRCR$) score. Plot (b) showing vulnerability priority comparison: $IRCR$ vs $CVSS$ results.

Figure 4b shows the patching order of the vulnerabilities based on the rank (or rating) assigned by $IRCR$ and $CVSS$. Along the x-axis, vulnerabilities plotted in the decreasing order of their $IRCR$ value. Whereas, along the y-axis, vulnerability with highest $CVSS$ Base Score is ranked first. After checking Table 3 and Fig. 4b as well, we can find that the CVSS ranking of the vulnerability *IIS_buffer_overflow* (CVE-2010-2370) is at 9th position. In contrast, through our proximity-based ranking, it comes to 1st, as shown in Table 3, which corresponds well to the estimated attacking scenario. In attack graph of Fig. 3, *IIS_buffer_overflow(0,0)* is the first vulnerability to be triggered by an adversary and it is very critical for vulnerability instance to stand out that no adversary can ignore or bypass while deploying attacks. Without issuing this vulnerability (i.e., CVE-2010-2370) successfully, no other vulnerability exploited.

Two vulnerabilities *Squid_port_ scan* and *LICQ_remote_ to_user*, share the same CVSS Base Score of 7.3 and given the same rank. These sort of rankings can frequently happen in CVSS, confusing on patching order and hindering decision on taking hardening measures. Checking ranking results, 3 vulnerability instances of *Squid_port_ scan* and 3 instances of *LICQ_remote_ to_user* have been ranked in Table 3. All the instances of *Squid_port_ scan* ranked before the instances of *LICQ_remote_ to_user*. It indicates that based on the view of the whole security level, the elimination of each *Squid_port_ scan* leads to more secure network than the elimination of *LICQ_remote_ to_user* vulnerability instances.

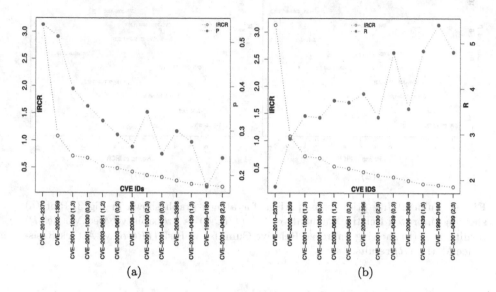

(a)   (b)

Fig. 5. Plot (a) showing the Improved Relative Cumulative Risk ($IRCR$) and Probability-based Metric (P) values for each vulnerability. Plot (b) showing the Improved Relative Cumulative Risk ($IRCR$) and Attack Resistance Metric (R) values for each vulnerability.

Table 4. Results comparison: top 5 vulnerabilities based on the different risk assessment techniques.

Risk assessment technique	Top 5 vulnerabilities instances
CVSS v3.0 [10]	**CVE-2002-1359**, CVE-2001-1030 (1,3), CVE-2001-1030 (0,3), CVE-2001-1030 (2,3), **CVE-2001-0439 (0,3)**
Probability-based Metric (P) [21]	CVE-2010-2370, CVE-2002-1359, CVE-2001-1030 (1,3), CVE-2001-1030 (0,3), **CVE-2001-1030 (2,3)**
Attack Resistance Metric (R) [22]	CVE-2010-2370, CVE-2002-1359, CVE-2001-1030 (0,3), **CVE-2001-1030 (2,3)**, CVE-2001-1030 (1,3)
Improved Relative Cumulative Risk (IRCR)	CVE-2010-2370, CVE-2002-1359, CVE-2001-1030 (1,3), CVE-2001-1030 (0,3), **CVE-2003-0661 (1,2)**

Next, we compared the Improved Relative Cumulative Risk ($IRCR$) metric with probability-based metric (P) [21] and attack resistance metric (R) [22]. We have chosen these two metrics for comparison because they take into account all

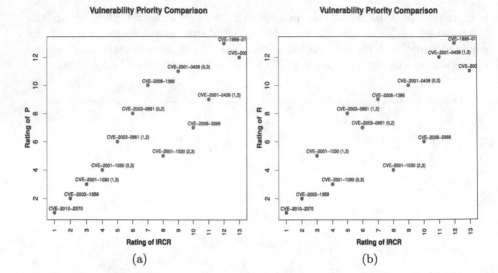

Fig. 6. Vulnerability priority comparison for attack graph shown in Fig. 3. Plot (a) showing Improved Relative Cumulative Risk ($IRCR$) vs Probability-based Metric (P) results. Plot (b) showing Improved Relative Cumulative Risk ($IRCR$) vs Attack Resistance Metric (R) results.

the vulnerabilities between the attacker's initial position and the target vulnerability. Further, these metrics reflect the cause-consequence relationship between vulnerabilities.

The comparative results for the top 5 vulnerability instances based on different risk assessment techniques presented in Table 4. As evident from the Fig. 5a and b, both probability-based metric (P) and attack resistance (R) metric choose the vulnerability instance CVE-2001-1030 (2,3) over CVE-2003-0661 (1,2). It is because the calculation steps for both P and R are roughly similar. Both P and R gives higher priority to the vulnerabilities that can be reachable and exploitable through more number of attack paths. There are three ways to reach and exploit the vulnerability instance CVE-2001-1030 (2,3). However, $IRCR$ gives priority to CVE-2003-0661 (1,2) over CVE-2001-1030 (2,3). It is because the attacker needs to spend less effort to reach and exploit CVE-2003-0661 (1,2). Figure 6a shows the patching order of the vulnerabilities based on the rank assigned by both $IRCR$ and probability-based metric (P). Whereas, the patching order of the exploitable vulnerabilities based on the rank assigned by $IRCR$ and attack resistance metric (R) shown in Fig. 6b. In the mitigation plan of top 5 vulnerabilities for our example attack graph illustrated in Fig. 3 based on P, R and IRCR consists of four common vulnerabilities. Even though the mitigation plan is 80% same for all the three risk assessment methods, the vulnerability patching order varies. It demonstrates that the proposed $IRCR$ metric can be complementary to the current attack graph-based metrics in measuring the influential levels of exploitable vulnerabilities.

5 Conclusion

A comprehensive, integrated measure called Improved Relative Cumulative Risk (IRCR) proposed for quantifying the security risk of exploitable vulnerabilities in a dynamic computer network. It incorporates (i) CVSS Base Score, (ii) proximity of a vulnerability from the attacker's initial position, (iii) vulnerability diversity along the attack path(s), and (iv) the risk of the neighboring exploitable vulnerabilities. We tested $IRCR$ metric on a synthetic network, and experimental results show that $IRCR$ effectively computes the security risk of exploitable vulnerabilities. We can use the resultant $IRCR$ score for the direct comparison of exploitable vulnerabilities in terms of their security risks, and hence for vulnerability prioritization. It helps administrators in accurately determining top vulnerabilities and in prioritizing vulnerability remediation activities accordingly. Further, $IRCR$ reflects the influential level of vulnerability instances more precisely, as the estimation performed by considering various network risk conditions. As an immediate future work, we propose to investigate the reduction in the attacker's work factor (vulnerability resistance) because of the repetition of vulnerabilities along the attack paths. Further, we want to improve the $IRCR$ metric and use it for investigating different aspects of network security.

References

1. Poolsappasit, N., Dewri, R., Ray, I.: Dynamic security risk management using Bayesian attack graphs. IEEE Trans. Depend. Secur. Comput. **9**, 61–74 (2012)
2. US-CERT: United states computer emergency response team. https://www.us-cert.gov/
3. SANS. http://www.sans.org/newsletters/cva/
4. NVD. https://nvd.nist.gov/
5. Vupen-Security. http://www.vupen.com/english/
6. Secunia. http://secunia.com/about_secunia_advisories/
7. Microsoft. http://www.microsoft.com/technet/
8. Mell, P., Scarfone, K., Romanosky, S.: Common vulnerability scoring system. IEEE Secur. Privacy **4**, 85–89 (2006)
9. Mell, P., Scarfone, K., Romanosky, S.: A complete guide to the common vulnerability scoring system version 2.0, June 2007
10. FIRST: Common vulnerability scoring system v3.0: Specification doc, June 2015
11. MITRE: Common weakness scoring system (2016). https://cwe.mitre.org/cwss/
12. Holm, H., Afridi, K.K.: An expert-based investigation of the common vulnerability scoring system. Comput. Secur. **53**, 18–30 (2015)
13. Holm, H.: Baltic cyber shield: research from a red team versus blue team exercise (2012)
14. Wang, L., Jajodia, S., Singhal, A., Cheng, P., Noel, S.: k-zero day safety: a network security metric for measuring the risk of unknown vulnerabilities. IEEE Trans. Depend. Secur. Comput. **11**, 30–44 (2014)
15. Sheyner, O., Haines, J., Jha, S., Lippmann, R., Wing, J.: Automated generation and analysis of attack graphs. In: Proceedings of the IEEE Symposium on Security and Privacy, pp. 273–284 (2002)

16. Ammann, P.: Scalable, graph-based network vulnerability analysis. In: Proceedings of the 9th ACM Conference on Computer and Communications Security, pp. 217–224. ACM Press (2002)

17. Ou, X., Boyer, W.F.: A scalable approach to attack graph generation. In: Proceedings of the 13th ACM Conference on Computer and Communications Security (CCS), pp. 336–345. ACM Press (2006)

18. Jajodia, S., Noel, S.: Topological vulnerability analysis: a powerful new approach for network attack prevention, detection, and response. In: Proceedings of Algorithms, Architectures, and Information System Security, Indian Statistical Institute Platinum Jubilee Series, pp. 285–305 (2009)

19. Ghosh, N., Ghosh, S.: A planner-based approach to generate and analyze minimal attack graph. Appl. Intell. **36**, 369–390 (2012)

20. Kordy, B., Piètre-Cambacédès, L., Schweitzer, P.: DAG-based attack and defense modeling: don't miss the forest for the attack trees. Comput. Sci. Rev. **13–14**, 1–38 (2014)

21. Wang, L., Islam, T., Long, T., Singhal, A., Jajodia, S.: An attack graph-based probabilistic security metric. In: Atluri, V. (ed.) DBSec 2008. LNCS, vol. 5094, pp. 283–296. Springer, Heidelberg (2008). https://doi.org/10.1007/978-3-540-70567-3_22

22. Wang, L., Singhal, A., Jajodia, S.: Measuring the overall security of network configurations using attack graphs. In: Barker, S., Ahn, G.-J. (eds.) DBSec 2007. LNCS, vol. 4602, pp. 98–112. Springer, Heidelberg (2007). https://doi.org/10.1007/978-3-540-73538-0_9

23. Chen, F., Liu, D., Zhang, Y., Su, J.: A scalable approach to analyzing network security using compact attack graphs. J. Netw. **5**, 543 (2010)

24. Wang, L., Jajodia, S., Singhal, A., Noel, S.: k-zero day safety: measuring the security risk of networks against unknown attacks. In: Gritzalis, D., Preneel, B., Theoharidou, M. (eds.) ESORICS 2010. LNCS, vol. 6345, pp. 573–587. Springer, Heidelberg (2010). https://doi.org/10.1007/978-3-642-15497-3_35

25. Suh-Lee, C., Jo, J.: Quantifying security risk by measuring network risk conditions. In: 2015 IEEE/ACIS Proceedings of the 14th International Conference on Computer and Information Science (ICIS), pp. 9–14 (2015)

26. Mukherjee, P., Mazumdar, C.: Attack difficulty metric for assessment of network security. In: Proceedings of the 13th International Conference on Availability, Reliability and Security, p. 44. ACM (2018)

27. Wang, L., Noel, S., Jajodia, S.: Minimum-cost network hardening using attack graphs. Comput. Commun. **29**, 3812–3824 (2006)

28. Phillips, C., Swiler, L.P.: A graph-based system for network-vulnerability analysis. In: Proceedings of the Workshop on New Security Paradigms. NSPW 1998, pp. 71–79. ACM, New York (1998)

29. Preuß, J., Furnell, S.M., Papadaki, M.: Considering the potential of criminal profiling to combat hacking. J. Comput. Virol. **3**, 135–141 (2007)

30. Ghosh, N., Ghosh, S.: An approach for security assessment of network configurations using attack graph. In: 1st International Conference on Networks and Communications, NETCOM 2009, pp. 283–288 (2009)

31. Ghosh, N., Ghosh, S.: An approach for security assessment of network configurations using attack graph. In: Proceedings of the International Conference on Networks & amp; Communications, pp. 283–288 (2009)

32. Bopche, G.S., Mehtre, B.M.: Exploiting curse of diversity for improved network security. In: Proceedings of the International Conference on Advances in Computing, Communications and Informatics (ICACCI), pp. 1975–1981 (2015)

33. Borbor, D., Wang, L., Jajodia, S., Singhal, A.: Diversifying network services under cost constraints for better resilience against unknown attacks. In: Ranise, S., Swarup, V. (eds.) DBSec 2016. LNCS, vol. 9766, pp. 295–312. Springer, Cham (2016). https://doi.org/10.1007/978-3-319-41483-6_21
34. Zhao, F., Huang, H., Jin, H., Zhang, Q.: A hybrid ranking approach to estimate vulnerability for dynamic attacks. Comput. Math. Appl. **62**, 4308–4321 (2011)

Man-in-the-browser Attack: A Case Study on Malicious Browser Extensions

Sampsa Rauti[✉]

University of Turku, 20014 Turku, Finland
sjprau@utu.fi

Abstract. Man-in-the-browser (MitB) attacks, often implemented as malicious browser extensions, have the ability to alter the structure and contents of web pages, and stealthily change the data given by the user before it is sent to the server. This is done without the user or the online service (the server) noticing anything suspicious. In this study, we present a case study on the man-in-the-browser attack. Our proof-of-concept implementation demonstrates how easily this attack can be implemented as a malicious browser extension. The implementation is a UI-level, cross-browser implementation using JavaScript. We also successfully test the extension in a real online bank. By demonstrating a practical man-in-the-browser attack, our research highlights the need to better monitor and control malicious browser extensions.

1 Introduction

In a man-in-the-browser (MitB) attack, a malicious program can change the structure and contents of web pages, modify data in HTTP messages, or steal sensitive data the user enters in the browser without the user or online service observing anything out of the ordinary [15]. There are several real-world examples of man-in-the-browser malware, such as SpyEye, Zeus, Torpig, URLZone and Silentbanker [4, 5].

The attack was originally presented by Augusto Paes de Barros in a talk about new backdoor trends in 2005. The name man-in-the-browser attack was later invented by Philipp Gühring, who also described the attack in more detail and discussed possible countermeasures against it [9]. Today, almost 15 years later, pieces of malware with man-in-the-browser functionality are still a significant threat for many online services. Online banking and web services of financial institutions, for example, are among the most popular targets for man-in-the-browser attacks [6].

This study presents a case study on the man-in-the-browser attack. We demonstrate how easy it is to build a malicious browser extension with man-in-the-browser functionality that stealthily changes the data the user has inputted in the browser. While our implementation is a Chrome extension, it could easily be utilized in Opera or Firefox as well, as the code is written in JavaScript and operates on the UI level. We also successfully test this extension in a real

© Springer Nature Singapore Pte Ltd. 2020
S. M. Thampi et al. (Eds.): SSCC 2019, CCIS 1208, pp. 60–71, 2020.
https://doi.org/10.1007/978-981-15-4825-3_5

online bank. This study shows that even a simple, easy-to-implement malware can successfully perform a man-in-the-browser attack, bypassing all traditional authentication mechanisms and other security solutions like TLS encryption. By demonstrating a practical man-in-the-browser attack, our research shows that MitB is still a serious threat for web applications and outlines the need to better monitor and control the malicious browser extensions.

The rest of the paper is organized as follows. Section 2 explains how a typical man-in-the-browser attack proceeds. Section 3 describes our proof-of-concept implementation for the attack. Section 4 describes the experiment we performed in a real online bank with our malicious extension. Section 5 discusses the implications and countermeasures of man-in-the-browser attacks. Finally, Sect. 6 concludes the paper.

2   The Attack

Because spying on and altering messages in the network is difficult due to encryption, many attackers are instead looking for an easier opportunity to perform man-in-the-middle attack at the endpoint of communication – the user's infected machine. Man-in-the-browser is a security threat that can be described as a deceitful proxy inside the browser. The goal of the malicious program is either to steal or alter the data exchanged by the user and the web service [20]. This can mean (1) fraudulently altering the contents of web pages before they are rendered (2) modifying the data in incoming or outgoing messages (3) generating additional malicious HTTP requests, or (4) capturing sensitive data and sending it to command and control server [9,22]. A MitB malware can contain some or many of these functionalities. The malicious program usually operates totally silently, without giving the user or the web service any visible clues about its existence.

In this paper, we will take a closer look at a type of man-in-the-browser attack that uses DOM (Document Object Model) modification to quietly alter the data inputted by the user before the data gets transmitted to the server. Such an attack usually proceeds as follows:

1. The user's computer gets infected by malware. Oftentimes, the malware resides in the browser and is implemented as a malicious browser extension.
2. The malware has a list of matching URLs and once the user visits a URL on the list, the man-in-the-browser functionality activates.
3. The malicious program waits until the user logs in and makes a transaction – for instance, the user transfers money from his or her bank account.
4. Before the data is sent to the server, the malware tampers with the request and modifies the data – for example by using the browser's DOM interface to change the bank account number of the receiver.
5. After the values submitted by the user have been modified, the man-in-the-browser malware lets the browser proceed with transmitting the data to the server.

6. The browser then delivers the deceptive HTTP request to the server. The server, however, has no way of telling this falsified request from a real one. It therefore accepts the request, believing this is the real intent of the user.
7. The user is then usually asked to verify the transaction. For instance, an online banking website shows the details of a bank transfer to the user once more so that they can be confirmed.
8. The MitB malware changes any details (e.g. the bank account number) on the displayed page so that they correspond to the original transaction that the user intended to make. The user thinks everything is fine and confirms the transaction.

The user and the online service involved in the exchange have been deceived. Later the user will probably notice that the transaction was altered (e.g. when receiving a reminder letter for the invoice). At this point, the money has probably already been irrevocably lost.

3   Implementation

We studied how a man-in-the-browser attack could be implemented as an extension for the Chrome web browser. Like in the example description of a man-in-the-browser attack in the previous section, we decided to make a malicious browser extension that manipulates the data the user has filled in on a web site before it is sent to the server. Later on, we perform an experiment with our extension by changing the recipient account number when making a transaction in an online bank.

For better security, changing HTTP messages has been made tricky in Chrome by restricting this functionality in the WebRequest API. We circumvent this problem by using an easier method of manipulating the data with the DOM API before it is sent to the server. This way, we do not even need to use any browser specific APIs, the extension will just consist of a few lines of very basic JavaScript.

When using DOM to replace the data given by the user with our own fraudulent data, we have to find a way to do this stealthily so that the user does not notice anything. Simply changing the value of a text field so that the user can easily spot the change does not work, for example. There are many possible approaches to modify the DOM and manipulate data, but in our implementation we used the following one:

1. Find the text field containing the value we want to change.
2. Make a fake copy of this original text field.
3. Make the original field invisible (with CSS).
4. Replace the value of the invisible original text field with a deceptive value.
5. Insert to fake field in the place of the original one.

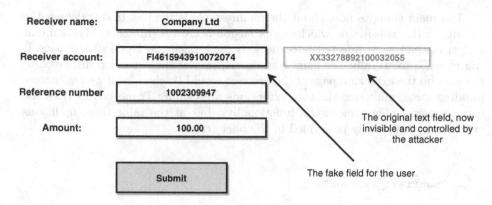

Fig. 1. A man-in-the-browser attack against the online bank application by substituting the receiver account field with a fake one. The user types a value in the fake field, which is never going to be submitted. Instead, the value in the original, invisible text field, controlled by the attacker, is transmitted to the server.

Now, the user will think that the fake field is the real one, and he or she will use this field to input the value in the application. However, what is really going to be sent to the server is the data in the original text field that is invisible and unreachable to the user. Figure 1 illustrates this situation. Of course, the same trick could be used with other text fields as well. For instance, the attacker could easily increase the amount of money that is being transferred.

The whole malicious modification functionality in the extension can be written in about 5 lines of basic JavaScript which uses the DOM API. We will not share the code here, because it is a piece of malware, but anyone with a moderate knowledge of JavaScript could write the extension in just a few minutes. The code is available upon request for research purposes.

There is one more minor thing to take care of: we want the malicious extension to also deceive the user when the verification page is displayed. On the verification page, the extension just searches the element that displays the data which has been sent to the server (e.g. payment information with an account number) and replaces its contents with the original value the user has inputted. This requires just a few lines of code: capture the data written by the user in the fake text field, store it and display it on the verification page instead of the fallacious data that has really been sent to the server. With this, our extension is pretty much finished.

The extension should normally only be installed through Chrome Web Store, but one can also test unpacked extensions by enabling Chrome's developer mode. To load the extension in Chrome, we just have to have two separate files in a folder: a manifest (manifest.json) and a content script (content.js) containing the malicious functionality that was described previously. The contents of the manifest file are shown in Fig. 2.

The main thing to note about the manifest file is the fact that it defines the website or the websites on which the extension activates (matches). The content script, content.js, is injected into the web page once the DOM of the page is complete [7]. Naturally, the name and description of the extension displayed to the user on the extension page of the browser would be changed if we really were building a real malware. Malware extensions are usually Trojans: they trick the user by performing some useful functionality, but at the same time, malicious activities are stealthily performed in the background.

```
{
    "manifest_version": 2,

    "name": "Bank transfer modifier",
    "version": "0.1.0",
    "description": "Sends your payments to the evil attacker",

    "content_scripts": [{
        "js": ["content.js"],
        "matches": ["*://bank.com/*"],
        "run_at": "document_end"
    }]

}
```

Fig. 2. The extension's manifest file.

4   Experiment

We used Chrome's developer mode and installed our extension. The extension was tested on a machine with Windows 10 and Chrome version 76.0.3809.132 installed. Figure 3 shows the extension on Chrome's extension page.

We proceeded to test our extension on a real online bank service. We will leave out the name of the bank from this study, suffice it to say it was a relatively large European bank. The experiment was a success, as our extension was able to divert the payment to a different bank account than given in the bank application.

Regarding the experiment, the following observations are especially noteworthy:

1. *Two-factor authentication is useless.* The bank uses two-factor authentication in the login process. This is useless against man-in-the-browser attacks that bypass the authentication phase and modify the transaction "on the fly" as the user makes the payment. Therefore, our extension did not experience any challenges in the login phase.

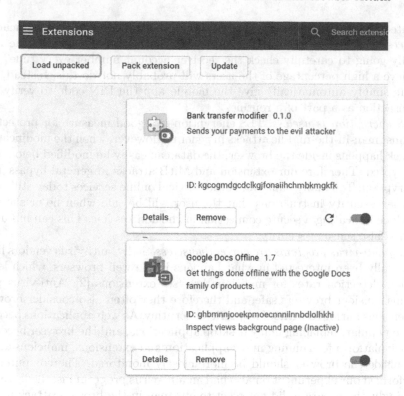

Fig. 3. Chrome's extension page.

2. *Out-of-band verification is useless to some extent.* The bank uses out-of-band (OOB) verification to confirm the transaction. OOB verification verifies the transaction using a second channel other than just the web browser [5,24]. This can be done with a mobile application (where the user gives a PIN code) or using a separate little device supplied by the bank. If the user uses the separate device, he or she gives the device a code on the bank's web page, and then gives the bank web page a code calculated by the device. However, the device never displays the receiver's account number to the user, and in this sense, the verification is not really complete and does not really protect against our MitB attack.

The other way of verification, the mobile application, is better, because the receiver account number is displayed to the user for verification. Of course, this can potentially stop a MitB attack and our extension, if the user notices the difference in account number is different from what he or she originally inputted in the browser. One problem in mobile verification is the fact that nowadays, many users can use their mobile phones for online banking. In this case, OOB verification may be rendered useless if the phone is infected, because there is no real second channel anymore in the verification process [3,10]. In addition, our most prominent concern with OOB verification is related to user errors and simple psychology. After a while, the verification process most likely becomes an automatic routine for the user. Is the user really going to carefully check the receiver account number every time? We believe a high percentage of the users will probably not do this. Instead, the users simply automatically give the mobile app the PIN code to verify the transaction as a part of a routine.

3. *TLS encryption is useless.* TLS encryption is a good measure for protecting against man-in-the-middle attacks in general. However, when the modification attack happens inside the browser, the data can easily be modified before it is encrypted. Therefore our extension and MitB attacks in general bypass TLS encryption. Too many banks and other critical online services today still state in their security instructions that the user will be safe when he or she sees the lock indicating a secure connection in the address bar. This can lull users into a false sense of security.

4. *Many anti-virus programs are currently useless.* Sadly, anti-virus vendors have not really been interested in what happens inside web browsers, which leads to low detection rates for malicious browser extensions [2]. Anti-virus programs consider browsers safe, and therefore they often also consider browser extensions harmless without any stricter scrutiny. As web applications become more popular, replacing many desktop applications, and the browser becomes a new platform for running many application and extensions, malicious activity inside the browser should be more closely monitored. The computer we performed our experiment on also had an anti-virus program installed. Unsurprisingly, the program did not react to our man-in-the-browser attack in any way.

5. *The bank did not question the transaction.* Finally, the transaction we tested was a success and the online bank did not notice anything suspicious was going on. It is not completely fair to criticize the bank about this, because we transferred a relatively small amount inside the same country (from a Finnish account to a Finnish account). Still, we want to make this observation here to remind that banks should check all transfers on the server side and require extra verification (for example by calling the customer and asking for verification) for payments that differ from the normal pattern of transactions. Also, banks could include some client side security measures in their web applications to mitigate MitB attacks, as we will see in the next section.

5   Discussion and Countermeasures

The proof-of-concept implementation for a malicious MitB extension presented in this study shows that in 2020, about 15 years after their appearance, man-in-the-browser attacks are still a significant threat and can effectively work against the modern online banking web systems which are supposed to be at the top of their game in terms of securing transactions. As already noted by Blom a couple of years earlier [1], it still seems that many banks do not consider man-in-the-browser attacks a serious threat.

As noted before, a malicious extension is regrettably easy to implement. Writing a few lines of rudimentary JavaScript and using the DOM interface is not difficult. However, to create an extension that changes data entered in a form, not even this is actually required. This is because the code of extension could be shared to less technically oriented attackers, who would then only need to fill in two details in the code: (1) the ID of the text field which we want to fabricate (or IDs for several text fields, if required), and (2) the ID of the corresponding element on the verification page so that it can be edited as well. Actually, the latter ID is not strictly necessary, because the extension could just scan the verification page and replace the value regardless where it is. Even more dangerously, why not make the extension the look for IBAN account numbers (or any other well-formatted data) in the text fields and replace all such fields? Then the extension would be completely automatic and probably work against several banks even without prior knowledge about the exact user interfaces of the banking web apps. At any rate, it should be clear that even when not automatized to this extent, our extension is really easy to parametrize. Anyone can search for IDs of HTML elements (e.g. using Chrome's inspect functionality) and then make the necessary replacements in the JavaScript code.

Google has continuously striven to make the process of reviewing extensions more rigorous [16], and in 2018, installation from web sites other than Chrome Web Store was disabled. However, many malicious authors have still succeeded in slipping their extensions into Chrome Web Store. With over 60 % market share, Chrome is still a very attractive choice for malware developers. Many malware authors also first publish a completely harmless extension and then integrate malicious functionality to the extension later. The adversary can also use malware that circumvent Chrome's installation restrictions and programmatically install the extension to Chrome without the user's knowledge and permission. For example, the notorious "Catch-All" extension for Chrome that stole all data user typed in the browser used a malicious installer program that started Chrome from command line with parameters that allowed the installation of the extension and circumventing many security features related to extensions [12]. Finally, the adversary could employ social engineering to get the user to install the harmful extension in developer mode.

Although Chrome's extension policy has become stricter in recent years, many other browsers, other browsers such as Firefox and Opera have looser policies when it comes to extension installation and permissions. It is also important to note that the JavaScript code we wrote does not use any browser specific features, and it could be directly used for Firefox and Opera extensions as well.

It is quite apparent additional countermeasures are needed against malware with man-in-the-browser functionality modifying the user's transactions. Scientific literature has proposed numerous different countermeasures over the years, but we will discuss just a few solutions in the context of our practical experiment here:

- *Stricter permission control for browser extensions.* Chrome has a system in place that makes the users confirm the permissions an extension can have.

However, many users are probably going to accept these permissions without really reviewing them or understanding what they mean. Firefox and Opera, on the other hand, do not have this fine-grained extension permission management. Therefore, new ideas and frameworks for permission and access control management and monitoring [8, 13, 23] are needed. For example, Liu et al. propose assigning different sensitivity levels for HTML elements [11]. It could be a good idea to restrict the ability of extensions to modify text fields, for example. At the very least, certain patterns such as an extension modifying an invisible text field (like in our example implementation) are highly suspicious. Also, it would not be that difficult to compile a list of the most critical web sites (such as online banks) where extensions would be completely turned off.

- *Out-of-band verification.* We already saw that out-of-the-band verification has its downsides. The process can become a boring routine for the user or both web banking and verification can be done on the same infected mobile phone. However, out-of-band verification is still a good security mechanism when used correctly. An uninfected second channel has to be used for verification and the transaction details have to be shown to the user. The user has to understand why verification is important and check the transaction carefully. Aside from a mobile device which may not be completely secure, for instance a separate USB gadget with a display can be used for verification [14, 18].
- *Monitoring web page integrity.* One way to protect against DOM-based man-in-the-browser attacks is to verify the integrity of the web pages [17]. The challenge here, of course, is that there are many legitimate extensions such as advertisement blockers that need to modify pages. On some web sites with critical functionality and sensitive information, however, this countermeasure could provide great benefits. Cryptography can be used to protect the integrity of web content [21]. As a mechanism to mitigate man-in-the-browser attacks, critical applications could add functionality guarding the integrity of the web page. An even more secure solution would be to integrate this check in the browser. This way, performing tricks such as adding extra text fields would become more difficult.
- *Hardening the browser.* Hardening refers to securing software by limiting the attack surface and implementing other mechanisms preventing cyber attacks. For example, a clean web browser can be loaded from an external tamper-proof device [19]. The hardened browser would use TLS to encrypt communication with the server and browser extensions would not be allowed. Therefore, setting up a man-in-the-browser attack would become difficult for the adversary. However, the usability of this solution is not as good as that of a normal browser, as the user has to attach the device and use a separate browser for critical transactions.

To summarize, thwarting man-in-the-browser attacks is a co-operative effort involving many parties. First, web browser vendors need to make sure permissions of extensions are controlled and users are informed about possible implications of granting these permissions. Installing malicious extensions should not be too easy. Intuitive mechanisms for turning off extensions on certain web sites should be provided. Second, providers of critical services such as banks should always provide appropriate out-of-band verification and emphasize the importance of carefully checking the transactions. Client-side mechanism such as DOM integrity checking can be used on client side. Third, anti-virus vendors should do even better job in analyzing what happens inside the browser (e.g. by analyzing activities of extensions and monitoring what kind of resources they access). Fourth, organizations need to pay attention to their policies on browser extensions. It would be a good idea to regularly review the installed extensions. Last but not least, it is important for the users to understand how powerful browser extensions are and select the extensions they use carefully. Many attacks could be proactively prevented by educating users.

Finally, although we have been mainly discussing online banks in our examples, it is worth noting that man-in-the-browser attacks are a threat to a wide variety of different web services. One can easily imagine replacing the content sent by the user in social media or webmail services with messages decided by the adversary. Tampering with online voting, input data for medical appliances, or industrial processes could potentially have even more serious consequences.

6   Conclusion

We have presented a case study on man-in-the-browser attacks and demonstrated how a practical attack can be carried out by building a malicious browser extension. It is concerning how simple the malicious code is and how effortlessly the attack can be deployed against users even 15 years after man-in-the-browser attacks were first discovered. While no security solution completely prevents man-in-the-browser attacks (and still preserves good usability), combining several countermeasures and enforcing these security approaches more effectively in modern web browsers and web applications should significantly alleviate the problem in the future. This goal can be reached with co-operative efforts of web developers, users, antivirus program vendors and browser manufacturers.

References

1. Blom, A., de Koning Gans, G., Poll, E., de Ruiter, J., Verdult, R.: Designed to fail: a USB-connected reader for online banking. In: Jøsang, A., Carlsson, B. (eds.) NordSec 2012. LNCS, vol. 7617, pp. 1–16. Springer, Heidelberg (2012). https://doi.org/10.1007/978-3-642-34210-3_1
2. DeKoven, L.F., Savage, S., Voelker, G.M., Leontiadis, N.: Malicious browser extensions at scale: bridging the observability gap between web site and browser. In: 10th USENIX Workshop on Cyber Security Experimentation and Test (CSET 2017). USENIX Association, Vancouver, BC (2017), https://www.usenix.org/conference/cset17/workshop-program/presentation/dekoven
3. Dmitrienko, A., Liebchen, C., Rossow, C., Sadeghi, A.R.: On the (in)security of mobile two-factor authentication. In: Christin, N., Safavi-Naini, R. (eds.) Financial Cryptography and Data Security, pp. 365–383. Springer, Berlin Heidelberg (2014). https://doi.org/10.1007/978-3-662-45472-5_24

4. Dougan, T., Curran, K.: Man in the browser attacks. Int. J. Ambient Comput. Intell. (IJACI) **4**(1), 29–39 (2012)
5. Entrust: Defeating Man-in-the-Browser Malware - How to prevent the latest malware attacks against consumer and corporate banking. White paper (2014)
6. Gezer, A., Warner, G., Wilson, C., Shrestha, P.: A flow-based approach for trickbot banking trojan detection. Comput. Secur. **84**, 179–192 (2019)
7. Google: Content scripts (2019). https://developer.chrome.com/extensions/content_scripts
8. Guha, A., Fredrikson, M., Livshits, B., Swamy, N.: Verified security for browser extensions. In: 2011 IEEE Symposium on Security and Privacy, pp. 115–130. IEEE (2011)
9. Gühring, P.: Concepts against man-in-the-browser attacks. Technical report (2006)
10. Konoth, R.K., van der Veen, V., Bos, H.: How anywhere computing just killed your phone-based two-factor authentication. In: Grossklags, J., Preneel, B. (eds.) FC 2016. LNCS, vol. 9603, pp. 405–421. Springer, Heidelberg (2017). https://doi.org/10.1007/978-3-662-54970-4_24
11. Liu, L., Zhang, X., Yan, G., Chen, S., et al.: Chrome extensions: threat analysis and countermeasures. In: NDSS (2012)
12. Marinho, R.: "Catch-All" Google Chrome Malicious Extension Steals All Posted Data (2017). https://morphuslabs.com/catch-all-google-chrome-malicious-extension-steals-all-posted-data-f2472e272101
13. Marouf, S., Shehab, M.: Towards improving browser extension permission management and user awareness. In: 8th International Conference on Collaborative Computing: Networking, Applications and Worksharing (CollaborateCom), pp. 695–702. IEEE (2012)
14. Migdal, D., Johansen, C., Jøsang, A.: DEMO: OffPAD - offline personal authenticating device with applications in hospitals and e-banking. In: Proceedings of the 2016 ACM SIGSAC Conference on Computer and Communications Security CCS 2016, pp. 1847–1849. ACM, New York, NY, USA (2016)
15. OWASP: Man-in-the-browser attack (2019). https://www.owasp.org/index.php/Man-in-the-browser_attack
16. Protalinski, E.: Google updates Chrome Web Store review process and sets new extension code requirements (2018). https://venturebeat.com/2018/06/12/google-disables-inline-installation-for-chrome-extensions/
17. Rauti, S., Leppänen, V.: Man-in-the-browser attacks in modern web browsers. In: Emerging Trends in ICT Security, pp. 469–480. Elsevier (2014)
18. Rautila, M., Suomalainen, J.: Secure inspection of web transactions. Int. J. Internet Technol. Secur. Trans. **4**(4), 253–271 (2012)
19. Ronchi, C., Zakhidov, S.: Hardened client platforms for secure internet banking. In: Pohlmann, N., Reimer, H., Schneider, W. (eds.) ISSE 2008 Securing Electronic Business Processes. Springer, Heidelberg (2009). https://doi.org/10.1007/978-3-8348-9283-6_39
20. Ståhlberg, M.: The trojan money spinner. In: Virus Bulletin Conference, vol. 4 (2007)
21. Toreini, E., Shahandashti, S.F., Mehrnezhad, M., Hao, F.: Domtegrity: ensuring web page integrity against malicious browser extensions. Int. J. Inf. Secur. 1–14 (2019)
22. Utakrit, N.: Review of browser extensions, a man-in-the-browser phishing techniques targeting bank customers (2009)

23. Wang, L., Xiang, J., Jing, J., Zhang, L.: Towards fine-grained access control on browser extensions. In: Ryan, M.D., Smyth, B., Wang, G. (eds.) ISPEC 2012. LNCS, vol. 7232, pp. 158–169. Springer, Heidelberg (2012). https://doi.org/10.1007/978-3-642-29101-2_11
24. Zhang, P., He, Y., Chow, K.: Fraud track on secure electronic check system. Int. J. Digit. Crime Forensics 10(2), 137–144 (2018)

Detection and Analysis of Drive-by Downloads and Malicious Websites

Saeed Ibrahim, Nawwaf Al Herami, Ebrahim Al Naqbi,
and Monther Aldwairi$^{(\boxtimes)}$

College of Technological Innovation, Zayed University, 144534, Abu Dhabi, UAE
{m80007514,m80006805,m80006809,monther.aldwairi}@zu.ac.ae

Abstract. A drive-by download is a download that occurs without user's action or knowledge. It usually triggers an exploit of vulnerability in a browser to downloads an unknown file. The malicious program in the downloaded file installs itself on the victim's machine. Moreover, the downloaded file can be camouflaged as an installer that would further install malicious software. Drive-by downloads is a very good example of the exponential increase in malicious activity over the Internet and how it affects the daily use of the web. In this paper, we try to address the problem caused by drive-by downloads from different standpoints. We provide in-depth understanding of the difficulties in dealing with drive-by downloads and suggest appropriate solutions. We propose machine learning and feature selection solutions to remedy the drive-by download problem. Experimental results reported 98.2% precision, 98.2% F-Measure and 97.2% ROC area.

Keywords: Drive by download · Malware detection · Web security

1 Introduction

Miscreants make use of malicious web content to perform attacks targeting web clients. Drive-by downloads (DBD) are unintentional downloads of malware or virus on to a mobile device or a computer. Due to the increased population of several web applications, DBD have become one of the most common malware spreading methods, thereby leading the security threats to cyber community. According to [29], query search results from Google contain more than 1.3% of the web pages that do DBD attacks. These downloads are located on normal-looking, but malicious websites [4]. They exploit vulnerabilities in out-of-date apps, browsers, plugins, or operating systems. Over the years, hackers have become much more sophisticated that just opening such web page could allow malicious code to be installed on the device without the knowledge and consent of the user. Downloaded malware takes complete control of the victim's platform [13]. Once the attacker gets full control, he can download and execute any code and run malicious activities on the victim's platform such as joining botnets, sending spam emails, and participating in distributed denial of service attacks

© Springer Nature Singapore Pte Ltd. 2020
S. M. Thampi et al. (Eds.): SSCC 2019, CCIS 1208, pp. 72–86, 2020.
https://doi.org/10.1007/978-981-15-4825-3_6

[14]. Attackers may also record keystrokes, steal passwords, and can access sensitive information. Use of DBD to steal confidential data is also a major threat to the financial companies and banks.

A DBD attack occurs in four steps. First, the attacker compromises a genuine website and uploads malicious content to it. When a user visits that website, the malicious program is downloaded by browser, installed by itself, and the attacker gets full control [14]. APT programs and methods used by cybercriminal groups to attack businesses make them more dangerous.

In 2015, almost two million cases of malware infections to steal money were registered, while 34.2 % of computer users were exposed to at least one such attack through the year [12]. In order to ensure protection against such attack, there is a vital need for new methods and technologies that can safeguard the users from DBD attacks [31]. There are couple of existing techniques to detect and prevent such attacks. The detection of attacks can be performed by tracking web addresses with a history of malicious behavior [29]. According to Microsoft, Bing normally detects huge numbers of DBD pages every month. However, after getting blocked by Bing, the attackers switch servers and thus the same attacks are reborn but with different domain names [33]. Intrusion detection systems monitor traffic and system activities and may be used to detect attacks [7].

In order to counter the innovative tactics employed by the hackers, there is a vital need to develop efficient techniques that could potentially counter DBD attacks. In this paper, we proposed a novel design, which uses machine learning to detect and prevent DBD attacks. We selected nine attributes from a dataset of benign URLs from University of California Irvine (UCI) machine learning repository and malicious URLs from malware domain list [5]. Each attribute was chosen carefully to measure its effectiveness on different characteristics of malicious URLs. Furthermore, we employed several machine learning models for the training the system to detect malicious URLs. However, after empirical performance evaluation of these models, we selected Naive Bayes (NB), JRip, and J48 classifiers.

The rest of the paper is structured as follows: Sect. 2 contains the related work. Section 3 describes the methodology. Results are discussed in Sect. 4 and Sect. 5 concludes our work.

2   Related Work

Below we classify the most relevant work on detecting DBDs.

2.1   Using Web Crawler to Detect Drive by Downloads

Harle and Pierre-Marc work does not offer a solution to DBDs, but tries to provoke more research in the area by suggesting possible ideas [15]. It provokes researchers to pay more attention to attacks that are large scale in nature and which do not use codes that are self-propagating. This is because current attacks are sophisticated and, therefore, a long-lasting solution may be one that uses the fault-tolerant and robust software in addition to ensuring the monitoring of web pages. A web crawler can be used to identify distribution points, however, due to the complexity of this detection, false positives risks can be lessened by either digital signing or obfuscating techniques can be avoided. Some of the characteristics of this web crawler would be; ability to analyze HTML pages as well as follows its links; ability to imitate web cookies; ability to imitate scripting languages in order to decode obfuscated code; and ability to use heuristics in the detection of possible exploits in web pages. It concludes that measures, which are semi-effective and multi-layered, and those that accept specific risks of both false positives and negatives offer much protection.

2.2   Antivirus Software to Detect Drive-by Downloads Malware

Narvaez et al., studied how antivirus software can be useful in the detection of drive-by malware installation by studying the effectiveness of the current antivirus tools [27]. A sample of malware was collected by use of a honeypot. The sample of the malware was categorized into whether the malware used either delivered payload or downloader. An evaluation of the results was made by common antivirus software to determine their effectiveness in detecting exploits. After 30 days, the sample of the malware was scanned again as it was expected that the antivirus would have made an update of signature databases. According to the initial results, Norton detected 66% of the collected malware, Kaspersky 91%, CA 61%, ClamWin 62% [9] and TrendMicro 69% [22]. The next scan, after 30 days, showed an increase in the rate of detection with Norton having 90%, Kaspersky 98%, TrendMicro 70%, ClamWin 75% and CA 81%. However, even though there was an improvement in the second scan, signature-based antivirus may not perform well in reality. This is because just as they had an opportunity to perform an update on their signatures similarly would attackers update malware. The initial detection, which was low, shows that malware authors use polymorphic capabilities. In 84% of attacks, downloaders are used instead of payloads. Antivirus products struggle to keep their signature databases up to date with the continuously changing threat landscape [32].

2.3   BrowserGuard as a Behavior-Based Solution

Hsu et al. [17] proposed a behavior-based BrowserGuard, which detects secret downloads and blocks the malware from being executed. BrowserGuard uses two phases to provide protection to its host. The first is the filtration phase, whereby BrowserGuard makes a distinction between malicious and benign files depending on the situations in which they are downloaded. The second is the prohibition phase, whereby a request for the execution of malicious files is denied. In order to test the technique in terms of false positives, BrowserGuard visited the 500 top-ranked websites from Alexa. As expected BrowserGuard did not issue any attack alert, therefore, BrowserGuard had zero false positives. To measure the false negatives, Metasploit framework was used to generate ten malicious web pages that are then hosted on a remote server. BrowserGuard blocked all ten pages, therefore, the authors claimed zero false negatives. To assess the performance overhead of BrowserGuard, the time to download fives web page, from Alexa, was measured 2000 times. BrowserGuard introduced a fixed delays time and the worst performance overhead was 2.5%. Unfortunately, we believe the test samples are insufficient to support the conclusions and BrowserGuard only works for Windows Internet Explorer 7.0.

2.4 A Framework for DBD Attacks with Users Voluntary Monitoring of the Web

Matsunaka et al. [24] proposed participative monitoring framework that fights DBDs with voluntary monitoring of websites by users and expert analysts. The framework provided a security ecosystem whereby users allow monitoring of their web activities, while security analysts do an inspection of the information in order to detect threats, devise countermeasures and provide feedback to the users. The framework enables users to provide data via the sensors and security analysts to give feedback through analyzing the data available at the center. The sensors are located in web proxies, DNS servers, and web browsers. Additionally, a web crawler was used to inspect web pages that are suspicious. The real-time data enabled the framework to previously detect unknown malicious web pages. However, advertisement hosts can cause false positives and further work is needed to address that.

2.5 HTML and JavaScript Feature for Detecting the Drive-by Download

Priya et al. [28] provided a static approach to the detect DBDs using JavaScript and HTML features [28]. A sample dataset was created with 311 malicious URLs, from www.malwaredomainlist.com, and 654 benign URLs from Alexa were used to test different classifiers. To view the source code of benign sites you just open the URL, however, opening a malicious web page is a problem because it will cause malware to be installed on the computer. Therefore, MATLAB parser was developed to extract the malicious source code without visiting and executing the code. The HTML code was parsed and JavaScript and HTML features were extracted. They used both WEKA and MATLAB to evaluate the classifiers performance with 92% best case detection accuracy.

2.6 Approach to Detect Drive-by Download Based on Characters

Matsunaka et al. [23] proposed FCDBD that includes monitoring sensors on the client side and analysis center on the network. The sensors include web browsers, web sensors or DNS sensors. The browser sensors extracted the user's data while DNS and web sensors monitored DNS-/HTTP- related traffic [3]. The analysis center collects the logs and analyzes them, if malicious websites are detected, the information is reported to monitoring sensors so the users may not access the websites. The approach was evaluated using D3M 2013 dataset. According to the results, false positives only occur when a transition of a sequence of web pages is terminated before the malware is downloaded. To compensate for that, advertisement or affiliates scripts are obfuscated and referrer field is empty.

2.7   Enhanced Approach for Malware Downloading

Adachi et al. [1] used two approaches to predict DBD through opcode and vulnerability evaluation. The first approach identified vulnerabilities CVE-IDs in the web pages to predict the of malware download. For analysis, Wepawet was employed to identify CVE-IDs in the web pages, and the National Vulnerability Database (NVD) provided information concerning the CVEs. To improve detection rates they are reduced unnecessary information by a grouping algorithm [26]. Features were then extracted and the prediction model computed malware-downloading probabilities. The second approach combined opcode with the first approach one because opcode by itself fails to detect attacks that do not use JavaScript. Pages from 2011–2014 D3M datasets and AlexaTop500 were used. The first approach had 83% prediction accuracy and low FPs rate, however it had high FNs rate. The second approach had a 92% prediction accuracy, 11% FNs and 6% FPs using Random Forest.

2.8   Analyze Redirection Code for Mining URLs

Takata et al. [30] MineSpider performed an analysis on JavaScripts that include browser fingerprinting and redirection code and extracted possible URLs through the execution of the redirection code. MineSpider applied program slicing to JavaScript in order to extract execution paths, the extracted code fragments are executed by an interpreter and URLs are extracted. The outcome is just URL extraction and no detection was done. However, the URLs extracted by this method can be analyzed for malice using other approaches. MineSpider could extract more than 30,000 URLs in seconds compared to other methods.

2.9   Visualize the Flow of HTTP Traffic

Kikuchi et al. [20] used decision trees to classify DBDs by using features such as object size and redirection methods. The first premise was that many code variations modify words that are user-defined without the structure of the script being affected. Second, the characteristics of the scripts do not protect from DBDs because of disguised transformations fabrication. Additionally, they used the prediction of latent behavior to detect large-scale DBDs by using the drive-by disclosure method, which bridges the gap in between static and dynamic approaches. The method captured models and learned latent behaviors as opposed to scanning web pages for content that is malicious. To evaluate the efficiency of the approach 50 malicious and 50 legitimate sessions were obtained from Alexa. It was found that the method had no false positives but had 0.06 chance of false negatives. The results showed that drive-by exposure can filter out scripts that are benign in nature, detect malicious scripts, and detect a variety of obfuscated patterns of DBDs as well as sort-out scripts that are disguised. In comparison to other high-tech solutions, drive-by disclosure was doubling accurate when compared to Cujo and it outdid JSAND by 29%.

2.10   Drive-by Download as a Large Scale Web Attacks

Jodavi et al. drive-by disclosure [2] used anomaly DbD hunter approach to train and detect using a collection of classifiers. In the training stage, inputs of benign web pages are run in a browser. Then, JavaScript byte codes are logged for the web pages and a feature vector generated for the sequence. The feature vectors are then used to construct the classifiers baseline. The detection stage involved logging JavaScript byte codes for web pages, after which a feature vector is generated and applied to all base classifiers. The detection performance of DbD hunter was evaluated and was found that it increased the rate of detection by 12.44%, while decreasing rates of false alarms by approximately 48.13%. It had an accuracy of 97%, a detection rate of 96.3% and false alarm rate of 1.8%. Anomaly detection approach [8] have been used to detect DBD. According to [19], attacks by DBDs make use of browser exploit packs (BEPs) that are deployed on compromised servers to spread malware. BEPs that are widely used include sweet orange, Black Hole, Angler, Nuclear, Sakura, Fiesta, Hunter, Magnitude and Styx. The study makes an analysis of features that are built-in, which allow successful attacks by DBDs. The study conclude that just as attacks by DBDs increase in sophistication, so should the solutions.

3   Methodology

We develop a novel mechanism to counter DBD attacks that employs machine learning techniques. The proposed mechanism is able to classify the URLs into benign and malicious categories accurately. The benign category refers to websites that are safe, whereas the malicious category relates to the websites created by attackers to gain access or retrieve sensitive information. We used Waikato Environment for Knowledge Analysis (WEKA) [16] to classify the URLs based on different attributes using machine learning based models. WEKA is a popular machine learning suite developed at the University of Waikato, New Zealand and is licensed under the GNU General Public License (GPL). It contains machine learning algorithms for data mining related tasks. Integration feature helps to integrate these algorithms with the application code. It also supports data preprocessing, classification, regression, clustering, association rules, and visualization. The following subsection summarize the methodology used to classify DBDs and evaluate the performance.

3.1 Dataset

We collected benign URLs from open source UCI Machine Learning Repository [21] and we used a list of 63 updated malware and spyware URLs from Malware Domain List [25].

3.2 Feature Selection

Feature selection, also known as variable selection or attribute selection, is a process to select relevant features from predictive models. Each instance of the dataset used by machine learning algorithms is represented by the same set of features. These features can be continuous, categorical, or binary. We selected multiple effective features to build our proposed model. Given a single URL, its features were extracted and categorized into eight attributes (plus class) that were used by WEKA as itemized below.

– HostRank: the URL's global Amazon Alexa ranking [10].
– CountryRank: the URL's Amazon Alexa website rank by country [11].
– ASNNumber: The autonomous system number (ASN), which is assigned to the URL's domain, and used in BGP routing [18].
– DotsInURL: number of dots in URLs [6].
– Lenghthofurl: length of the URL.
– IPaddress: is the host name using ip address rather than name address.
– Lengthofhostname: length of host name.
– Safe Browsing: rating of Google safe browsing.

Two attribute evaluators: Correlation Attributes Evaluation (CAE) and Information Gain Attributes (IG) have been used on the dataset. Correlation Attributes Evaluation is used to choose best attributes for model training. It measures the correlation between attribute and the class and evaluates its worth. Information Gain picks attributes by measuring IG with respect to the class. For this work, eight features were selected to be used with WEKA. Referring to the Fig. 1, most of the attributes have scored a high ranking except IPaddress and ASNnumber for which, IG was 0.0521 and 0.1691, respectively. On the CAE, the IPaddress and ASNnumber scored 0.247 and 0.148, which are the lowest scores in the precision test. Thus, these two attributes were eliminated from the attribute set. We finalized six features that include Host Rank, Country Rank, Dots in URL, Length of the URL, length of the host name, in addition to the class: malicious or benign.

3.3 Classification

Many classifiers were chosen to train on the selected dataset, however, NB, JRip, and J48 outperformed all others. Therefore, we experimentally determined that those three are the best classifiers based on their performance on a given dataset. To evaluate the trained model, we employed 10 folds cross validation. Cross-validation is a technique to evaluate predictive models by splitting the original

```
Rank    Attribute                    Rank    Attribute ranking
0.921   1 hostrank                   0.899   8 SafeBRowsing
0.8823  5 lengthoftheurl             0.699   5 lengthoftheurl
0.7094  8 SafeBRowsing               0.574   4 dotsinURL
0.6565  2 countryrank                0.532   7 lengthofhostname
0.6115  7 lengthofhostname           0.345   1 hostrank
0.5162  4 dotsinURL                  0.247   6 IPaddress
0.1691  3 ASNnumber                  0.148   2 countryrank
0.0521  6 IPaddress                  0.148   3 ASNnumber
(a) Information Gain Ranking Filter  (b) Correlation Ranking Filter
```

Fig. 1. Information gain and correlation ranking attributes ranking

dataset sample into a training and test sets to train and evaluate the model respectively. The process is repeated k times, with each of the k sub-samples used exactly once as the validation data. For this problem, data was split into 10 sets of size $n/10$, training with 9 subsets and testing on the remaining one subset. This process was repeated ten times while using a different subset for the test each time. The final results were then calculated by taking the mean accuracy of ten tests.

4   Results

Figure 2 shows the comparison of each classifier for malicious, benign, and average instance by using precision metric. We observed that NB scored 97% Malicious, 99% Benign, and 98% Average whereas JRip scored 97% Malicious, 99% Benign and 98% Average. Finally, J48 scored 95% Malicious, 97% Benign and 96% Average. Among all the three classifiers, the J48 scored the lowest with the average score of 96%. Naive Bayes and JRip have scored the highest in the tests, with similar results of average being 98%. Therefore, NB and JRip classifiers are used in the following analysis.

4.1   Metrics

Confusion Matrix. The confusion matrix summarizes the performance of classification model. True Positive (TP), False Negative (FN), False Positive (FP), and True Negative (TN) are elements of confusion matrix as shown in Fig. 3. Columns represent the predicted class while rows represent the actual class. Higher values in the main diagonal reflect better accuracy in the classification.

True Positive Rate. A true positive rate is the proportion of positives that are correctly identified by classifier. The TP rate is defined as follows.

$$TPRate = \frac{TP}{TP + FN} \tag{1}$$

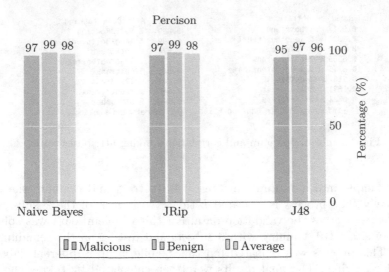

Fig. 2. Precision of different classifiers

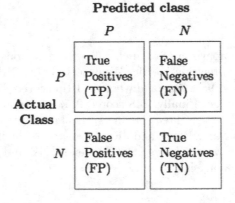

Fig. 3. Confusion matrix

False Positive Rate. A False Positive rate is the proportion of the outcome that is incorrectly predicted as yes (or positive) when it is actually no (negative). The FP rate is defined as follows.

$$FPRate = \frac{FP}{FP + TN} \tag{2}$$

Precision. Precision is the fraction of relevant instances among the retrieved instances.

$$Precision = \frac{TP}{TP + FP} \tag{3}$$

Recall. Recall is the fraction of relevant instances among the retrieved instances.

$$Recall = \frac{TP}{TP + FN} \qquad (4)$$

F-measure. The F-measure is defined as a harmonic mean of precision and recall.

$$Precision = \frac{2xPrecisionxRecall}{Recall + Precision} \qquad (5)$$

Matthews Correlation Coefficient (MCC). MCC ranges from 1.0 (worst) to 1.0 (best) and is defined as follows.

$$MCC = \frac{(TPxTN) - (FPxFN)}{\sqrt{(TP + FP)(TP + FN)(TN + FP)(TN + FN)}} \qquad (6)$$

4.2 Naive Bayes

The results of the NB classifier are shown in Table 1. The average score of TP is 98.20%, which indicates that the attributes have been correctly identified. The FP averaged 1.70%, which indicates that the result is scoring low on the error scale of the attributes. Therefore, the results can be identified as viable and true in this test. Table 2 shows the confusion matrix containing the details of the predicted and actual classes done by the NB classifier. Using these numbers we can calculate the TP and FP rates.

Table 1. Naive Bayes classifier results

	Malware	Benign	Average
TPR	98.40%	98%	98.20%
FPR	2%	1.60%	1.70%
Precision	96.90%	99%	98.20%
Recall	98.40%	98%	98.20%
F-measure	97.60%	98.50%	98.20%
MCC	96.20%	96.20%	96.20%
ROC area	98.70%	99.50%	99.20%
PRC area	96%	99.70%	98.30%

Table 2. Confusion matrix Naive Bayes

	a = Malicious	b = Benign
a = Malicious	61	2
b = Benign	1	100

Applying formula 1 and 2 to the confusion matrix of NB, we get the following results.

$$TPRate = \frac{61}{61 + 2} = 0.968 \tag{7}$$

$$FPRate = \frac{1}{1 + 100} = 0.009 \tag{8}$$

4.3 JRIP

Table 3 shows that average TP of 98.20%, which indicates that JRip is able to correctly classify the URLs. The FP score is 1.70%, which indicates the classification had a low number of errors.

Table 3. JRip classifier results

	Malware	Benign	Average
TPR	98.40%	98%	98.20%
FPR	2%	1.60%	1.70%
Precision	90.60%	99%	98.20%
Recall	98.40%	98%	98.20%
F-measure	97.60%	98.50%	98.20%
MCC	96.20%	96.20%	96.20%
ROC area	97.20%	97.20%	97.20%
PRC area	92.80%	98%	96%

In Table 4 the confusion matrix is presented, which contains the details about the predicted and actual classification done by the JRip classifier. The count of TP is 62, FN is 1, and FP is 1 whereas TN is equal to 100. Using these numbers we can calculate the TP rate and FP rate.

Table 4. Confusion matrix JRip

	a = Malicious	b = Benign
a = Malicious	62	1
b = Benign	1	100

$$TPRate = \frac{62}{62 + 1} = 0.984 \tag{9}$$

$$FPRate = \frac{1}{1 + 100} = 0.009 \tag{10}$$

4.4   J48

From Table 5, we can deduce that the average TP is 96.30%, which indicates that most of the URLs are correctly classified. The FP score is 4.10%, which indicates that the classification had a low number of errors.

Table 5. J48 classifier results

	Malware	Benign	Average
TPR	95.20%	97%	96.30%
FPR	3%	4.80%	4.10%
Precision	95.20%	97%	96.30%
Recall	95.20%	97%	96.30%
F-measure	95.20%	97%	96.30%
MCC	92.30%	92.30%	92.30%
ROC area	95.60%	95.60%	95.60%
PRC area	91.60%	96.10%	94.40%

Table 6. Confusion matrix J48

	a = Malicious	b = Benign
a = Malicious	60	3
b = Benign	3	98

Table 6 shows the confusion matrix, which contains the details about the predicted and actual classification done by the J48 classifier. Using these numbers we can calculate the TP rate and FP rate.

$$TPRate = \frac{60}{60 + 3} = 0.952 \tag{11}$$

$$FPRate = \frac{3}{3 + 98} = 0.029 \tag{12}$$

5   Conclusions

In this paper, we proposed an approach to filter benign and malicious websites. The URL based analysis is performed that helped by removing the runtime latency and delay of loading the websites. Furthermore, the proposed design protects the users from attacks induced by browser vulnerabilities. The proposed approach can be applied via a blacklisting content and system-based evaluation of site content and behavior of the site. By selecting the right features and algorithms, our system has achieved 98% accuracy in detecting and classifying the malicious URLs. The limitation of the work include the small dataset, number of classifiers used and actual real time testing. Future work would include creating a browser plugin and testing the system with real data, using a much larger dataset and investigating deep learning methods.

Acknowledgment. This research was supported, in part, by Zayed University Research Office, Research Incentives Grant # R18054.

References

1. Adachi, T., Omote, K.: An approach to predict drive-by-download attacks by vulnerability evaluation and opcode. In: 2015 10th Asia Joint Conference on Information Security (AsiaJCIS), pp. 145–151. IEEE (2015). https://doi.org/10.1109/AsiaJCIS.2015.17
2. Al-Taharwa, I.A., Lee, H.M., Jeng, A.B., Ho, C.S., Wu, K.P., Chen, S.M.: Drive-by disclosure: a large-scale detector of drive-by downloads based on latent behavior prediction. In: 2015 IEEE Trustcom/BigDataSE/ISPA, vol. 1, pp. 334–343. IEEE (2015). https://doi.org/10.1109/Trustcom.2015.392
3. Aldwairi, M., Guled, M., Cassada, M., Pratt, M., Stevenson, D., Franzon, P.: Switch architecture for optical burst switching networks. In: Proceedings of the First Workshop on Optical Burst Switching, OPTICOMM 2003, October 2003
4. Aldwairi, M., Alsalman, R.: MALURLs: Malicious URLs classification system. In: Annual International Conference on Information Theory and Applications (2011). https://doi.org/10.5176/978-981-08-8113-9_ITA2011-29
5. Aldwairi, M., Alsalman, R.: MALURLs: a lightweight malicious website classification based on URL features. J. Emerg. Technol. Web Intell. **4**(2), 128–133 (2012). https://doi.org/10.4304/jetwi.4.2.128-133
6. Aldwairi, M., Alwahedi, A.: Detecting fake news in social media networks. Procedia Comput. Sci. **141**, 215–222 (2018). https://doi.org/10.1016/j.procs.2018.10.171. http://www.sciencedirect.com/science/article/pii/S1877050918318210. ISSN 1877-0509. The 9th International Conference on Emerging Ubiquitous Systems and Pervasive Networks (EUSPN-2018), The 8th International Conference on Current and Future Trends of Information and Communication Technologies in Healthcare (ICTH-2018), Affiliated Workshops
7. Aldwairi, M., Hasan, M., Balbahaith, Z.: Detection of drive-by download attacks using machine learning approach. Int. J. Inf. Secur. Priv. (IJISP) **11**(4), 16–28 (2017). https://doi.org/10.4018/IJISP.2017100102
8. Aldwairi, M., Mardini, W., Alhowaide, A.: Anomaly payload signature generation system based on efficient tokenization methodology. Int. J. Commun. Antenna Propag. (IRECAP) **8**(5) (2018). https://doi.org/10.15866/irecap.v8i5.12794. ISSN 2533-2929
9. Aldwairi, M., Mhaidat, K., Flaifel, Y.: Efficient pattern matching hardware for network intrusion detection systems. In: International Conference on Electrical, Electronics, Computers, Communication, Mechanical and Computing (EECCMC). IEEE (2018). https://arxiv.org/pdf/2003.00405.pdf
10. Amazon: Alexa. https://www.alexa.com/
11. Amazon: Alexa: the top 500 sites on the web. https://www.alexa.com/topsites/countries

12. Anton, I., Makrushin, D., Van Der Wiel, J., Garnaeva, M., Namestnikov, Y.: Kaspersky security bulletin 2015. Overall statistics for 2015. Securelist Information about Viruses Hackers and Spam. AO Kaspersky Lab (2015)
13. Cova, M., Kruegel, C., Vigna, G.: Detection and analysis of drive-by-download attacks and malicious Javascript code. In: Proceedings of the 19th International Conference on World Wide Web, pp. 281–290. ACM (2010). https://doi.org/10.1145/1772690.1772720
14. Egele, M., Wurzinger, P., Kruegel, C., Kirda, E.: Defending browsers against drive-by downloads: mitigating heap-spraying code injection attacks. In: Flegel, U., Bruschi, D. (eds.) DIMVA 2009. LNCS, vol. 5587, pp. 88–106. Springer, Heidelberg (2009). https://doi.org/10.1007/978-3-642-02918-9_6. ISBN 978-3-642-02918-9
15. Harley, D., Bureau, P.M.: Drive-by downloads from the trenches. In: 3rd International Conference on Malicious and Unwanted Software, MALWARE 2008, pp. 98–103. IEEE (2008). https://doi.org/10.1109/MALWARE.2008.4690864
16. Holmes, G., Donkin, A., Witten, I.H.: WEKA: a machine learning workbench. In: Proceedings of the 1994 Second Australian and New Zealand Conference on Intelligent Information Systems, pp. 357–361. IEEE (1994). https://doi.org/10.1109/ANZIIS.1994.396988
17. Hsu, F.H., Tso, C.K., Yeh, Y.C., Wang, W.J., Chen, L.H.: BrowserGuard: a behavior-based solution to drive-by-download attacks. IEEE J. Sel. Areas Commun. 29(7), 1461–1468 (2011). https://doi.org/10.1109/JSAC.2011.110811
18. Huston, G.: Exploring autonomous system numbers. Internet Protocol J. 9(1), 2–23 (2006). https://www.kiv.zcu.cz/~ledvina/DHT/ipj_9-1.pdf
19. Jodavi, M., Abadi, M., Parhizkar, E.: DbDHunter: an ensemble-based anomaly detection approach to detect drive-by download attacks. In: 2015 5th International Conference on Computer and Knowledge Engineering (ICCKE), pp. 273–278. IEEE (2015). https://doi.org/10.1109/ICCKE.2015.7365841
20. Kikuchi, H., Matsumoto, H., Ishii, H.: Automated detection of drive-by download attack. In: 2015 9th International Conference on Innovative Mobile and Internet Services in Ubiquitous Computing (IMIS), pp. 511–515. IEEE (2015). https://doi.org/10.1109/IMIS.2015.71
21. Lichman, M.: UCI machine learning repository (2013). http://archive.ics.uci.edu/ml
22. Masri, R., Aldwairi, M.: Automated malicious advertisement detection using VirusTotal, URLVoid, and TrendMicro. In: 2017 8th International Conference on Information and Communication Systems (ICICS), pp. 336–341, April 2017. https://doi.org/10.1109/IACS.2017.7921994
23. Matsunaka, T., Kubota, A., Kasama, T.: An approach to detect drive-by download by observing the web page transition behaviors. In: 2014 Ninth Asia Joint Conference on Information Security (ASIA JCIS), pp. 19–25. IEEE (2014). https://doi.org/10.1109/AsiaJCIS.2014.21
24. Matsunaka, T., Urakawa, J., Kubota, A.: Detecting and preventing drive-by download attack via participative monitoring of the web. In: 2013 Eighth Asia Joint Conference on Information Security (Asia JCIS), pp. 48–55. IEEE (2013). https://doi.org/10.1109/ASIAJCIS.2013.15
25. MDL: Malware Domain List featuring a list of malware-related sites plus a discussion forum on new threats (2009). https://www.malwaredomainlist.com/mdl.php
26. Mohammad, M.: A numerical solution of Fredholm integral equations of the second kind based on tight framelets generated by the oblique extension principle. Symmetry 11(7), 854 (2019). https://doi.org/10.3390/sym11070854. ISSN 2073-8994

27. Narvaez, J., Endicott-Popovsky, B., Seifert, C., Aval, C., Frincke, D.A.: Drive-by-downloads. In: 2010 43rd Hawaii International Conference on System Sciences (HICSS), pp. 1–10. IEEE (2010). https://doi.org/10.1109/HICSS.2010.160

28. Priya, M., Sandhya, L., Thomas, C.: A static approach to detect drive-by-download attacks on webpages. In: 2013 International Conference on Control Communication and Computing (ICCC), pp. 298–303. IEEE (2013). https://doi.org/10.1109/ICCC.2013.6731668

29. Provos, N., Mavrommatis, P., Rajab, M.A., Monrose, F.: All your iFRAMEs point to us. In: Proceedings of the 17th Conference on Security Symposium, SS 2008, pp. 1–15. USENIX Association, Berkeley, CA (2008). http://dl.acm.org/citation.cfm?id=1496711.1496712

30. Takata, Y., Akiyama, M., Yagi, T., Hariu, T., Goto, S.: MineSpider: extracting URLs from environment-dependent drive-by download attacks. In: 2015 IEEE 39th Annual Computer Software and Applications Conference (COMPSAC), vol. 2, pp. 444–449. IEEE (2015). https://doi.org/10.1109/COMPSAC.2015.76

31. Vergelis, M., Shcherbakova, T., Demidova, N.: Kaspersky security bulletin. Spam in 2014. Secure List, p. 68 (2015)

32. Yaseen, Q., Jararweh, Y., Al-Ayyoub, M., AlDwairi, M.: Collusion attacks in internet of things: detection and mitigation using a fog based model. In: 2017 IEEE Sensors Applications Symposium (SAS), pp. 1–5, March 2017. https://doi.org/10.1109/SAS.2017.7894031

33. Zhang, J., Seifert, C., Stokes, J.W., Lee, W.: Arrow: generating signatures to detect drive-by downloads. In: Proceedings of the 20th International Conference on World Wide Web, pp. 187–196. ACM (2011). https://dl.acm.org/doi/pdf/10.1145/1963405.1963435

Intrusion Detection Systems for Smart Home IoT Devices: Experimental Comparison Study

Faisal Alsakran[1], Gueltoum Bendiab[1], Stavros Shiaeles[2(✉)], and Nicholas Kolokotronis[3]

[1] CSCAN, University of Plymouth, Plymouth PL4 8AA, UK
faisal.alsakran@postgrad.plymouth.ac.uk, bendiab.kelthoum@umc.edu.dz
[2] School of Computing, University of Portsmouth, Portsmouth PO1 2UP, UK
sshiaeles@ieee.org
[3] Department of Informatics and Telecommunications, University of Peloponnese, 22131 Tripolis, Greece
nkolok@uop.gr

Abstract. With the growing number of IoT related devices, smart homes promise to make our lives easier and more comfortable. However, the increased deployment of such smart devices brings a lot of security and privacy risks. In order to overcome such risks, Intrusion Detection Systems are presented as pertinent tools that can provide network-level protection for smart devices deployed in home environments. These systems monitor the network activities of the smart home-connected devices and focus on alerting suspicious or malicious activity. They also can deal with detected abnormal activities by hindering the impostors in accessing the victim devices. However, the employment of such systems in the context of smart home can be challenging due to the devices hardware limitations, which may restrict their ability to counter the existing and emerging attack vectors. Therefore, this paper proposes an experimental comparison between the widely used open-source NIDSs namely Snort, Suricata and Bro (currently known as Zeek) to find the most appropriate IDS for smart homes in term of resources consumption including CPU and memory utilisation. Experimental Results show that Suricata and Bro are the best performing NIDS for smart homes.

Keywords: Internet of Things (IoT) · Smart-home · Anomaly detection · Attack mitigation · Intrusion Detection System

1 Introduction

Smart home technology enables the whole home to be automated, where the related smart home devices can be remotely controlled and managed, from any location in the world, through a smartphone application or other network devices [11]. In recent years, smart home technology is gaining tremendous ground at

© Springer Nature Singapore Pte Ltd. 2020
S. M. Thampi et al. (Eds.): SSCC 2019, CCIS 1208, pp. 87–98, 2020.
https://doi.org/10.1007/978-981-15-4825-3_7

all levels. Economic reports affirm that connected home market becomes the largest IoT segment at seven billion related smart devices in 2018, which present 26% of the global IoT devices market [12]. According to Gartner [30] this segment is expected to grow to 20.4 billion devices by 2020. Further, the number of householders with smart systems has grown to nearly 150 million smart householders' worldwide in 2019 [12]. The main reasons for the large adoption of such technology are comfort, convenience, safety, and energy and cost savings [11] However, connecting smart devices such as lights, appliances and locks introduces tremendous cybersecurity risks. All security reports warn that more than 80% of connected smart home devices are vulnerable to a wide range of attacks [9,23]. A recent study by the cybersecurity firm Avast found that two out of five smart homes are exposed to cyberattacks [4]. Exploiting such unsecured devices by hackers can lead to all kinds of potential harm [9,15], like switching the security system to unlock a door [9], or cracking the smart oven until overheats and burns the house down [9]. In other cases, the smart home network is infected with ransomware that requires the homeowner to pay in order to regain access to the home network [23]. Even a simple smart light bulb can be exploited by hackers to gain wider access to the smart home network and cause potential physical damage [15].

In the light of all of this, it is clear that there is a major gap between security requirements and security capabilities of currently available smart home IoT devices. One of the main reasons that make these devices insecure is the hardware limitations [3,28]. More specifically, restricted resources including low power sources, small amounts of memory and limited processing power, which means minimizing the number of processes, and consequently, the size of the applications. These limitations hinder the execution of complexes security tasks that generate massive computation and communication load [3]. Consequently, security solutions for these devices should maintain a balance between the smart home high-security requirements and supporting infrastructures' hardware limitations. Because smart home technology has a direct influence on people's security and privacy, this issue must become the priority for security and home automation experts [16]. In this context, there is a need for efficient Intrusion Detection Systems (IDSs), which can protect smart devices used in home environments with a minimum of resources consumption [16,23].

This paper aims to address this issue by examining the existing IDSs, in order to find the most appropriate solution for smart homes in terms of resources consumption. To this end, several open-source network-based intrusion detection systems (NIDS) are available such as ACARM-ng, AIDE, Bro IDS, Snort, Suricata, OSSEC HIDS, Prelud Hybrid IDS, Samhain, Fail2Ban, Security Onion, etc. Open-source systems are considered as a cost-effective way to improve the security of smart home environments by monitoring the home network and detect internal or external cyber-attacks [24]. However, in this experimental study we will focus on Snort, Suricata and Bro-IDS as these three NIDSs are the most efficient and become the de-facto industry standard for intrusion detection engines [2,21,25,27]. The main contribution of this paper is a comparison of those three

IDSs based on CPU and RAM utilisation. The chosen IDSs are deployed inside different Linux containers known as Dockers, instead of running them directly on a VM base operating system. Each container has its resources that are separated from other containers. By doing this, Snort, Suricata and Bro-IDS will be deployed on the same virtual machine, they will have the same network and resource setup, the resources needed will be minimal to simulate resource limitation on smart homes gateways and finally comparison will. The experiments evaluate the difference in resource usage between these NIDSs while monitoring live network traffic under various attacks.

The rest of the paper is structured as follows. In Sect. 2, we give an overview of some prior work that is similar to our work. Section 3 gives an overview of the chosen IDSs Snort, Suricata and Bro. Section 4 explains our evaluation experiments and the results, and Sect. 5 concludes the paper and outlines the potential future work.

2   Related Work

In recent years, researchers have increased their interests in studying the performance of different NIDSs in different environments, from different perspectives. In this context, the performance of the Snort IDS has been extensively investigated in research studies [7,20,26,27]. For instance, in [26] authors carried out experimental evaluation and comparison of Snort NIDS in term of performance when operating under the two popular OSs Linux and Windows. The evaluation is done for both normal and malicious traffic, and the metrics used were the throughput and the packet loss. Those experiments showed that Snort is performing better on Linux than on Windows. In another work [20], authors examined the performances of snort 2.8.0 NIDS by considering CPU and memory usage, system bus, network interface card, hard disc, logging technique, and the pattern matching algorithm. This study showed that hardware resources have a clear impact on the overall snort IDS performance. While authors in [7] studied the limitations of snort IDS by conducting several experiments on a real network environment. The performance of Snort IDS is analysed by using some metrics including the number of packets received, analysed, filtered and dropped. The experiments results noted that the Snort IDS failed to process high-speed network traffic and the packet drop rate was more significant.

Several other studies conducted performance comparison between the two popular open IDS systems Snort and Suricata [1,2,6,32]. In [2], authors investigated the performance of Snort and Suricata on three different platforms: Free BSD, Linux 2.6 and ESXi virtual server. The experiments were carried out for different packet sizes and speeds, and measure the rates of packet drop and alerts. Authors reported that Suricata gave better performance on Linux, while FreeBSD is the ideal platform for Snort especially when the later run on the high-speed network traffic. In [1], the performance comparison study of Snort and Suricata IDSs focused on identifying the computer host resource utilisation performance and detection accuracy. The experiments were conducted on two different machines with different CPU, RAM and network interface configurations. This study showed that Snort requires less processing power to perform well compared to Suricata. However, Suricata is more accurate in detecting malicious traffic with high computing resources and its ruleset is more effective. In another recent study [6], authors analysed and compered Snort and Suricata performances on Windows and Linux platforms. Experiment results showed that both IDSs use more resources on the Linux operating system. Authors concluded that CPU usage is highly affected by the operating system on which the IDS is deployed for both solutions. Study in [13] reached the same conclusions as in [6]. Authors reported that Linux-based execution of both IDSs consumes more system resources than its windows-based counterpart. With a similar intention, the study in [27] examined the performance of Snort and Suricata for correctly detecting the malicious traffic in networks. The performance of both IDSs was evaluated on two computers with the same configuration, at 10 Gbps network speed. The evaluation revealed that the Snort IDS processes a lower speed of network traffic than Suricata with higher packet drop, but it uses lower computational resources. In [8], authors focused on packet drops. They found that both Snort and Suricata performed with the same behaviour with larger packets and larger throughputs.

Few studies have considered other IDSs in the comparison such as in [29], where authors studied the performance and the detection accuracy of Snort, Suricata and Bro. The evaluation is done using several types of attacks including DoS attack, DNS attack, FTP attack, Scan port attack and SNMP attack. Further, each type of attacks is examined under various traffic rates with different sets of active rules. The metrics used in the evaluation include the CPU usage and the number of packets lost and alerts. In this study, Bro IDS showed better performance than Suricata and snort when evaluated under different attack types for some specific set of rules. Also, authors concluded that the high traffic rate has a significant effect on the CPU usage, the packets lost and the number of alerts for the three IDSs. In a previous work [22], author compared the three above-mentioned IDSs, looking for advantages and disadvantages of each one. The evaluation was performed at different network speeds. The experimental results showed that Suricata and Bro IDSs can handle 100 Mbps and 1 Gbps network speeds with no packet drops. In a similar context, authors in [31] proposed a new methodology to assess the performance of the intrusion detection systems snort, Ourmon and Samhain in a simulated environment. The simulation experiments were carried out on tow kind of machines (physical and virtual) to measure the CPU, RAM and input/output memory usage, and bandwidth constraint. Authors concluded that Snort imposes more impact on network traffic than Ourmon and Samhain IDSs. In [17] a high-level comparison is done between Snort and Bro. In this study, the authors affirmed that Snort is the best lightweight IDS but it not good for high-speed networks. Whereas, Bro is more effective for Gbps networks but it is more complex to deploy and understand. In more recent work [24] authors provided a high-level analysis and performance evaluation of popular IDSs including Snort, Suricata, Bro IDS, Open WIPS-ng,

OSSEC, Security Onion and Fragroute. The survey concluded that most of the existing IDSs have low detection accuracy with minimum hardware and sensor support.

3   Intrusion Detection Systems Snort, Suricata and Bro

Network-based intrusion detection systems (NIDS) collect information about incoming and outgoing network traffic to detect and mitigate potential attacks (Fig. 1) [1,10]. These systems utilise a combination of signature-based and anomaly-based detection methods [10]. Signature-based detection involves comparing the collected data packets against signature files that are known to be malicious, while anomaly-based detection method uses behavioural analysis to monitor events against a baseline of "normal" network activity. When malicious activity arises on a network, NIDSs detect the activity and generate alerts to notifying administrators, or blocking the source IP address from reaching the network [10].

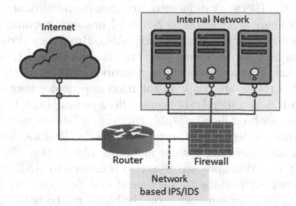

Fig. 1. IDS/IPS in a network architecture.

There are various open-source NIDS/NIPS that simplify the process of intrusion detection, and Snort is one of the most suitable solutions for small networks [25]. It was developed in 1998 by Martin Roesch from Sourcefire[1] and is now owned by Cisco, which acquired Sourcefire in 2013 [4]. Snort is the most widely deployed IDS/IPS worldwide over the last decades [27]. According to The Snort website, this IDS has been downloaded over 5 million times so far and currently has more than 600,000 registered users [4]. It has a single-threaded and multi-stage packet processing architecture, which uses the TCP/IP stack to capture and examine network packets payload [19,27]. However, their last version Snort 3.0 has added the multiple packet processing threads in order to address

---

[1] Sourcefire: www.sourcefire.com.

the limitation of single-threaded architecture in the previous versions. It uses both signature-based (SIDS) and anomaly-based (AIDS) methods for anomaly detection.

The Suricata IDS is a recent NIDS compared to Snort, it was developed in 2010 by the Open Information Security Foundation (OISF)[2] in an attempt to meet the requirements of modern infrastructures [27]. This NIDS introduced multi-threading to help speed up the network traffic analysis and overcome the computational limitations of single-threaded architecture [18,29]. Like Snort; Suricata is rules-based and offers compatibility with Snort Rules [27], it also provides intrusion prevention (NIPS) and network security monitoring [6], and uses both signature-based and anomaly-based methods to detect malicious network traffic [29]. Unlike Snort, Suricata provides offline analysis of PCAP files by using a PCAP recorder. It also provides excellent deep packet inspection and pattern matching which makes it more efficient for threat and attack detection [1]. Many studies assume that Suricata a powerful adversary to Snort and thus they are often compared with each other.

Bro-IDS is an open-source Unix-based NIDS and passive network traffic analysis [33]. It was originally developed in 1994 by Vern Paxson and renamed Zeek in late 2018 [33]. Bro IDS work differently from Snort and Suricata because of its focus on network analysis. It works as NIDS by passively monitors the network traffic and looks for suspicious activity [21]. Also, Bro policy scripts (—rules||) are written in its own Bro scripting language thatdoes not rely on traditional signature detection. Further, Suricata and snort are under GNU GPL licence [27], support IPv6 traffic and their installation and deployment are easy [27]. In contrast, Bro-IDS is under BSD license, does not support IPv6 traffic and their installation can be difficult [27,29,32]. In fact, Bro is more difficult and consume more time to deploy and to understand [5]. Besides, Snort and Suricata can run on any operating system including Linux, Mac OS X, FreeBSD, OpenBSD, UNIX and Windows, whereas Bro is limited to UNIX operating systems, which limits their portability. Like snort and Suricata, Bro IDS also uses both signature-based intrusion and anomaly-based methods to detect unusual network behaviour [5,29].

Table 1 shows a high-level comparison between the three IDSs and gives an overview of the different parameters can be assembled. This high-level comparison reveals that the three intrusion detection systems Suricata, Snort and Bro have some benefits for smart homes security and no one is dominant over the others.

4   Experimental Methodology

As mentioned above, smart homes security becomes a challenging topic, in which the security and home automation experts try to maintain a balance between the smart home high security requirements and supporting infrastructures' hardware

---

[2] OISF: https://suricata-ids.org/about/oisf/.

Table 1. Comparison table of Snort, Suricata and Bro IDSs

Parameters	Snort	Suricata	Bro IDS
Provider	Cisco system	OISF	Vern Paxson
Open source licence	GNU GPL licence	GNU GPL licence	BSD license
Operating system	Win/Unix/Mac	Win/Unix/Mac	Unix/FreeBSD
Installation/deployment	Easy	Intermediate	Typical
Intrusion prevention capabilities	Yes	Yes	No
Network traffic	IPv4/IPv6	IPv4/IPv6	IPv4
Intrusion detection technique	SIDS, AIDS	SIDS, AIDS	SIDS, AIDS
Configuration GUI	Yes	Yes	No
Support to high speed network	Medium	High	High

limitation. In general, these environments suffer from inherent hardware limitations, which restrict their ability to implement comprehensive security measures and increase their exposure to vulnerability attacks. To select the appropriate security solutions, it is indispensable to examine these hardware limitations and make sure that they will not affect the performance of these solutions in protecting the smart home-related devices. To this end, we aim in these experiments to examine the well-known intrusion detection systems Snort 3.0, Suricata 3.0.1 and ID Bro 2.5 to find the most suitable one for smart homes in term of resources consumption. More concretely, we examined the real-time performances of these IDSs while monitoring live network traffic from the smart home. Performance information from the CPU and RAM will be recorded, analysed and compared.

4.1 Experimental Setup

The experiments were performed on a virtual machine running Ubuntu 16.04 OS, with 8 GB of RAM, 40 GG of HDD and Intel Xeon CPU E5-2650 v2 running at 2.6 GHz. In the simulation scenarios, we first take a snapshot of the clean machine before executing any malicious sample. Then, after executing the malicious sample and recorded all information related to resources consumption and VM state, the VM is reverted to its original form. In order to emulate the smart home environment, we used Docker Enterprise (EE) to run the three IDSs inside Linux containers than running them directly on the VM base operating system. Several studies affirm that Docker is more convincing when compared to normal VM or hypervisor in terms of processing performance including CPU, disk and memory management, start-up and compilation speed, etc. [14]. In these experiments, each IDS was individually installed on identical custom Docker containers with default performance parameters (Fig. 2).

The performance evaluation of each IDS is done for 20 PCAP samples of malicious traffic generated by different types of attacks. The PCAP files were collected from (malware-traffic-analysis.net). The same malicious pcap files were used to monitor the resources used by the three IDSs while doing analysis of traffic and generating alerts. For the performance evaluation of the three IDSs, the information recorded during the execution of the malicious pcap samples include CPU and RAM use. Tcpreplay is used to replay the malicious pcap files to the NIDSs (Fig. 2). Table 2 shows the PCAP samples of malicious traffic used in the experiments.

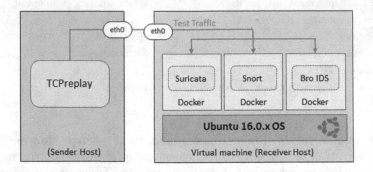

Fig. 2. Overview of the Testbed.

Table 2. PCAP samples of malicious traffic

#Id	Type of the malware in the PCAP file	Size of the PCAP file
#1	Malspam traffic	1.03 MB
#2	Necurs Botnet Malspam	448 KB
#3	Payment Slip Malspam	3.0 MB
#4	MedusaHTTP malware	669 kB
#5	Adwind Malspam	1.7 kB
#6	KainXN EK	1.93 MB
#7	Cyber Ransomware	584 KB
#8	Locky-malspam-traffic	285 KB
#9	Facebook Themed Malspam	1.4 MB
#10	BOLETO Malspam infection traffic	2.4 MB
#11	Pizzacrypt	254.4 KB
#12	BIZCN Gate Actor Nuclear	0.98 MB
#13	Fiesta Ek	1.52 MB
#14	Nuclear EK	2 MB
#15	Fake-Netflix-login-page-traffic	768 KB
#16	URSNIF Infection with DRIDEX	2.5 MB
#17	Dridex Spam traffic	999 KB
#18	Brazil malware spam	12.7 MB
#19	Info stealer that uses FTP to exfiltrate data	1.4 MB
#20	Hookads-Rig-EK-sends-Dreambot	595 KB

4.2   Experiments Results

CPU Utilisation. Figure 3 compares the results for the CPU utilisation rate for each malware sample, for the three IDSs Snort, Suricata and Bro IDS. From the obtained results, it is observed that the Snort IDS recorded the highest CPU utilisation rates for most of the PCAP samples, between 60% and 70%. While Suricata and Bro recorded relatively lower rates for the same malware attack tests. The CPU utilisation for Both IDSs are ranging from 20% to 40%, however, Suricata gives the lower rates for most of the tests compared to Bro and Snort. It is also observed that the type of malware traffic has a significant effect on the CPU usage, each IDS gives different CPU usage rates for the same test attack as they act quite differently for each attack.

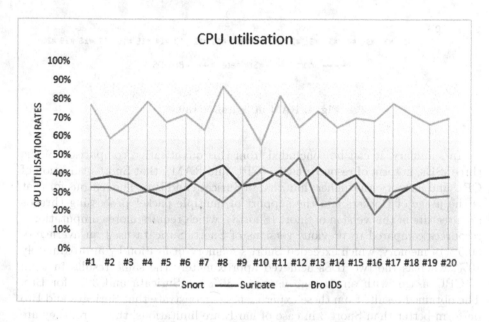

Fig. 3. CPU utilisation results.

RAM Utilisation. Figure 4 compares the results for the RAM utilisation rate for each malware sample, for the three IDSs Snort, Suricata and Bro IDS. From the obtained results, we can also have the same conclusions for the CPU usage; the Snort IDS gives the highest RAM utilisation rates for most of the PCAP samples. The rates are in the range of 60% and approximately 80%. While the highest rates were recorded for samples #4, #13 and #19. Suricata recorded relatively lower rates than Snort ranged from 20% to approximately 40%. While Bro IDS was the Best IDS in term of RAM usage by recording the lowest rates for most of the tests (From 20% to approximately 34%). Like in the CPU tests, it is also observed that the type of malware traffic has a significant effect on the RAM usage for the three IDSs.

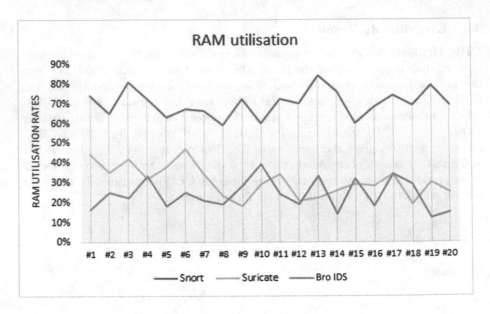

Fig. 4. RAM utilisation results.

In summary, it can be concluded from this quantitative comparison of the three ISDs, in term of resource usage (CPU and RAM), that Snort utilisation of CPU and memory was higher than that of Suricata and Bro. The reasons for that is the usage of Dockers and the support of multiple packet processing threads architecture in this version of Snort (Snort3), which require more computational resources compared to previous versions of Snort. Suricata used an average of 30.5% of memory, which exceeded Snort's memory utilisation by approximately 10%, whereas the two IDSs achieved approximately the same results in term of CPU usage, with an average usage of 36% for Suricata and 32% for Bro. The obtained results from these experiments demonstrate that Suricata and Bro perform better than Snort 3 in case of hardware limitations, therefore, they are more suitable for smart homes.

5   Conclusion

In this paper, we compared the performance of the open-source IDS systems Snort, Suricata and Bro to find the most suitable one for smart homes in term of resources consumption including CPU and memory usage. This study using Dockers, showed that each system had its strengths and weaknesses and the experimental results demonstrated that Suricata and Bro utilised less resources than Snort 3, which make them more appropriate to smart homes than Snort 3. In the future, we expect to improve this work by conducting more experiments on the three IDSs in term of detection accuracy as well as resources using larger pcap files. Finally, we are intend to use real smart home environment to perform the experiments.

Acknowledgement. This project has received funding from the European Union's Horizon 2020 research and innovation programme under grant agreement no. 786698. This work reflects authors view and Agency is not responsible for any use that may be made of the information it contains.

References

1. Albin, E., Rowe, N.C.: A realistic experimental comparison of the Suricata and Snort intrusion-detection systems. In: 2012 26th International Conference on Advanced Information Networking and Applications Workshops, pp. 122–127. IEEE (2012)
2. Alhomoud, A., Munir, R., Disso, J.P., Awan, I., Al-Dhelaan, A.: Performance evaluation study of intrusion detection systems. Procedia Comput. Sci. **5**, 173–180 (2011)
3. Anthi, E., Williams, L., Słowińska, M., Theodorakopoulos, G., Burnap, P.: A supervised intrusion detection system for smart home IoT devices. IEEE Internet Things J. **6**(5), 9042–9053 (2019)
4. Avast: Avast smart home security report 2019. https://bit.ly/2Ns2ju2. Accessed 29 Aug 2019
5. Bhosale, D.A., Mane, V.M.: Comparative study and analysis of network intrusion detection tools. In: 2015 International Conference on Applied and Theoretical Computing and Communication Technology (iCATccT), pp. 312–315. IEEE (2015)
6. Brumen, B., Legvart, J.: Performance analysis of two open source intrusion detection systems. In: 2016 39th International Convention on Information and Communication Technology, Electronics and Microelectronics (MIPRO), pp. 1387–1392. IEEE (2016)
7. Bulajoul, W., James, A., Pannu, M.: Network intrusion detection systems in highspeed traffic in computer networks. In: 2013 IEEE 10th International Conference on e-Business Engineering, pp. 168–175. IEEE (2013)
8. China, R., Avadhani, P.: A comparison of two intrusion detection systems. IJCST **4**(1), 316–319 (2013)
9. Dietrich, T.: Smart home product security risks can be alarming. https://www.insurancejournal.com/news/national/2019/01/03/513394.htm. Accessed 28 Mar 2019
10. Ghosh, A.K., Schwartzbard, A., Schatz, M.: Learning program behavior profiles for intrusion detection. In: Workshop on Intrusion Detection and Network Monitoring, vol. 51462, pp. 1–13 (1999)
11. Hargreaves, T., Wilson, C., Hauxwell-Baldwin, R.: Learning to live in a smart home. Build. Res. Inf. **46**(1), 127–139 (2018)
12. InsightDiy: TechUK and GfK: The state of the connected home. https://bit.ly/2oz4nbf. Accessed 11 Aug 2019
13. Isa, F.M., Saad, S., Fadzil, A.F.A., Saidi, R.M.: Comprehensive performance assessment on open source intrusion detection system. In: Kor, L.-K., Ahmad, A.-R., Idrus, Z., Mansor, K.A. (eds.) Proceedings of the Third International Conference on Computing, Mathematics and Statistics (iCMS2017), pp. 45–51. Springer, Singapore (2019). https://doi.org/10.1007/978-981-13-7279-7_6

14. Joy, A.M.: Performance comparison between Linux containers and virtual machines. In: 2015 International Conference on Advances in Computer Engineering and Applications, pp. 342–346. IEEE (2015)
15. Lin, H., Bergmann, N.: IoT privacy and security challenges for smart home environments. Information **7**(3), 44 (2016)
16. Liu, K., Fan, Z., Liu, M., Zhang, S.: Hybrid intrusion detection method based on k-means and CNN for smart home. In: 2018 IEEE 8th Annual International Conference on CYBER Technology in Automation, Control, and Intelligent Systems (CYBER), pp. 312–317. IEEE (2018)
17. Mehra, P.: A brief study and comparison of snort and bro open source network intrusion detection systems. Int. J. Adv. Res. Comput. Commun. Eng. **1**(6), 383–386 (2012)
18. Murphy, B.R.: Comparing the performance of intrusion detection systems: Snort and Suricata. Ph.D. thesis, Colorado Technical University (2019)
19. O'Leary, M.: Snort. In: O'Leary, M. (ed.) Cyber Operations, pp. 947–982. Apress, Berkeley (2019). https://doi.org/10.1007/978-1-4842-4294-0_19
20. Paulauskas, N., Skudutis, J.: Investigation of the intrusion detection system "snort" performance. Elektron. Elektrotech. **87**, 15–18 (2008)
21. Paxson, V.: Bro: a system for detecting network intruders in real-time. Comput. Netw. **31**(23–24), 2435–2463 (1999)
22. Pihelgas, M.: A comparative analysis of open-source intrusion detection systems. Tallinn University of Technology & University of Tartu, Tallinn (2012)
23. Rambus: Smart home: Threats and countermeasures. https://www.rambus.com/iot/smart-home/. Accessed 02 July 2019
24. Resmi, A.: Intrusion detection system techniques and tools: a survey (2017)
25. Roesch, M., et al.: Snort: lightweight intrusion detection for networks. In: LISA 1999, pp. 229–238 (1999)
26. Salah, K., Kahtani, A.: Performance evaluation comparison of snort NIDS under Linux and windows server. J. Netw. Comput. Appl. **33**(1), 6–15 (2010)
27. Shah, S.A.R., Issac, B.: Performance comparison of intrusion detection systems and application of machine learning to Snort system. Future Gener. Comput. Syst. **80**, 157–170 (2018)
28. Sivaraman, V., Gharakheili, H.H., Fernandes, C., Clark, N., Karliychuk, T.: Smart IoT devices in the home: security and privacy implications. IEEE Technol. Soc. Mag. **37**(2), 71–79 (2018)
29. Thongkanchorn, K., Ngamsuriyaroj, S., Visoottiviseth, V.: Evaluation studies of three intrusion detection systems under various attacks and rule sets. In: 2013 IEEE International Conference of IEEE Region 10 (TENCON 2013), pp. 1–4. IEEE (2013)
30. Van Der Meulen, R.: Gartner says 6.4 billion connected 'things' will be in use in 2016, up 30 percent from 2015. STAMFORD, Conn (2015)
31. Wang, X., Kordas, A., Hu, L., Gaedke, M., Smith, D.: Administrative evaluation of intrusion detection system. In: Proceedings of the 2nd Annual Conference on Research in Information Technology, pp. 47–52. ACM (2013)
32. White, J.S., Fitzsimmons, T., Matthews, J.N.: Quantitative analysis of intrusion detection systems: Snort and Suricata. In: Cyber Sensing 2013, vol. 8757, p. 875704. International Society for Optics and Photonics (2013)
33. Zeek: Introduction: Bro overview. https://bit.ly/2mRmeKd. Accessed 29 Aug 2019

A Resilient Hierarchical Checkpointing Algorithm for Distributed Systems Running on Cluster Federation

Houssem Mansouri[1]([✉]) and Al-Sakib Khan Pathan[2]

[1] Laboratory of Networks and Distributed Systems, Computer Science Department,
Faculty of Sciences, Ferhat Abbas Setif University 1, Sétif, Algeria
`mansouri_houssem@univ-setif.dz`
[2] Department of Computer Science and Engineering, Southeast University, Dhaka, Bangladesh
`spathan@ieee.org`

Abstract. In distributed systems, checkpointing method can be used to ensure fault-tolerance, which in turn could help the system's security and stability. In simple terms, checkpointing means saving status information of a system. In this work, a novel hierarchical checkpointing algorithm for distributed systems is proposed, which runs on cluster federation. This algorithm is based on two well-known techniques in the literature and it ensures that a locally consistent state is always maintained in each cluster with a global optimistic logging technique between clusters. The proposed algorithm synchronizes the intra- and inter-cluster checkpointing process in such way that each checkpoint taken locally in any cluster is a segment of the consistent global state. Compared to other works, our scheme has low message cost as it makes sure that only few processes in each cluster record checkpoints for any execution operation.

Keywords: Checkpointing · Cluster-based · Consistent global state · Distributed systems · Fault tolerance · Non-blocking · Optimistic logging · Recovery

1 Introduction

Today, cluster architectures are very widely spread in the research arena and in the industries. However, the use of computer cluster raises a number of problems related to several factors imposed by the nature of the distributed computing environment. In this kind of environment, resources can be volatile because the nodes can get disconnected when the connection is lost or hardware failure occurs, or voluntarily during proprietary use. In addition, the cluster may be exploited by a large number of users with very large distributed applications with long runtime. Thus, the risks of occurrence of faults become very high; these faults would cause failures that prevent the correct execution of the distributed applications – eventually, threatening the stability and security. Hence, to deploy computing applications on a large number of nodes, it is a necessity to have effective fault-tolerance mechanism.

In distributed systems, fault-tolerance can be ensured by using checkpointing techniques. A checkpointing technique basically maintains the records of the system on

© Springer Nature Singapore Pte Ltd. 2020
S. M. Thampi et al. (Eds.): SSCC 2019, CCIS 1208, pp. 99–110, 2020.
https://doi.org/10.1007/978-981-15-4825-3_8

some stable storage when the system is running without any fault (i.e., fault-free operation state). In case of any system failure, it could then restart from a previously recorded consistent global checkpoint state (i.e., according to the preserved record). Though fault-tolerance and security are two different terms, they are often interrelated. If a system is not fault-tolerant, unstable state of it or not functioning in the expected way (after a failure) could open several security loopholes as well that could be exploited by rogue entities.

Usually, in distributed environments, application processes communicate by passing messages among themselves. In this kind of computing environment, some kind of casual dependency is induced by a message between a transmitter process and a receiver process. The global dependency of the distributed application is defined by the transitive dependencies of the messages. Hence, only restarting any faulty process is not enough after a fault occurrence. The employed checkpointing algorithm must also ensure that all the related processes are coherent after the recovery operation is executed and it must maintain the dependencies between the applications. Hence, all these are also very important for the system's overall level of security.

In the existing literature, there are various types of checkpointing recovery algorithms. In general, all of the algorithms could be classified into two major categories:

– *Checkpoint-based techniques*: Each process periodically saves its state into a stable storage disk. After occurrence of fault, all processes roll back to a coherent global state. In this way, the strategy limits the amount of lost computation.
– *Message logging techniques*: Messages are saved so that they can be replayed in the same order in case of fault; only the faulty processes roll back to a coherent local state.

Main contribution of this paper is proposing a hierarchical checkpointing algorithm for distributed systems running on cluster federation. Our proposed algorithm results from a thorough comparative study of different algorithms/techniques proposed in the literature. Essentially, it is a combination of a *non-blocking* type checkpointing technique and the pessimistic message logging technique [1]. Here, the cluster is the main component in which the non-blocking checkpointing algorithm will be executed in a simultaneous way and the inter-cluster messages will be saved using a pessimistic logging technique based on the receiver process.

After this introductory section, in Sect. 2, our system model is presented. Section 3 discusses the related works. Section 4 proposes our checkpointing strategy. Performance evaluation along with comparisons is presented in Sect. 5. Section 6 presents the simulation results. The paper is concluded with Sect. 7 in which we also mention the possible future research directions.

2   System Model

Cluster federation (Fig. 1) is a union of n number of processes distributed on m number of clusters where k processes are contained by each cluster [2–4]. A SAN (System Area Network) connects the processes within a cluster. A Local Area Network (LAN) or

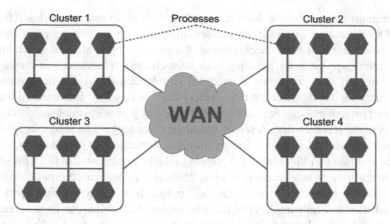

Fig. 1. Clusters in a cluster federation.

Wide Area Network (WAN) connects the clusters in the federation. In such environment of cluster computing, a running distributed application is divided into several modules which communicate with each other. The modules run on different process from different clusters.

Let us consider that there are n number of concurrent processes, $P1, P2, P3,..., Pn$ which are running on n clusters, at a rate k processes by cluster, $P1, P2, P3,..., Pk$. In this setting, we assume a *Fail-stop* mode. This means that when there is a process failure, it would immediately stop its execution. In this way, it would refrain from doing any malicious operation. Otherwise, it could threaten the security of the system. Reliable inter-cluster and intra-cluster message deliveries are also assumed in this setting. This means that during normal computation, there would not be any loss or alteration of message. In addition, there is no shared memory, no common or synchronized clock, or any central coordinator. Message passing is the only mode of communication between any pair of processes (inter- or intra-cluster). It is possible that the checkpointing process can be initiated by any process. There are finite but arbitrary delays when the message exchanges take place [5–8].

3 Related Work

In this section, some related works have been discussed. These are the representative previous works that helped us come up with our scheme.

There are three prominent schemes for checkpointing and rollback recovery in the existing literature. They are (i) *central file server checkpointing*, (ii) *checkpoint mirroring*, and (iii) *skewed checkpointing*. Using these schemes, the researchers in [9] develop a stochastic model to evaluate the expected total recovery overhead for a cluster computing system. Their work also presents a comparative study considering expected total recovery overhead. Generally, in a cluster system, there could be either single-process failure or multi-process failure. Hence, it is often difficult to assess the closed form of expected total recovery overhead. By performing various quantitative comparisons, the authors show that the skewed checkpointing is superior to other alternative schemes.

A recovery approach for handling both inter-cluster orphan and lost messages is proposed in [10]. This algorithm is executed simultaneously by all the clusters in a cluster federation for determining the recovery line. In this way, it is ensured that any inter-cluster orphan message may not exist between any pair of cluster level checkpoints belonging to the recovery line. A sender-based message logging technique is applied to handle inter-cluster lost messages for ensuring the correctness of computation.

A single-phase non-blocking checkpointing scheme is presented in [8]. This scheme ensures that after a failure-recovery, all processes in a system in different clusters can restart from their respective most recent checkpoints. In this way, *domino-effect* could be avoided. This basically implies that the most recent checkpoints can form a consistent recovery line for the cluster federation almost in all cases. The work takes advantage of message logging which enables the initiator process in each cluster to log minimum number of messages. One good feature of this approach is that it does not depend on the number of processes that may concurrently fail in a given setting.

A hierarchical checkpointing protocol is presented in [3], which is suitable for code coupling applications. The degree of interdependence between software modules is called coupling (generally). This is basically a measure of how closely two modules are connected with each other or the strength of their relationships. Code coupling applications show good level of code relationships. In this work, the authors' approach relies on a hybrid method of combining coordinated checkpointing within clusters. In between the clusters, some communication-induced checkpointing works. Though the work is fine, the algorithm needs some enhancements by adding some transitivity in the dependency tracking mechanism. In fact, as the claim is that the algorithm could tolerate multiple faults in a cluster, this also means that the redundancy is more for implementation of stable storage.

A fast and efficient recovery algorithm is proposed in [11] for cluster computing environment. The key aspect of this algorithm is that it does not depend on the cluster federation's architecture. This algorithm can also be run simultaneously by all participating clusters when determining a federation-level recovery line. Also, when compared with the approach in [3], it shows that it reduces computational overhead significantly.

In [5], the authors propose a low-cost non-blocking checkpointing algorithm for cluster federation. The time interval between successive invocations of the algorithm is significant here as that ensures minimum number of lost or delayed messages. Major aspects of the scheme are: (a) minimum number of processes take the checkpoints, (b) the communications between clusters are kept at a minimum, (c) for speedy execution, a decentralized approach is used which ensures that each cluster would maintain its own data structures to store the checkpointing dependency information, and (d) bandwidth wastage is kept at a minimum. In [6], the proposed *non-blocking* checkpointing/recovery algorithm limits the effect of domino phenomenon by the time interval between successive invocations of the algorithm. Recovery in this approach is as simple as that in the synchronous approach presented in [5]. A key aspect of this approach is that it employs some kind of responsibility taking strategy of the sender of a message to make it *non-orphan*.

In [7], another hybrid checkpointing algorithm is proposed which combines coordinated and communication-induced checkpointing methods. Based on the network and application communication pattern, this algorithm can be tuned accordingly. The authors have evaluated the algorithm via simulation studies and showed that the algorithm is suitable for applications that can be divided into several modules where many communications happen within a single module but communications in between the modules are relatively less.

4 Proposed Algorithm

4.1 Basic Idea

The basic idea of our new checkpointing algorithm is to combine the non-blocking checkpointing technique [12, 13] applied within clusters with the pessimistic message logging technique [14] applied between clusters. However, within the clusters, processes will be coordinated by the checkpointing process using non-blocking technique. The advantage of using this solution in intra-cluster setting is that during its execution, the logging protocol could run (at the same time) on the inter-cluster messages. These saved messages may not be part of the calculation for the system's global state, since they will be replayed only in case of failure.

For the adaptive algorithm to switch to this combination, the number of exchanged messages (by the processes) between clusters must reach to a sufficiently high threshold value. The experiments allowed the threshold to be set at five (5) messages per second (5 msg/s). Hence, if the frequency of inter-cluster communication messages exceeds this threshold, the logging of these messages degrades the performance of the distributed applications. At the same time, to save the process states, the non-blocking coordinated checkpoint algorithm will be used synchronously (and simultaneously) inside each cluster at a checkpointing frequency of 180 s.

The purpose of our proposed algorithm is to reduce the message cost during normal execution, and also to avoid a too-long recovery procedure that could slow down the operation of the distributed system in the event of a failure. For this, it is assumed at first that the running distributed application generates a few intra-cluster messages under a maximum frequency threshold.

4.2 Checkpointing Implementation

The combined checkpointing algorithm is presented in Subsect. 4.3 (Fig. 2 and Fig. 3). In this algorithm, each process has an identifier Pi and the identifier of its cluster Cj. At the start of the distributed application execution, it is the optimistic logging-based checkpointing algorithm that runs *intra-cluster* [1]. Here, all inter-cluster messages are saved by applying optimistic logging-based technique on the receiver process memory in the *InpMsg* set. Similarly, the determinant of each message is recorded at the level of receiver memory in the *DetMsg* set. The determinant is composed of: the sending date, the receipt date, and the message sequence number. To save a new process checkpoint, the algorithm stores the following data on a stable storage: the state of the process, the state of the incoming channels, and the state of the outgoing channels. At the same time, the non-blocking coordinated checkpoint-based algorithm [15, 16] runs synchronously (and simultaneously) inside each cluster. In our scheme, It is launched in every one hundred and eighty seconds (180 s), in which, *Pi* (which is basically the initiator process) saves a temporary checkpoint. Then a checkpoint request is sent by *Pi* to its directly dependent process, *Pj* $\in$ *DepProcsi* (*Pj* is the process that sends a computing message to *Pi* after taking its last snapshot). The *Ckpti* index and a value t = *1/Card(DepProci)* (*Card* refers to the cardinal function) are piggybacked by this request. This implies that element number in *DepProci* set is provided by *Card(DepProci)*.

If a checkpoint request is received by process *Pj* from another process *Px* during the running period of the algorithm, an answer is sent by *Pj*, then it piggybacks *t*'s value to the initiator process if the set *DepProcj* is empty. If not, it sends a checkpoint request piggybacking a new value, t = *t/Card(DepProcj)* to its directly dependent process (which is in fact, indirectly dependent on *Pi*), and so on. Whenever *Pi* (i.e., the initiator process) receives an answer, it collects the value *t* in *Termi*. If *Termi* is equal to 1, it sends a validation request to all other processes running in the cluster. If a process receives that validation request, it is required to store its temporary checkpoint as a permanent/stable one. Then, it would reset its data structure.

4.3 Data Structure and Pseudo Code

Every process *Pi* in different clusters has the following data structure:

- P_i: *process id (i $\in$ [1...n]).*
- C_j: *cluster id (j $\in$ [1...m]).*
- *Ckpt$_i$: index of the last checkpoint saved.*
- *DepProc$_i$: set of dependant processes in the same cluster.*
- *Term$_i$: algorithm termination detection.*
- *TempCkpt$_i$: last temporary snapshot.*
- *PermCkpt$_i$: last permanent snapshot.*
- *InpMsg$_i$: set of messages sent by the process.*
- *DetMsg$_i$: set of determinants of messages receipt by the process.*

Every message determinant has the following data structure:

- *SeqNbr: sequence number.*
- *SntDate: sent date.*
- *RcpDate: receipt date.*

Algorithm Part 1: *Checkpointing Process*

Part executed always by every process on each cluster

    <u>*Upon receiving a message Msg:*</u>

      if $(C_{Receiver} \neq C_{Sender})$

        Save *Msg to* $InpMsg_{Receiver}$;

        Save *Determinant to* $DetMsg_{Receiver}$;

      else

        if $(Ckpt_{Receiver} < Ckpt_{Sender})$

          Save $(TempCkpt_i)$;

          $Ckpt_{Receiver} \leftarrow Ckpt_{Sender}$;

        endif

      endif

Part executed simultaneously on each cluster every 180 s

Part executed by the initiator process Pi

      Save $(TempCkpt_i)$;

      $Ckpt_i := Ckpt_i + 1$;

      for All $(P_x \in DepProc_i)$

      Send *Checkpoint Request* $(Ckpt_i, t)$;

      endfor

      <u>*Upon receiving : Answer Request (t)*</u>

      $Term_i := Term_i + t$;

      if $(Term_i = 1)$

        for All $(P_x / x \in [1..k])$

          Send *Conformation Request ()*;

        endfor

      endif

Part executed by every process Pj in the cluster

    <u>*Upon receiving : Checkpoint Request* $(Ckpt_x, t)$</u>

      if $(Ckpt_j < Ckpt_x)$

        Save $(TempCkpt_j)$;

        $Ckpt_j := Ckpt_j + 1$;

        if $(DepProc_j = \varnothing)$

          Send *Answer Request (t)*;

        else

          for All $(P_x \in DepProc_j)$

            Send *Checkpoint Request* $(Ckpt_j, t)$;

          endfor

        endif

      endif

    <u>*Upon receiving : Conformation Request ()*</u>

    $PermCkpt_j \leftarrow TempCkpt_j$;

    $InpMsg_j \leftarrow \varnothing$;

    $DetMsg_j \leftarrow \varnothing$;

    $Term_j \leftarrow 0$;

Fig. 2. Algorithm part 1.

Algorithm Part 2: *Recovery Process*

Part executed by the faulty Process
      for All *(P_x / x ∈ [1..n])*
        Send *Recovery Request ();*
      endfor

Part executed by every process Pj in the system
    <u>*Upon receiving a Recovery Request ()*</u>

    if *($C_{Receiver} = C_{Sender}$)*
      Resume execution at the last recorded checkpoint PermCkpt$_j$;
    else
      Replay the reception event of Msg ∈ InpMsg$_j$ based on DetMsg$_j$;
    endif

Fig. 3. Algorithm part 2.

4.4 Recovery Implementation

After resuming from fault, all the processes in the cluster containing the faulty process resume execution at the last checkpoint recorded during the last coordinated checkpointing process. At the same time, all processes in others clusters replay the reception event of all the messages received from the cluster containing the faulty process (after its last recorded checkpoint). Here, their reception orders are saved in the determinants recorded in *DetMsg* at the time of execution (without fault).

5 Comparison of the Performances of Various Algorithms

Table 1 shows the performances of various checkpointing algorithms for cluster federation. Nine significant evaluation criteria are used for this comparative study. It is clear that our algorithm shows some advantages compared to other existing alternatives.

The main aspects that make our proposed mechanism relatively more efficient than the other alternative mechanisms are:

(1) The basic idea of our algorithm is independent of all system architectures.
(2) As concurrent failures are taken care of, single failures are also well-tackled.
(3) For the recovery process, there is no *domino-effect*. The algorithm can guarantee the minimum re-computation in this process.
(4) Just the messages that a process has received after its most recent permanent checkpointing (from only intra-cluster processes) need to be logged by a process at its recent local checkpoint.
(5) The most recent local permanent checkpoint needs to be only saved by a process. Hence, the number of trips to stable storage during recovery per cluster is merely, *k*.
(6) In this approach, blocking of the execution of the distributed application is not needed.

Table 1. Comparative chart.

Criteria	[2]	[7]	[8]	[10]	[11]	[17]	Our algorithm
1. Dependent on architecture	Yes	No	Yes	No	No	No	No
2. Domino-effect free	No	No	Yes	Yes	No	Yes	Yes
3. Concurrent failures	No	No	Yes	No	No	Yes	Yes
4. Logging message inter-cluster	No	No	Yes	Yes	No	Yes	Yes
5. Blocking time	0	0	0	0	0	0	0
6. Simultaneous execution (by clusters)	Yes	Yes	Yes	Yes	Yes	Yes	Yes
7. Number of checkpoints by process	>1	>1	1	1	>1	1	1
8. Stable storage related number of trips	$k + r$	$k + r$	k	k	$k + r$	k	k
9. Message complexity	$O(kn)$	$O(kn^2)$	$O(n)$	$O(kn)$	$O(kn)$	$O(n^2)$	$O(n)$

(7)   The algorithm is run simultaneously by all the clusters in the system.

(8)   Message complexity is pretty simple: $O(n)$.

Table 1 explains that our proposed algorithm is of clear advantage over the algorithms proposed in [7, 10, 11], and [17]. We can also note that there are two algorithms which may be close to our proposed algorithm in terms of performance; especially, based on the message complexity criterion – these two are the algorithms in [2] and [8]. Hence, for these cases, we need to compare the message cost of the three algorithms against the number of processes and clusters in the system through different simulation scenarios. That is why we have also done some simulation studies to show the efficiency and clear superiority of our algorithm.

6   Simulation Results

Message costs for [2, 8], and our algorithm to complete checkpointing processes considering the best case scenario are shown in Fig. 4(a), (b), and (c). We consider three clustering schemes: with 5, 10, and 20 clusters, against the number of processes in the system. *ChkSim* [18] simulator is used for these experiments. As the simulator is written in Java language, it is possible to run it on various platforms as long as the Java Virtual Machine (JVM) is available. We implemented the three checkpointing algorithms as Java classes.

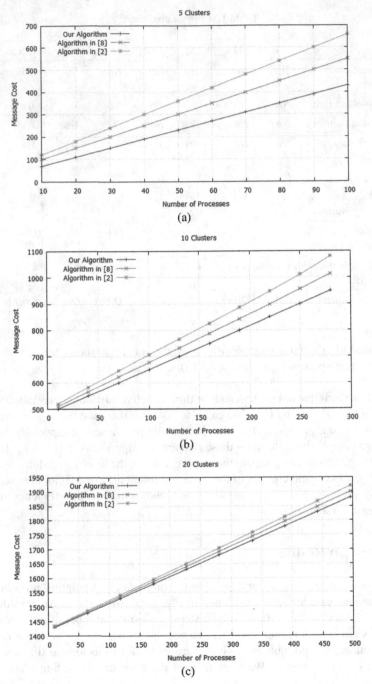

Fig. 4. Message cost vs. number of processes in the system when: (a) m = 5 (b) m = 10 (c) m = 20.

In our experiments, we changed the number of clusters (5, 10, and 20) and varied the number of processes (from 10 to 20 * m) to see the corresponding changes of the message cost. Especially, we tried to compare the performance of our algorithm with the algorithms in [2] and [8].

It is evident that the other two algorithms in question show relatively higher message costs to determine a global consistent state as the numbers of processes and/or clusters increase in the system. It could also be noticed that the message cost of the algorithm in [2] is higher than that of the algorithm proposed in [8]. Hence, it is fair to state that our algorithm shows better efficiency in terms of message cost. In fact, when the numbers of processes and/or clusters decrease, our algorithm's message cost would be even lesser comparatively. Thus, this is relatively more suitable for saving a consistent global state compared to any other alternative approach.

7 Conclusions and Future Research Direction

Here, we proposed a hierarchical checkpointing algorithm combining an optimistic logging method applied to inter-cluster messages and a non-blocking checkpoint technique used in intra-cluster setting. This adaptive algorithm is of coordinated type and it avoids the blocking of the distributed application. It also minimizes the message cost to the strict necessary, which significantly decreases network traffic in favor of the distributed application. Overall, by this technique, the system's requirement of fault-tolerance and security could be supported. A performance evaluation and simulation comparison of our proposition with other reference algorithms proves the efficiency of our algorithm.

Further investigations can be done on this issue. For instance, taking various complex deployment scenarios, the algorithms could be tested for their performance. There is another direction for research; that the algorithm could be tested against multiple simultaneous executions.

References

1. Elnozahy, M., Alvisi, L., Wang, Y.-M., Johnson, D.B.: A survey of rollback-recovery protocols in message-passing systems. ACM Comput. Surv. **34**(3), 375–408 (2002)
2. Cao, J., Chen, Y., Zhang, K., He, Y.: Checkpointing in hybrid distributed systems. In: Proceedings of the 7th IEEE International Symposium on Parallel Architectures, Algorithms and Network, pp. 136–141. IEEE Press, New York (2004)
3. Monnet, S., Morin, C., Badrinath, R.: A hierarchical checkpointing protocol for parallel applications in cluster federations. In: Proceedings of the 9th IEEE Workshop on Fault-Tolerant Parallel, Distributed and Network-Centric Systems, pp. 211–218. IEEE Press, New York (2004)
4. Sharma, K., Tomar, A., Kumar, M.: Clustering and recovery mechanism using checkpointing to improve the performance of recovery system. Int. J. Sci. Res. Dev. **4**(7), 827–832 (2016)
5. Kumar, M.: An efficient recovery mechanism with checkpointing approach for cluster federation. Int. J. Comput. Sci. Appl. **4**(6), 33–45 (2014)
6. Gupta, B., Rahimi, S., Ahmad, R.: A new roll-forward checkpointing/recovery mechanism for cluster federation. Int. J. Comput. Sci. Netw. Secur. **6**(11), 292–298 (2006)

7. Monnet, S., Morin, C., Badrinath, R.: Hybrid checkpointing for parallel applications in cluster federations. In: Proceedings of the 4th IEEE/ACM International Symposium on Cluster Computing and the Grid, pp. 773–782. IEEE Press, New York (2004)
8. Gupta, B., Rahimi, S.: Novel crash recovery approach for concurrent failures in cluster federation. In: Abdennadher, N., Petcu, D. (eds.) GPC 2009. LNCS, vol. 5529, pp. 434–445. Springer, Heidelberg (2009). https://doi.org/10.1007/978-3-642-01671-4_39
9. Bessho, N., Dohi, T.: Comparing checkpoint and rollback recovery schemes in a cluster system. In: Xiang, Y., Stojmenovic, I., Apduhan, B.O., Wang, G., Nakano, K., Zomaya, A. (eds.) ICA3PP 2012. LNCS, vol. 7439, pp. 531–545. Springer, Heidelberg (2012). https://doi.org/10.1007/978-3-642-33078-0_38
10. Gupta, B., Nikolaev, R., Chirra, R.: A recovery scheme for cluster federations using sender-based message logging. J. Comput. Inf. Technol. 19(2), 127–139 (2011)
11. Gupta, B., Rahimi, S., Ahmad, R., Chirra, R.: A novel recovery approach for cluster federations. In: Cérin, C., Li, K.-C. (eds.) GPC 2007. LNCS, vol. 4459, pp. 519–530. Springer, Heidelberg (2007). https://doi.org/10.1007/978-3-540-72360-8_44
12. Mansouri, H., Badache, N., Aliouat, M., Pathan, A.-S.K.: Adaptive fault tolerant checkpointing protocol for cluster based mobile ad hoc networks. Procedia Comput. Sci. 73, 40–47 (2015)
13. Mansouri, H., Badache, N., Aliouat, M., Pathan, A.-S.K.: A new efficient checkpointing algorithm for distributed mobile computing. J. Control Eng. Appl. Inform. 17(2), 43–54 (2015)
14. Mansouri, H., Pathan, A-S.K.: An efficient minimum-process non-intrusive snapshot protocol for vehicular ad hoc networks. In: Proceedings of the 13th ACS/IEEE International Conference on Computer Systems and Applications, pp 83–92. IEEE Press, New York (2016)
15. Mansouri, H., Pathan, A.-S.K.: Checkpointing distributed application running on mobile ad hoc networks. Int. J. High Perform. Comput. Netw. 11(2), 95–107 (2018)
16. Mansouri, H., Pathan, A.-S.K.: Checkpointing distributed computing systems: an optimization approach. Int. J. High Perform. Comput. Netw. 15(3–4), 202–209 (2019)
17. Gupta, B., Rahimi, S., Allam, V., Jupally, V.: Domino-effect free crash recovery for concurrent failures in cluster federation. In: Wu, S., Yang, L.T., Xu, T.L. (eds.) GPC 2008. LNCS, vol. 5036, pp. 4–17. Springer, Heidelberg (2008). https://doi.org/10.1007/978-3-540-68083-3_4
18. ChkSim: A Distributed Checkpointing Simulator. https://dcomp.sor.ufscar.br/gdvieira/chksim/. Accessed 20 Oct 2019

Towards Evaluating the Robustness of Deep Intrusion Detection Models in Adversarial Environment

S. Sriram[1]([✉]), K. Simran[1], R. Vinayakumar[1,2], S. Akarsh[1], and K. P. Soman[1]

[1] Center for Computational Engineering and Networking, Amrita School of Engineering, Amrita Vishwa Vidyapeetham, Coimbatore, India
sri27395ram@gmail.com, simiketha19@gmail.com
[2] Division of Biomedical Informatics, Cincinnati Children's Hospital Medical Centre, Cincinnati, OH, USA
Vinayakumar.Ravi@cchmc.org, vinayakumarr77@gmail.com

Abstract. Network Intrusion Detection System (NIDS) is a method that is utilized to categorize network traffic as malicious or normal. Anomaly-based method and signature-based method are the traditional approaches used for network intrusion detection. The signature-based approach can only detect familiar attacks whereas the anomaly-based approach shows promising results in detecting new unknown attacks. Machine Learning (ML) based approaches have been studied in the past for anomaly-based NIDS. In recent years, the Deep Learning (DL) algorithms have been widely utilized for intrusion detection due to its capability to obtain optimal feature representation automatically. Even though DL based approaches improves the accuracy of the detection tremendously, they are prone to adversarial attacks. The attackers can trick the model to wrongly classify the adversarial samples into a particular target class. In this paper, the performance analysis of several ML and DL models are carried out for intrusion detection in both adversarial and non-adversarial environment. The models are trained on the NSLKDD dataset which contains a total of 148,517 data points. The robustness of several models against adversarial samples is studied.

Keywords: Intrusion detection · Deep learning · Machine learning · Cyber security · Adversarial attacks

1 Introduction

In today's world, cyber-attacks and threats on Information and Communication Technologies (ICT) systems are growing rapidly. Various new attacks are invented daily by attackers to bypass the current security systems and steal crucial information. To detect and prevent these attacks on ICT systems, we need flexible and reliable integrated network security solutions. Various security structures and methods are used to deal with these malicious attacks namely

© Springer Nature Singapore Pte Ltd. 2020
S. M. Thampi et al. (Eds.): SSCC 2019, CCIS 1208, pp. 111–120, 2020.
https://doi.org/10.1007/978-981-15-4825-3_9

firewalls, Intrusion Detection System (IDS), software updates, encryption and decryption methods, etc. In that, IDS plays a big role in defending the network from all kinds of intrusion and malicious acts, both from outside and inside the network. IDS has been actively studied area from the 1980s, a seminal work by [2] on the computer security threat monitoring and surveillance. IDS is mainly categorized into two types. One is Network IDS (NIDS): It is utilized to monitor and analyze network traffic records to safeguard a system from network-based attacks. The next type is Host-based IDS (HIDS): it monitors the system in which it is installed to detect both internal and external intrusion and misuse and it responds by recording the activities and alerts the authority. NIDS monitors the network traffic and classifies the network records between normal ones and malicious ones. Since this is a classification problem, various Machine Learning (ML) and Deep Learning (DL) models are widely used in these detection systems and have achieved good results. However, ML and DL models are prone to adversarial attacks. Attackers can fool the detection system by using adversarial samples and make the classifier misclassify those sample data [3]. Therefore, it is necessary to check the robustness of those models that are used in NIDS against adversarial samples. In this paper, Several DL and ML models are trained on the openly available NSLKDD dataset for IDS. The robustness of those models against adversarial samples is studied. The main contributions of this work are the following:

– We have trained several DL and ML models using NSLKDD dataset in a non-adversarial environment and reported their performance using standard metrics.
– We have also studied the robustness of the trained models in the adversarial environment using the samples generated by two different adversarial attack techniques.

The rest of the paper is arranged as follows. Section 2 presents the related works. Section 3 includes the background information. Sections 4 and 5 presents description of the dataset and statistical measures respectively. Sections 6 and 7 covers the experimental results and conclusion.

2   Related Work

Various ML-based solutions have been proposed for IDS in the past. The authors Tsai et al. utilized Support Vector Machine (SVM), Self-organizing maps, Artificial Neural Networks (ANN), Naive Bayes (NB), K-Nearest Neighbor (KNN), Genetic algorithms, Decision Tree (DT), Fuzzy logic, etc for detecting the intrusion [4]. Buczak and Guven have done a comprehensive survey [5] on ML-based NIDS where many ML classifiers such as DT, ensemble learning, SVM, clustering, Hidden Markov Models (HMM), NB, etc. Since ML techniques require manual features, DL based approaches are proposed. DL architectures can obtain salient features from the input data automatically. In [10], the authors have proposed multiple Deep Neural Network (DNN) models for both network and host-based intrusion detection. They have trained models using several bench-mark datasets and compared its performance with ML-based approaches. Similar to [10,11] proposes a DNN based IDS for Software Defined Networking (SDN) environment. The proposed model only takes 6 basic features from 41 features of the NSLKDD dataset. [12] studies the effectiveness of DL networks such as DNN, Convolutional Neural Network (CNN), and Hybrid CNN for binary and multi-class classification. [14] compares the performance of many shallow and deep neural networks in detecting intrusion and [15] proposes a recurrent neural network and its variants for intrusion detection.

ML and DL models are prone to adversarial attacks. This vulnerability, which was discovered in recent years, limits the application of ML and DL models in various security-critical areas like IDS, autonomous vehicles, health care, etc. The authors Szegedy et al experimented on AlexNet with some adversarial sample images [6]. AlexNet [7] is the name of a convolutional neural network, designed by Alex Krizhevsky. They showed that by making very small variations in the input image, they could make the model misclassify it. Since then, the profound implications of this vulnerability sparked several researchers to develop various adversarial attacks and defenses. Some of the most commonly known attacks are Jacobian based Saliency Map Attack (JSMA) [9] and Fast Gradient Sign Method (FGSM) [8]. In this paper, the effects of adversarial samples generated by [8,9] on various ML and DL models are studied.

3   Background

3.1   Adversarial Attacks

Fast Gradient Sign Method (FGSM): It is a straightforward method of creating adversarial samples, which was proposed by Goodfellow et al. In FSGM, a small deviation is calculated in the direction of the gradient and it is defined as follows.

$$p = \epsilon sign(\triangledown_x L(\theta, x, y)) \tag{1}$$

where p is the perturbation, ϵ is a small constant, $\triangledown x L(\theta, x, y)$ is the gradient of loss function L which is used for training the model, θ denotes the model, x denotes the input and y denotes the class of input x. This perturbation p is added to the input data to generate adversarial samples:

$$x^{adversarial} = x + p \tag{2}$$

FGSM is computationally more efficient when compared to JSMA. But it has a lower rate of success.

Jacobian-Based Saliency Map Attack (JSMA): It uses the concept of saliency maps to generate adversarial samples. A saliency map gives insights about the features of the input data that are most likely to create a change of targeted class. In other words, saliency maps rate each feature of how influential it is for causing the model to predict a target class. JSMA causes the model to misclassify the resulting adversarial sample to a specific erroneous target class by modifying the high-saliency features. The formulation of the saliency map is given as:

$$A^+(x_{(i)}, y) = \begin{cases} 0 \; if \frac{\partial f(x)_{(y)}}{\partial x_{(i)}} < 0 \; or \sum_{y' \neq y} \frac{\partial f(x)_{(y')}}{\partial x_{(i)}} > 0 \\ -\frac{\partial f(x)_{(y)}}{\partial x_{(i)}} \cdot \sum_{y' \neq y} \frac{\partial f(x)_{(y')}}{\partial x_{(i)}} \; otherwise \end{cases} \quad (3)$$

where $x_{(i)}$ is input feature, y is a class, and $A^+(.)$ is the measure of positive correlation of $x_{(i)}$ with class y and negative correlation of $x_{(i)}$ with all other classes. If both cases in the formulation fail, then the saliency is zero. JSMA can create adversarial samples with less degree of distortion and has a better success rate while compared to FGSM.

3.2   Intrusion Detection System (IDS)

IDS is a tool that deals with unauthorized access and threats to systems and information by any type of user or software. Intrusion can be external or internal. External intrusion is when an intruder tries to gain access to a protected internal network. Internal intrusion is when an insider with a motive tries to misuse, attack or steal information. This is also called an insider threat. Two major categories of IDS are HIDS and NIDS. HIDS is a tool that monitors the system in which it is installed to detect both external and internal intrusion, misuse and responds by recording activities and alerts the authority. NIDS is utilized to monitor and analyze network traffic to safeguard a system from network-based attacks. Figure 1 shows a model of Intrusion detection system. Signature-based NIDS uses signatures that are extracted from previously known attacks. Signatures are manually generated and stored in the database whenever a new attack is identified. New attacks will not be detected by this system. Anomaly-based NIDS models the normal behavior of the network and raises alarm whenever it detects an anomalous behavior. Hybrid NIDS uses the combination of the above two approaches.

3.3   Deep Learning (DL) Models

The DL models are used for solving various research problems in a wide range of fields like biomedical, speech processing, natural language processing, etc since DL models have the capability of extracting salient features automatically with very less or no human intervention. The Deep Neural Network (DNN) model used in work has 5 hidden layers and overall it has a total of 1,399,557 trainable parameters. These five layers have 1024, 768, 512, 256, 128 neurons respectively. The dropout regularization technique is also employed to avoid overfitting.

The Convolutional Neural Network (CNN) model is widely used in the area of computer vision as it is capable of extracting location invariant features automatically. The CNN model, which is used in this work, has four convolution

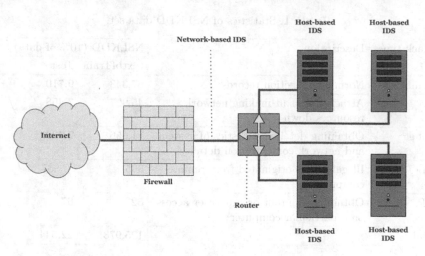

Fig. 1. Intrusion detection system model.

layers followed by a fully connected layer of 128 neurons. The CNN model has a total of 251,205 trainable parameters whereas the Long Short-Term Memory (LSTM) model, which is also used in this work has 1,26,533 trainable parameters.

4 Description of Dataset

One of the most used datasets is KDDCUP 99 which was obtained from the DARPA'98 dataset. The KDDCUP 99 dataset has several issues that are resolved by a newly refined version called NSL-KDD [1]. In this dataset, the invalid and redundant connection records are omitted from the entire train and test data. Table 1 represents the statistics of the NSLKDD dataset. This dataset has various attacks that belong to four major families such as User to Root (U2R), Probing attacks, Denial of Service (DoS) and Remote to Local (R2L). The purpose of the DoS attack is to work against resource availability. U2R attacks represent attempts for privilege escalation. R2L attacks attempt to exploit a vulnerability and gain remote access to a machine. Probe attacks are mainly information gathering attempts by scanning parts of the networks. The dataset contains a total of 41 features.

5 Statistical Measures

The performance evaluation of the models against adversarial attacks is conducted based on some of the popular performance metrics such as precision, accuracy, f1-score, and recall. Accuracy gives an oversight of the performance of the classifier. F1-score gives the harmonic mean between recall and precision. In a binary classification setting, true labels versus the predicted labels are represented by confusion matrix and the matrix contains four terms. The first one

Table 1. Statistics of NSLKDD data set.

Attack types	Description	NSLKDD (10% of data)	
		textbfTrain	Test
Normal	Normal connection records	67,343	9,710
DoS	Attacker aims at making network resources down	45,927	7,458
Probe	Obtaining detailed statistics of system and network configuration details	11,656	2,422
R2L	Illegal access originated from remote computer	995	2,887
U2R	Obtaining the root or superuser access on a particular computer	52	67
Total		125,973	22,544

is True Positive (TP). It denotes the amount of malicious traffic records that are correctly predicted as malicious. The second one is False Positive (FP). It denotes the amount of normal traffic records that are incorrectly predicted as malicious. The next one is True Negative (TN) and it denotes the amount of normal traffic records that are correctly predicted as normal. The final one is False Negative (FN) and it denotes the amount of malicious traffic records that are incorrectly predicted as normal. Based on these four terms, we can define several metrics:

- **Accuracy:** It denotes the total amount of correct predictions (TP and TN) over the total number of predictions.

$$Accuracy = \frac{TP + TN}{TP + FP + FN + TN} \tag{4}$$

- **Precision:** It denotes the amount of correct positive results over the amount of positive results predicted by the model.

$$Precision = \frac{TP}{TP + FP} \tag{5}$$

- **Recall:** It denotes the total amount of correct positive results over the amount of all relevant samples.

$$Recall = \frac{TP}{TP + FN} \tag{6}$$

- **F1 score:** F1 score denotes the harmonic mean between recall and precision.

$$F1score = 2 * \frac{precision * recall}{precision + recall} \tag{7}$$

The adversarial attacks reduce the overall performance of the model by tricking it to perform misclassification. Therefore, the above-mentioned metrics which show the performance of the system can be used to measure the robustness of the model in the adversarial environment.

6   Experimental Results

The adversarial attacks such as FGSM and JSMA are implemented using Adversarial Robustness Toolbox v0.10.0 [4] and the ML and DL models are implemented using Scikit-Learn and Keras python libraries respectively. The models implemented Table 2 represents the performance of models such as Long Short-Term Memory (LSTM), Convolutional Neural Network (CNN) and Deep Neural Network (DNN), Support Vector Machine (SVM), Naive Bayes (NB), K-Nearest Neighbour (KNN), Logistic Regression (LR), Decision Tree (DT), Random Forest (RF), Adaboost (AB) in non-adversarial environment. The performance of the trained models is compared with the performance of the Soft-Max Regression (SMR) classifier [13].

Table 2. Performance of baseline models for test set.

ML model	Accuracy	Precision	Recall	F1-score
DNN	77.39	78.36	77.39	75.80
CNN	75.37	80.61	75.37	71.88
LSTM	74.65	71.73	74.65	70.01
SMR [13]	75.23	86.71	62.30	72.14
LR	63.32	55.88	63.32	57.07
NB	44.41	63.22	44.41	48.29
KNN	73.50	74.13	73.50	70.02
DT	74.78	74.58	74.78	71.95
AB	43.12	51.08	43.12	45.84
RF	73.84	81.28	73.84	69.33
Linear-SVM	66.51	68.20	66.51	61.59
RBF-SVM	64.71	60.13	64.71	59.08

It can be observed from Table 2 that the DNN performed better than all the other models that are trained in this work. Based on the accuracy metric, the DNN, CNN, and DT are the top three models that are trained in this work and their accuracies are 77.39%, 75.37%, and 74.78%. Adaboost classifier gives the least performance in terms of accuracy. In terms of F1-score, both SMR and DT models performed better than CNN and LSTM models. All the models that are trained in this work are also tested on adversarial samples generated by FGSM and JSMA to evaluate how robust they are under an adversarial environment. The Table 3 and Table 4 represents the performance of all the models tested on adversarial samples generated by FGSM and JSMA methods respectively. It can be observed from both the tables that the adversarial attacks tremendously reduced the performance of the baseline models that are trained in a non-adversarial environment.

Table 3. Performance of models for the adversarial sample generated by FGSM.

ML model	Accuracy	Precision	Recall	F1-score
DNN	16.74	30.62	16.74	16.02
CNN	37.83	35.82	37.83	35.82
LSTM	24.51	32.47	24.51	25.36
LR	62.27	54.81	62.27	55.43
NB	33.76	22.64	33.76	25.31
KNN	66.35	61.79	66.35	61.47
DT	17.65	23.85	17.65	17.49
AB	17.28	19.71	17.28	14.74
RF	39.97	29.88	39.97	30.81
Linear-SVM	63.25	56.98	63.25	57.32
RBF-SVM	63.05	56.79	63.05	56.18

Table 4. Performance of models for the adversarial sample generated by JSMA.

ML model	Accuracy	Precision	Recall	F1-score
DNN	10.87	3.93	10.87	3.05
CNN	10.06	24.24	10.06	7.44
LSTM	46.49	45.44	46.49	0.33
LR	14.38	25.84	14.38	1
NB	43.61	29.39	43.61	30.58
KNN	49.27	47.95	49.27	38.50
DT	12.21	38.41	12.21	6.98
AB	3.88	20.12	3.88	6.05
RF	14.18	47.63	14.18	10.95
Linear-SVM	46.60	38.54	46.60	34.04
RBF-SVM	62.01	54.59	62.01	54.11

The performance of the models is affected tremendously by both FGSM and JSMA techniques. The top three most affected models by FGSM in terms of accuracy are DNN, LSTM, and DT. The FGSM attack reduced the performance of DNN from 77.39 to 16.74 (78% reduction), LSTM from 74.65 to 24.51 (76% reduction), and DT from 74.78 to 17.65 (67% reduction). The least affected models by FGSM attack is RBF-SVM (2% reduction), LR (2% reduction), and LSVM (4% reduction). The top three most affected models by JSMA in terms of accuracy are CNN, DNN, and DT. The JSMA attack reduced the performance of CNN from 74.65 to 10.06 (87% reduction), DNN from 77.39 to 10.87 (86% reduction), and DT from 74.78 to 12.21 (83% reduction). The least affected models by JSMA attack are NB (2% reduction), RBF-SVM (4% reduction), and LSVM (30% reduction).

It can be observed from both the tables that, FGSM worked well in the case of LSTM and NB and JSMA worked better than FGSM in all other cases. RBF-SVM, LSVM, KNN, and NB are the models which show more robustness against both adversarial attacks when compared to the rest of the models. The adversarial samples that are created using the DNN model generalize well over other DL and ML models as well. In other words, the attack samples, which are created by both FGSM and JSMA for the DNN model as the target, also affect the performance of other ML and DL models.

7   Conclusion

In this paper, we have observed that the adversarial samples can lower the accuracy of many DL and ML classifiers with varying degrees of success. This shows that it is necessary to test the robustness of any DL or ML model against adversarial samples especially when they are used in security-critical applications. In this paper, the models that are trained did not perform well when compared to other state-of-the-art approaches, but its robustness towards adversarial attacks are studied. In the future, we will further focus on the defense techniques that avoid such attacks.

Acknowledgement. This research was supported in part by Paramount Computer Systems and Lakhshya Cyber Security Labs. Also, the authors would like to express gratitude to NVIDIA India for supporting the research by providing the GPU hardware. They would also like to express gratitude to Computational Engineering and Networking (CEN) department for encouraging the research.

References

1. Tavallaee, M., Bagheri, E., Lu, W., Ghorbani, A.A.: A detailed analysis of the KDD CUP 99 data set. In: 2009 IEEE Symposium on Computational Intelligence for Security and Defense Applications, pp. 1–6. IEEE, July 2009
2. Anderson, J.P.: Computer Security Threat Monitoring and Surveillance. James P. Anderson Co., Fort Washington (1980)
3. Rigaki, M.: Adversarial deep learning against intrusion detection classifiers (2017)
4. Tsai, C.-F., et al.: Intrusion detection by machine learning: a review. Expert Syst. Appl. **36**, 11994–12000 (2009). https://doi.org/10.1016/j.eswa.2009.05.029
5. Buczak, A.L., Guven, E.: A survey of data mining and machine learning methods for cyber security intrusion detection. In: IEEE Communications Surveys Tutorials 18.2 (Second Quarter 2016), pp. 1153–1176 (2015). ISSN: 1553–877X. https://doi.org/10.1109/COMST.2015.2494502
6. Szegedy, C., et al.: Intriguing properties of neural networks. In: arXiv preprint arXiv:1312.6199 (2013)
7. Krizhevsky, A., Sutskever, I., Hinton, G.E.: Imagenet classification with deep convolutional neural networks. In: Advances in Neural Information Processing Systems, pp. 1097–1105 (2012)
8. Goodfellow, I.J., Shlens, J., Szegedy, C.: Explaining and harnessing adversarial examples, arXiv preprint arXiv:1412.6572 (2014)

9. Papernot, N., McDaniel, P., Jha, S., Fredrikson, M., Celik, Z.B., Swami, A.: The limitations of deep learning in adversarial settings. In: 2016 IEEE European Symposium on Security and Privacy (EuroS & P), pp. 372–387. IEEE (2016)

10. Vinayakumar, R., Alazab, M., Soman, K.P., Poornachandran, P., Al-Nemrat, A., Venkatraman, S.: Deep learning approach for intelligent intrusion detection system. IEEE Access **7**, 41525–41550 (2019)

11. Tang, T.A., Mhamdi, L., McLernon, D., Zaidi, S.A.R., Ghogho, M.: Deep learning approach for network intrusion detection in software defined networking. In: 2016 International Conference on Wireless Networks and Mobile Communications (WINCOM), pp. 258–263. IEEE, October 2016

12. Vinayakumar, R., Soman, K.P., Poornachandran, P.: Applying convolutional neural network for network intrusion detection. In: 2017 International Conference on Advances in Computing, Communications and Informatics (ICACCI), pp. 1222–1228. IEEE, September 2017

13. Javaid, A., Niyaz, Q., Sun, W., Alam, M.: A deep learning approach for network intrusion detection system. In: Proceedings of the 9th EAI International Conference on Bio-inspired Information and Communications Technologies (Formerly BIONETICS), pp. 21–26. ICST (Institute for Computer Sciences, Social-Informatics and Telecommunications Engineering), May 2016

14. Vinayakumar, R., Soman, K.P., Poornachandran, P.: Evaluating effectiveness of shallow and deep networks to intrusion detection system. In: 2017 International Conference on Advances in Computing, Communications and Informatics (ICACCI), pp. 1282–1289. IEEE, September 2017

15. Vinayakumar, R., Soman, K.P., Poornachandran, P.: Evaluation of recurrent neural network and its variants for intrusion detection system (IDS). Int. J. Inf. Syst. Model. Des. (IJISMD) **8**(3), 43–63 (2017)

Privacy Preserving Profile Matching in Mobile Social Networks: A Comprehensive Survey

Rohini Bhosale$^{(\boxtimes)}$ and Madhumita Chatterjee

Pillai HOC College of Engineering and Technology (Affiliated to University of Mumbai), Khalapur, HOC Colony Road, Taluka, Rasayani, Maharashtra, India
{rbhosale,mchatterjee}@mes.ac.in

Abstract. The advancements in wireless communication technologies and smart mobile devices enabled the proliferation of Mobile Social Networks (MSN). MSN is more flexible and popular than Online Social Network (OSN). It provides a platform for intelligent device users to search on the Internet and connect to people in close proximity to obtain the required information. Connecting with other people in close proximity is the prominent feature of MSN. In social network connections are built based on common interest and location traces. To connect with more people who have similar interest profile matching is one of the essential steps. A new connection is built by comparing the profile of two strange users. During this process, private information of a user may get leaked. A major issue greatly raised and potentially vulnerable in MSN is user privacy preservation. During profile matching the ill-intended user may receive the private information of another user and misuse it. The issue of privacy in profile matching is focused by many researchers. This paper reviews the work done in the domain of privacy and security issues of profile matching and provides a comprehensive analysis on it.

Keywords: Mobile social network · Profile matching · Privacy preservation

1 Introduction

In recent years, tremendous growth in Online Social Network (OSN) has changed the way we communicate and share ideas, news, and information with our friends and relatives. The use of OSN is explosively increased because of its versatile platforms and various benefits in almost all aspects of our life. Facebook is the third most visited site on the Internet [1]. It has 2.375 billion monthly active users in that over 1 billion of those are mobile-only users. 47% of Facebook users access the platform through mobile [7].

Users get attracted to different platforms of OSN for various purposes. OSN helps the user to connect with other people who share similar interests and stimulate the sharing of information in the form of text, images, video, etc. The use of the social network is not limit to enforcing real-life relations but much more than that. Now job-seekers credibility is verified by checking their social networking profiles such as LinkedIn [2]. In business, the social network is used for the marketing of a product. It is more useful than conventional marketing as targeted marketing is feasible with it.

© Springer Nature Singapore Pte Ltd. 2020
S. M. Thampi et al. (Eds.): SSCC 2019, CCIS 1208, pp. 121–134, 2020.
https://doi.org/10.1007/978-981-15-4825-3_10

Advancement in wireless communication technology and Internet-enabled smart mobile devices; use of Mobile Social Network (MSN) proliferated. It is an extension of OSN on mobile devices. Location-based MSN is the category of social network where a user uses his mobile device location to enquire for Point of Interests (POIs) nearby such as a petrol pump, restaurant to the Location Based Service (LBS) provider. An example of such MSN is Foursquare [3]. People are not using OSN to communicate with whom they are already known in real life but also to extend their social network by finding new users who are having similar interests. MSN provides friend-finding on a much larger scale then OSN. MSN users can find a friend in particular vanity at any time e.g. a patient sitting in the hospital can find another patient who is having a similar symptom by using mHealthcare social networking (MHSN) app. They can exchange their experiences and give moral support to each other. It is also useful for forwarding patients' health information wirelessly to a related mhealthcenter. User profile contents user details which may include sensitive information that the user doesn't want to share any stranger. Data security issues are the major obstacles to the application of MHSN [4].

Vanity based friend-finding is a prominent feature of MSN and which reflects a more realistic connection than OSN. Some most common MSNs are Tinder, Sonar.me and Twitter [5]. Facebook also provides features like MSN. MSN allows mobile users to discover and interact with friends who are in their nearby physical vicinity. Consider you went to a new city and visited a mall there. You wanted to take a suggestion from people who are interested in shopping. MSN helps you in this situation by finding people with similar interests who are there at that moment. With this flexibility and benefits it also suffers from various security and privacy issues.

The privacy of the users' data in the MSN environment is a serious issue that requires special considerations. Numerous academic analysis and reality incidents have shown that users' profile information can be easily disclosed to the unintended audience during profile matching and unintended information disclosure can result in very negative consequences, e.g. identity theft, blackmailing, and stalking. All these attacks are performed because of the leakage of private information. Existing MSNs have provided some privacy settings, to safeguard the private data of user but these solutions are not sufficient. The motivation behind this paper is to analyze the existing work and provide future research direction in this domain.

The rest of this paper is organized as follows: in Sect. 2 we have discusses about the process of profile matching. Section 3 covers the privacy and security issues in MSN and profile matching. In Sect. 4, we have presented a taxonomy of privacy preservation in profile matching. Section 5 focuses on various approaches proposed by researchers to perform secure profile matching. Critical analysis and future directions on privacy protected profile matching are done in Sect. 6. Finally, we conclude our review work in Sect. 7.

2 Profile Matching in Mobile Social Network

MSN can work efficiently if a user can find people who share the same interest and contact anywhere, at any time. To stand with this requirement one of the important steps is speedy and accurate profile matching. MSN is consists of set of users $V = \{u_1, u_2, u_3,$ $u_4 \dots u_n\}$ with N users. When a user wants to use MSN she needs to download the MSN app on her intelligent device like a Smartphone and install it. Create a profile on MSN. Each user in the social network has user profile u_i with m attributes and represented as, $u_i = \{a_1, a_2, a_3, a_4 \dots a_m\}$. Various types of attributes are included in the user profile. The values of these attributes vary from numerical to text i.e. few attributes may take numerical values between 0 to 10 and some may take fixed one word or a sentence. For the profile matching, user may specify her interest or all attributes of the profile are considered for finding people with similar interests. The interest of users ranges from the type of movie user likes to a political view. The specified profile is a query profile. It is a subset of the user profile in which the user is interested to connect with other people. Based on it a user receives recommended friends list.

In the process of profile matching the initiator defines the query profile that includes her interest. Initiators broadcast query profile and it is received by nearby people. The nearby people who have received this request are called as responders. The initiator and responder calculate the intersection of two profiles. If the intersection factor is more than the threshold value then they can communicate with each other else the request is discarded. The process of profile matching using hybrid approach is shown in the Fig. 1. As shown is Fig. 1 Rina, Viaan and Siddhi are in close proximity.

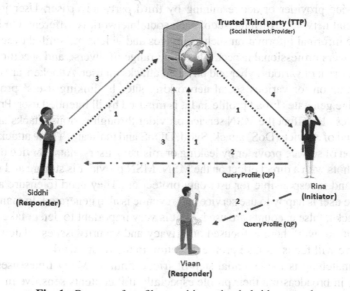

Fig. 1. Process of profile matching using hybrid approach

- **Step 1.** Rina, Viaan and Siddhi downloaded mobile application registered themselves with Social Network Provider (SNP) which also plays the role of Trusted Third Party (TTP).

- **Step 2.** Rina (initiator) broadcasts a request. When Siddhi (responder) and Viaan (responder) receive the request they process it. Siddhi and Viaan can communicate with Rina only if the result of the profile matching is more than the threshold value.
- **Step 3.** Each responder sends result of profile matching to TTP for verification
- **Step 4.** TTP verifies the result and sends it to Rina.

3   Privacy and Security Issues in Mobile Social Networks

The privacy and security issues have brought serious upshots for users and MSN service providers. Social network is an open space and everyone can decide what to share publically and how much personal data to hide. Finding the real identity of the user is difficult as there is no restriction on who can create profiles and how many profiles user may have. Anyone can create accounts with the same or different name in various social networks. Because of this whole system of social networking as become complicated and vulnerable to attacks. Users share huge amount of personal data on social network including unique identification number, interest, hobbies, location, feeling, social status, relationship, political view etc. Users are affected due to unseemly sharing of sensitive information. This happens because of ill-treatment to users personal data by service provider or active mining by third party advertiser. User joins more than one social network. Attribute set of each social network is different. On Facebook people share informal information such as images and videos of familial event whereas Linked In covers professional aspect. This wide range of diverse and specific information increases risk of various cyber and physical attacks on user. Attackers are collecting users' information for various social networking sites by linking users' profile. User profile linkage generates broad profile and it is misused by ill intended user. Privacy and security issues also affect the MSN service provider through various attacks and threats such as Denial of Service (DoS) attack, Sybil, DDoS and malware. These attacks damage the reputation of service provider by leaking or misusing users' data, service disruption, or other upshots with a direct effect on the MSN. MSN provider is storing and managing users' data and is responsible for user data protection. They need to ensure a business model where user is happy to use service and revenue is also generated. In many of these types of attacks, false accounts are used. So it is very important to detect fake accounts. The scope of our work here is focused on privacy and security issues related to profile matching. We will focus on fake profile detection in the future work.

Profile matching is the essential step of friend finding. Many times users are not comfortable in broadcasting their profile especially if it contents sensitive information. Many times users keep their personal and professional life separately. They don't share their details at the workplace. Some pre-shared parameters between users are more likely to leak while profile matching. If ill-intended co-worker of the user can link her account on the social network from an interest in that case also she loses her privacy. In another scenario user privacy is compromise when malicious user systematically changes his interest to match with initiator profile. In the profile matching process, private information of the user may leak and misused by other participants. Because of this privacy is the big concern in profile matching and it increases a lot while performing profile matching with a stranger. So attributes of any profile must not be revealed to other users till they become friends. Profile matching process suffers with various attacks by insider or external users. Collusion Attack, Runaway Attack, Dictionary Profiling, Cheating, Fake Profile, Attribute Inference Attack, Sybil attack and Man-in-the-Middle Attack are some of the attacks that may occur during profile matching.

This paper provides a comprehensive review of privacy issues and solutions related to profile matching in MSNs.

4   Taxonomies of Privacy Preservation Profile Matching

Recently, many researchers have targeted issues of security and privacy in MSN. There are quite a few proposals for privacy preservation in profile matching, which allows two users to compare their profiles without revealing private information to each other. In this process, both users should not able to get details of each other.

Privacy-preserving profile matching can be broadly divided into two categories coarse-grained and fine-grained. In the coarse-grained approach, a similarity match between user profiles is defined as a set intersection or cardinality of a set. [6–15] have implemented coarse-grained private matching schemes. The limitation of this approach is the user can not further discriminate users for a better choice with further degrees of attributes. The other approach is the fine-grained private matching approach. In this approach, the similarity between users profile is defined as a dot product between two user profiles. In [16–21] authors have implemented fine-grained private matching scheme. It enables finer discriminate among users having different degrees of interest in the same attribute. Consider the following scenario; Rina initiates the process of friend-finding with movie as her interest. She got two choices Viaan and Siddhi who are nearby her. Rina watches movies trice a month, Viaan, twice and Siddhi once a month. Three of them are interested in the movie but the degree of interest is different. As per this scenario, Viaan is the better choice for Rina but the coarse grained scheme will give both the profile as a match whereas in fine grained the choice is further differentiated by checking the degree of interest and gives the finest match.

Based on the process of profile matchmaking, it is further classified into the following approaches. The user profile is saved as an attribute set or attribute vector and the concept of set theory is proposed by many researchers. Private Set Intersection (PSI) or a Private Cardinality of Set Intersection (PSICA) and Private Dot-Product (PDP) are used in existing work. If the user profile is treated as an attribute set then choice is PSI or PSICA. PSI-based matching approach only considers the number of common attributes. It gives results in coarse-grained. It does not take the degree of interest into account. Because of this it cannot provide a fine-grained private matching. PDP method is applicable if the profile is described as vector. PDP provides results in the fine-grained match of two profiles. To make security mechanism stronger public-key cryptosystem is used by researchers. For ensuring privacy in finding common interest PSI or PSICA and PDP adopt the public-key cryptosystem such as Homomorphic cryptography encryption which inevitably yields high computational overhead.

On the basis of architecture of profile matching system it is categorized into three categories: distributed, centralized and hybrid approaches. In a centralized approach, a server is a trusted entity and keeps a record of all users with it. Whenever a user wants to connect with other users, he sends the request to the server and the server performs matchmaking. Here server plays the role of a Trusted Third Party (TTP) among participants. The centralized approach is proposed by many researchers. Easy implementation is the advantage of this approach. However, it suffers from limitations too. First, to manage user at different location service provider needs to deploy a dedicated local server. Second, it is a single point of failure thus if the server is attacked then whole data will be leaked. The third reason is the user may not always have access to the central server through the internet. Low scalability is another problem with TTP based approach. It is not suitable for a larger social network. These are the reason why a centralized approach is not appropriate for MSN. The distributed approach is a more appealing solution for MSN. In the distributed approach, the initiator broadcasts his profile and subsequently, profile matcher protocol executes. Profile matcher protocol is the program which is used for finding people who are having similar interest. The drawback of this approach is user's information may get leaked and the ill-intended user may get users sensitive information. To overcome the limitations of a centralized and distributed approach hybrid approach is used. In the hybrid approach, the trusted server is used for information management and verification of matchmaking results. In verification, the server ensures the any of the users should not cheat another user with manipulated results but it does not take part in the matchmaking phase. The process of profile matching is performed on a user's device. The benefit of using a hybrid approach is the verification of results. Here it is assumed the server is trustworthy.

5 Related Work

Various solutions have been proposed by the researcher to address the issue of privacy in profile matching. We have classified research work as follow:

5.1 Coarse-Grained and Centralized Approach

Li et al. in the paper [6] proposed a scalable friend matching and recommendation system without disclosing the private information of users to the honest-but-curious cloud. In this system, the obfuscation technique is used. Before uploading the user's data on the cloud XOR operation is performed on every bit and masking sequence which is generated with a certain probability. Thus in the friend matching process, the server has no idea of the original sensitive data but it can still perform the friend matching and recommend friends. The design of SPFM ensures the same data maintain a statistical similarity after obfuscation while different data can be statistically classified without leaking the original data. This scheme works even better when the original data is large.

Luo et al. in [7] proposed a dual authentication scheme that combines Identity authentication and key agreement. Trusted Third Party is responsible for friend discovery and to secure data from TTP and other attacker one way hash function is applied on data. Bilinear cryptography and Diffie Hellman Key Exchange algorithm makes this scheme resistant against internal and external attacker. Symmetric cryptography is used at user side and asymmetric cryptography is at server side. It provides resistance to Man-in-the-Middle (MitM), replay attack and brute force attack. Algorithm used in [7] system is quite complex. Result of profile matching is coarse grained, user does not get exact matching friend.

5.2   Coarse-Grained and Distributed Approach

Li, Cao, et al. in the paper [8] proposed FindU, a privacy-preserving personal profile matching schemes for MSNs. To make system Secure Multiparty Computation (SMC) based on Shamir Secret Sharing Scheme (SS) and additive Homomorphic Encryption is used. Match making is based on an intersection of interest sets. User with maximum matching attributes considered as best match for the initiator. Each user computes his match locally and no verification of results is done. Three levels of privacy are implemented in it and as the level of privacy increases the minimum information is disclosed and less information is exchanged during profile matching. In [8] authors have proposed a distributed reliable friend matching scheme which takes much less computational cost. Limitation of FindU is the high communication cost. It also does not verify results calculated by the participants and as a result, cannot prevent any participant from forging the computation result to match with query requirements.

Zhu, Du, et al. [9] proposed a privacy-preserving and fairness aware friend matching protocol. In this system the user profile is separated from his interest profile and both are encrypted by using Paillier cryptosystem. Bind Vector Transforming (BVT) technique is used to attain privacy guarantee and fairness assurance. In BVT two users transform their profile into blind ones by performing blind add, append, reverse and shuffle on their interest vector and encrypted profile vector of another user. These operations are performed in the same order. As same steps are followed by both the users result of profile comparison will be same. Single user cannot recover original vector alone. Runway attack is prevented in [9] by blind append, reverse which hide the exact matching number. A verifier verifies the results computed by both the users. The verifier is considered as an honest entity. However collusion attack may launch by verifier and one of the participants. This attack is inhibited by performing BVT on result vector before sending it to verifier. The computational overhead of the protocol is low. Limitation of [9] is the randomness of key. It is not truly random thus is it not really very secured.

Cui, Du, et al. in the paper [10] proposed a novel distributed scheme based on special Ciphertext-Policy Attribute-Based Encryption (CP-ABE). A trusted central server is called as attribute authority and role of it is to generate public key and private key for each user at the time of registration. A preference-profile works as a hidden access policy. The initiator sends an encrypted preference-profile along with random number N and remainder vector to nearby users. Only the user whose profile contents preference-profile will able to decrypt the message. Matched user replies to the initiator by sending encrypted N and shared communication key KS The reply is encrypted by using public key of initiator. If the N is same as sent by the initiator then the result is considered as valid. KS is used by the matched pair to established secure communication between them. Number of attribute linearly affects the encryption and key generation time whereas decryption time is constant. Very few interactions are required between initiator and responder for the process of profile matching.

Shewale and Babar in the paper [11] propose two protocols with full anonymity for user profile matching explicit Comparison-based Profile Matching protocol (eCPM), that runs between parties, initiator, and a responder and an implicit Comparison-based Profile Matching protocol (iCPM) which allows the initiator to obtain directly some messages instead of the comparison result from the responder. The Homomorphic encryption scheme is used prominently in this system. Responder divides the message unrelated to the user in multiple categories. The initiator implicitly selects open categories about which responder are not aware of. The responder prepares two messages in each category, and the initiator can obtain only one message according to the similarity result on a single attribute. Then further, generalize the iCPM to an implicit Predicate-based Profile Matching protocol (iPPM) which allows complex similarity criteria spanning multiple attributes.

Sommers et al. in the paper [12] proposed a matching scheme that precisely pairs matching users while protecting user's data from the malicious user. No third party is used for matching the results. A comparison of the user profile is done on the users' device. The issue of malicious users' access is addressed by applying differentially private techniques to user's interest data. Laplace distribution is used to generate random noise. Subsequently querying on the randomized data will not leak any sensitive data of the user. It ensures that even if a differentially private system does not match a user to the user with the highest similarity score, it will be one of the top six. When more features are used to calculate the similarity between two users, similarity scores decrease. The limitation of this method is if more noise is added to the data accuracy of match losses.

Zhang, Li, et al. in the paper [13] proposed a lightweight protocol for privacy-preserving profile matching with a secure communication channel. It is a distributed method and results of comparison are verified by initiator. Request Profile (RP) is interest vector of the initiator. Profile privacy is achieved by applying SHA-256 to each attribute of RP. It capitalizes on the fact that the intersection result of initiator and responder is a common secret shared by them so the hash of RP acts as a key to encrypt the message and only the exact matched user can decrypt the message efficiently and correctly. To enable fuzzy search hint matrix is constructed, which enable users to also find people who are similar to them. Advanced Encryption Standard (AES) is used to encrypt the secret message. Dynamic attribute such as location is added to the profile vector with static vector to improve the profile privacy. The communication cost for the proposed protocol is quite small, but computation overhead is relatively high. Attribute values of users are not authenticated by any authority. It makes the scheme is vulnerable to dictionary attack and collusion attack as a user may change its attribute values quickly and easily. Another limitation of this method is, relay users, need to calculate all possible subset to with request subset and it is infeasible with a large set of attributes.

5.3 Coarse-Grained and Hybrid Approach

Wang, Hou, et al. in the paper [14] they find the best match and combine the identity and interest verification server into a single server. However, their criterion of the best match only depends upon the number of matches. A candidate with most matches is considered to be the best match. In reality, a user may wish to know the matched interests to decide the best match. This method suffers from the problem of cheating. The performance of this system is better when users are less but it decreases as a count of users increases. It uses expensive Public Key Infrastructure (PKI) with separate encryption-decryption process is done for each user to send the matching interest when multiple matches are there, because of this it is slow and expensive in case of multiple matches.

Abbas, et al. in the paper [15] proposed efficient privacy protection and interest sharing protocol referred to as PRivacy- aware Interest Sharing and Matching (PRISM). In this system, the hybrid approach is used where the role of a Trusted Third Party (TTP) is to verify identity and resolve the conflict. A Private Set Intersection (PSI) with commutative encryption used to make a system secure. Sybil attack is restricted by limiting the number of users' identity to one, on a single device. The security of the protocol is based on the Decisional Diffie- Hellman Hypothesis (DDH). In the case of multiple users, PRISM is faster as hash values are used for sharing interest values. For less number of users, the performance is a bit less. An important limitation of this method is high communication complexity because of dummy interests. Collusion attack is not considered in this scheme. Limiting user identity to device-specific is not a proper solution.

5.4 Fine-Grained and Distributed Approach

In [16] Niu, Zhu et al., proposed a system in where the number of common interest and the priority of attribute is also considered which results in fine-grained match for the user's friend request. Each user defines weight for interest and matches users by both interest and the corresponding priority of interest. They have opted for a distributed matching scheme for friend finding. The computation cost of this scheme is more due to the exchange of attribute priority. In [16] verification of result is not done which increases the chance of manipulation of the result. Computationally expensive encryption is used but still doesn't protect from the malicious user who tries to interfere with users based on interest.

In paper [17] Zhang et al. proposed a fine-grained private profile matching approach. The attribute values specify the exact level of user interest and help in finding an accurate match. Paillier Cryptosystem is used which is semantically secure for large sizes of N and g. Efficient SMC method is adapted for quick and reliable results. A malicious user may be initiator or responder and tries to match with a requested profile by creating a fake account. This type of attack is handling in [17] by limiting the attempts malicious users can do to compare his profile with other users. But proposed solution in is not sufficient and need to have a much prominent one. An adversary can easy modify the result to match with the required interest of the initiator.

Luo, Liu, et al. in the paper [18] have proposed a privacy-preserving multi-hop profile-matching protocol for Proximity-based Mobile Social Networks (PMSNs). Proposed methods allow the user to customize profile attributes by setting different preference weights for different profile attributes. The result of profile matching is precise than other similar methods. In this approach, multi-hops are used for profile matching. To improve the efficiency of the profile matching and achieve high privacy in the system, a lightweight Confusion Matrix Transformation (CMT) algorithm with Attribute-Based Encryption (ABE) is proposed instead of a public-key cryptosystem and Homomorphic encryption. This method is efficient and gives accurate profile matching. Deficiencies in the protocol are anonymity, cheat and verification of data integrity is not perfect. Commutation and computing cost is greatly affected by the number of attribute and their weights.

In paper [19] Gao et al. have proposed cloud assisted user profile matching scheme for MSN using multiple keys. System is designed using proxy re-encryption with additive Homomorphic encryption which makes it more secure. It is fine grained decentralized computation system. Cloud environment is consists of two servers. User has to encrypt is profile and store it on cloud server. Initiator requests to cloud for the friend finding. Computations on re-encrypted data is done by sever and encrypted result of dot product is sent to the user. It is provides resistance to collusion attack by participants and once of the cloud server. Private data of user can be revealed only if both the server colludes. In [19] computation burden on user device is reduced effectively.

Zhu, Liu, et al. in paper [20] match users with similarity calculations based number of common interests and the weight of the interest. Prioritizing and weighting individual interests is done due to which system works efficiently. It does not depend on any TTP. The lightweight Confusion Matrix Transformation (CMT) algorithm used to perform private profile matching which improves the efficiency of a friend-finding process. Time and energy requirement by [18] is less due to noncomplex cryptographic computations. However, authentication of matches is not done thoroughly which raises the risk of attribute inference attack. A malicious user may try to match the interest with the user by infer interest.

Li, et al. in the paper [21] proposed a highly efficient perturbation-based scheme for fine-grained private profile matching. The similarity between the two profiles is calculated by using the secure dot-product protocol. The original data of the user is secured by adding noise in private data. Whenever data is shared between two entities it is either noise or a vector mixed with noise; thus no private data is revealed. Verification of result is done with the corporation of helpers. To achieve further data privacy and security from the collusion attack distributed cooperative framework is used. To attain high robustness requires more helpers. The limitation of the proposed method is high computational overhead as many helpers are involved in the computation.

Table 1 gives a summary of the technique that we have reviewed in the related work.

6   Critical Analysis and Future Directions

Many researchers have proposed that if the security aspect of MSN improved it can be utilized more efficiently by many entities for various purposes such as marketing companies, healthcare systems, etc. All the aforementioned private profile matching proposed solutions are suffering with various limitations. The literature review helped us to know the current security and privacy issues in the MSN environment. Many researchers have proposed cryptographic methods [7–19] to secure users' private data. Very few schemes are based on non cryptographic mechanisms [6, 12, 20, 21]. Cryptographic methods are much secured than non cryptographic approaches. However cryptographic approaches suffer with high computation cost. Verifiability is one of the important points that need to be considered while designing a solution for private profile matching. In verifiability result of profile matching is verified and authenticated by authorized entity. It ensures

Table 1. Summary of existing solutions

Sr. No.	Refer. No.	Fine grain/Coarse-grained	Centralized/Distributed/Hybrid approach	Mechanism Used	Resistance to Attack
1	[6]	Coarse-Grained	Central	Obfuscation Techniques	Data Privacy Leakage
2	[7]	Coarse-Grained	Central	Bilinear Cryptography and Diffie Hellman Key Exchange Algorithm	Replay attack, Man in the Middle Attack and Brute Force attack
3	[8]	Coarse-Grained	Distributed	Private Set-Intersection (PSI), Secure Multiparty Computation (SMC) based on Shamir Secret Sharing Scheme (SS), Additive Homomorphic Encryption	Resist Active Attacks such as All zero polynomial attack
4	[9]	Coarse-Grained	Distributed	Blind Vector Transformation Technique (BVT), Paillier Encryption	Runaway Attack, Collusion Attack
5	[10]	Coarse-Grained	Distributed	Cipher text-Policy Attribute-Based Encryption (CP-ABE)	Dictionary Profiling, Cheating
6	[11]	Coarse-Grained	Distributed	Homomorphic Encryption	Fake Profile
7	[12]	Coarse-Grained	Distributed	Differential Privacy, Laplace Distribution	Attribute Inference Attack
8	[13]	Coarse-Grained	Distributed	Symmetric Cryptography and Request Profile is considered as key	Dictionary Profiling, Cheating, Man in the Middle Attack
9	[14]	Coarse-Grained	Hybrid	Public Key Infrastructure (PKI)	Malicious and Semi Honest Attacks
10	[15]	Coarse-Grained	Hybrid	A Private Set Intersection (PSI) with Commutative Encryption	Sybil attack, Man-in-the-middle Attack, impersonation attack
11	[16]	Fine-Grained	Distributed	Commutative Encryption Function and Weight aware interest matching, Secure Multiparty Computation (SMC)	Attribute Inference Attack, Cheating and Denial-of-service (DoS) attack

(continued)

Table 1. (*continued*)

Sr. No.	Refer. No.	Fine grain/Coarse-grained	Centralized/Distributed/ Hybrid approach	Mechanism Used	Resistance to Attack
12	[17]	Fine-Grained	Distributed	Secure Dot-Product Computation (SDC) Based on Paillier Encryption	Man-in-the-Middle attack
13	[18]	Fine-Grained	Distributed	Confusion Matrix Transformation (CMT)Algorithm, Attribute Based Encryption (ABE)	Fake Profile
14	[19]	Fine-Grained	Distributed	Dot product, Proxy re-Encryption with Additive Homomorphic Encryption	Collusion Attack
15	[20]	Fine-Grained	Distributed	Confusion Matrix Transformation (CMT) Algorithm	Protection from outside adversary, Attribute Inference Attack
16	[21]	Fine-Grained	Distributed	Secure Dot-Product Protocol, Perturb Individual Records	Collusion Attack

that none of the participant able to manipulate the comparison result and cheat another participant. The verifiability also reduces the risk of attribute inference attack by any of the computing party. From above mentioned methods [10–15] and [20, 21] verification of results of profile matching is carried out. In [14, 15] central server works as verifier whereas in [13] initiator verifies the results of profile matching by using random number. In [20] helpers are cooperating with participant to verify results of profile comparison. Collusion attack is covered in [8, 9, 18, 19]. Solution for Sybil attack is given in [15] whereas in [13] and [16] Attribute Inference attack is focused. Solutions for Runaway attack, Dictionary profiling, and Man-in-the-Middle attack are given in [4, 6, 13]. All these are attacks are focused to ensure the security of users' data from malicious user.

The security and privacy issues of the MSN environment still need to be practically seen to understand to the extent of next level utilization. However the aforementioned protocols can provide private matching, most of them have used complex cryptographic computation such as Homomorphic cryptosystems to ensure privacy and incurs with very high computational overhead. It is infeasible to use these techniques in mobile devices as the computation power and batty life of mobile device is limited. Many schemes are using the centralized approach. When a centralized Trusted Third Party (TTP) is used for profile matching high computational cryptosystem is useful. However, the centralized approach suffers from single-point failure. If the central system is infected by malicious data of the all the users in that network will be leaked. Centralized approach is not suitable for MSN always it is not possible to connect with central server using Internet. User must able to connect with each other by using wireless technologies such as Bluetooth or

Wi-Fi. The distributed approach is the better choice as in this approach it is not require to connect with central server and depend on the Internet for friend finding.

In many existing works, results are not verified because of which the attacker may adjust the results of matchmaking as per requirement and may gain access to another user's sensitive information by becoming his/her friend. Attribute inference leads to serious privacy attacks. The efficiency of profile matching can be increased by filtering out an irrelevant profile. Profile filtering is implemented in few existing systems. In very few solutions secure communication channel is considered as an important aspect of privacy and security of user's data. The insecure channel may lead to attacks active and passive attacks such as Man-in-the-Middle (MitM).

7 Conclusion

Millions of Smartphone users are using MSN for communication and collaboration. MSN stared as next generation marketing and earn revenue with no or very less cost Many companies are using MSN for promoting their products and influencing the market. MSN can be efficiently used if the user can find people with the same interest and contacts anywhere at any time. This requirement can be satisfied by performing quick, accurate, secure and privacy-preserving user profile matching. The existing MSN pays little heed to the privacy concerns associated with users' personal information and the growing reliance on MSN is impaired by an increasingly more sophisticated range of attacks that undermine the very usefulness of the MSNs. Recent research papers conclude that MSN is useful for information exchange, but still needs more work in this domain to make the MSN more secure and privacy protected. To summarize, improvising MSN security and privacy the current solution needs more focus to enhance the utilization of MSN. However current solutions are suffering from various security and privacy threats as shown in the literature review. Users' sensitive data is not secure from the malicious users. A solution designed for this issue must be lightweight and less power consuming. To make MSN truly mobile user must able to connect with strangers securely without central trusted party as it is not always possible to connect central authority through Internet.

References

1. 53 Incredible Facebook Statistics and Facts. https://www.brandwatch.com/blog/facebook-statistics/
2. The Top 10 Most Popular Sites of 2019. https://www.lifewire.com/most-popular-sites-3483140
3. Foursquare (2012). https://foursquare.com/
4. Nissenbaum, H.: A contextual approach to privacy online. Daedalus 140(4), 32–48 (2011)
5. Abbas, A., Khan, S.: A Review on the state-of-the-art privacy-preserving approaches in the e-Health clouds. IEEE J. Biomed. Health Inform. 18(4), 1431–1441 (2014)
6. Li, M., Ruan, N., Qian, Q., Zhu, H., Liang, X., Yu, L.: SPFM: scalable and privacy-preserving friend matching in mobile cloud. IEEE Internet Things J. 4(2), 583–591 (2017)

7. Luo, E., Guo, K., Tang, Y., Ying, X., Huang, W.: Hidden the true identity and dating characteristics based on quick private matching in mobile social networks. Future Gener. Comput. Syst. (2018). https://doi.org/10.1016/j.future.2018.04.088

8. Li, M., Cao, N., Yu, S., Lou, W.: Findu: privacy preserving personal profile matching in mobile social networks. In: Proceedings of IEEE INFOCOM (2011)

9. Zhu, H., Du, S., Li, M., Gao, Z.: Fairness-aware and privacy-preserving friend matching protocol in mobile social networks. IEEE Trans. Emerg. Top. Comput. 1(1), 192–200 (2013)

10. Cui, W., Du, C., Chen, J.: CP-ABE based privacy-preserving user profile matching in mobile social networks. PLoS ONE 11(6), e0157933 (2016)

11. Shewale, K., Babar, S.D.: An efficient profile matching protocol using privacy preserving in mobile social network. Procedia Comput. Sci. 79, 922–931 (2016)

12. Sommer, M., Lim, L., Li, D.: A differentially private matching scheme for pairing similar users of proximity-based social networking applications. In: Proceedings of the 51st Hawaii International Conference on System Sciences (2018)

13. Zhang, L., Li, X.-Y., Liu, K., Jung, T., Liu, Y.: Message in a sealed bottle: privacy-preserving friending in mobile social networks. IEEE Trans. Mob. Comput. 14(9), 1888–1902 (2015)

14. Wang, Y., Hou, J., Xia, Y., Li, H.-Z.: Efficient privacy preserving matchmaking for mobile social networking. Concurr. Comput.: Pract. Exp. 27(12), 2924–2937 (2015)

15. Abbas, F., Rajput, U., Oh, H.: PRISM: privacy-aware interest sharing and matching in mobile social networks. IEEE Access 4, 2594–2603 (2016)

16. Niu, B., Zhu, X., Zhang, T., Chi, H., Li, H.: P-match: priority-aware friend discovery for proximity-based mobile social networks. In: Proceedings of the IEEE MASS, pp. 351–355 (2013)

17. Zhang, R., et al.: Privacy-preserving profile matching for proximity-based mobile social networking. IEEE J. Sel. Areas Commun. 31(9), 656–668 (2013)

18. Luo, E., Liu, Q., Abawajy, J.H., Wang, G.: Privacy-preserving multi-hop profile-matching protocol for proximity mobile social networks. Future Gener. Comput. Syst. 68, 222–233 (2017)

19. Gao, C.-Z., Cheng, Q., Li, X., Xia, S.-B.: Cloud-assisted privacy-preserving profile-matching scheme under multiple keys in mobile social network. Cluster Comput. 22(1), 1655–1663 (2019)

20. Zhu, X., Liu, J., Jiang, S., Chen, Z., Li, H.: Efficient weight-based private matching for proximity-based mobile social networks. In: Proceedings of the IEEE ICC, pp. 4114–4119 (2014)

21. Li, R., et al.: Perturbation-based private profile matching in social networks. IEEE Access 5, 19720–19732 (2017)

Deep Learning Approach for Enhanced Cyber Threat Indicators in Twitter Stream

K. Simran[1(✉)], Prathiksha Balakrishna[2], R. Vinayakumar[1,3], and K. P. Soman[1]

[1] Center for Computational Engineering and Networking,
Amrita School of Engineering, Amrita Vishwa Vidyapeetham, Coimbatore, India
simiketha19@gmail.com

[2] Graduate School, Computer Science Department,
Texas State University, San Marcos, USA
prathi.93april8@gmail.com

[3] Division of Biomedical Informatics, Cincinnati Children's Hospital Medical Centre,
Cincinnati, OH, USA
Vinayakumar.Ravi@cchmc.org, vinayakumarr77@gmail.com

Abstract. In recent days, the amount of Cyber Security text data shared via social media resources mainly Twitter has increased. An accurate analysis of this data can help to develop cyber threat situational awareness framework for a cyber threat. This work proposes a deep learning based approach for tweet data analysis. To convert the tweets into numerical representations, various text representations are employed. These features are feed into deep learning architecture for optimal feature extraction as well as classification. Various hyperparameter tuning approaches are used for identifying optimal text representation method as well as optimal network parameters and network structures for deep learning models. For comparative analysis, the classical text representation method with classical machine learning algorithm is employed. From the detailed analysis of experiments, we found that the deep learning architecture with advanced text representation methods performed better than the classical text representation and classical machine learning algorithms. The primary reason for this is that the advanced text representation methods have the capability to learn sequential properties which exist among the textual data and deep learning architectures learns the optimal features along with decreasing the feature size.

Keywords: Information extraction · Twitter · Cyber Security · Deep learning

1 Introduction

As social media is an interactive platform where individuals share thoughts, information, professional interests and different types of expression via virtual

© Springer Nature Singapore Pte Ltd. 2020
S. M. Thampi et al. (Eds.): SSCC 2019, CCIS 1208, pp. 135–145, 2020.
https://doi.org/10.1007/978-981-15-4825-3_11

communities and systems, it introduces a rich and timely source of information on events occurring everywhere throughout the world [13]. Social media giants like Facebook, Twitter, WhatsApp, etc enable a lot of applications like recognizing the area of missing people during catastrophic events or earthquake detection. Past work on event extraction has depended on a large amount of labeled information or taken an open-domain approach in which general events are extracted without a particular core interest. Information analyst is often interested in tracking a very specific type of event, for example, data breaches or account hijacking and probably won't have time or expertise to build an information extraction framework from scratch in response to emerging incidents. To address this challenge we introduce a deep learning approach for rapid training cyber threat indicators for the Twitter stream.

Open-Source Intelligence (OSINT) provides a vital source of information and has proven to be an important asset for Cyber Threat Intelligence (CTI). One of OSINT rich sources is Twitter. Twitter's popularity in the society provides an environment for defensive and offensive Cyber Security practitioners to debate, and promote timely indicators of different type of cyber events such as attacks, malware, vulnerabilities, etc. Various initial reports of recent major cyber events like the exposure of multiple "0-day" Microsoft Windows vulnerabilities, exposure of ransomware campaigns [1] and user reports on DDoS attacks [2] exhibits the value of Twitter data to CTI analysts.

Multiple frameworks for detecting as well as analysing the treat indicators in Twitter stream have come from the research on Twitter-based OSINT collection. However, most of these proposals have a high false-positive rate in detecting the relevant tweets as they are using heavily manual heuristics like keyword lists that are relevant to Cyber Security are used to detect and filter tweets. Furthermore, potentially valuable information in tweets is getting neglected by the emergence of new terminology and flexible typography. In recent days, the applications of deep learning with natural language processing methods leveraged in various Cyber Security tasks [13–17]. These methods have obtained good performance and most importantly, these methods performed well compared to the classical machine learning classifiers.

The major contribution of this proposed work are given below:

1. This work proposes a deep learning based framework for cyber threat indicators in the Twitter stream. The framework is highly scalable on using commodity hardware.
2. To identify a proper tweet representation, various state-of-the-art text representation exists in the domain of natural language processing (NLP) are leveraged for cyber threat indicators in Twitter Stream.
3. To identify an optimal machine learning approach, we have carried out a comprehensive and in-depth study of the application of classical machine learning and deep learning theory in the context of cyber threat indicators in Twitter stream.
4. In particular, we discuss several parameterization options for classical machine learning, deep learning, and tweet representation and we present

a large variety of benchmarks which have been used to either experimentally validate our choices or to help us to take the adequate decision.

The remaining of this paper is arranged in the following order: Sect. 2 documents a survey of the related literature, followed by background related to NLP and deep learning concepts in Sect. 3. Section 4 provides a description of Cyber Security related tweets data set used in this work. Section 5 describes the details of the proposed architecture. Section 6 reports the experiments and observations made by the proposed architecture. Section 7 concludes the paper as well as tells the remakes on future work of research.

2 Literature Survey

Classification and detection of CTI extraction from Twitter are less investigated compared to the other area, for example, crime prevention [3], identification of cyber-bullies [4], and disaster response [5]. To distinguish three sorts of threats and events ie., account hijacking, data breaches, and Distributed Denial of Service (DDoS) attacks, Khandpur et al. [6] proposed an architecture to separate cyber threat as well as security information from the Tweets. Target domain generation, event extraction, and dynamically typed query expansion are the three major segments of this framework. This methodology is powerful as it abuses syntactic, semantic analysis and dependency tree graph yet it requires the persistent tracking of features for each type of threat. It likewise requests a high computational overhead to produce as well as keep the focus on corpus space of tweet content for query extension. Also, this architecture can't flawlessly stretch out to more classifications of threats and events.

Furthermore, categorizing Cyber Security events from tweets was proposed by Le Sceller et al. [7]. The detection of events uses the taxonomy of Cyber Security and a set of keywords that describes the event type. Expanding of the set of seed keywords are performed by not only identifying but also attaching new words with comparative meaning with regards to word embeddings utilizing a physically indicated edge in the cosine similarity distance between word vectors. Term frequency - inverse document frequency (TF-IDF) method which produced events as groups of tweets was used in this framework. Inadvertent biasing effects of the initial seed keywords caused this algorithm to give a high false-positive rate.

Security Vulnerability Concept Extractor (SVCE) was utilized to process tweets in the structure proposed in [8]. SVSE is trained on a data set containing reports of the national vulnerability database to recognize as well as label the terms and ideas identified with CTI, for example, affected software, consequences of the attack and so forth. To additionally improve the extracted information, the ideas and substances extracted by SVCE are examined dependent on outside freely accessible semantic learning bases such as DBPedia. The client needs to specify a target framework profile included data about installed software or hardware, as this system is produced for client-based applications. As per the information provided, an ontology is produced and utilized alongside SWRL rules to address as well as organize time-delicate CTI entries. Later conversion from separated and labeled CTIs to RDF triple proclamations is finished. The ready alert system can reason over the information as RDF connected information portrayal is put away in the knowledge base. This framework is incapable of distinguishing novel threat types and indicators.

In [9], ontology-based technique and Named Entity Recognition (NER) were utilized to classify tweets as related events or not related events. This framework performs topic identification by means of cross-referencing NER results with other external knowledge bases, for example, DBPedia utilizing Wikipedia's Current Event Portal just as human info gathered using Amazon Mechanical Turk, produced an annotated data set of tweet event type and CTI. Different machine learning algorithms, for example, naive bayes, support vector machines (SVM) and deep learning architectures such as long short term memory (LSTM), recurrent neural network (RNN) used this annotated data set and the best outcome was delivered by LSTM architecture with word embedding. They additionally show that particular classifications of NER are useful in classifying the classes as well as event type, though the nonexclusive class of NER is useful in binary classification. Pagerank algorithm was used in this work for topic recognizable proof.

[10] proposed a framework which recognizes influential user or community of people to prioritize CTI information. This was finished utilizing a scoring strategy that is scores were given to the user and community who produced CTI-related tweets. This work has four segments. For gathering information from the Twitter platform, a social media connector is referred as the principal segment. The second segment is a module for recognizing and stretching out the rundown of specialists to discover developing themes. The third segment comprises of weight contribution and fitness calculation. Lastly, to recognize emerging threats the author proposed a topic detection algorithm. Anyhow, threat indicators are not adequately referred by the specialists in this work.

The framework proposed in [11] is a weekly supervised learning approach that trains a model for extracting new classes of Cyber Security events. This framework does extraction by seeding a little amount of positive event tests over a fundamentally amount of unlabeled data. The target to learn in this work is done by regularizing the label distribution over the unlabeled distribution. This work is vigorously reliant on historical seed and neglects to give the details of coordinating named entities into an event category.

3   Background

3.1   Text Representation

To represent the tweet into numeric form, we used various text representations in this works. The basic idea behind these text representations is discussed below.

Bag-of-Words (TDM, TF-IDF): Bag-of-words is basically a collection of words. So the texts (tweets) are represented as a bag of its words. Every unique word passed as an input will have a position in this bag (vector). The vector records the frequency of the words in the tweets. Term document matrix (TDM) and Term frequency-inverse document frequency (TF-IDF) are features extracted from the documents. They are the measures used to understand the similarities between the tweets. TDM will have each corpus word as rows and document (tweet) as columns. The matrix represents the frequencies of the words occurring in that particular tweet. The most used words are highlighted because of their high frequency. TF-IDF tells how frequently a word occurs in a specific record contrasted with the whole corpus. The uncommon words are featured to demonstrate their relative significance.

N-gram: N-gram is a contiguous order of n items from a given sample of content (tweets). N-gram with $N = 1$ is known as a unigram and it takes one word/character at once. $N = 2$ and $N = 3$ are called bigram and trigram respectively and will take two and three words/characters at a time. If n words/characters are to be taken at once then N will be equal to n.

Keras Embedding: Word Embedding basically converts words into a dense vector of real numbers in such a way that sequence and word similarities are additionally safeguarded. Keras offers an Embedding layer which is initialized with random weights. It will learn embedding of all the words in the training set but the input word should be represented by a unique integer. Keras is an open-source neural network library which contains various executions of generally utilized neural network building blocks. It also supports convolutional, recurrent neural networks and other common utility layers like pooling, batch normalization, and dropout.

fastText: fastText chips away at character n-gram level instead of just word level (word2vec) and it is better for morphologically rich dialects. To convert words into vectors it utilizes skip-gram and subword model. Given the present word, skip-gram model predicts the surrounding words. In the event that window size is 2, at that point we see just 5 vectors at once. The subword model will see the internal structure of the words. In this model n-grams per word are extracted. For example, 'her' will have distinctive vector and n-gram 'her' from the word 'where' will have a different vector.

3.2 Deep Learning

To understand which deep learning approach works for enhanced cyber threat indicators in the Twitter stream, we used various deep learning architectures. The basic idea behind different deep learning approaches is given below.

Deep Neural Network: A deep neural network (DNN) is a neural network with multiple layers which makes it somewhat mind-boggling. DNN contains one input layer, at least one hidden layer, and one output layer. Each hidden layer contains a rectified linear unit (ReLU). ReLU is an activation function which characterized the positive piece of its argument. It has less vanishing gradient problems and computationally efficient. Hidden layer is also called a fully connected layer since every neuron in one layer is associated with every neuron in the following layer.

Convolutional Neural Network: A convolutional neural network (CNN) otherwise called ConvNet is a deep neural network which is based on shared-loads architecture. It lessens the number of free parameters enabling the network to be deeper with fewer parameters. Generally, CNN architecture contains convolution, pooling, and fully connected layers. The convolution operation is performed using a number of filters which slide through the input and learns the features of the input data. Pooling layer is used to decrease the size of the feature matrix. The pooling can be min, max, or average. At the end of the CNN, there will be at least one fully connected layer where all the neurons are connected to all the neurons of its previous layer. Also in between these layers batchnomralization and dropout can be used. Batch normalization layer allows the network to learn by itself a little bit more independently of other layers and in turn reduces overfitting as it has slight regularization effects. Dropout is a regularization technique in which some neurons are randomly ignored during training the model. This method is treated like a layer and makes neural networks with different architectures to train in parallel.

Recurrent Structures (RNN, LSTM, GRU): A recurrent neural network (RNN) is a recurrent structure where associations between nodes form a directed graph along a sequence. This enables RNN to display temporal dynamic behavior for a time sequence that is applied to natural language processing (NLP). RNNs can utilize their internal state to process arrangements of inputs yet can do it for just a short amount of time i.e., they can not remember long term data.

Long short-term memory (LSTM) network is another recurrent structure that contains a cell, and three gates namely, input, output, and forget gate. A cell recalls esteems over discretionary time intervals and the three gates direct the stream of data in and out of the cell. This makes LSTM remember long term information. LSTMs were created to manage the vanishing and exploding gradient problems that can be experienced when training conventional RNNs.

Gated recurrent unit (GRU) is an enhanced version of standard RNN and is also considered as a minor variation from LSTM. To tackle the disappearing gradient problem of a standard RNN, GRU utilizes update gate and reset gate. These two vectors choose what information ought to be passed to the output. They are exceptional in light of the fact that they can be trained to keep information from a long prior time, without washing it through time or evacuate information which is superfluous to the expectation.

4   Description of the Data Set

The data set for data analysis of tweets from Twitter social media resource is provided by [12]. The authors used a stream listener to listen to the streaming of tweets from Twitter. They selected a set of keywords in order to filter as well as narrow down the results of the stream listener. The words like "0day" and "vulnerability" were selected for applicability to CTI. For producing more targeted filters, words related to a particular type of threat were selected. Preprocessing of the data set is also performed in [12]. The detailed statistics are tabulated in Tables 1 and 2.

Table 1. Binary class Twitter data samples.

Data set	Relevant	Irrelevant
Train	11,781	5,313
Test	2,989	1,285

Table 2. Multiclass Twitter data samples.

Category	Train data set	Test data set
Vulnerability	5,926	1,428
Ransomware	2,549	654
DDoS	1,776	469
Data leak	106	30
General	5,588	1,410
Day	585	145
Botnet	564	138

5   Proposed Architecture

The proposed architecture is shown in Fig. 1. The preprocessed tweets are sent to Keras embedding layer where the words are converted into dense vectors. These numerical features are passed into CNN and then to GRU layer for feature generation. Finally, the output from GRU is sent to a fully connected layer for classification.

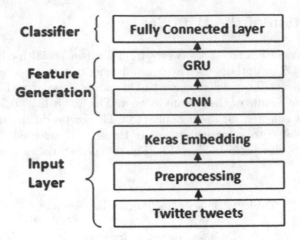

Fig. 1. Proposed architecture.

6   Experiments, Results and Observations

Scikit-learn[1] and TensorFlow[2] with Keras[3] framework were utilized to implement classical machine learning algorithms and deep learning architectures respectively. All the models are trained on GPU enabled TensorFlow. Various statistical measures are utilized in order to evaluate the performance of the proposed framework.

Preprocessing steps given in the proposed architecture section is followed for the data set to convert the unstructured format into a structured format. In this work, various text representation methods such as TDM, TF-IDF, 3-gram, and embedding are employed. SVM is implemented along with TDM and TF-IDF. SVM uses rbf kernel and c value of 100. Scikit-learn default parameters of TDM and TF-IDF are used. As the tweet length is not huge and there are a lot of important keywords used in tweets that might be the reason why TF-IDF has performed better than TDM. We followed n-gram representation specifically 3-gram is employed and we constructed a feature vector whose length will very huge. So in order to decrease the dimension be employed featurization technique to decrease the length of the sequence. This 1,000 length vector is passed into a deep neural network (DNN). DNN contains three layers, the first layer contains 1,024 neurons, the second layer contains 512 neurons and the third layer contains 128 neurons. In a sequential model, initially random weights are given to the model and these random values will be updated based on the loss of the function while backpropagation. When Keras embedding is employed along with the deep learning model, updation of weight will take place upto the embedding layer during backpropogation and not just stop at the deep neural layers. Since the

---

[1] https://scikit-learn.org/.

[2] https://www.tensorflow.org/.

[3] https://keras.io/.

Table 3. Average performance metrics.

Model	Accuracy (%)	Precision (%)	Recall (%)	F1-Score (%)
Binary class classification				
SVM-TDM	81.9	68.8	72.8	70.7
SVM-TF-IDF	82.2	69.2	73.6	71.3
DNN-3gram	82.9	73.5	67.6	70.4
CNN-Keras word embedding [12]	83.6	71.4	75.9	73.6
RNN-Keras word embedding	83.1	71.7	72.1	71.9
LSTM-Keras word embedding	84.3	70.1	83.1	76.0
GRU-Keras word embedding	84.7	73.9	76.0	74.9
CNN-GRU-Keras word embedding	**85.8**	**73.7**	**82.3**	**77.8**
fastText	84.4	74.6	73.2	73.9
Multiclass classification				
SVM-TDM	86.2	86.2	86.2	86.2
SVM-TF-IDF	86.3	86.4	86.3	86.3
DNN-3gram	86.9	87.0	86.9	86.9
CNN-Keras word embedding [12]	87.5	87.8	87.5	87.6
RNN-Keras word embedding	87.0	87.1	87.0	87.0
LSTM-Keras word embedding	88.0	88.1	88.0	88.0
GRU-Keras word embedding	88.4	88.8	88.4	88.5
CNN-GRU-Keras word embedding	**89.3**	**90.3**	**89.3**	**89.3**
fastText	87.9	88.0	87.9	87.9

data set is not huge, word embedding like word2vec is not followed in this work. Various deep learning classifiers like CNN, RNN, LSTM, GRU, CNN-GRU are used along with Keras word embedding in order to find the best deep learning model. Embedding size of 128, batch-size of 32, learning rate of 0.01, 128 hidden units, and Adam optimizer are hyperparameter value used by RNN, LSTM, GRU, CNN, and CNN-GRU classifiers. The output layer consists of 1 neuron in binary classification and 7 neurons for multiclass classification. In CNN, the number of filters used is 64 and the filter length is 3. In CNN-GRU as well as GRU, the number of hidden units used is 50. Finally, fastText is employed as fastText has given better performance in recent day applications. The value of parameters for fastText are learning rate of 0.1, dimension of 128, minimum word count of 1, 100 epochs, and 2 N-grams. The average performance metrics of all the models for binary and multiclass data set are reported in Table 3. Among all, CNN-GRU along with Keras word embedding has performed better in both binary and multiclass classification. For all the models, the training data set is used for training the models and testing data set is used to test the trained models.

7   Conclusion and Future Work

Twitter is one of the most popular social networks, where users share their opinions on various topics. The tweet could be related to security. This work evaluates the performance of various text representation techniques along with various deep learning models for cyber threat indicators in the Twitter stream. CNN-GRU with Keras embedding performed better than any other architecture in both binary as well as multiclass classification. The best part about the proposed architecture is that it does not require any feature engineering technique to be employed. Present and future work focus on event tracking and event detection of cyber threats using social media resources like Twitter, Facebook, etc.

Acknowledgements. This research was supported in part by Paramount Computer Systems and Lakhshya Cyber Security Labs. We are grateful to NVIDIA India, for the GPU hardware support to research grant. We are also grateful to Computational Engineering and Networking (CEN) department for encouraging the research.

References

1. Sapienza, A., Bessi, A., Damodaran, S., Shakarian, P., Lerman, K., Ferrara, E.: Early warnings of cyber threats in online discussions. In: 2017 IEEE International Conference on Data Mining Workshops (ICDMW), pp. 667–674. IEEE (2017)
2. Sabottke, C., Suciu, O., Dumitras, T.: Vulnerability disclosure in the age of social media: exploiting Twitter for predicting real-world exploits. In: USENIX Security Symposium, pp. 1041–1056 (2015)
3. Mackey, T., Kalyanam, J., Klugman, J., Kuzmenko, E., Gupta, R.: Solution to detect, classify, and report illicit online marketing and sales of controlled substances via Twitter: using machine learning and web forensics to combat digital opioid access. J. Med. Internet Res. **20**(4), e10029 (2018)
4. Galán-García, P., de la Puerta, J.G., Gómez, C.L., Santos, I., Bringas, P.G.: Supervised machine learning for the detection of troll profiles in Twitter social network: application to a real case of cyberbullying. Logic J. IGPL **24**(1), 42–53 (2016)
5. Ashktorab, Z., Brown, C., Nandi, M., Culotta, A.: Tweedr: mining Twitter to inform disaster response. In: ISCRAM (2014)
6. Khandpur, R.P., Ji, T., Jan, S., Wang, G., Lu, C.-T., Ramakrishnan, N.: Crowdsourcing cybersecurity: cyber attack detection using social media. In: Proceedings of the 2017 ACM on Conference on Information and Knowledge Management, pp. 1049–1057. ACM (2017)
7. Le Sceller, Q., Karbab, E.B., Debbabi, M., Iqbal, F.: Sonar: automatic detection of cyber security events over the Twitter stream. In: Proceedings of the 12th International Conference on Availability, Reliability and Security, p. 23. ACM (2017)
8. Mittal, S., Das, P.K., Mulwad, V., Joshi, A., Finin, T.: CyberTwitter: using Twitter to generate alerts for cybersecurity threats and vulnerabilities. In: Proceedings of the 2016 IEEE/ACM International Conference on Advances in Social Networks Analysis and Mining, pp. 860–867. IEEE Press (2016)
9. Edouard, A.: Event detection and analysis on short text messages. Ph.D. dissertation, Universite Côte d'Azur (2017)
10. Lee, K.-C., Hsieh, C.-H., Wei, L.-J., Mao, C.-H., Dai, J.-H., Kuang, Y.-T.: Secbuzzer: cyber security emerging topic mining with open threat intelligence retrieval and timeline event annotation. Soft Comput. **21**(11), 2883–2896 (2017)
11. Ritter, A., Wright, E., Casey, W., Mitchell, T.: Weakly supervised extraction of computer security events from Twitter. In: Proceedings of the 24th International

Conference on World Wide Web, pp. 896–905. International World Wide Web Conferences Steering Committee (2015)

12. Behzadan, V., Aguirre, C., Bose, A., Hsu, W.: Corpus and deep learning classifier for collection of cyber threat indicators in Twitter stream. In: 2018 IEEE International Conference on Big Data (Big Data), pp. 5002–5007 (2018)

13. Vinayakumar, R., Alazab, M., Jolfaei, A., Soman, K.P., Poornachandran, P.: Ransomware triage using deep learning: Twitter as a case study. In: 2019 Cybersecurity and Cyberforensics Conference (CCC), pp. 67–73. IEEE, May 2019

14. Vinayakumar, R., Soman, K.P., Poornachandran, P., Menon, V.K.: A deep-dive on machine learning for cyber security use cases. In: Machine Learning for Computer and Cyber Security, pp. 122–158. CRC Press (2019)

15. Vinayakumar, R., Soman, K.P., Poornachandran, P., Alazab, M., Jolfaei, A.: DBD: deep learning DGA-based botnet detection. In: Alazab, M., Tang, M.J. (eds.) Deep Learning Applications for Cyber Security. ASTSA, pp. 127–149. Springer, Cham (2019). https://doi.org/10.1007/978-3-030-13057-2_6

16. Vinayakumar, R., Soman, K.P., Poornachandran, P., Akarsh, S., Elhoseny, M.: Deep learning framework for cyber threat situational awareness based on email and URL data analysis. In: Hassanien, A., Elhoseny, M. (eds.) Cybersecurity and Secure Information Systems. ASTSA, pp. 87–124. Springer, Cham (2019). https://doi.org/10.1007/978-3-030-16837-7_6

17. Vinayakumar, R., Soman, K.P., Poornachandran, P., Akarsh, S., Elhoseny, M.: Improved DGA domain names detection and categorization using deep learning architectures with classical machine learning algorithms. In: Hassanien, A., Elhoseny, M. (eds.) Cybersecurity and Secure Information Systems. ASTSA, pp. 161–192. Springer, Cham (2019). https://doi.org/10.1007/978-3-030-16837-7_8

Improving Sentiment Analysis
of Arabic Tweets

Abdulrahman Alruban[1], Muhammed Abduallah[2], Gueltoum Bendiab[2],
Stavros Shiaeles[3(✉)], and Marco Palomino[2]

[1] Department of Information Technology, College of Computer and Information
Sciences, Majmaah University, Al-Majmaah 11952, Saudi Arabia
a.alruban@mu.edu.sa
[2] CSCAN, University of Plymouth, Plymouth PL4 8AA, UK
muhammed.abduallah@postgrad.plymouth.ac.uk, bendiab.kelthoum@umc.edu.dz,
marco.palomino@plymouth.ac.uk
[3] University of Portsmouth, Portsmouth, UK
sshiaeles@ieee.org

Abstract. Twitter popularity grew rapidly the last years and become a
place where people express their opinions, views, feelings and ideas. This
popularity and the vast amount of information triggered the interest of
companies as well as researchers on sentiment analysis trying to export
meaningful results from this information. Even if there is a tremendous
amount of work on Latin originated languages, such as English, there is
not much research available on native languages such as Arabic, Greek
etc. This research aims to develop a new system able to bridge the gap in
Arabic users and sentiment analysis by providing a novel dictionary able
to classify Arabic Tweets with different Arabic dialects and emotions, as
positive, negative or natural. The study provides a quantitative analysis
to gain an in-depth understanding of the phenomenon under investigation and the findings of the study show that the designed system is very
promising.

Keywords: Sentiment analysis · Security · Arabic language ·
Twitter · Lexicon · Bots

1 Introduction

Nowadays, social networks offer powerful platforms where millions of people can
easily share their thoughts, feelings and opinions about a wide variety of topics
[17]. A recent report by Twitter Inc affirms that there are over 326 million of
monthly active users involved with Twitter in 2019, where 46% of them use
the platform daily, sending over 6,000 tweets every second, which corresponds
to over 350,000 tweets per minute and 500 million tweets per day [13]. On the
other side, Facebook boasts 2.7 billion monthly active users, 74% of them visit
the platform daily, with 4.75 billion pieces of content shared daily and 510,000
comments posted every 60 s [23].

© Springer Nature Singapore Pte Ltd. 2020
S. M. Thampi et al. (Eds.): SSCC 2019, CCIS 1208, pp. 146–158, 2020.
https://doi.org/10.1007/978-981-15-4825-3_12

The inherent capability of these platforms in exchanging information in the form of opinions, sentiments, and emotions, makes them an ideal place for consuming and spreading negative and extremist beliefs that promote terrorist activities for the achievement of political, economic, religious, or social goals [16]. For instance, the stunning mass-shootings in Christchurch were planned to get huge attention, leveraging Facebook, YouTube, Twitter, and Instagram platforms to make sure that a lot of people would hear about the deaths and the hate underpinned them. Official authorities had reported that before the attack, a Twitter account was used to post a racist message in which the attackers identified the mosques that were later attacked [19]. Other criminal activities that followed these tactics include the Mumbai terrorist attack on 29 November 2008, Virginia shooting in 25 august 2015, the Brussels airport bombing on 22 Mar 2016, Manchester Arena bombing on 22 May 2017 and London Bridge attack on 3 Jun 2017. In all these cases, attackers used social media to spread their radical thoughts and criminal activities before the attacks. A study conducted in [22], affirm that nearly 1 million accounts that promote terrorism and spread extremist thoughts were identified on Twitter, in the last two years. Further, it is estimated there are over than 100,000 tweets of hate, racism and ethnic generated daily on Twitter [27]. This new reality means that governments, police forces and others involved in public safety, should pay attention to social media valuable content to track these criminal's activities, and determine how to react effectively before they become a real problem [29]. Previous studies have argued that these platforms have the hidden potential to reveal valuable insights when analysis techniques are applied to their unstructured data. In this context, Sentiment Analysis (SA) or Opinion Mining (OM) [20] is one of the key emerging technologies that help to navigate the large volume of sentiment rich data generated by users on social networking websites. SA is defined as a process that automates extracting of opinions, attitudes and emotions from a piece of text, through Natural Language Processing (NLP) methods [12,20]. It involves detecting whether the text expresses a positive, a negative, or a neutral opinion toward an entity (e.g., individual, organisation, event, topics, etc.) [17]. Unlike traditional data mining methods, sentiment analysis deal with unstructured data which is usually textual and messy such as documents, emails, user posts and comments on social media [24]. In the last years, Sentiment Analysis techniques have been intensively exploited to identify user's interests or behaviours through the information extracted from social media, especially towards the distorted beliefs and negative sentiments [5,11,25,30]. Most of the proposed approaches in this area showed promising results and high accuracy in classifying negative user's sentiments and opinions. However, most of these studies deal with English texts, while other languages, especially Arabic, have received less attention. Despite being one of the fastest-growing languages in term of users on social media, the field of Arabic NLP is rather not mature compared to English and other Latin originated languages, for various reasons such as language complexity, variety of related dialects where insufficient number of research publications and datasets gathered and analysed for such purpose [6]. Therefore, effective and more accurate Arabic sentiment analysis becomes the fundamental demand for analysing the vast amount of Arabic data available on social media and detect suspicious behavior.

This paper aims to bridge the gap in research concerning Arabic sentiment analysis, which can lead to a better understanding of the driving changes in different Arab countries and their impact on a global scale. To this end, we build a lexicon that contains positive and negative tokens (words). For the purpose of this study, a corpus of 500 mix feelings tweets is collected from random tweets regarding the Saudi-Qatari conflict [26]. The conflict led to relation cut off between the two countries until the writing of this paper. Most of the conflict was waged through social media platforms, especially Twitter, where a huge number of Arabic tweets were spreading hate and negative thoughts through fake accounts known as "bots" trying to manipulate the public opinion, according to a BBC Arabic investigation [26]. The hate tone in these tweets created a big tension between people in those two countries. The main contribution of this paper is to understand to what extent the existing publicly available systems and algorithms are able to classify a given Arabic tweet polarity. In addition, a more comprehensive lexicon of Arabic tokens is developed and evaluated based on manual annotation of the tweets from 6 native Arabic speakers. The results are then compared with other well-known systems and algorithms in order to demonstrate the efficacy and efficiency of our lexicon.

The rest of the paper is organised as follows. Section 2 presents a review of current state-of-the-art literature on opinion mining and sentiment analysis of Twitter data. Section 3 describes the process of collecting the corpora from the Twitter platform. Then, the generated mixed lexicon and the linguistic analysis of the obtained corpus are presented in Sect. 4. Section 5 presents the experimental results of the study and the findings are discussed in Sect. 6. Finally, Sect. 7 reviews the content of the paper, presents the conclusions and outlines the future work.

2   Related Work

In recent years, sentiment analysis becomes one of the fastest-growing research areas. In this context, many studies have been applied to effectively improve the understanding of user opinion on diverse challenging issues. For instance, authors in [25] used the sentiments expressed by the Turkish people in tweets to understand the public opinion towards the Syrian refugee crisis. Similarly, in [11], the authors exploited the sentiment analysis of Twitter data to provide graphical visualisations about potential terrorism scenarios. The study demonstrated that social media and sentiment analysis technologies can play a critical role in the effective response to terrorism physical activities. In another recent work [5], authors proposed a sentiment analysis approach to classify the user-generated posts on Twitter as extremist and non-extremist. This approach achieved 90% of accuracy in the classification of the user's sentiments. In [30], the authors focused on studying the influence of hate tone on the behaviour of twitter users. They reached 78.4% accuracy in detecting whether a tweet is hateful or not.

With regard to the Arabic language, there is a lack of research that addresses the sentiment analysis in this language, especially for detecting and classifying distorted beliefs and extremist sentiments [25,30]. The proposed studies in this area used two main approaches for sentiment analysis; Machine learning and lexicon-based approach. The Lexicon-based Approach is an unsupervised method that relies on a sentiment lexicon [17], which is a lexicon of known and pre-compiled sentiment terms, phrases and even idioms. It matches the words in the lexicon with the data to determine the polarity [17,25]. In this approach, sentiment scores are assigned to the opinion words describing how positive, negative and neutral the words are, based on the lexicon [6,17]. Lexicon-based approaches can be classified into lexicon-based approaches [17] and corpus-based approaches [20]. The later relies on human experts to annotate a set of data that can be used to train a classification model. The trained model can then be used to classify any new data item [17]. Machine learning techniques like Naive Bayes (NB), Maximum Entropy (ME), and Support Vector Machines (SVM) are usually used to classify the data into different classes [6,17,20].

The first interesting method for sentiment analysis(SA) of Arabic documents was proposed in [2]. In this study, the authors used a hybrid method for sentiment analysis. First, a lexicon-based approach is used to classify some documents, which will be used as a training dataset for the method, which subsequently classifies some other documents. Then, the k-nearest model is used to classify the rest of the documents. To validate this approach, authors used a dataset that was collected from 1,143 posts which contained 8,793 opinions expressed in Arabic from three different domains: "education", "politics" and "sports". Authors reported an accuracy equal to 80.29% on detecting negative and positive statements. In one of the few attempts of Arabic extremist SA, authors considered a binary (positive or negative) SA approach of English and Arabic hate/extremist web forum posts [1]. This approach focused on feature selection by using a wide array of English and Arabic stylistic attributes, including lexical, structural, and function-word style markers. For efficient feature selection for each sentiment class, they also developed an Entropy Weighted Genetic Algorithm (EWGA). The effectiveness of this approach was evaluated on two small datasets, each consisting of 1,000 posts written in English or Arabic. This approach achieved accuracy over 91% on both datasets. The main drawback of this approach was the extreme lack of pre-processing which is crucial for Arabic text.

Given the cultural and linguistic differences across the Arab world, inducing variations in semantics, some studies focused on developing SA for the different Arabic dialects used in the social media [9,10,14]. According to [31] there are four dominant dialects in the Arab world: Egyptian, Levantine, Gulf, Iraqi and Maghrebi. In this context, authors in [10] introduced a sentiment model for the Levantine dialect (ArSenTD-LEV)[1]. The proposed model used a corpus composed of 4,000 tweets retrieved from Levantine countries (Jordan, Lebanon, Palestine and Syria). For each tweet, the corpus specifies its overall sentiment and topic, the target to which the sentiment was expressed and how it is expressed

---

[1] The ArSenTD-LEV corpus is available at http://www.oma-project.com.

(explicitly or implicitly). The experimental results confirmed the relevance of these annotations at improving the accuracy of SA classifiers. Other works in this direction proposed a lexicon-based technique to deal with dialectal Arabic [9]. In this approach, the authors used an online game[2] that enables users to annotate large corpuses of text in a fun manner. For the text analysis and classification, they used the sentimental tag patterns and the sentimental majority approach. Authors reported 60.50% of accuracy for the sentimental majority approach while the sentimental tag patterns reached the lower accuracy of 60.32%. In [14], authors discussed in details the challenges faced by SA of dialectal Arabic on social media, especially the Egyptian dialect. Later they proposed a method for automatically constructing sentiment lexicon for Egyptian dialect [15].

Some other studies focused on the scarcity of available datasets by providing new resources to support research advances in Arabic SA [20–23]. In [28], authors introduced the Opinion Corpus for Arabic (OCA), one of the earliest public Arabic corpus for SA. The dataset contains 500 movie reviews collected from different web pages and blogs in Arabic, 250 of them considered as positive reviews, and the other 250 as negative opinions. While AWATIF [3] was the first corpus for Arabic SA that employed both regular and crowdsourcing annotation techniques. AWATIF contains 5342 sentences taken from 30 Wikipedia talk pages, Twitter and 2532 threaded conversations taken from seven Arabic forums. Later, the authors proposed SANA [4], a large-scale, multi-domain, multi-dialect, and multi-genre lexicon for sentiment analysis of the Arabic language and dialects. The lexicon automatically extends two manually collected lexicons HUDA (4,905 entries extracted from chat records in the Egyptian dialect) and SIFFAT (3,325 Arabic adjectives). In [21], authors prepared a sentiment analysis dataset gathered from Arabic tweets, called Arabic Sentiment Tweets Dataset (ASTD). ASTD consists of 10,000 tweets which are classified as objective, subjective positive, subjective negative, and subjective mixed. The authors constructed a seed sentiment lexicon from the dataset. In [8] authors presented an Arabic lexicon-based tool called Arabic Opinions Polarity Identification (AOPI). This tool relies on domain-specific lexicon approach for extracting opinions in posts written in Modern Standard Arabic (MSA) and dialectal Arabic. They compared it with SocialMention[3] and SentiStrength[4]. Their results showed that AOPI is more accurate than other tools. Studies in [7,18] showed that most of SA tools are inefficient for extracting opinions in reviews written in MSA or in dialectal Arabic.

From the state of the art, it can be concluded that despite the speedy growth in the volume of Arabic opinionated posts on social media, Research in the area of Arabic SA is progressing at a very slow rate compared to English and other languages. Moreover, most of the available resources in this area are either of limited size, domain-specific or not publicly available. In addition, most of them

---

[2] http://kalimat.afnan.ws/.

[3] SocialMention: http://www.socialmention.com/.

[4] SentiStrength: http://sentistrength.wlv.ac.uk/.

had issues in terms of the quality of its content and annotation, which limits advancement in Arabic sentiment analysis. Moreover, there is no study that compares publicly available sentiment analysis algorithms on limited Arabic text (tweets) with Lexicon and human opinions of both male and females.

3 Corpus Collection

The corpus samples were collected manually by three different people from the Twitter platform. The reason that corpus was collected manually instead of using an automated API, is because this research uses the Saudi-Qatar political conflict as a case study. The use of API with pre-defined keywords would have resulted many unrelated samples that would needed to be filtered later on. Also, there were no specific selection criteria followed, instead, the collectors were asked to browse Twitter platform in which they tag any tweet that they found related to the matter (Saudi-Qatari politic conflict). In total, 500 tweets were collected during the period from 1 to 8 January 2019 and the focus of this research was to evaluate the lexicon that was constructed. Table 1 provides some statistical information about the collected corpus.

Table 1. Corpus statistics

Item	Corpus overall stats						
	Mean	Std	Min	25%	50%	75%	Max
Token	21.30	10.47	1	16	20	24	55
Char	139.48	63.18	3	110	124	145	305
Special char	0.22	0.88	0	0	0	0	13
Link	0.44	0.54	0	0	0	1	2
Hashtag	1.65	1.59	0	1	1	2	10
Emojis	0.23	0.76	0	0	0	0	7
@	0.18	0.55	0	0	0	0	3

The table shows the mean (average), standard deviation, min, max and quartiles of the listed items for the corpus tweets. The token expresses any single word, term, or symbol exist in a tweet that is separated by white space. However, the definition of the token can be controversy. In this paper context, the above definition is what we followed. For example; the tweet below has five tokens.

"SA محمد بن سلمان طموحنا عنان السماء#"

1. محمد بن سلمان#: means: *person*: Mohammed bin Salman
2. طموحنا: means: *noun*: Our ambition
3. عنان: means: *noun*: highest

4. السماء: means: *noun*: sky

5. SA: means *acronym*: Saudi Arabia

The given translation is not very accurate as is word by word instead as a whole sentence in which the English meaning is not well expressed. From the table, it can be seen that the average tweet has around 21 words. The char indicates any single character in a tweet, for instance, the word طموحنا has the following characters: ط، م، و، ح، ن and ا. Since October 2018, Twitter allows a max of 280 characters per tweet from the initial of 140 characters. The averaged tweet in the collected corpus has around 139 characters. The special char expresses exclamation (!) and question marks (?). The existing of such marks in a tweet could express a type of feeling. For example, the exclamation mark in a short sentence could express very strong feeling, while the existing of question mark could indicate that the tweet is a question in a way that the author do not agree with the context or the point expressed by someone else. From the table, the existing of these marks in the corpus tweet is around 0.22 per tweet, which means that one in every five tweets could include such mark. Finally, "@" indicates the existence of "@" in the corpus tweets whether it belongs to a username or email or any type of context. Table 2 lists the most common tokens in the collected corpus.

Table 2. Most frequent tokens

Token	English translation	Frequency	Token	English translation	Frequency
في	In	245	من	From	212
على	On	117	محمد بن سلمان #	That	73
ولي العهد #	crown prince	71	السعودية #	Saudia	65
أن	That	63	بن	Son	62
و	And	60	مع	With	59
سلمان	Salman	56			

It can be seen that most of the listed word are stop words and name of the crown prince of Saudi Arabia as well as the king of the country.

4   Lexicon Generation

In this study, a mixed lexicon was used since the current literature review did not provide a suitable Arabic lexicon that could fulfil the aims of this study. The lexicon created was a combination of "AraSentiLexicon V 1.0" made by Nora Al-Tweiresh in 2016, along with an Arabic translation of Bing Liu's Lexicon. The translated Bing Liu lexicon has been manually edited and numerous sentiment words added in order to include all cases of sentiments in the Arabic language for male, female, past, present, future, formal, informal as well as other cases that can cause differences in the Arabic language. In the end, the positive lexicon produces was consisted of more than 61,600 positive words and the negative lexicon consisted of more than 77,900 negative words. The generated lexicon includes words that belong to different Arabic dialects which makes it a comprehensive lexicon.

Both lexicons can be downloaded from the link below[5]. Table 3 lists the most common usernames in the corpus from which the tweets were collected. Any user who has four or more tweets is included in the figure along with their number of tweets. Those 22 users (out of 202) from 44% of the total percentage of tweets in the corpus. While 157 tweets out of 500 tweets (total corpus samples) belong to only the top seven accounts most of which are news accounts.

Table 3. Most accounts in the corpus

Screen name	Count of tweets	Screen name	Count of tweets
@AJABreaking	30	@TurkiShalhoub	6
@mshinqiti	30	@m3takl	6
@Benguennak	29	@AjelNews24	5
@hureyaksa	25	@spagov	5
@ELHAMBADER1	15	@AlkhaleejOnline	4
@DrMahmoudRefaat	8	@HashKSA	4
@AJArabic	7	@MALHACHIMI 4	4
@GamalSultan1	7	@MBNsaudi	4
@Saudi_24	7	@aa_arabic	4
@Raed_Fakih	6	@jamalrayyan	4
@SaudiNews50	6	@saudibus222	4

5   Experimental Analysis

In order to measure the performance of the examined approaches, two aspect were considered; word aspect and general overview aspect. The word aspect is when the matching is based on the words within a tweet, with the lexicon been applied in order to find the negative and positive words within a tweet. This also includes how comprehensive are the positive and negative lexicon. The other aspect is the general polarity aspect which is how accurately can the method/software understand the general sentiment of the tweet and be able to

---

[5] Abduallah Arabic Lexicon: http://shiaeles.net/datasets/Arabic_Lexicon_Abduallah. 7z.

classify it. The corpus tweets were classified and annotated into one of three classes; positive, negative or neutral. This is done by requesting 6 adult people (3 males and 3 females) speak different Arabic dialects to perform a manual annotation of the 500 tweets in order to be use as a reference point and validate the accuracy of our lexicon system developed. The annotators ages were between 20 and 40 years old. There were no specific protocol used for the recruitment, however, having different backgrounds and nationalities and mix gender was taken into consideration. The raw tweets were used in the analysis without performing typical pre-processing steps such as removing stop-words, normalisation and root words etc. This is because this study focuses on evaluating how the developed dictionary would perform in comparison to publicly available tools and classifiers without modifying the raw data. Also, the polarity of the tweets were classified by the developed lexicon that this study used. Table 4 presents the overall corpus sentiment polarity. It can be seen that, the developed lexicon positive sentiment rate is close to the human based rate, while the negative and neutral sentiment is different.

Table 4. Corpus sentiment polarity

Sentiment	Method	
	Lexicon	Human
Positive	43%	41%
Negative	33%	14%
Netrutal	25%	45%
Total points	1,330	N/A

In comparison with publicly available sentiment analysis algorithms, such as SentiStrength, uClassify and Vader, the developed Arabic dictionary (lexicon) has higher accuracy to human annotation results as illustrated in Fig. 1. However, this also shows that the problem of analysing Arabic sentiment is not an easy task as the results are significantly vary among the tested approaches. Moreover, it does not only vary among the examined algorithms but also among those required human annotators. As illustrated in Fig. 2, around 75% percentage of the corpus has an agreement with 4 or more annotators, while the rest agreed with three or less people. This reveals how human can interpreted differently written tone feelings, proving that a sentiment analysis system is not a simple task.

To fairly evaluate and compare those selected approaches and systems with human annotations, we filtered the corpus to have only those tweets where there is an agreement among the human annotators of minimum 4. This resulted in a reduction on the samples to 379 tweets (out of 500) which means that 121 tweets have three or less agreements among the annotators. Table 5 presents the agreements as percentage and number of those tweets for each approach and the developed lexicon along with that of the 4 human agreement.

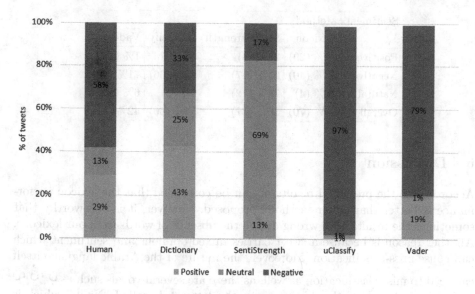

Fig. 1. Overall corpus sentiment polarity

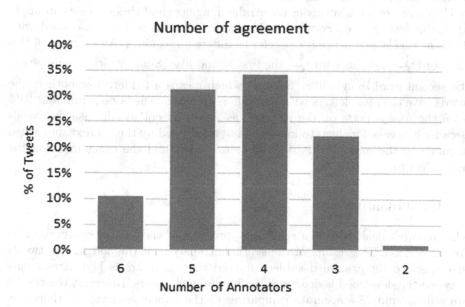

Fig. 2. Human annotation agreements

Table 5. Agreement of tools with human annotations

Sentiment	Method			
	Lexicon	SentiStrength	uClassify	Vader
Positive	83% (29)	23% (8)	0% (0)	1% (1)
Negative	57% (40)	24% (17)	94% (66)	71% (49)
Natural	20% (4)	75% (12)	0% (0)	6% (1)
Overall	60% (70)	30% (37)	54% (66)	42% (51)

6   Discussion

According to the presented results, it can be concluded that the lexicon performance is better than other methods proposed. However, it is noteworthy that
sometimes the results were wrong due to the absence of words from our lexicons.
Another reason is because a tweet carries mixed opinions and sentiment which
can cause miss-classification. Moreover, the nature of the Arabic language itself
can lead to miss-classification as well, as there are several vocals such as نَ ، نُ ، نِ
and many other vocal. In this example, the letter ن is called "Noon" which is
similar to the letter N in English. However, the letter ن was written with different vocals which will make the sound different in each case. In the first case
where the letter was نَ, the letter sounds "Na", in the second case the letter نُ
sounds like "No", and in the last case of the example the letter نِ sound like
"Ni". There are more vocals in the Arabic language and these vocals can apply
to Arabic letters in every word and sometimes it can be the same word with
different vocals, and hence it can refer to different meanings. An example of this
the word سِلم and the word سُلَّم, the first sound like "Silm" which means peace,
the second word sounds like "Sollum" which means a ladder, now both of the
words have the same letters with just different vocals. The issue is in about 95%
from the Arabic posts on the internet, as Arabs do not usually use the vocals
because it is easy for them to know the intended word by the context, but when
it comes to the computer, it is an issue to understand the exact meaning the
user refers to.

7   Conclusion

This research dealt with the significant problem of the lack of comprehensive
Arabic lexicon. The results of the sentiment analysis of the 500 Arabic tweets
in respect to the examined subject showed that there are is high agreements
between the developed lexicon and the human annotators. However, the results
are still around 75% accurate comparing to the human annotators, therefore,
there is a strong need to investigate other approaches such as machine learning
and deep learning-based methods along with the lexicon, more able to capture
the latent meaning and feelings of the tweets.

Acknowledgement. The authors of this paper would like to thank Salam Ketab, Hussam Mohammed, Mona Almana, Aysar Hasan and Yasameen Mahih for the time devoted in annotating the tweets manually.

References

1. Abbasi, A., Chen, H., Salem, A.: Sentiment analysis in multiple languages: feature selection for opinion classification in web forums. ACM Trans. Inf. Syst. (TOIS) **26**(3), 12 (2008)
2. Abdul-Mageed, M., Kuebler, S., Diab, M.: SAMAR: a system for subjectivity and sentiment analysis of Arabic social media (2012)
3. Abdul-Mageed, M., Diab, M.T.: AWATIF: a multi-genre corpus for modern standard Arabic subjectivity and sentiment analysis. In: LREC, vol. 515, pp. 3907–3914. Citeseer (2012)
4. Abdul-Mageed, M., Diab, M.T.: SANA: a large scale multi-genre, multi-dialect lexicon for Arabic subjectivity and sentiment analysis. In: LREC, pp. 1162–1169 (2014)
5. Ahmad, S., Asghar, M.Z., Alotaibi, F.M., Awan, I.: Detection and classification of social media-based extremist affiliations using sentiment analysis techniques. Hum.-Centric Comput. Inf. Sci. **9**(1), 24 (2019)
6. Al-Ayyoub, M., Khamaiseh, A.A., Jararweh, Y., Al-Kabi, M.N.: A comprehensive survey of Arabic sentiment analysis. Inf. Process. Manag. **56**(2), 320–342 (2019)
7. Al-Kabi, M., Al-Qudah, N.M., Alsmadi, I., Dabour, M., Wahsheh, H.: Arabic/English sentiment analysis: an empirical study. In: The Fourth International Conference on Information and Communication Systems (ICICS 2013), pp. 23–25 (2013)
8. Al-Kabi, M., Alsmadi, I., Khasawneh, R.T., Wahsheh, H.: Evaluating social context in Arabic opinion mining. Int. Arab J. Inf. Technol. **15**(6), 974–982 (2018)
9. Al-Subaihin, A.S., Al-Khalifa, H.S.: A system for sentiment analysis of colloquial Arabic using human computation. Sci. World J. **2014**, 1–8 (2014)
10. Baly, R., Khaddaj, A., Hajj, H., El-Hajj, W., Shaban, K.B.: ArSentD-LEV: a multitopic corpus for target-based sentiment analysis in Arabic levantine tweets. arXiv preprint arXiv:1906.01830 (2019)
11. Cheong, M., Lee, V.C.: A microblogging-based approach to terrorism informatics: exploration and chronicling civilian sentiment and response to terrorism events via Twitter. Inf. Syst. Front. **13**(1), 45–59 (2011)
12. Danneman, N., Heimann, R.: Social Media Mining with R. Packt Publishing Ltd. (2014)
13. Dorsey, J.: Twitter by the numbers: stats, demographics & fun facts, [online] OMNICORE. https://www.omnicoreagency.com/twitter-statistics/. Accessed 1 Sept 2019
14. El-Beltagy, S.R., Ali, A.: Open issues in the sentiment analysis of Arabic social media: a case study. In: 2013 9th International Conference on Innovations in Information Technology (IIT), pp. 215–220. IEEE (2013)
15. ElSahar, H., El-Beltagy, S.R.: A fully automated approach for Arabic slang lexicon extraction from microblogs. In: Gelbukh, A. (ed.) CICLing 2014. LNCS, vol. 8403, pp. 79–91. Springer, Heidelberg (2014). https://doi.org/10.1007/978-3-642-54906-9_7
16. Hossain, M.S.: Social media and terrorism: threats and challenges to the modern era. South Asian Surv. **22**(2), 136–155 (2015)

17. Kharde, V., Sonawane, P., et al.: Sentiment analysis of Twitter data: a survey of techniques. arXiv preprint arXiv:1601.06971 (2016)
18. Khasawneh, R.T., Wahsheh, H.A., Al-Kabi, M.N., Alsmadi, I.M.: Sentiment analysis of Arabic social media content: a comparative study. In: 8th International Conference for Internet Technology and Secured Transactions (ICITST-2013), pp. 101–106. IEEE (2013)
19. Lopatto, E.: The mass shooting in New Zealand was designed to spread on social media, [online] The Virage. https://www.theverge.com/2019/3/15/18266859/new-zealand-shooting-video-social-media-manipulation. Accessed 1 Sept 2019
20. Medhat, W., Hassan, A., Korashy, H.: Sentiment analysis algorithms and applications: a survey. Ain Shams Eng. J. 5(4), 1093–1113 (2014)
21. Nabil, M., Aly, M., Atiya, A.: ASTD: Arabic sentiment tweets dataset. In: Proceedings of the 2015 Conference on Empirical Methods in Natural Language Processing, pp. 2515–2519 (2015)
22. Breaking News: Twitter suspends almost a million accounts for promoting terrorism in two years, [online] Breaking News. https://www.breakingnews.ie/tech/twitter-suspends-almost-a-million-accounts-for-promoting-terrorism-in-two-years-806566.html. Accessed 1 Sept 2019
23. Noyes, D.: The top 20 valuable Facebook statistics - updated September 2019, [online] ZEPHORIA. https://zephoria.com/top-15-valuable-facebook-statistics/. Accessed 1 Sept 2019
24. Oza, K.S., Naik, P.G.: Prediction of online lectures popularity: a text mining approach. Procedia Comput. Sci. 92, 468–474 (2016)
25. Öztürk, N., Ayvaz, S.: Sentiment analysis on Twitter: a text mining approach to the Syrian refugee crisis. Telemat. Inform. 35(1), 136–147 (2018)
26. Pinnell, O.: The online war between Gatar and Saudi Arabia, [online] BBC Arabic News. https://www.bbc.co.uk/news/blogs-trending-44294826. Accessed 1 Sept 2019
27. Relia, K., Li, Z., Cook, S.H., Chunara, R.: Race, ethnicity and national origin-based discrimination in social media and hate crimes across 100 US cities. In: Proceedings of the International AAAI Conference on Web and Social Media, vol. 13, pp. 417–427 (2019)
28. Rushdi-Saleh, M., Martín-Valdivia, M.T., Ureña-López, L.A., Perea-Ortega, J.M.: OCA: opinion corpus for Arabic. J. Am. Soc. Inform. Sci. Technol. 62(10), 2045–2054 (2011)
29. Stanton, J.: Examining the use of social media by United States senators. Ph.D. thesis, Information and Design Technology State University of New York (2014)
30. Watanabe, H., Bouazizi, M., Ohtsuki, T.: Hate speech on Twitter: a pragmatic approach to collect hateful and offensive expressions and perform hate speech detection. IEEE Access 6, 13825–13835 (2018)
31. Zaidan, O.F., Callison-Burch, C.: Arabic dialect identification. Comput. Linguist. 40(1), 171–202 (2014)

Energy Awareness and Secure Communication Protocols: The Era of Green Cybersecurity

Marco Castaldo[1], Aniello Castiglione[2] (ID), Barbara Masucci[1] (ID), Michele Nappi[1] (ID), and Chiara Pero[1]([✉]) (ID)

[1] Department of Computer Science, University of Salerno, Fisciano, Italy
m.castaldo92@gmail.com, {bmasucci,mnappi,cpero}@unisa.it
[2] Department of Science and Technology,
University of Naples Parthenope, Naples, Italy
castiglione@ieee.org, castiglione@acm.org

Abstract. The computational effort required to guarantee the security of a communication, due to the complexity of the cryptographic algorithms, heavily influences the energy consumption and consequently the energy demand of the involved parties. This energy request makes secure communication with low energy consumption a non-trivial issue. The aim of this work is to study, as well as evaluate, the way in which the cryptographic primitives used in secure communication protocols affect the workload of the CPU and, therefore, the energy expenditure of the interacting devices. Through the aforementioned analysis, attention will be focused on the need to consider with greater sensitivity the possibility of operating/undergoing cyber-attacks using the power consumption induced by secure communications. The main focus is to exaggerate the workload of the target devices in order to produce the maximum energy consumption and have a kind of Denial-of-Service attack. The paper studies the contribution of energy consumption introduced by the different part of "secure" primitives within the TLS protocol. As a conclusion, it is shown how Cryptography is often used not in the proper way, i.e., it may introduce costs that are sometimes higher than the value of the "goods" to protect.

Keywords: Energy · Green computing · Cybersecurity · Network security · Applied cryptography · TLS protocol

1 Introduction

The right compromise between security and performance it is always known to depend on the implementations. After the recent EU regulations and the always more restrictive security policies adopted by the leading companies operating on the Internet it is essential and unavoidable to adopt policies, protection methods as well as encryption of data and communications. The main focus of the paper

© Springer Nature Singapore Pte Ltd. 2020
S. M. Thampi et al. (Eds.): SSCC 2019, CCIS 1208, pp. 159–173, 2020.
https://doi.org/10.1007/978-981-15-4825-3_13

is to study and measure how cryptographic primitives impact on the CPU usage, and consequently on the power consumption of the involved devices. There is the need to consider new kind of attacks that (are both distributed and local) lead to resource starvation. Such kind of attacks aim at exploiting the consumption of some hardware resources of the victim host that, for example, is the CPU time, the memory amount, the free space on disk and many others. Those attacks are characterized for being "no noise", hence not perceivable by the traditional IDS but only by custom agents located close the single machines. A specific implantation of such attacks is the one that see as the main objective the energy consumption of the target system. Those are what we called power-attacks. Those attacks have, as their main disruptive purpose, not just the objective of the saturation of the system's resources but also the exacerbation of the system workload that brings to an high level of energy consumption. Being such attacks particularly stealth, they result to be more and more dangerous since the caused damage could have been detected after a long time together with an irreparable financial-loss. This study therefore highlights that the "protection" methods should not be more expensive than the value of data themselves.

2 Related Works

Security protocols as well as cryptographic primitives, are known to have a significant impact in terms of computational overhead. In fact, several studies have demonstrated that the above-mentioned elements (i.e., security protocols and cryptographic primitives) have a significant impact on the usage and on the workload of the adopted CPUs [9,13,17,23,24].

However, researchers have proposed interesting approaches aimed at engineering and implementing "light-weighted" security protocols describing different ways of operational modes as w ell as different usages in order to minimize the energy consumption. In [6] and [14] it has been analyzed the impact of "lightweight" Cryptography on the energy consumption of sensor nodes, observing that such kind of algorithms allows to reduce in a remarkable manner the electricity consumption of devices that were not powered, in most cases, by a source of constant energy but from small batteries.

In [10] and [26] have been proposed ad-hoc protocols that have low power involvement for the mutual authentication among peers. In [15] and [16], instead, have been analyzed the energetic constraints related to network protocols and in the key management in the domain of Wireless Sensor Networks (WSN). In a more specific way, in [12] has been proposed an encryption model that is power-adaptive for a WSN characterized by devices powered by solar energy. In [7], instead, has been analyzed the computational burden, and so the energy consumption, inducted by the TLS-based communications among IoT devices. Using a more high level approach, on the contrary, in [11] have proposed operational techniques aimed at minimize the energy consumption of the devices involved in the secure wireless sessions. Analogously, in [18] as a suggestion for eventual future directions for engineering new security mechanisms that are *energy-efficient*, has been done a detailed empirical analysis made on the most used security protocols among Internet communications, with the aim of easily identify *energy-bottlenecks* within the context of those mechanisms of secure communication. The work [3] instead, offers a (*cross-devices*) parametric mathematical formulation that allows to evaluate the energetic/computational impact introduced by the secure communication on mobile devices.

3   Energy-Efficient Security Protocols

The goal to execute/configure a secure protocol that will result to be efficient from an energy point of view, can be achieved in two different ways:

Efficient Cryptography Strategies, by making efficient the cryptographic primitives that define the functioning of the security protocol choosing in an accurate and pertinent way the usage of some specific cryptographic algorithms depending on the needed security level as well as on the operating scenario. This is achieved by using in a combined manner hardware and software techniques [5,19,20] in order to improve the encryption performances and, in turn, the energy consumption inducted by such operations.

Energy-Cognizant Security Protocol, by making the security protocols able to dynamically adapt their functioning depending on the working environment by means of the adoption of a set of empirical rules that describe the best operational mode, in some given circumstances, to the advantage of the energy preserving.

In both scenarios, the challenge to obtain secure communications that results efficient from the energy point of view may be dealt with in a very efficient way by analyzing in depth its mode of operation, its security requirements and also the computational bottleneck of the security protocols. The security protocols commonly used, such as SSL/TLS or IPSec, offer indeed the possibility to satisfy security objectives by choosing specific cryptographic primitives within a predefined set. Moreover, the corresponding peers may preliminary agree on the security parameters that influence the operational working modes of the cryptographic algorithms chosen for the secure communication. The computational efforts made by the adopted mechanisms with the aim of obtaining secure communications, influence in a considerably way the consumption of energy and, as a consequence, the energy demand of the devices involved in the communication.

4   A Parametric Assessment Model: Evaluate Energy Consumption of Cryptography Process in Secure Communications

Today, many research efforts in the fields of energy efficiency and power management are concentrated on portable computers and mobile devices without constant power. Approximately 80% of the energy consumed by a mobile terminal is used to transmit data on the different communication channels available [1]. In particular, these entities are connected to radio access subsystems that can be considered "legacy" network nodes, in which the generated traffic originates and ends. These radio subsystems are defined by an IEEE 802.11 Access Point in Extended WLAN network topologies or by a UMTS/LTE Radio Access in the cellular or WWAN scenario. It is necessary, in any case, to point out that the modern wireless devices are often equipped with multiple network interfaces, each characterized by an antenna and a power amplifier. In particular, this amplifier is the component with the greatest impact on overall energy consumption. Therefore, the amount of energy required for a device to support communications can be divided into two different components:

- **Fixed part.** Fixed component based on specific hardware and software features of the device.
- **Variable part.** Variable component, characterized by a proportional request of energy that varies over time in relation to the activities of the device.

Processing the above, each wireless network interface requires a fixed amount of energy, measured $Watt = Joule/second\ (W = J/s)$, so that it can remain operational. Furthermore, it is noted that in order to minimize this energy expenditure, technological research has defined and introduced different operating states for network interfaces. However, even in these states the interface consumes a fixed amount of energy, although significantly lower than that required by the same device in full operation. In addition to these fixed consumption, the energy required for the implementation of a communication is also characterized by consumption that varies proportionally to the transmission time, as well as to the amount of transmitted data (this amount of energy is typically expressed in $\mu J/bit$ or, in an equivalent manner, in $W/Gbps$). As expressed, it is considered, the total energy drained by the data transmission process as the sum of the fixed and variable energy consumption of all the network interfaces of the specific device.

4.1 Encryption Energy Consumption

It has been shown in [8] that private-key cryptographic techniques are about a thousand times faster than public-key ones, since the latter require much more computational power and are therefore more expensive in terms of energy consumption. Therefore, in an energy-saving perspective, guaranteeing the best compromise between safety and energy consumption, a sort of "hybrid approach" is needed, characterized by the combined use of both cryptographic techniques. To formulate a mathematical model for estimating the energy consumption of the overexposed cryptographic operations on a device, it is necessary to take into consideration different aspects: the different processing capacities of the devices, the available network interfaces as well as the number of active sessions for each interface. In order to realistically represent the energy consumption of mobile devices, it is also necessary to consider some form of dependence on their mobility profile. A *mobility scheme* is a structure capable of modeling the behavior of a mobile terminal in relation to different endpoints; this structure should be able to describe the movement patterns of the devices (the so-called "mobility model") whose operational variables must include the position, speed and acceleration of the mobile node, as well as how these parameters vary over time. This information appears to be necessary for a reliable estimation of the transmission power required by mobile devices, in particular when performing secure communications in motion. More in detail, the mobility factor μ_i, can be considered as a measure that characterizes the behavior of the node i during a sample time interval Δt and can be modeled, as described in [25]. Formally:

$$\mu_i = \frac{1}{k\Delta t} \sum_{k=0}^{k-1} \mid A_i(k\Delta t) - A_i((k+1)\Delta t) \mid \qquad with\ A_i(t) = \frac{1}{N-1} \sum_{j=1}^{N} D_{i,j}(t) \quad (1)$$

where N is the total number of nodes in the network, $D_{(i,j)}(t)$ is the distance between nodes i and j at time t, and with $k = \frac{T}{\Delta t}$ where T is the total observation time.

4.2 Modelling Encryption Energy

Informally, "session" is defined as the interaction between two endpoints in order to exchange messages in a certain amount of time. For each session s, the energy consumption related to cryptographic operations of the device, indicating it with $\varepsilon(s)$, combining the two different energy factors defined in Sect. 4: a fixed amount of energy, not dependent on the data transmitted, and a variable quantity, depending on the quantity of traffic exchanged between the parties and which takes into account the energy-proportional behavior of modern hardware equipment. The variables C_1, C_2, C_3, respectively denote the energy consumption related to a single Authentication operation, Key Exchange and Key Setup. To estimate the energy consumption for each session, it is therefore necessary to define the number of security operations (Authentication, Key Exchange and Key Setup) that a given endpoint performs with respect to another. To this end, the variables R_1, R_2, R_3 denote the number of operations performed (per session) by a device, respectively for Authentication operations, Key Exchange and key initialization. The *data-independent* (fixed) contribution of Authentication, Key Exchange and key configuration operations for each s, taking into account the mobility and communication models of the involved devices, can be modeled via a parameter ϕ_s, formally defined in Eq. 2.

$$\phi_s = \left(C^{(AU)} * R^{(AU)}(s) \right) + \left(C^{(KX)} * R^{(KX)}(s) \right) + \left(C^{(KS)} * R^{(KS)}(s) \right) \quad (2)$$

The part of data-dependent energy consumption necessary, instead, to establish a secure session s is proportional to the amount of data to be processed denoted by p. In particular, it depends (per session) on the amount of energy needed to encrypt a single byte, which is based on several factors; therefore, it is easy to appreciate how the amount of data to be processed influences energy consumption. The energy values associated with the various cryptographic activities can be further determined by considering the specific power characteristics of the CPU, together with the number of cycles required to manage cryptographic processing, which depend on both the efficiency of the encryption and the size of the *payload* p. Each individual Ψ component that characterizes the energy consumption of an given *mobile terminal* within a secure session, can be estimated generically, based on the architecture's implementation and specifications, using Eq. 3:

$$\Psi = M_X \cdot Y \cdot F \cdot V^2 \tag{3}$$

where M_X is the number of machine instructions necessary to execute the operation X, Y is the average number of CPU cycles necessary for the execution of the machine instruction, F is the switching capacity of the CPU (measured in *Farads*) and V is its voltage in exit input (measured the *Volts*).

Clearly, the number of instructions/cycles performed increases with the algorithmic complexity of the associated safety activity, leading to greater energy consumption/demand. Therefore, the energy required for the cryptographic operations for each session is characterized s, through the sum of the fixed and variable energy consumption, as shown in Eq. 4

$$\varepsilon(s) = \phi_s + p \cdot \varepsilon\left(c_{enc}(s), key_{enc}(s), mode(s)\right) \tag{4}$$

As a result, the amount of energy needed to perform cryptographic operations on a device n during a certain time interval Δt, represented with $\varepsilon^n(\Delta t)$, is obtained from the summation of all the individual energy requests associated with each secure session $s \in \sum_n$ involving the device n in the aforementioned time interval, as described in Eq. 5.

$$\varepsilon^n(\Delta t) = \sum_{s \in \sum_n(\Delta t)} \varepsilon(s) \tag{5}$$

5 "Benchmarking" Energy Consumption of a TLS Secure Communication

The *Transport Layer Security* (TLS), successor and evolution of the Secure Socket Layer (SSL), is an IEFT standard and, to date, is one of the most widely used security protocols on the Internet. This security layer allows you to obtain secure communications between two corresponding parties (end-to-end) on TCP/IP networks by offering certain security services: encryption, authentication and integrity protection of data exchanged on unprotected networks. Its most common use is to establish secure web connections: HTTPS (HTTP over TLS). However, although less clearly, this level of security is widely used to encrypt data sent to/from e-mail or together with many other Internet protocols where secure communications are needed. With reference to the Internet Protocol Suite, better known as the TCP/IP suite, TLS is typically superimposed on the Transport Layer or integrated with the higher level applications (e. g., the web browsers) and is divided into two sub-layers: the *TLS Protocol Layer* and the *TLS Record Layer*. The TLS Record Layer operates directly above the transport level and is used, mainly, to encapsulate what comes from the higher level protocols: TLS Handshake Protocol, TLS Change Cipher Specification Protocol and TLS Alert Protocol. The TLS Protocol Layer operates, instead, immediately below the Application Layer, allows the authentication between the peers, the negotiation of the security parameters and the initialization of the same. Of the three protocols that defining it, the TLS Handshake is certainly the most complex. This *"handshake"* consists of a sequence of back-and-forth communications between the corresponding parties aimed at mutual authentication and negotiation of the cryptographic parameters necessary for the establishment of a secure session. For example, the cipher suite ECDHE-RSA-AES128-SHA256 makes explicit the use of ECDH for Key Agreement, RSA for Authentication, while AES-1287 and SHA-256, respectively, for Data Encryption/Decryption operations and Integrity Check (Fig. 1).

Fig. 1. TLS: cipher suite name construction

With reference to the other two protocols of the TLS Protocol Layer it is observed that the TLS Change Cipher Specification allows the corresponding parties to dynamically update the cryptographic suites used in a secure connection. The TLS Alert, on the other hand, allows the forwarding, therefore the reception, of any warning and/or error messages to the corresponding parts.

5.1 TLS Cryptography Overhead

The speed of communication in a network is determined by two main factors: *bandwidth* and *latency*. Bandwidth is a measure that describes the amount of data that can be sent in a unit of time; the latency represents the delay between the forwarding of a message and its reception. Between the two just mentioned factors, bandwidth is certainly the least relevant because, in general, it is possible to buy more and more bandwidth. Latency, on the other hand, is a limiting factor whenever an interactive message exchange between two corresponding parties is required. In fact, in a typical request-response protocol a certain amount of time is required before a request sent by a client reaches the desired destination and, consequently, so that the eventual reply reaches the applicant. After the latency related to the communication between corresponding parties, the higher cost related to the use of Transport Layer Security derives from the execution of cryptographic operations. The cost is strictly determined by a number of factors including the *private key algorithm* chosen by the server, the *key size* and the *Key Exchange algorithm*.

- *Key size.* The effort required to break a cryptographic key is strictly dependent on its size. The bigger the key, the better its strength.

– *Key Algorithm.* In the current state of the art, the most widely used private key algorithms are: RSA and ECDSA. The RSA, although it is still the most widely used algorithm, is considered to be particularly under-performing from the moment in which it is considered that the minimum size of a cryptographic key, in order to be considered robust, is 2048 bits. ECDSA, on the other hand, is significantly faster than RSA, therefore definitely more suitable for obtaining better performances.
– *Key Exchange Algorithm.* From a theoretical point of view, it is possible to choose between three different algorithms for the key exchange operations: RSA, DHE and ECDHE. The choice of a key exchange algorithm that offers the best ratio between performance and security is definitely ECDHE. The best performances of the two DH-based algorithms are to be attributed to the robustness, therefore to the size of the security parameters negotiated during the configuration phase. It is considered, however, that in a concrete context it is not possible to make an arbitrary combination of the elements mentioned above. It is necessary, in fact, to use one of the four combinations proposed by the security protocol: RSA, DHE_RSA, ECDHE_RSA and EDCDHE_ECDSA.

5.2   TLS Key Exchange CPU Usage Evaluation

In order to evaluate the performance of the Key exchange procedures indicated in Subsect. 5.1, the experimentation method proposed in [22] was followed, appropriately modifying the microbenchmarking tool for OpenSSL proposed by Vincent Bernat [2]. The experimentation was performed in a Linux environment (Ubuntu 14.04 LTS) and taking advantage of the cryptographic library OpenSSL 1.0.1.f (preset by default from the version of the operating system in use) on a HP g6-2338sl laptop with an Intel Core i5-3230M processor at 2.60 GHz. In particular, the test tool included the parallel execution of two different threads (one for client and one for the server) and in the sequential execution of 1000 TLS Handshake, measuring the CPU consumption of the two different threads. It should also be noted that the different suites have been tested by appropriately tuning the key values and safety parameters, based on the values commonly used in a real context. Analyzing the results of this experimentation (Fig. 2), it is possible to observe that, with an RSA key of 2048 bits, a server need computational power about 6 times higher than that of the client. The diametrically opposite scenario is the one described by the use of DH, in which a client needs about two times the computational power of the server. It should be noted, in fact, that the exchange of keys operated with DH is the slowest among the algorithms also used with "weak" security parameters (1024 bits), but it is definitely slower, approximately 15 times, if used with parameters at 2048 bits. However, the most efficient server-side suite seems to be ECDH where the ratio of CPU usage time between client and server is about 2 and the processor usage time values are significantly smaller. Furthermore, with respect to ECDHE, it is noted that the exchange of DHE keys also affects the size of the server-side handshake from 320 to 450 bytes, depending on the robustness of the security parameters used. Finally, it is agreed that the use of DHE, as well as of ECDHE, imposes on the client a workload greater than that of the server. It is necessary to highlight that although these results are fully representative of a possible real implementation, they have been obtained in a virtual scenario and are strictly dependent on the specific release of OpenSSL adopted. In fact, it is explicit that in a concrete operating scenario the performance of Transport Layer Security varies according to the libraries, devices and CPUs involved.

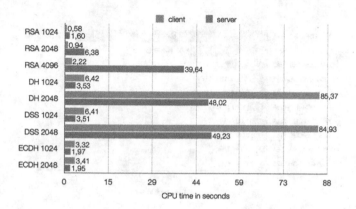

Fig. 2. Experimental results: CPU usage performance comparison of TLS key exchange algorithms

5.3   TLS Symmetric Encryption CPU Usage Evaluation

In terms of CPU consumption, the TLS Handshake is certainly the most CPU-intensive process. It is, however, known that cryptographic operations, particularly those relating to symmetric key cryptographic processes, have a significant impact on the CPU usage load. This overhead is strictly dependent on the encryption algorithm used, on its operating mode and on the integrity checking functions performed. Therefore, with reference to the experimental setup described in Subsect. 5.2, we worked to determine the performance characteristics of the various cipher suites. The performed tests, like the previous ones, were divided into two different threads (one for the client and one for the server). In particular, the client thread sends about 1 Gb of data to the server thread, in blocks of 16 kB, according to the cryptographic suites, to date, most used and deemed safe. In accordance with what is considered in [22], in evaluating the results obtained and reported in Fig. 3, the suite AES-128-CBC was considered as a reference element since, to date, widely used and considered safe. From the above graph, it is possible to consider that AES clearly offers the best performances. It is possible to observe, in fact, that without an hardware accelerator it is faster than all the other ciphers except for RC4. With the AES-NI module, instead, it is agreed that AES-128-CBC is 2.77 times faster than CAMELLIA-128-CBC. Compared to the faster execution of AES, AES-128-GMC-SHA256, it is observed that CAMELLIA-128-CBC is four times slower. AES-128 in authenticated mode (GCM), on the other hand, is 1.4 times faster than the reference AES suite. These results are rather encouraging, considering that, to date, AES is one of the most "robust" available algorithm that can be used. In conclusion it is correct to observe that, although it is common practice to operate server-side benchmarks, it is good practice to evaluate the performance of the encryption also on the client side. This consideration comes from the need to evaluate the effects of secure communications on mobile devices.

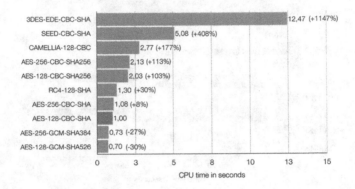

Fig. 3. Experimental results: CPU usage performance of various cipher suites

6   TLS Communication Energy Consumption Evaluation

From the previous tests it emerged that client and server employ a different amount of computational resources in the implementation of a secure communication, finding a different performance profile for each of the possible cipher suites. It is precisely from this performance gap that the idea of evaluating the energy impact of secure communications is born in order to assess how much the application of Cryptography can rise possible energy-oriented attacks. By virtue of the above-mentioned considerations, in order to evaluate the energy expenditure caused by secure communications, hence cryptographic operations, a further experimentation scenario has been defined. In particular, this scenario for secure client server communications consists of two devices interconnected with each other on a LAN using wireless access points. Specifically, the server is represented by the same device used for the previous experiments while the client is a laptop equipped with an Intel Core i5-4278U processor with a clock rate of 2.60 GHz. It is explicit that the server is defined by an Apache Web Server configured in such a way as to make HTTPS connections through the use of a suitably defined self-signed certificate with RSA key at 2048 bits. The energy consumption due to the use of the individual cryptographic suites operated for the definition and implementation of a secure communication were obtained by using a series of repeated requests from the client to the server, with different levels of concurrency, measuring the current absorbed by the power supply. The measurement of the amount of energy absorbed by the server was performed using the TP-Link HS100 smart plug on which the server was powered. By defining appropriate scripts, it was then possible to detect the instantaneous values about the energy absorption of the device. In Fig. 4 the results obtained from the execution of the previously described tests are made explicit. With reference to what is reported in the aforementioned graphic representation, and in relation to the testing method described above, it should be noted that the obtained results, although fully indicative of the problem under analysis, appear to be purely illustrative. From the reported bar graph, in fact, it is not possible to fully appreciate the different amount of energy needed to implement a secure communication by means of the different cryptographic primitives. A more in depth analysis, in fact, should not be limited to assessing the standard variation of the amount of energy drained by the server to satisfy in parallel requests made by n users, but should consider these values in relation to the amount of time needed to satisfy the same requests.

7   "NoCrypto Client TLS Communication": A TLS Energy Oriented Attack

By virtue of the contents of Sect. 5.2, the most complex cryptographic operation performed in a TLS Handshake is the *RSA decryption*. This operation is performed by the server in order to obtain the pre-master secret sent to it by the client in encrypted form. In this scenario, a potential attacker could operate by sending a large number of requests to a target server causing it to perform the aforementioned decryption operation for the sole purpose of exacerbating its computational load. The described modus operandi requires that the same client performs some cryptographic operations, significantly less expensive than server-side operations, but that however involve a significant computational overhead. According to what reported in the previous section and using the strategy proposed in [21] as framework, the script described below has been developed. How much in reference has been elaborated through the use of the Libevent library in order to manage the events, such as the reading of the reply messages sent by the server and the forwarding of further messages to the target. In this script, the messages needed to define the TLS Handshake (Client Hello, Client Key Exchange, Change Cipher Specification and Finished messages) are prepared based on what are the formatting specifications of the protocol [4]. More specifically, the Client Hello message consists of the client Hello header and the body of the message. The client key exchange message is constructed based on the length of the server's RSA key. The Change Cipher Specification message consists of a single byte with value 1. The Finished message, finally, is a structure containing a random data sequence. Analyzing the execution of this script, we observe that the attack begins with the creation of a new socket. This socket is used to open a connection to the server and send the first record structure containing the Hello Client message. Once the receipt of the corresponding Hello message server is

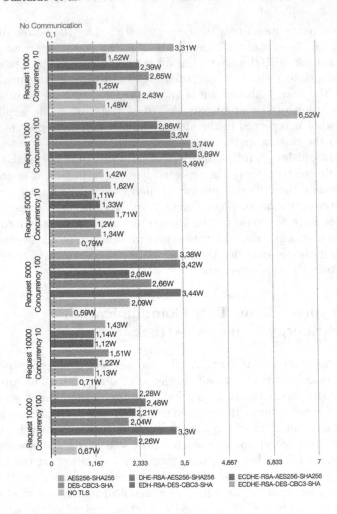

Fig. 4. Experimental results: energy consumption of various cipher suites

confirmed, the tool continues sending the rest of the preassembled message from the Client Key Exchange message followed by a single additional record containing the Change Cipher Specification message and the finished message. The server, having received the Key Exchange message client, decrypts it, verifying, however, that the message received is not properly formatted, and thus closing the connection. It is therefore necessary to highlight the need to correctly configure these messages. Indeed, the forwarding of random or malformed handshake messages would lead to the closure of the server-side connection. The proposed script operates in such a way that the client uses and sends to the server hardcoded handshake messages and therefore does not operate any cryptographic operation.

7.1   Attack Evaluation

Analyzing the output shown in Fig. 5 and obtained from the execution of the script, it is explained that each "Success" indicates that the web server has operated in order to decrypt the dummy message received and then return a bad record MAC message for each one.

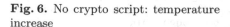

Fig. 5. No crypto script: running

Furthermore, by observing the runtime client system parameters during the long execution of the script in a time interval of five minutes, confirmed the fact that being exempt from cryptographic procedures this operating mode does not burden the workload of the CPU, it is possible to highlight that the computational load of the client appears to be almost entirely related to I/O operations. The server side scenario, however, is diametrically opposed. From the graphs shown below (Figs. 6, 7) it is possible to immediately appreciate that after a few seconds from the execution of the script the CPU load and the processor temperature have reached values close to their maximum limit with a consequent increase in the energy consumption of the device. From the obtained results it is not trivial to observe that a client with a modest computing power can easily overwhelm a server with better computational capabilities simply by executing a large number of requests in parallel. It is further necessary to agree that, by

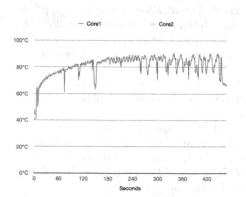

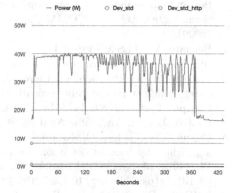

Fig. 6. No crypto script: temperature increase

Fig. 7. No crypto script: energy consumption

making the most of the different computational complexity that exists between a client and a server, related to the different cryptographic procedures performed by the corresponding parties during the initialization of a secure communication, it is possible to define the suitable scenario for the implementation of a DoS attack.

8   Conclusions

The technological development and the ever increasing computational power of the devices implies an increase in the energy consumption of the resource itself: costs decrease, capacities increase, but, at the same time, energy consumption increases. Implementing policies and techniques for the protection of data and communications has become essential and indispensable. However, it is known that the cryptographic operations are particularly onerous in terms of CPU workload and, consequently, in terms of energy consumption. In this perspective an energy-aware approach is not yet fully disseminated. A total awareness of the type of data to be protected and on the type of network in which the communication is operated is necessary, in order to address the overexposed problems related to the different needs and different contexts. Therefore, it is necessary to carefully evaluate the choice of cryptographic primitives for a given context, considering the energy expenditure induced by cryptographic operations as a new constraint for the definition and realization of secure communications. An energy-oriented approach contributes to the reduction of the overall energy consumption of telecommunications systems, as well as of the devices that operate these communications, helping their sustainable growth and decreasing the environmental impact.

References

1. Balasubramanian, N., Balasubramanian, A., Venkataramani, A.: Energy consumption in mobile phones: a measurement study and implications for network applications. In: 9th ACM SIGCOMM Conference on Internet Measurement, pp. 280–293 (2009)
2. Bernard, V.: TLS & Perfect Forward Secrecy (online). https://vincent.bernat.ch/en/blog/2011-ssl-perfect-forward-secrecy
3. Castiglione, A., Palmieri, F., Fiore, U., Castiglione, A., De Santis, A.: Modeling energy-efficient secure communication in multi-mode wireless mobile device. J. Comput. Syst. Sci. **81**, 1464–1478 (2015)
4. Castro-Castilla, A.: Traffic Analysis of an SSL/TLS Session (online)
5. Chang, J.K.-T., Liu, C., Gaudiot, J.-L.: Hardware acceleration for cryptography algorithms by hotspot detection. In: Park, J.J.J.H., Arabnia, H.R., Kim, C., Shi, W., Gil, J.-M. (eds.) GPC 2013. LNCS, vol. 7861, pp. 472–481. Springer, Heidelberg (2013). https://doi.org/10.1007/978-3-642-38027-3_50
6. DelBello, C., Raihan, K., Zhang, T.: Reducing energy consumption of mobile phones during data transmission and encryption for wireless body area network applications. Secur. Commun. Netw. **8**(17), 2973–2980 (2015)

7. Gerez, A.H., Kamaraj, K., Nofal, R., Liu, Y., Dezfouli, B.: Energy and processing demand analysis of TLS protocol in internet of things applications. In: IEEE Workshop on Signal Processing System (2018)
8. Hardjono, T., Dondeti, L.: Security in Wireless LANs and MANs. Artech House (2005)
9. Jain, A., Bhatnagar, D.: Comparative study of symmetric key encryption algorithms. Int. J. Comput. Sci. Netw. **3**(5), 298–303 (2014)
10. Jakobsson, M., Pointcheval, D.: Mutual authentication for low-power mobile devices. In: Syverson, P. (ed.) FC 2001. LNCS, vol. 2339, pp. 178–195. Springer, Heidelberg (2002). https://doi.org/10.1007/3-540-46088-8_17
11. Karri, R., Mishra, P.: Minimizing energy consumption of secure wireless session with QoS constraints. In: IEEE International Conference on Communication, pp. 2053–2057 (2002)
12. Kim, J.M., Lee, H.S., Yi, J., Park, M.: Power adaptive data encryption for energy-efficient and secure communication in solar-powered wireless sensor networks. J. Sens. **2016**, 1–9 (2016). https://doi.org/10.1155/2016/2678269
13. Kolamunna, H., et al.: Are wearable devices ready for secure and direct internet communication. GetMob. Mob. Comput. Commun. **21**(3), 5–10 (2017)
14. Lara-Nino, C.A., Diaz-Perez, A., Morales-Sandoval, M.: Energy and area costs of lightweight cryptographic algorithms for authenticated encryption in WSN. Secur. Commun. Netw. **2018**, 1–14 (2018). https://doi.org/10.1155/2018/5087065
15. Law, Y., Dulman, S., Etalle, S., Havinga, P.J.: Assessing Security-Critical Energy-Efficient Sensor Networks. Centre for Telematics and Information Technology (2002)
16. de Meulenaer, G., Gosset, F., Standaert, F., Pereira, O.: On the energy cost of communication and cryptography in wireless sensor networks. In: IEEE International Conference on Wireless and Mobile Computing, Networking and Communications (2008)
17. Naylor, D., et al.: The cost of the "S" in HTTPS. In: 10th ACM International Conference on Emerging Networking Experiments and Technologies, pp. 133–140 (2014)
18. Potlapally, N.R., Ravi, S., Raghunathan, A., Jha, N.K.: A study of the energy energy consumption characteristics of cryptographic algorithms and security protocols. IEEE Trans. Mob. Comput. **5**(2), 128–143 (2006)
19. Potlapally, N.R., Ravi, S., Raghunathan, A., Lakshminarayana, G.: Optimizing public-key encryption for wireless clients. In: IEEE International Conference on Communications, vol. 2, pp. 1050–1056 (2002)
20. Ravi, S., Raghunathan, A., Potlapally, N., Sankaradass, M.: System design methodologies for a wireless security processing platform. In: IEEE Design Automation Conference, pp. 772–782 (2002)
21. Rescorla, E.: SSL/TLS and Computational DoS (online)
22. Ristić, I.: Bulletproof SSL and TLS. Feisty Duck (2014)
23. Salama, D., Kader, H., Hadhoud, M.: Studying the effect of most common encryption algorithms. Int. Arab J. e-Technol. **2**(1), 1–10 (2011)
24. Singelee, D., Seys, S., Batina, L., Verbauwhede, I.: The communication and computation cost of wireless security. In: 4th ACM Conference on Wireless Network Security, pp. 1–4, June 2011
25. Song, J., Miller, L.: Empirical analysis of the mobility factor for the random waypoint model. In: OPNETWORK, pp. 600–700 (2002)
26. Wong, D., Chan, A.: Mutual authentication and key exchange for low power wireless communications. In: MILCOM Proceedings Communications for Network-Centric Operations: Creating the Information Force (2001)

Towards a Privacy Web Scanner
for End-Users

Myriam Massardier-Meca and Antonio Ruiz-Martínez[✉][iD]

Department of Information and Communications Engineering,
Faculty of Computer Science, University of Murcia, Murcia, Spain
{myriam.m.m,arm}@um.es

Abstract. Internet users progressively have realized that due to our online activities our privacy can be compromised and that much personal information can be gathered. To cope with this problem, both technological solutions and regulations have emerged which are steadily being improved. But, apart from these privacy-preserving tools, we need tools to show privacy risks and that end-users be aware the risks they might be exposed to when they access a website. Currently, there are some tools of this kind. However, they are not oriented to end-users (users with not a high/moderate knowledge on technical issues related to tracking). To address this issue, we have started the development of a Web scanner, named Privacy Web Scanner, that is, in charge of analyzing a website and provide in a simple and graphical way the privacy implications of accessing that site for end-users. In the paper, we present the main issues that should be considered in this kind of scanner, its design and the features of the current beta version.

Keywords: Privacy · Tracking · Web scanner

1 Introduction

Surfing on the Web is a common activity that every Internet user makes a lot of times along the day. In general, the content that is accessed is "for free". In return this free access, the Web content provider or publisher makes revenues from showing adverts in the content that is provided or by gathering personal information that is used to offer us personalized services. This information later will be sold to other third parties.

So that the different adverts are customized and, therefore, it is more probable that they are clicked by the users, different entities try to create a user's profile that associates to this user (identified or not) what his/her preferences are, browsing behaviour, and so on. Thus, advertisers can show customized adverts according to the user's interests. This is what is called Online Behavioral Advertising (OBA) [3]. In these profiles, although the user, in general, is not identified, he/she can be tracked when he/she is surfing due to when the user access to a website he/she is also accessing to the same time to third-parties that are tracking the user into the different sites. These third parties can be web analytics

S. M. Thampi et al. (Eds.): SSCC 2019, CCIS 1208, pp. 174–185, 2020.
https://doi.org/10.1007/978-981-15-4825-3_14

services, advertisers, social networks. This unidentified profile could be linked to a user if, in some transactions, the user reveals some personally identifiable information. Furthermore, nowadays, as we are "hyperconnected" to the Internet, we are widely traceable by third-parties [6].

The tracking of the users is made using different kinds of mechanisms [5,11]. The most well known is the use of cookies. There are also other mechanisms such as tracking the IP address, fingerprinting techniques, and local storage [8,9,11].

To protect from this tracking, users have used different types of tools such as cookie erasers, ad blockers, privacy-aware browsers or anonymous communication networks such as Tor [2,8,9,11].

So far many users were not aware that they were being tracked. However, some regulations, such as the General Data Protection Regulation (GDPR) that have made that a website has to inform users about the use of the cookies and third-party trackers, whether they are gathering user's information, what they are going to do with that information and how the can query, modify and delete their information.

Recently, different web scanner services have appeared to show the different risks we are exposed to when we access a website. The aim of these web scanners is that a user obtains information on the different mechanisms that the website is using to track him/her by showing information on cookies used, the third parties the website is working with, and so on. Thus, users can be aware of the impact a website can have on their privacy. From our point of view, this kind of solution is quite interesting to promote users' literacy in privacy. However, from our point of view, the main problem these tools have is that, in most of the cases, the information they are providing will only be understood by advanced users (with a technical background on privacy). However, the information shown can be overwhelming to non-experts users and they might not understand it.

As a response to this problem, in this paper, we present a web scanner, named PrivacyWebScanner (PWS), whose aim is showing privacy risks associated with a website in a simple way that can be understood by end-users. Thus, this paper presents the goals that should satisfy this kind of scanner, what kind of information should be shown, the design of the scanner we have made and a use case where we show the information that the scanner presents to an end-user.

The rest of this paper is organized as follows. In Sect. 2 we present related work. Section 3 presents the requirements and goals established for our privacy web scanner, and the architecture of the tool we consider it should have. In Sect. 4 we present some implementation issues. The results of the access to a website are shown in Sect. 5. After that, in Sect. 6, we present the limitations of PWS and, finally, in Sect. 7, we present conclusions and future work.

2   Related Work

This section introduces the different mechanisms that can be used to track a user. These mechanisms has to be taken into account in a Privacy Web Scanner to show the possible risks a user is exposed to when he/she is going to access a website. After that, we present the main web tools developed so far to analyze a website.

2.1 Tracking Mechanisms

A user can be tracked in a website by using a plethora of mechanisms. As commented by Estrada-Jiménez et al. [5], most of the mechanisms are based on the use of cookies and they could be classified on first-party tracking, third-party tracking, cookie matching, fingerprinting, flash cookies, canvas fingerprinting, and HTML5 local storage. Although there are other mechanisms such as Etags, or using iframes and social widgets [9].

In first-party tracking, the publisher tracks the user by means of cookies and information released by the user agent. Third-party tracking is produced when the user is accessing the publisher and within the content, there are links to other contents placed in other parties different from the publisher such as social networks, content providers, advertisers, demand-side platforms, supply-side platforms, etc. Thus, the user is accessing these third-parties and they gather information from the users and create the profile to offer later personalized advertising [10]. In general, this tracking is made using Web bugs, cookies and the Referer header of the HTTP request. However, as the cookies received from third-parties can be blocked by means of adblockers, other mechanisms have been developed such as evercookies, cookies matching, fingerprinting, and the use of HTML5 storage, canvas fingerprinting or iframes. In general, these mechanisms are based on the use of two main components: Javascript and data storage mechanisms on the client, which allow the storage of unique identifiers in multiple storage locations [9].

To protect from tracking, there are different privacy-enhancing technologies achieving different levels of privacy protection and that in many cases should be combined to achieve the best level of privacy protection. Some of these tools are anonymous communications tools, adblockers, cookies erasers, etc. More details can be found in different works [1,2,8,9,11]. We are not going enter into detail because the purpose of this paper is not to analyze protection mechanisms, we are interested in providing a view of the elements that we should analyze in a web page to determine if a user is exposed to some kind of privacy risk.

Taking into account the different tracking mechanisms previously mentioned, to know if we are being tracked, we should analyze whether a web page is using or including some of these elements: cookies, web bugs, Javascript, canvas, iframes, and HTML5 storage. In the case of Javascript, to be more specific, we should consider if Javascript is performing some kind of fingerprinting or storing some data on client storage.

2.2 Websites Showing Privacy Risks

Nowadays, due to privacy is becoming a more important issue in society by both end-users, regulators, data protection authorities and data protection non-governmental organizations, different (privacy) website scanning services are available. Next, we present some of the most well-known: urlscan.io[1], webbkoll[2],

---

[1] https://urlscan.io.
[2] https://webbkoll.dataskydd.net/.

WebCookies[3], and PrivacyScore[4]. In all these scanners, the scanner access as if an end-user was browsing the web page and records some information. The information gathered depends on the scanner and we comment it next.

urlscan.io provides information about domains and IPs accessed, resources (Javascript, CSS, images, etc), HTTP requests, cookies, certificates, a screenshot of the site, indicators of compromise, and technologies used.

webbkoll allows a user to check the different data-protecting measures considering a web browser without plug-ins and with Do Not Track disabled. Namely, this tool offers information about the use of HTTPs, content security policy, strict transport security (HSTS), referrer policy, cookies, third-parties, HTTP headers protection, local storage, and information about the server location.

WebCookies is a scanner for Web application vulnerability and privacy. It mainly provides information about cookies (third-party, persistent, and session). Furthermore, it provides information about SSL/TLS security, security-related HTTP headers, HTML5 storage (local and session), advertising publisher identifiers, and resources (images, CSS, Javascript, web fonts, audio and video files, and iframes). One interesting information this scanner provides is a privacy impact score mainly based on the cookies' information gathered.

PrivacyScore is a web scanner that aims to show the security and privacy measures that websites are taking [7]. It shows information about third-parties (tracking or advertising companies), cookies, if Google Analytics is used, compliance with GDPR, whether web server and mail server are located in the same country, different tests about the encryption of Web traffic (certificates, HTTPS, HSTS, TLS, attacks as CRIME, BREACH, POODLE, etc.), the use of security-related headers, and encryption of mail traffic. Thus, they do not only cover tracking mechanisms but also software development errors can could lead to user's privacy is put at risk [4]. Based on this information they provide an overall rating.

After analyzing the different (privacy) web scanners mentioned, we consider that they reflect the importance of being aware of the different privacy risks we are exposed to when we access a website, how we can be tracked and by whom. Our analysis also reveals that not all the web scanners analyze all the information mentioned in the previous section and depending on the tool are more focused on some issues, e.g., some are more focused on cookies or in HTTP information. But there are elements such as iframes or canvas that are not analyzed and that can also be a privacy risk. Another important issue we have found is that, in many cases, the information is shown in a quite technical and difficult way to be understood by an end-user since it is not presented in a simple way that helps its understanding because of the amount technical and detailed information shown in the results.

---

[3] https://webcookies.org/.
[4] https://privacyscore.org/.

3   PrivacyWebScanner: A Web Scanner for Privacy Risks Identification

In this section we present the web scanner for privacy risk identification we have developed and named PrivacyWebScanner or PWS for short. Next, we define the goals and requirements that we establish for it, we describe its architecture and how it has been developed.

3.1   Goals and Requirements for PWS

The main goal of PWS is to offer a web scanner that helps any end-user without any technical skills to understand and interpret the different privacy risks associated with the access to a website.

As requirements, we establish that PWS should allow a user to access a website where he/she can indicate a URL to be analyzed, then, the system should detect the elements previously mentioned in Sect. 2.1, next, the results should be presented in a simple way and using categories, finally, the system should work correctly both in desktop and mobile devices.

3.2   PrivacyWebScanner Architecture

PWS is a web application that runs on a web server, so that the user can access it by just using a web browser. The proposed architecture follows a modular approach, which is depicted in Fig. 1. This architecture has been designed so that the following information can be gathered and shown as result of the analysis: web beacons, cookies, fingerprinting variables, resources (Javascript, iframes, canvas, and images), third-parties, and HTML web storage (more details are provided in Sect. 3.3). Next, we describe the different modules of PWS.

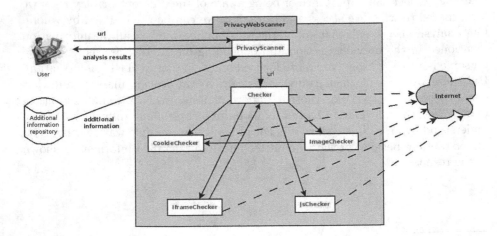

Fig. 1. PrivacyWebScanner system architecture.

As depicted in Fig. 1, *PrivacyScanner* module takes as input the URL of the target web page, loads the necessary information from the repository of additional information and passes the URL to the *Checker* module. Then, it will receive the final information on the analysis of the web page obtained from the other modules. Finally, it processes all the information to compose a graph with the results and shows it to the user along with other relevant information.

The *Checker* module is the PWS processing core. It checks if the target URL is valid and retrieves its HTML code. Next, it gets the DOM model and parses it to find web elements that can be malicious. For each element type, it invokes the module responsible for its analysis and stores all the information collected from the other modules. It also gets a snapshot of the target website.

The *CookieChecker* module is responsible for collecting all cookies. It gets a resource as input and returns a list of cookies including both HTTP cookies and those generated by script code. To obtain the latter, it uses a tool integrated into the system that executes JavaScript code[5].

As Fig. 1 depicts, the *ImageChecker* module receives a list of images and cookies. For each image, this module checks whether it is a canvas or a web beacon. It also checks if the image belongs to a third party and invokes the CookieChecker module to obtain cookies. As a result, the module obtains a list of web beacons, a list of images containing canvas, a list of cookies generated when consulting the images, and a list of third parties.

The *IframeChecker* module receives a list of iframe resources and the collected cookies. For each iframe, it invokes the Checker module to perform a complete scan of the resource. As a result, it returns a list of the third-parties detected and all the elements referenced in the iframes.

The *JsChecker* module is responsible for script code processing. It takes both the URL and the DOM document of a script as input. Then, it parses the resource in order to find fingerprinting variables or calls to other scripts. Finally, this module provides as output a list of variables that could be used to perform fingerprinting and another list of suspicious scripts.

The *Additional information repository* has also been defined with additional information about the most common trackers and cookies that are usually used by web pages. More in detail, we have distinguished three types of trackers:

- Advertising: third-parties that collect information about the user to create a profile and thus offer personalized advertising.
- Web analytics: third-parties that collect information of the user mainly to generate statistics about certain website parameters.
- Social: third-parties associated with social networks. For example, the well-known *Like* button is also used to track users.

Therefore, when the target website makes use of a known third party, our tool will indicate what type of tracker is and it will show information about such a third party. To elaborate on the list of *known* third-parties, we have considered the works of Zimmeck et al. [13] and Starov and Nikiforakis [12].

---

[5] ChromeDriver, http://chromedriver.chromium.org/.

It is also interesting to provide users with information about cookies. To prepare the list of cookies, we rely on the Google Analytics cookies[6] and the Cookiepedia[7] as primary sources. The rest of the list has been created during the evaluation of our tool.

3.3 PWS Output

From the information gathered in the analysis, PWS shows the following items:

- A diagram with the third-parties detected in the analysis of the website, detailing, for each of them its type, the number of web beacons, cookies, iframes, fingerprinting variables, JavaScript files and web storage.
- A summary of the number of third-parties and suspect elements detected, with a link to detailed information.
- A screenshot of the website so that the end-user can easily see if the website contains many advertising elements.
- A list of the third-parties detected on the target website split by category. If the tool has information in the repository about the third parties, this information will also be displayed.
- A list of the images used on the website, indicating their size and highlighting those that are web beacons or canvas.
- A list of session and persistence cookies with their properties. We include relevant parameters of a cookie such as the domain, value, expiration date, if it is safe or has the "http" field. Furthermore, additional information about the cookie is also displayed if it has been cataloged as known.
- A list of HTML5 web storage where we distinguish between local and session storage.
- Finally, a list of scripts used on the website.

4 Implementation Issues

PWS has been developed with J2EE and two JSF Frameworks: JSFs Primefaces[8] and BootsFaces[9]. These frameworks facilitate the development of a responsive design. Furthermore, the open-source library Jsoup[10] has been used to manage HTTP requests. For more detailed processing of the web page, we have used the Selenium[11] WebDriver API with the browser driver implementation for Chrome, i.e., ChromeDriver[12] in headless mode, and HtmlUnitDriver[13].

Hereafter, we describe the implementation for each of the system modules.

---

[6] https://policies.google.com/technologies/types.
[7] https://cookiepedia.co.uk/.
[8] https://www.primefaces.org/.
[9] https://www.bootsfaces.net/.
[10] https://jsoup.org/.
[11] https://www.seleniumhq.org/projects/webdriver.
[12] https://github.com/SeleniumHQ/selenium/wiki/ChromeDriver,
   http://chromedriver.chromium.org/.
[13] https://github.com/SeleniumHQ/htmlunit-driver.

4.1   PrivacyScanner

This module is responsible for initializing PWS. It verifies that the user entered a valid URL. Then, it invokes the *Checker* module and, it processes its output to show the result of the risk analysis.

PrivacyWebScanner uses the additional information repository of trackers and cookies. It has been implemented as JSON files that are processed by the open-source library Gson[14].

This module is also responsible for the user interface and builds a graph in which the central node is the target website and the rest of the nodes represent the third-parties used by the website. Each node shows the information on the suspicious elements analyzed by also indicating whether the third party is a well-known tracker.

4.2   Checker

This module manages the HTTP connection with the target website and processes the obtained HTML code. Next, it selects on that page the resources corresponding to the web elements that are suspicious. For this goal, it calls each module by passing the elements found and the cookies. This module also obtains the HTML5 Web Storage by invoking the *Chrome Driver API* and, finally, it takes a snapshot of the website.

4.3   CookieChecker

The main goal of this module is to retrieve the cookies. On the one hand, it searches the cookies that appear in the header (e.g. *Cookie, Set-Cookie, Cookie2,* and *Set-Cookie2* fields) of the HTTP requests to the resources of the analyzed web page. On the other hand, it retrieves cookies that are generated by script code by using the *HtmlUnitDriver*.

4.4   ImageChecker

This module processes the images obtained from the target website. For each image, it checks if it is a canvas or a web beacon by calculating its size. Later, the *CookieChecker* module is called by passing the cookies of the target website, if the image belongs to the domain, or third-party cookies, if there were otherwise.

4.5   IframeChecker

This module receives a list of iframes and cookies. For each iframe, it invokes the *Checker* module to perform a complete analysis. Depending on the domain of the iframe, the module invokes with the cookies of the domain or with those of the third-party and updates the *Referer* header of the HTTP request header.

---

[14] Google Gson, https://github.com/google/gson.

4.6   JsChecker

This module receives script elements and analyzes them to detect if they use
variables that can be used to perform fingerprinting. For this goal, the script
is parsed. In the case of external scripts, we use the *HtmlUnitDriver* driver
to retrieve the script code and analyze the variables suspicious to be used to
perform fingerprinting. Besides, this module detects the use of three social networks[15,16,17] by using regular-expression patterns.

5   Use Cases

We have tested PWS by accessing to a tourism website, namely, the Official
Guide to New York City[18]. The main results of the PWS analysis are shown in
Fig. 2.

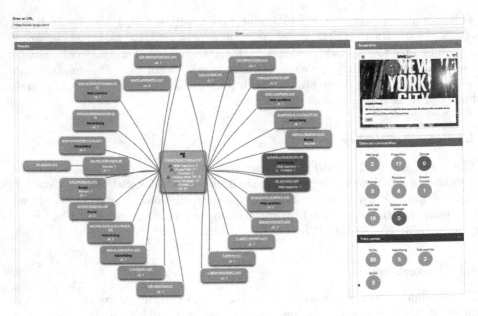

Fig. 2. Analysis of the website https://www.nycgo.com

Based on the analysis performed, we observe that the website delegates to
a large number of third-parties. Among them, we find usual third-parties for
advertising as Google, Doubleclick, and Chartbeat, social networks third-parties

---

[15] https://developers.facebook.com/docs/javascript/quickstart/.

[16] https://developer.twitter.com/en/docs/twitter-for-websites/javascript-api/guides/
set-up-twitter-for-websites.html.

[17] https://developers.pinterest.com/docs/sdks/js/.

[18] https://www.nycgo.com.

and third-parties that perform web analytics. It should also be noted that the website includes three iframes, two of which belong to Facebook and are possibly embedded pages that communicate and share information with the well-known social network.

On the other hand, we check that the analyzed website contains many elements that may threaten the privacy of users when surfing the net. We can see that they are 8 persistent cookies, one of which is a cookie from a third-party (it is marked in red in Fig. 3). This persistent third-party cookie indicates that this website actually tracks the user. In addition, the third-party that uses this cookie is an advertising third-party that also inserts a web beacon on the website to carry out the user tracking.

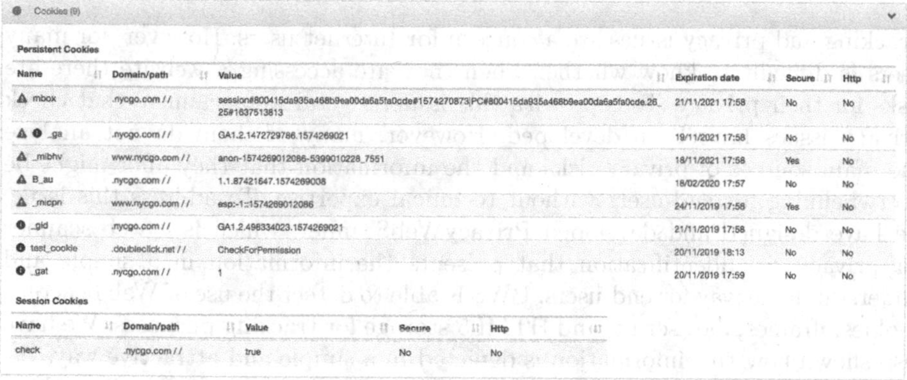

⊘ Cookies (9)						⌄

Persistent Cookies

Name	Domain/path	Value	Expiration date	Secure	Http	
⚠ mbox	.nycgo.com / /	session#800415da935a468b9ea00da5a5fa0cde#1574270873|PC#800415da935a468b9ea00da5a5fa0cde.26_25#1637513813	21/11/2021 17:58	No	No	
⚠ ⬤ _ga	.nycgo.com / /	GA1.2.1472729786.1574269021	19/11/2021 17:58	No	No	
⚠ _mibhv	www.nycgo.com / /	anon-1574269012086-5399010228_7551	18/11/2021 17:58	Yes	No	
⚠ B_au	.nycgo.com / /	1.1.87421847.1574269008	18/02/2020 17:57	No	No	
⚠ _micpn	www.nycgo.com / /	esp:-1:1574269012086	24/11/2019 17:58	Yes	No	
⬤ _gid	.nycgo.com / /	GA1.2.496334023.1574269021	21/11/2019 17:58	No	No	
⬤ test_cookie	.doubleclick.net / /	CheckForPermission	20/11/2019 18:13	No	No	
⬤ _gat	.nycgo.com / /	1	20/11/2019 17:59	No	No	

Session Cookies

Name	Domain/path	Value	Secure	Http	
check	.nycgo.com / /	true	No	No	

Fig. 3. Cookies from the website https://www.nycgo.com analysis

By observing the cookies obtained in Fig. 3, we verify that the majority of persistence cookies are long-term cookies and that the website uses the known tracking cookies _ga, _gid, and _gat.

Based on the use of web beacons, social media iframes, long-term cookies and third-parties of web analytics, advertising and social networks, we can conclude that this website puts the user's privacy at risk.

6   Limitations

Some limitations of the current solution have been detected when carrying out the testing phase, namely, we can mention:

– Websites that require acceptance of a web certificate cannot be analyzed because the current version of PWS does not include a certificate repository. As a result, a handshake exception is thrown.

- The system cannot consult all the resources of the websites that use dynamic module load frameworks, such as RequireJs[19]. These frameworks do not include inline scripts. Instead of that, they load the script require.js that dynamically loads the other scripts.
- We have not implemented any mechanism to solve the problem of script code obfuscation. As a result, it may happen that no fingerprinting variables or calls to other scripts are detected.
- A Chrome browser driver has been used. Therefore, the analysis depends on this browser. Not all the browsers manage web pages in the same manner, so using another browser might give slightly different results.

7   Conclusions and Future Work

Tracking and privacy issues are a concern for Internet users. However, for many users is difficult to know whether when they are accessing a website there are risks for their privacy. To cope with this issue, several web scanners that check privacy issues have been developed. However, many of them do not analyze the main sources of privacy risks and the information that they offer might be overwhelming for end-users without technical expertise. To address this issue, we have designed and developed PrivacyWebScanner, which is a web scanner for privacy risk identification that presents the information in a simple and understandable way for end-users. PWS is able to detect the use of Web beacons, cookies, iframes, Javascript, and HTML5 storage for tracking purposes. We have also shown how this information is depicted in a simple and attractive way.

This solution is developed to be in the beta permanent state since there are issues that require not only more development but also more research as is the case of detecting the use of Javascript or canvas for tracking. Thus, our future work will focus on studying detection mechanisms for these issues and performing a users' evaluation.

Acknowledgements. This work has been sponsored by the Spanish Ministry of Economy and Competitiveness through the PERSEIDES (contract TIN2017-86885-R), Spanish Ministry of Science, Innovation and Universities, grant number RTI2018-095855-B-I00, and European Union's Horizon 2020 research and innovation program under grant agreement No. 786725 (OLYMPUS project).

References

1. Alidoost Nia, M., Ebrahimi Atani, R., Ruiz-Martínez, A.: Privacy enhancement in anonymous network channels using multimodality injection. Secur. Commun. Netw. **8**(16), 2917–2932 (2015)
2. Alidoost Nia, M., Ruiz-Martínez, A.: Systematic literature review on the state of the art and future research work in anonymous communications systems. Comput. Electr. Eng. **69**, 497–520 (2018)

---

[19] https://requirejs.org.

3. Boerman, S.C., Kruikemeier, S., Borgesius, F.J.Z.: Online behavioral advertising: a literature review and research agenda. J. Adver. **46**(3), 363–376 (2017)
4. Cozza, V., Tsiatsikas, Z., Conti, M., Kambourakis, G.: Why snoopy loves online services: an analysis of (lack of) privacy in online services, February 2017
5. Estrada-Jiménez, J., Parra-Arnau, J., Rodríguez-Hoyos, A., Forné, J.: Online advertising: analysis of privacy threats and protection approaches. Comput. Commun. **100**, 32–51 (2017)
6. Estrada-Jiménez, J., Parra-Arnau, J., Rodríguez-Hoyos, A., Forné, J.: On the regulation of personal data distribution in online advertising platforms. Eng. Appl. Artif. Intell. **82**, 13–29 (2019)
7. Maass, M., Wichmann, P., Pridöhl, H., Herrmann, D.: PrivacyScore: improving privacy and security via crowd-sourced benchmarks of websites. In: Schweighofer, E., Leitold, H., Mitrakas, A., Rannenberg, K. (eds.) APF 2017. LNCS, vol. 10518, pp. 178–191. Springer, Cham (2017). https://doi.org/10.1007/978-3-319-67280-9_10
8. Mazel, J., Garnier, R., Fukuda, K.: A comparison of web privacy protection techniques. Comput. Commun. **144**, 162–174 (2019)
9. Merzdovnik, G., et al.: Block me if you can: a large-scale study of tracker-blocking tools. In: 2017 IEEE European Symposium on Security and Privacy (EuroS&P), pp. 319–333, April 2017
10. Palos-Sanchez, P., Saura, J.R., Martin-Velicia, F.: A study of the effects of programmatic advertising on users' concerns about privacy overtime. J. Bus. Res. **96**, 61–72 (2019)
11. Ruiz-Martínez, A.: A survey on solutions and main free tools for privacy enhancing web communications. J. Netw. Comput. Appl. **35**(5), 1473–1492 (2012)
12. Starov, O., Nikiforakis, N.: Extended tracking powers: measuring the privacy diffusion enabled by browser extensions. In: Proceedings of the 26th International Conference on World Wide Web, WWW 2017, Perth, Australia, pp. 1481–1490 (2017)
13. Zimmeck, S., Li, J.S., Kim, H., Bellovin, S.M., Jebara, T.: A privacy analysis of cross-device tracking. In: Proceedings of the 26th USENIX Conference on Security Symposium, SEC 2017, Vancouver, BC, Canada, pp. 1391–1408. USENIX Association (2017)

Security of Quantum Cryptography

Anindita Banerjee[✉]

QuNu Labs Pvt Ltd., MG Road, Bangalore, India
anindita@qunulabs.in

Abstract. Quantum cryptography is one of the most mature area of quantum information. In the past few decades, active research has taken place in theoretical as well as implementation security of a practical quantum key distribution system. This resulted in hardening of theoretical proofs for a robust implementation against implementation loopholes and realistic attacks on QKD system. Particularly, many hacking strategies on the source, link, and detection system have been demonstrated. This paved way to the development of robust engineering of QKD system. The emphasis of this paper is twofold, we bring forth the newer security techniques paving way for information-theoretic security proofs leading to high QKD performance for market deployment, and discuss the recent quantum hacking on different QKD protocols. This has led to the strengthening of the QKD system and enabled active monitoring against possible eavesdropping activities.

Keywords: Quantum cryptography · Information-theoretic security · Secure key generation · Coherent attack · Blinding attack · Authentication · Quantum hacking

1 Introduction

Cryptography is an art of secret writing and has played a crucial role since early human civilization. With the progress in science and technology, the cryptography has beautifully evolved itself with time. Today a new technology (quantum technology) is on the horizon and we need to be proactive in strengthening the present cryptographic architecture against rising quantum adversary. In any encryption algorithm, the security lies in the secrecy of the key. The distribution of the keys is very critical as they need to be shared by the legitimate parties, without divulging the keys to an adversary. A simple way to do this is to meet in person and share the key. This system is currently prevalent in high-level security applications. The foundation of conventional cryptosystem lies in computational security which remains vulnerable to the human ingenuity, increased computational power, and quantum computing. Recent accomplishments in quantum experiments and global efforts towards quantum supremacy have posed a substantial threat to the existence of today's state-of-art cryptosystem. Government security agencies of the US and UK, standardization bodies such as European

© Springer Nature Singapore Pte Ltd. 2020
S. M. Thampi et al. (Eds.): SSCC 2019, CCIS 1208, pp. 186–197, 2020.
https://doi.org/10.1007/978-981-15-4825-3_15

Telecommunications Standards Institute (ETSI), National Institute for Standards and Technology (NIST), International Organization for Standardization (ISO) and Cloud Security Alliance (CSA) believe that transition to quantum-safe encryption is inevitable. Quantum-safe implies being resistant to attacks by the quantum computer. Quantum Key Distribution (QKD) is an essential approach of quantum-safe encryption. As the saying goes the negative principles of quantum information like non-commutativity, no cloning, non-realism has led to a powerful cryptographic technique which is based on general principles of quantum physics. This generates the possibility of guaranteeing security without imposing any restriction on the power of the eavesdropper. It is based on the fact that any measurement on the quantum system will perturb the state and leave a footprint somewhere. This calls for very careful and active monitoring at both source and detection systems. The work on QKD was first published in an IEEE conference in India more than 3 decades back [1]. From the first step of 32 cm free space QKD [2] to present large scale deployments, field tests, ground-satellite, free space, fiber based QKD, commercial deployments [[3–6] and References therein] has called for rigorous theoretical and experimental research followed by engineering challenges in the past few decades.

2   Scientific Security

The first step before establishing a QKD is to identify and authenticate the sender Alice and the receiver Bob. Both the parties share an authentication key which can be prior distributed or established in the two systems through secure means. The key is enough to perform the required authentication schemes. QKD is an art of key growing, it does not create a secret key out of nothing but expands a short key into a long one. Key growing cannot be done using classical means alone and QKD keys need to be composable in nature as it will be engaged for next round of authentication. We have briefly described below an information-theoretic scheme called Wegman and Carter protocol, which is mostly implemented in QKD for authentication.

1. A security parameter t is chosen which is basically the tag length.
2. Alice wants to authenticate message M of length m.
3. Alice divides the m into blocks of length $2s$.
4. Alice and Bob considers first $2s$ bits as a number a and next $2s$ bits as number b.
5. They discard a and b and compute p_i' for each block such that $p_i' = ap_i + b \pmod{2^s}$ where $s = t + \log_2 \log_2 m$ and p_i is the number represented by the block.
6. The resulting string is concatenated and this operation is performed repeatedly till the final length is s.
7. Finally a tag is generated and authentication is performed across both the parties.

After the parties are authenticated QKD is performed. It involves transmission of quantum signals from Alice to Bob and post processing the classical data through error correction, privacy amplification and reconciliation. The nature of an ideal key string is such that it is identical at both ends and uniformly distributed. Let k_A and k_B be the key bit strings of length m generated at Alice and Bob, respectively. They form an ideal key set $\{k_A, k_B\}$. The joint probability distribution satisfies,

$$\text{Prob}(k_A, k_B) = \begin{cases} 2^{-m} & k_A = k_B \\ 0 & k_A \neq k_B \end{cases} \tag{1}$$

In quantum mechanics an ideal key state can be represented by density matrix as below

$$\rho_{\text{ideal}} = 2^{-m} \sum_k |k_A k_B\rangle \langle k_A k_B| \otimes \rho_E \tag{2}$$

where A, B and E are Alice, Bob, and Eve. It is interesting to note that in an ideal case Eve's state is independent of the key k. However, in realistic implementations Alice and Bob cannot generate an ideal key at both sides thus, some failure probability gets associated with the process. In probability theory, the total variation distance is used to characterize two probability distributions. This variation distance would imply the probability to distinguish the key generated from real experiment from an ideal one. It is given by

$$\epsilon = \frac{1}{2} \sum_k |P(x) - P_{\text{ideal}}(x)| \tag{3}$$

where, x is the key bit string, the summation takes over the entire key space, $P(x)$ is the probability distribution from a realistic implementation and $P_{\text{ideal}}(x)$ are the probability distributions an ideal implementation for the key. In quantum language it can be written using the trace distance [8] as

$$\epsilon = \frac{1}{2} \|\rho_{\text{key}} - \rho_{\text{ideal}}\|_1 \tag{4}$$

where ρ_{key} is the realistic case i.e. the key shared by Alice, Bob, and Eve after the final key measurement.

2.1   Composable Security

A composable definition of security is the one based on the trace-norm [7,8] discussed earlier. This is the modern definition of security. We will write it in slightly different manner as below:

$$\frac{1}{2} \|\rho_{KE} - \tau_k \otimes \rho_E\|_1 \leq \epsilon \tag{5}$$

where ρ_{KE} is the actual state containing some correlations between the final key (between Alice and Bob) and Eve, the τ_k is a completely mixed state for all possible final keys. The state ρ_E is the state of Eve. The parameter ϵ represents the maximum failure probability of QKD. It bounds the guessing probability for Eve on the final key generated by QKD.

2.2   Conjugate Coding

QKD unfolded with BB84 protocol [1], which was based on earlier ideas of Wiesner [9]. In the BB84 protocol, bits are coded in two complementary bases of qubit which is then transmitted to the legitimate receiver, Bob. The principle of security in conjugate coding protocols are non-realism and non-commutativity. Due to non-commutativity we cannot distinguish non-orthogonal states with certainty. The principle of non-realism does not allow us to measure a system without disturbing it. It is also interesting to learn that the quantum hacking strategies apply to most QKD protocols based on their security feature. For example certain attacks on detection system can be primarily performed on protocols which are basis dependent like BB84.

2.3   Bell's Inequality

It was not until 1991, when Ekert, independently worked on quantum key distribution protocol and proposed an entanglement based algorithm [10] which gained huge popularity. According to Ekert if an eavesdropper eavesdrops then it introduces some "elements of reality" into the correlations between legitimate parties. If Alice and Bob observe correlations that violate Bell inequality then they don't abort the key generation process and finally generate secure keys at both ends.

2.4   Entanglement Distillation

The main idea of the Lo-Chau [11] security proof lies on quantum error correction, which proved the security of an entanglement-based QKD protocol. We have listed the steps of execution of this security technique.

1. Alice creates n EPR pairs $|\phi^+\rangle^{\otimes n}$.
2. She sends the second qubit of each of these pairs to Bob.
3. Alice and Bob share imperfect EPR pairs because of channel noise, Eve's interference and decoherence.
4. Alice and Bob perform some local operations and classical communication (LOCC) on their halves of the imperfect pairs to distill a smaller number k of perfect EPR pairs, by entanglement distillation.
5. Alice and Bob perform measurements on their qubits k distilled EPR pairs to obtain a random, private key of length $(k < n)$.

Thus, the amount of distillable entanglement from quantum transmission would give a lower bound on the key generation rate. The Shor-Preskill proof [12] is an entanglement-based protocol which modifies Lo-Chau protocol by replacing entanglement distillation using quantum memory and quantum computers with entanglement distillation using the CSS quantum error-correcting codes. Subsequently, they reduce the modified Lo-Chau protocol to a protocol where entanglement is eliminated. In order to remove the requirement of quantum memory or quantum computer, one can move the final measurement ahead of the two error correction steps. The bit error correction becomes classical error correction, and the phase error correction becomes privacy amplification [12]. Quantum bit and phase error correction operations commute. The Shor-Preskill proof is given below:

1. Alice creates n random check bits, a random m-bit key k, and a random $2r$-bit string b (consider basis with $b = 0$ in X and $b = 1$ in Z), all in state $(\Phi^+)^{\otimes m}$.
2. Alice chooses r-bit string of each X basis and Z basis, at random.
3. Alice encodes her key $|k\rangle$ using the CSS code.
4. Alice chooses r positions (out of $2r$) and puts the check bits in these positions and the code bits in the remaining positions.
5. Alice applies a Hadamard transformation to those qubits in the positions where $b = 1$.
6. Alice sends the resulting state to Bob.
7. Bob acknowledges receipt of the qubits.
8. Alice announces b, the positions of the check bits, the values of the check bits, and the X and Z determining the code.
9. Bob performs Hadamards on the qubits where $b = 1$.
10. Bob examines whether too many of the check bits have been corrupted and hence decides whether to abort or continue with the protocol.
11. Bob decodes the key bits and uses them for the key.

Precisely, Alice and Bob will compare their measurements and evaluate the syndromes through which they can compute the locations of the bit and the phase flips. Thereafter, they can then correct the errors to obtain m perfect EPR pairs. The advantage of CSS codes is that error correction for the two phases is decoupled from that for the bit values, as shown above. If one needs to correct all errors on at most $t = \delta n$ qubits (t of each errors can be corrected), the best codes that we know exist satisfy the quantum Gilbert-Varshamov bound. For asymptotically increasing n, these codes can asymptotically protect against δn bit errors and δn phase errors and can encode $[1 - 2H(2\delta)]n$ qubits. In the case of random errors, it can encode $[1 - 2H(\delta)]n$ qubits against δn random bit and δn random phase errors.

2.5 Uncertainty Principle

Mayer's proof [13] was the first proof of unconditional security of BB84 QKD. This is based on uncertainty principle. Koashi's complementarity [14] for unconditional security is also based on the same spirit and further use Shor-Preskill and Lo-Chau tools. The BB84 protocol is converted into an equivalent entanglement-based protocol with a particular method for generating final key through information reconciliation and privacy amplification. In this approach, there is an actual protocol (AP) and a virtual protocol (VP), and there is a complementary control on both the protocols which Alice and Bob can select, but they cannot execute it simultaneously. The VP is not physically carried out and must be theoretically indistinguishable from Eve's perspective. It is important to mention that this would imply that any information revealed to Eve is identical for VP and AP. It is interesting to note that while the AP is bound by the Alice's and Bob's operation on a realistic setup, in the VP one can perform any operation that is allowed by quantum physics. In the AP the basis of key generation is declared, while in the VP, Alice and Bob collaborate to create an eigenstate in a complementary basis. Koashi proved in [14] that the necessary and sufficient condition for the secure key distillation is to be able to execute whichever protocol was chosen.

2.6   GLLP

The Gottesman, Lo, Lütkenhaus, and Preskill (GLLP) [15] established a general framework for security analysis with realistic devices. Suppose the total error rate is e then the key rate formulae is given by $r \geq -H(e) + (1 - \triangle)[1 - H\left(\frac{e}{1-\triangle}\right)]$. There are two kind of qubits discussed in GLLP, tagged qubits and untagged qubits. Tagged qubits are not secure, as the name suggests they have their basis information revealed to Eve in some manner. The untagged qubits are secure and single photons is the only source for untagged qubits. The key generated from these will be private and random. Both the legitimate parties can separate the tagged and untagged qubits. They will perform privacy amplification to the untagged qubits. The final key will be bitwise XOR of keys that could be obtained from the tagged and untagged qubits.

3   Categories of Protocols

There are two categories of QKD protocols based on the preparation technique:

1. Prepare-and-measure protocol (P&M): In these protocols the sender (Alice), randomly encodes the quantum state from a prescribed set and sends it to receiver (Bob). Bob will perform quantum measurement on the state according to the protocol.
2. Entanglement based protocol: In these protocols a third party generate maximally entangled state and sends them to both the parties. The parties then perform measurements in two mutually unbiased bases and if the output is perfectly correlated then key is established. Ekert 91 is an example of such a protocol.

3.1   General Eavesdropping Attack

Eve is considered to be all powerful and can perform any operation on the channel which is allowed by quantum mechanics. In QKD, the quantum link is the channel through which quantum states will travel to reach Bob. Eve can apply various strategies to get information from the travelling quantum states. She can choose to measure or entangle her probe with the quantum states. Various theoretical and experimental attacks on the link, detection system and source have been prescribed, analysed and some of them have been experimentally performed on the QKD system (academic and commercial) to understand the impact from a realistic perspective and develop a security cover for the same. Most of these attacks are incoherent in nature. It can be again classified into 3 categories: (1) with quantum memory and quantum computer, (2) with quantum memory and no quantum computer and (3) no quantum memory and no quantum computer. There is no technology available to perform full scale implementation of collective and coherent attack on QKD system. Security against these can be achieved from the security techniques mentioned earlier. There are device independent QKD protocols for higher security, from device perspective, but, it has a lesser performance in terms of key rate and distance. Most of the experimental attacks performed so far on QKD system are Intercept-and-Resend (IR) attack or it is also called fake state attack. These mostly belong to category (3). We will look at the different classification of attacks from Eve's strategy perspective.

Incoherent Attack or Individual Attack: In Fig. 1, we have shown the schematic of incoherent attack. Eve entangles each of Alice's photon independently with a 2-qubit probe P_i and use same strategy for all. She performs a measurement say, U (the most general unitary) which entangles the initial state of Eve's probe E_i to Alice's photon A_i. A simpler strategy would be Eve intercepts all the photons and measures them one by one and sends fake states to Bob according to her measurement. She can measure and store the results. Examples of such an attack are beam splitter attack (BS) and photon-number-splitting (PNS) attack (no quantum memory). However, she is smart and can always choose to either measure them instantaneously or save it in quantum memory and wait till sifting is done after which she can measure each probe one after the other. If we consider BB84 with polarization encoding using two bases B_1 for Rectilinear basis and B_2 for Diagonal basis then Eve's attack after U for both the bases can be modeled as below: $|E_i\rangle \left|A_p^{B_k}\right\rangle \mapsto \left|E_{lm}^{B_k}\right\rangle$ where $k = \{0,1\}, l = \{0,1\}, m = \{0,1\}, p$ can be two different polarization states corresponding to particular basis, $\left|E_{lm}^{B_1}\right\rangle$ are unnormalized states of P_i and $\left|E_{lm}^{B_2}\right\rangle$ can be written in terms of $\left|E_{lm}^{B_1}\right\rangle$ using linearity relation. Eve will select the measurement such that the probability of disturbance is small, precisely, $\left\langle E_{lm}^{B_1} \middle| E_{lm}^{B_1}\right\rangle$ and $\left\langle E_{lm}^{B_2} \middle| E_{lm}^{B_2}\right\rangle$ when $l \neq m$ are small and, an efficient strategy such that she can maximize her probability of guessing correct bit (after she learns which bases were used by Bob).

Collective Attack: In this attack Eve can entangle her system similar to individual attack however, she can perform a global measurement on all her probes, i.e. Eve can perform POVM on all the probes considering it as a single quantum system. This will allow her to take the advantage of the correlations from the classical communication during post processing. This attack is a subclass of coherent attack. It is powerful than individual attack as Eve has an access to quantum memory and quantum computer. For example PNS attack is

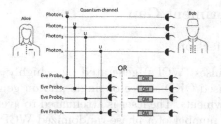

Fig. 1. Individual attack: with and without quantum memory (QM).

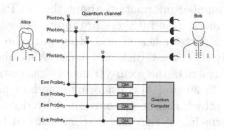

Fig. 2. Collective attack with quantum memory (QM) and all-powerful quantum computer (QC).

stronger when performed with quantum memory. In Fig. 2, we have shown the schematic of collective attack.

Coherent Attack: In Fig. 3, we have presented coherent attack. This is the most general and powerful attack. Eve will entangle her system with a probe of huge dimensionality with Alice's transmitted photons. It is extremely difficult to establish security against these attacks. However, mostly the proofs against collective attacks are extended for generalized attacks using quantum de Finetii theorem.

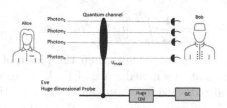

Fig. 3. Coherent attack with huge quantum memory (QM) and quantum computer (QC).

4   Theory-Experiment Gap

4.1   Source Imperfection

The weak coherent pulses (WCPs) generated by a highly attenuated laser are most the commonly used QKD source of single photon generation in academic and commercial deployments. The laser is attenuated to average photon number 0.1. Since the photon number of a phase-randomized WCP follows the Poisson distribution, there is a finite chance for emission of multiple-photon pulses. In PNS attack, Eve first performs a quantum non-demolition (QND) measurement to obtain the photon number information about the WCP. If she observes one photon then, she will block it and if there àre multiphotons then she will split the pulse into two, one part for herself and other part she sends to Bob. This attack does not directly effect the QBER and hence, Alice and Bob do not notice Eve. The PNS attack restricts the secure transmission distance of particularly BB84 typically about 25–30 km [15] considering standard parameters of experiment. However, this attack can be circumvented by decoy [16] method. The insight of the decoy principle is that the PNS attack can be detected by evaluating the quantum channel during QKD process. One crucial assumption in the decoy-state QKD is that the signal state and decoy state or states are identical except for their average photon numbers. Thus Eve has no way of telling whether the resulted photon number state is originated from the signal state or decoy states. Hence, the yield Y_n and QBER e_n can depend on only the photon number, n, but not which distribution (decoy or signal) the state is from. That is, $Y_{n(signal)} = Y_{n(decoy)}$ and $e_{n(signal)} = e_{n(decoy)}$. In Fig. 4, we have presented the key generation of BB84 with different sources, single photon source, weak coherent source with average photon number 0.1 and with decoy at different distances. In decoy method, GLLP technique of security was applied for establishing unconditional security. It clearly shows that decoy has an added advantage of increasing the distance of QKD and also making the system robust against PNS attack. We had mentioned that for a coherent state, a photon number channel model is used, which assumes the phase of the coherent state is randomized,

$$\rho = \frac{1}{2\pi} \int_0^{2\pi} \left| \alpha e^{i\theta} \right\rangle \left\langle \alpha e^{i\theta} \right| d\theta \tag{6}$$

A physical interpretation behind is that when the phase of a coherent state is randomized, it is equivalent to a mixed state of Fock states whose photon number follows a Poisson distribution with a mean of $|\alpha|^2$. In other words, the Fock states are totally decohered from each other with continuous phase randomization. It can also be interpreted to an eavesdropper with no a priori knowledge of the phase, a signal whose phase is selected uniformly at random is indistinguishable from the state ρ_μ which is a Poisson distributed mixture of photon number eigenstates. Therefore, for a security analysis, we consider that it is actually emitting signals in the state ρ_μ. The state ρ_μ is represented by a diagonal density matrix with respect to photon-number basis. By using a combination of an

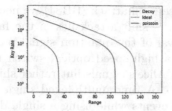

Fig. 4. Secure key generation vs distance for BB84 QKD with different sources.

unambiguous-state-discrimination (USD) measurement and a photon-number-splitting (PNS) attack, it is shown in [17] that the final key generated by the non-phase-randomized system can be compromised. Hence in a decoy state QKD it is very important to randomize the phase of the quantum signals.

4.2 Detection Imperfection

One of the basic assumptions involved in the security proof of any quantum key distribution protocol is that all the components used in the process are ideal, whereas in a practical QKD system it is not so. Attacks on detection [18] arises due to manufacturing precision in the detector and the electronics. The difference in optical path length will slightly misalign the two detector gates resulting in detector-efficiency mismatch. Hence a QKD system that employs such pair of detectors will carry a risk of an attack due to detector efficiency mismatch. The time-shift attack [19] is a simple yet strong attack, owing to the fact that it can be performed on almost all the QKDs possible and can be performed in a number of ways. Also the fact that such an attack is possible with the present technology, makes it even more powerful. To understand the attack, let us consider Fig. 5.

We can see that the efficiency of detection of bit 0, at $t_0, \eta_0(t_0)$, is greater than the efficiency of detection of bit 1 at $t_0, \eta_1(t_0)$. Therefore, $\eta_0(t_0) > \eta_1(t_0)$. Similarly, we find that $\eta_1(t_1) > \eta_0(t_1)$. Using symmetry assumption we can define r as the ratio of efficiencies $r = \frac{\eta_1(t_0)}{\eta_0(t_0)} = \frac{\eta_0(t_1)}{\eta_1(t_1)}$. The ratio r, gives us a qualitative idea of the possibility of an attack being successful. The value of r also helps us in determining the quantum bit error rate (QBER) introduced in

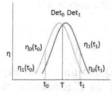

Fig. 5. The time dependent efficiencies $\eta(t)$ of SPDs. The yellow line indicates the detection efficiency of bit 0 and the blue indicates the detection efficiency of bit 1. (Color figure online)

the system. To make a successful attack (BB84) we need the value r, such that $r < 0.2$. The bases of time - shift attack lies in the fact that Eve can simply delay or advance the arrival of the quantum signal pulses in Bob's subsystem randomly by introducing a high speed optical switch in between the channel. Eve need not measure the Alice's signals but rather shifts them such that they reach Bob at time t_0 or t_1. A time multiplexed single photon detector (SPD) can detect more than one events while using a single detector only. In such an SPD, the detection is done by the use of separation in time of arrival of the bit. In this case, Bob's SPDs are in gated mode and has to open exactly twice for each incoming pulse. Because there is no overlap between the two gate openings the system is similar to $r = 0$. Eve can thus have complete information on the sifting key without introducing any error. In the detector blinding attack [20], by sending a strong light to Bob, Eve can force Bob's SPDs to work in a Linear mode instead of Geiger mode. In the Linear mode, the SPD, is only sensitive to bright illumination. This detector operation mode is called detector blinding. To use the control of Bob's detectors to her advantage, Eve can conduct an intercept-resend attack, where she measures the phase of Alice's photons in random bases and resends her results to Bob in the superimposed classical pulses, the power of each pulse being just above Bob's detectors threshold.

5   Conclusion

We have discussed the security techniques for unconditional proofs of QKD protocols. It is very important to state the failure probability (leakage) of each key using the modern definition of security since the quantum signals generating the final key is finite and there will be errors due to realistic implementations. It quantifies the security of the protocol. Using the current technology Eve can successfully make certain attacks on the source (targeting multiphoton states and phase) and detection system (detectors and optical components at Bob based on specific QKD protocol) to perform phase attacks, time-shift attack, blinding attack and trojan horse attack etc on almost any QKD system. But while doing so, Eve will have to face certain challenges. The manufacturers can certainly take precautions and add security patches to prevent these attacks. Better engineering of the detectors like efficiency of the detectors must be very close to each other, monitoring devices in Alice and Bob unit and sifting strategies need to be devised to identify any realistic eavesdropping. A direct application of standard security proofs, without taking into account such loopholes, will remain insecure.

References

1. Bennett, C.H., Brassard, G.: Quantum cryptography: public key distribution and coin tossing. In: Proceeding of the IEEE International Conference on Computers, Systems and Signal Processing, pp. 175–179 (1984)
2. Bennett, C.H., Bessette, F., Brassard, G., Salvail, L., Smolin, J.: Experimental quantum cryptography. J. Cryptol. 5, 3–28 (1992). https://doi.org/10.1007/BF00191318

3. Elliott, C., Colvin, A., Pearson, D., Pikalo, O., Schlafer, J., Yeh, H.: Current status of the DARPA quantum network (Invited Paper). In: Quantum Information and Computation III. Proceedings of SPIE, vol. 5815, p. 138 (2005). https://doi.org/10.1117/12.606489

4. Pan, J.-W.: Quantum science satellite. Chin. J. Space Sci. **34**, 547–549 (2014)

5. Lo, H.-K., Curty, M., Tamaki, K.: Secure quantum key distribution. Nat. Photonics **8**, 595 (2014)

6. Diamanti, E., Lo, H.-K., Yuan, Z.: Practical challenges in quantum key distribution. npj Quant. Inf. **2**, 16025 (2016)

7. Ben-Or, M., Horodecki, M., Leung, D.W., Mayers, D., Oppenheim, J.: The universal composable security of quantum key distribution. In: Kilian, J. (ed.) TCC 2005. LNCS, vol. 3378, pp. 386–406. Springer, Heidelberg (2005). https://doi.org/10.1007/978-3-540-30576-7_21

8. Renner, R., König, R.: Universally composable privacy amplification against quantum adversaries. In: Kilian, J. (ed.) TCC 2005. LNCS, vol. 3378, pp. 407–425. Springer, Heidelberg (2005). https://doi.org/10.1007/978-3-540-30576-7_22

9. Wiesner, S.: Conjugate coding. ACM SIGACT News **15**, 78–88 (1983)

10. Ekert, A.K.: Quantum cryptography based on Bell's theorem. Phys. Rev. Lett. **67**, 661 (1991)

11. Lo, H.-K., Chau, H.F.: Unconditional security of quantum key distribution over arbitrarily long distances. Science **283**, 2050–2056 (1999)

12. Shor, P.W., Preskill, J.: Simple proof of security of the BB84 quantum key distribution protocol. Phys. Rev. Lett. **85**, 441 (2000)

13. Mayer, D.: Unconditional security in quantum cryptography. J. ACM (JACM) **48**, 351–406 (2001)

14. Koashi, M.: Simple security proof of quantum key distribution based on complementarity. New J. Phys. **11**, 045018 (2009)

15. Gottesman, D., Lo, H.-K., Lütkenhaus, N., Preskill, J.: Security of quantum key distribution with imperfect devices. Quant. Inf. Comput. **5**, 325–360 (2004)

16. Lo, H.-K., Ma, X., Chen, K.: Decoy state quantum key distribution. Phys. Rev. Lett. **94**, 230504 (2005)

17. Tang, Y.-L., et al.: Source attack of decoy-state quantum key distribution using phase information. Phys. Rev. A **88**, 022308 (2013)

18. Jain, N., Stiller, B., Khan, I., Elser, D., Marquardt, C., Leuchs, G.: Attacks on practical quantum key distribution systems (and how to prevent them). Contemp. Phys. **57**, 366–387 (2016)

19. Qi, B., Fung, C.-H.F., Lo, H.-K., Ma, X.: Time shift attack in practical quantum cryptosystems. Quant. Inf. Comput. **7**, 73–82 (2007)

20. Lydersen, L., Wiechers, C., Wittmann, C., Elser, D., Skaar, J., Makarov, V.: Hacking commercial quantum cryptography systems by tailored bright illumination. Nat. Photonics **4**, 686–689 (2010)

The Impact of a Security Model in a Fog Computing Environment

Nhlakanipho C. Fakude, Paul Tarwireyi(✉) (iD), and Mathew O. Adigun

Department of Computer Science, University of Zululand, Private Bag X1001,
KwaDlangezwa 3886, South Africa
ncfakude30@gmail.com, tarwireyip@unizulu.ac.za

Abstract. The Internet of Things (IoT) is an emerging technology that has received much attention in recent years due to its ability to process data in real-time, speed up awareness and respond quickly to events. IoT aims to bring every object online, thereby generating increasing amounts of data. This exponential growth of network traffic calls for faster, efficient and scalable ways of processing. Critical IoT applications such as health monitoring, emergency response and industrial control require high availability and very low latency to guarantee good user experiences. Fog computing has been proposed as a solution to decrease latency and network congestion in IoT environments. However, security in the fog-IoT layer is still a very open area that is yet to receive much attention. This paper presents a security model that addresses data security, both at rest and in transit on end-devices and fog devices. The study uses a latency-sensitive online application (EEG tractor game) to evaluate the performance impact of the security model in an IoT based fog environment. *iFogSim* was used to model IoT and Fog environments and measure the effect of security in terms of latency, network congestion, energy consumption, and cost. Experimental results demonstrate the viability of our model.

Keywords: Edge computing · Fog computing · Internet of Things (IoT) · Security model · Hybrid cryptosystem

1 Introduction

The Internet of Things (IoT) is an emerging paradigm that enables advanced services through ubiquitous interconnection of smart devices over the Internet. According to a recent Visual Networking Index forecast by Cisco[1], in 2022, there will be about 28.5 billion connected sensors and devices worldwide, and more traffic will be created than in the 32 years since the Internet started. Cloud computing, which plays a significant role in managing and storing the increasing amounts of data generated by the IoT devices, presents various challenges to meet the peculiar requirements of IoT. Fog computing, to a certain extent has been used to solve the bottleneck problem and the aforementioned cloud computing challenges. Fog computing improves performance by bringing

---

[1] https://www.cisco.com/c/en/us/solutions/collateral/service-provider/visual-networking-index-vni/white-paper-c11-741490.html.

© Springer Nature Singapore Pte Ltd. 2020
S. M. Thampi et al. (Eds.): SSCC 2019, CCIS 1208, pp. 198–212, 2020.
https://doi.org/10.1007/978-981-15-4825-3_16

computation to the edge, closer to the data source. It enables decentralised on-demand applications and services for managing and processing large volumes of data at the network's edge [1].

IoT aims to bring every object (e.g. smart cameras, wearable, environmental sensors, home appliances, and vehicles) online, hence generating a massive amount of data that require high processing to provide event responses in real-time [2]. This paradigm opens doors to new innovations that build new types of interaction among things or objects and humans and enables the realisation of smart cities, infrastructures, and services for enhancing the quality of life and use of resources [3].

The proliferation of interconnected devices widens the attack surface; thereby expanding opportunities for threat actors assume device control. IoT has made networks and devices more vulnerable than ever. This has seen IoT devices being increasingly compromised and used in a wide variety of attacks. A case in example is the Mirai Botnet[2]. Another example is that of potentially life-threatening vulnerability that was discovered in wireless-enabled implantable cardiac pacemakers. This vulnerability could allow hackers to easily gain access to implanted cardiac defibrillators and interfere with operation[3].

Even though IoT devices have undisputable benefits, such benefits may be obviated if the IoT devices themselves are a hazard [4]. Security challenges are prevalent in all layers of the IoT architecture because security has always been an afterthought in the design of IoT devices. Fog computing has the potential to alleviate some of the IoT security challenges. Nevertheless, it has its own privacy and security issues such as authentication, access control, trust management and privacy.

Confidentiality, data integrity, and non-repudiation are often used as security yardsticks for any platform [5, 6]. Enabling IoT devices to exchange data should be preceded by authentication of the endpoints and mechanisms to provide integrity and protecting the confidentiality of exchanged data [6]. In the context of fog computing and IoT, there is a need for security mechanisms that do not result in considerable additional power consumption, complexity and cost.

In this work, we demonstrate the effect of security in fog computing by articulating research challenges in fog security and propose a security model that uses hybrid (encryption algorithm) cryptosystem which is the combination of both the symmetric and asymmetric encryption algorithms [7]. Hybrid cryptosystem has been chosen because it allows the exchange of cryptographic keys and encryption as two concurrent processes. The hybrid encryption algorithm will address how confidentiality, data integrity, and non-repudiation are achieved. The security model will be evaluated for performance using a latency-sensitive online game scenario. To summarize, the contributions of the paper are the following.

- We present a security model that uses a hybrid cryptosystem, that utilizes both symmetric and asymmetric encryption algorithms.
- We demonstrate the applicability, utility and impact of the proposed model using a latency-sensitive simulation scenario.

---

[2] https://www.cloudflare.com/learning/ddos/glossary/mirai-botnet/.

[3] https://fortune.com/2017/08/31/pacemaker-recall-fda/.

The remainder of the paper is organized as follows: Sect. 2 presents a review of existing studies. Section 3 presents an overview of fog computing and the scenarios chosen for simulation. Section 4 presents the proposed model. Section 5 discusses the simulation and evaluation results, whilst the paper is concluded in Sect. 6.

2 Related Work

In [8] the authors discussed security and privacy issues in the fog computing environment and identified authentication, as the main security issue. In [9], the major security and privacy challenges that were discussed include Authentication, Trust, Rogue Node Detection, Privacy, Access Control, Intrusion Detection, Data Protection, and others. Authors in [10], proposed the use of the AES algorithm to encrypt the data in the fog-computing environment. Fog devices need to serve end devices through wireless connections; hence, a secure communication model is necessary. The work did not explain how secure communication is achieved between the two entities.

In [11], the authors discussed the sharing of critical medical data and challenging security measures. Thus, the authors built a novel healthcare system utilising the flexibility of the cloudlet platform. The Number Theory Research Unit (NTRU) method was used to encrypt data collected from wearable devices. However, the trust model proposed does not accommodate non-medical data (e.g. videos, images, etc.). Thus, the considered literature has not adequately addressed the challenge of secured transmission and storage in a fog environment. In [12], the authors designed a cloud computing security model for data at rest and in transit. The authors opted into using a new encryption algorithm, which enables Biometrics to be used instead of passwords for access control. However, due to some mobile devices not supporting biometric technology, the model designed cannot be applied to fog computing, as it does not accommodate a mobile device (end-devices) and fog device autonomous communication.

Moreover, in [13], the authors proposed a security solution by using hybrid encryption algorithm. The authors enhanced RSA asymmetric encryption algorithm by increasing the length of the key so that it can generate big primes. The authors further merged AES symmetric encryption algorithm with the enhanced RSA algorithm. However, this study only considered lightweight data on the cloud storage service. It did not address the security of scalable data and the deployment of the security solution to a fog-computing paradigm.

IoT devices may generate massive amounts of security sensitive data, making them a target for data breach and other security attacks. The constrained nature of the IoT device architecture makes it difficult to embed robust security mechanisms in the devices. Hence, the need to investigate other solutions that can be employed to mitigate the risks. Even though fog is reported to have the potential to address some of the cloud computing and IoT challenges, on its own, it is a high risk from a security perspective. This is because it exposes the public APIs that are used to provide services to connected users. Security is a very challenging domain where the introduction of a new component to address existing vulnerabilities always widens the attack surface and introduce yet other vulnerabilities. Fog enabled IoT systems bring together heterogeneous devices and networks resulting in potential attacks from anywhere.

Although there has been a lot of research on IoT and fog computing, many essential matters remain. Prior works discuss the security issues faced by fog computing and IoT in isolation. Not much attention has been paid to the security challenges that arise at the intersection of heterogeneous fog and IoT networks. Lack of standardisation in this area is also evident. The present study proposes the design of a security model that uses a hybrid encryption algorithm to provide end-to-end security in fog enabled IoT deployments.

3   Fog Computing Environment Overview

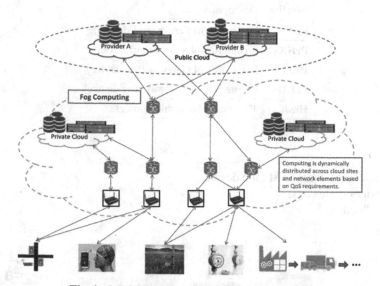

Fig. 1. IoT based fog computing environment [2]

As highlighted before, fog computing is as an intermediary that enables decentralised on-demand services for managing and processing large volumes of data between IoT devices and the cloud. It allows the seamless convergence of heterogeneous infrastructure stretching from the public cloud to edge devices such as ISP gateways and cellular base stations a (see Fig. 4) [2, 14]. This architecture has the benefits of offloading computation from end devices to the public cloud while limiting the use of the cloud whose higher latency could negatively affect the user experience. In Fig. 1, the overview of the IoT based fog environment in which the security model will be integrated, is provided, where the two applications will be deployed. The model processes are then implemented in the fog environment, as illustrated in Fig. 4.

This section presents the proposed security model. The techniques used to secure data in transit and at rest are also highlighted. The notations in Table 1 were used in defining the encryption process flow in Figs. 2, 3, and 4. The proposed model includes the components which are depicted in Fig. 4.

4 Proposed Security Model

Table 1. Security model notations

Notation	Description
PKS	Public Key of Sensor (end-device)
PrKS	Private Key of Sensor (end-device)
PKG	Public Key of Gateway (fog device)
PrKG	Private Key of Gateway (fog device)
Hash	The result of a hashing process

- End-devices (Sensors or Mobile devices)
- Fog devices (gateways)
- Public Cloud

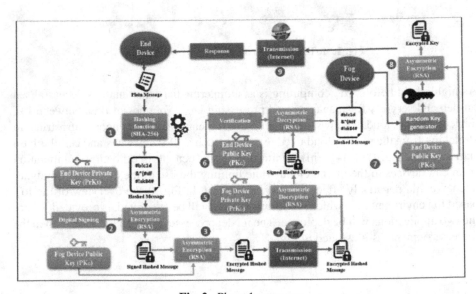

Fig. 2. Phase 1 processes

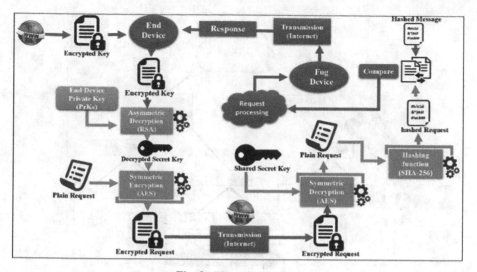

Fig. 3. Phase 2 processes

To demonstrate the utility and applicability of the proposed model, we implemented it using iFogSim simulator. We measured the impact of the model in terms of latency, network congestion, energy consumption and cost [2, 14]. iFogSim is a tool which enables simulation of resource management and application scheduling policies across edge and cloud resources under different scenarios and conditions. The scenario used in our simulation is a sensitive-latency online game with operational requirements such as low latency, low energy consumption and low network usage. The specifications of the application are described in Table 2.

The gateway acts as an intermediary for the end-device and the cloud. Moreover, the end-device – fog device communication consists of a trust management system which enables only eligible entities to access the information/data [1]. This is achieved by the use of hybrid cryptosystem that is the combination of both the asymmetric and the symmetric encryption algorithms. The model proposed in this paper aims to enable end-device to fog-device communications that do not suffer from security vulnerabilities such as replay, message tampering and eavesdropping. Before an end-device can communicate with the gateway, it needs to know the identification and authentication information. Because many IoT devices do not have user interfaces that can be used to configure this information, the norm is to provision the information securely to the end devices during manufacturing time or later depending on the envisioned deployment model.

This is usually done using standard procedures such as configuration files in operating systems, firmware packages or EEPROM chips. Just like any situation where devices have joined a network, a certain amount of configuration is inevitable. It is assumed in this paper that the hardware and physical security needed to protect the provisioned credentials is in place. Provisioning this information in advance is desirable in IoT networks because it is both computationally and bandwidth-efficient.

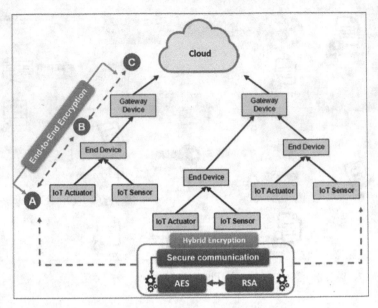

Fig. 4. IoT-based end-to-end encryption

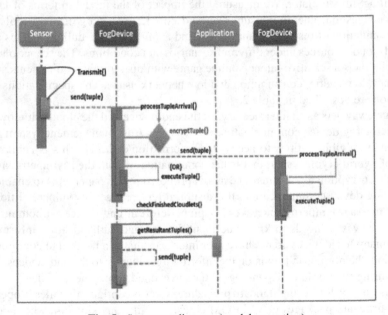

Fig. 5. Sequence diagram (model execution)

While the identification information to be provisioned can include addresses of end-points and IP addresses, authentication mechanisms can include pre-shared keys, public keys and certificates. Literature has pointed out that a secure system should address the following security properties; confidentiality, data integrity, and non-repudiation [2, 3]; thus our study proposes a model that aims address these major properties.

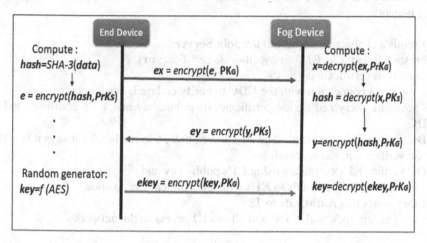

Fig. 6. Handshake protocol

Figure 2 and 3 highlights some of the crucial processes of the model. They show interactions between the end device (sensor) and the fog device (gateway). Figure 4 shows a general overview of the implemented security model in the IoT based fog environment. The deployment of the model enables end-to-end encryption from the sensor or actuator to the cloud via the fog gateway. As the number of IoT devices continues to grow, access control is becoming an increasingly critical security concern. As the first layer of defence, it is essential to enable certain levels of trust by ensuring that end-devices are identified and verified before being allowed on the network.

4.1 Network Join Authentication

If inadequate attention is paid to it, authentication can easily become the weakest part of fog computing security. This work proposes an authentication mechanism inspired by the security-as-a-service paradigm [15]. When an end-device tries to connect to an IoT gateway, it has to go through authentication and authorisation procedures, where certificates are shared and verified. The model presented in this paper proposes that the credentials be stored and managed centrally on a resourceful distributed server using standard secure AAA mechanisms such as OAuth, Kerberos, EAP-TLS and RADIUS. The network join server is responsible for enforcing the policies that govern access to network resources and behaviour of nodes on the network. This server can be located in the cloud. Another distributed server, Certificate Distribution Centre (CDC), which is used for generating the certificates whose url's are provisioned on the end devices is also in the cloud. These certificates are issued after verifying the identities of the end devices. Assuming an environment that has m end nodes as shown in Fig. 4, $endNoes = (E_1, E_2, E_3, E_4 \ldots E_m)$. We propose that the join server (JS) be located in the cloud.

The following steps illustrate the authentication steps, using E1 as an example. To protect the credentials from prying eyes while in transit, a secure channel is used during the negotiations. If a device has been authenticated, it is allowed to start sending traffic on the network.

- E1 sends a connection request to the **Join Server**
- **JS** responds and asks **E1** for or AuthCode certificate **url**
- **E1** sends its certificate url to **JS**
- **JS** initiates a connection with the **CDC** to verify end node certificate
- **JS** sends its encrypted digital certificate, its public key and **E1's** certificate **url** to **CDC**
- **CDC** verifies JS's certificate. The step proves that **JS** is really who it says it is
- If the verification was successful
- **CDC** verifies **E1's** certificate using **E1's** public key and
- If successful **CDC** responds to **E1's** with and Authentication code
- **E1** then sends this **AuthCode** to **JS**
- **JS** verifies this code with **CDC** and allows **E1** access to the network.

This mechanism ensures that the nodes become part of the same domain of trust before exchanging data and minimises the computations that need to be done on the end devices. For example, the certificate verification tasks are offloaded to the cloud, which has abundant resources.

4.2 Data Transmission

In Fig. 2, the end device (sensor) establishes a connection with the fog device. For the subsequent procedures and exchanges, the model assumes all the information required for the authentication mechanisms in use has been distributed and verified before the data protection interactions start. This includes public keys and certificates.

Message Signing and Verification

- The end device will first generate a *hash* from the data to be transmitted using an SHA-3 hashing algorithm, thereafter encrypt the *hash* with its private key (PrK_S) using RSA to get a *signed hash x = encrypt (hash, PrK$_s$)*.
- The x will then be encrypted with the fog device's public key (PK_G) to get an *ex = encrypt (x, PK$_G$)*.
- The *ex* is then sent to the fog device by the end device over the internet and waits for a response.
- As soon as the *ex* is received, the fog device will decrypt it using its private key (PK_G) to get *x = decrypt (ex, PK$_G$)*.
- A *hash* will be obtained when the *x* is further decrypted (verified) with the end device's public key (PK_S) *hash = decrypt (x, PK$_S$)*.
- At this point, the fog device (gateway) would have had validated the authenticity of the communication with the end device, because only the public key of the end device (PKs) can be used to decrypt the signed hash which was signed with the end device's

private key (**PrK$_S$**). Also, the digital signature in the certificate is used to bind the public key to the end device. The *hash* is then kept for later use.

- The fog device (gateway) sends back a (response) **signed hash2** (signed with its private key (**PrK$_G$**)) to the end device which follows the above processes to validate the authenticity of the communication with the fog device.

Key Exchange (RSA)

- The processes above perform mutual authentication. The fog device authenticates the end device, and similarly, the end device proves the authenticity of the fog device. Subsequently, the fog device generates a secure random key for sharing with the other authenticated endpoint. For the experiments carried out in this work, 128-bit AES keys were used.
- The fog device encrypts the random key using the verified end device's public key (**PK$_S$**) and then sends the key to the end device.
- As soon as the **encrypted key** is received, the end device will decrypt it using its private key (**PrK$_S$**) to get the **shared key** that will be used to secure the payload.

Data Encryption and Confidentiality

- This model uses the AES cryptographic primitive with modes of operation, methods and techniques for integrity protection and encryption. AES is a well-tested, FIPS 140-2 compliant cryptographic algorithm that is widely adopted as a best practice for resource-constrained devices.
- Now that the end device is satisfied that it is communicating with the expected fog device and also has the **shared key** sent by the fog device. The payload is encrypted end-to-end between the end-device and the fog node using AES. Encryption of data to and from end nodes is critical because it could contain sensitive information such as information to control the amount of insulin delivery on a patient. If such information is intercepted and tampered with, it could have life-threatening consequences.
- The end device initiates data encryption using the **shared key** (AES), which results in encrypted data that is then sent to the fog device.
- Once the fog device receives the encrypted data, it can easily decrypt it using the **shared key** to get the actual data.

Confidentiality is achieved by the encryption of the data using the AES. In this scenario, the end device and the fog device achieve confidentiality because no other device can intercept and decipher the communication without the appropriate shared key.

Data Integrity and Non-repudiation

After the above processes both entities (end device and fog device) have a secure communication channel, but to verify that the data sent by the mobile device has not been tampered with, the fog device will firstly generate a hash from the decrypted data to get hash2. Since the fog device kept the hash received from the end device, the fog device will compare the hash with hash2 to validate that the data has not been altered.

In the message signing and verification processes, the fog device verifies the authenticity of the end device. Thus, the hash has been signed with the end device's private key ($\mathbf{PrK_s}$), and it can only be decrypted with the end device's public key ($\mathbf{PK_G}$), hence the fog device is sure that the message was sent by the anticipated end device which also cannot deny that they have sent the message.

4.3 Data Storage

The transmitted data is stored in the cloud via the fog device. The following steps will take place for the storage of encrypted data: (1) the fog device will send the encrypted data to the cloud for storage using the same transmission process as described in the data transmission Sect. 2). On receiving the response, the fog device will pass it to the end device.

The reason for not allowing the end device to send a request directly to the cloud is to maximize the performance, that is, it is essential to delegate the fog device to perform the complex tasks and return fewer heavy responses to the end device. However, the average time of deploying hybrid encryption algorithm is slightly higher than symmetric encryption; this is because both symmetric and asymmetric encryption algorithms are used concurrently. Hence the time required to compute both is higher than symmetric encryption algorithm alone [12].

5   Experiments and Results

This section provides the simulation configurations, application specifications, and the results obtained from the simulation. The latency-sensitive online game application scenario called EEG tractor was used to evaluate the security model under the conditions of the IoT based Fog computing environment. The performance metrics considered are; latency, network usage, and energy consumption.

Table 2. Network links for EEG tractor game

Source	Destination	Latency, ms
EEG headset	Smartphone	6
Smartphone	Wi-Fi gateway	2
Wi-Fi gateway	ISP gateway	4
ISP gateway	Cloud Data Center	100

The minimum latencies between the interconnections of the EEG headset, Smartphones, Wi-Fi gateway, and ISP gateway are shown in Table 2. Table 3 shows the simulation configurations. The column smartphones ($\sum$) denotes the total number of smartphones connected to the gateways in a configuration. Smartphones gain internet connection through Wi-Fi gateways that connected to the ISP gateway, and the number of smartphones and gateways are varied, which results in different scenarios of the

Table 3. Configuration of devices

Configurations	Gateways	Smartphones/GW	Smartphones $(\sum)$
1	2	4	8
2	3	4	12
3	4	4	16
4	4	8	32
5	4	12	48
6	4	16	64

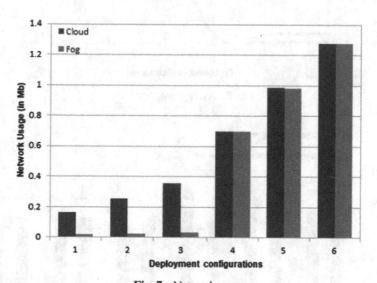

Fig. 7. Network usage

IoT-based Fog computing environment. The EEG tractor application generates different types of data (tuples) and transmits it to the fog device (Wi-Fi gateway) which processes and executes the data (tuples) (Fig. 5). The security model is integrated between the end device (sensor) and the fog device (gateway).

Fog environment provides a platform for filtering and analysis of the data generated by the end devices (sensors) using resources of the edge devices or fog devices. Hence the integration of the security model in this architecture enables secure communication between the end devices and fog devices. In this work, devices were configured to evaluate the effect of the security model in fog based IoT based infrastructure. Performance evaluation experiments were carried out using three performance metrics. These are namely: network usage, energy consumption, latency. The following sections provide a discussion of the experimental results (Fig. 6).

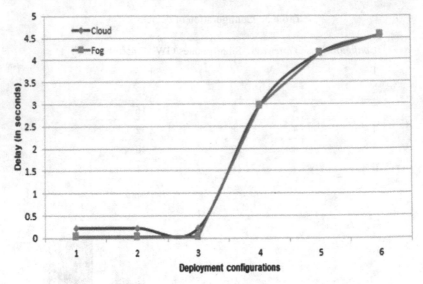

Fig. 8. Average latency

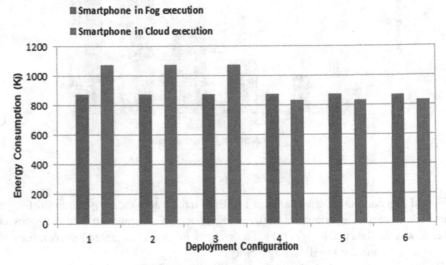

Fig. 9. Average energy consumption

5.1 Network Usage

The network usage which is measured as the amount data (in Megabytes) sent and received by the online game application installed on the smartphone. Figure 7 shows that there is a positive correlation between number of devices and network usage. When the number of devices increase, the network usage also increases. The network usage is higher for the cloud architecture, compared to Fog, because as the number of smartphones (end devices) increase, the network becomes congested leading to the degradation of the application's performance. Fog has generally better network usage and less network congestion due to fog devices being closer to the end devices.

5.2 Average Latency

The average latency is the measure of how long an end device (smartphone) has to wait until it is served by the fog device or the cloud. The most critical requirement for the latency-sensitive online game application is low latency, which results in real-time communication between the end devices and the fog devices. Delay in the IoT configurations may result in the user experience being affected. Figure 8 illustrates the average latency in the execution of the security model in the fog enabled IoT environment and shows that the delay is constant for the fog execution up until the number of smartphones is increased, whereas the cloud execution latency is higher. As the number of gateways is kept constant (four gateways) and the number of smartphones is increased the delay increases as well.

5.3 Average Energy Consumption

As shown in Fig. 9, the energy consumption of the gateways is higher due to the number of smartphones being higher than the gateways in both architectures. This means the gateways have a congestion of smartphones when communicating with the cloud but starting from configuration 4, the number of smartphones increases while the gateways remain the same. The Cloud architecture becomes congested and consumes more energy while the Fog architecture can distribute (offload) to other free fog devices, which result in better energy consumption. The energy consumption for the fog execution is the same throughout, and that is because the smartphones are being hosted by the gateways locally, and the cloud infrastructure is not called upon.

6 Conclusion and Future Work

In this paper, we have presented a security model that secures data transmission and data storage between IoT end devices and fog devices. The model takes advantage of a hybrid encryption algorithm, which combines the asymmetric and symmetric encryption algorithms. The security model addressed the three basic security properties (confidentiality, data integrity, and non-repudiation) in detail. The simulation results demonstrated that the model affects the overall performance of an IoT-based Fog computing environment. Deploying this model in the fog is better because of the performance benefits. However, some limitations are worth noting. Even though the proposed solution addresses some of the security problems like authentication, it does not fully address trust issues. Furthermore, the proposed work does not have a way of detecting compromised nodes that can be used for insider attacks. Future work should, therefore, include follow up works to ensure trust and detect anomalies caused by insider attacks.

References

1. Khan, S., Parkinson, S., Qin, Y.: Fog computing security: a review of current applications and security solutions. J. Cloud Comput. **6**(1), 19 (2017
2. Gupta, H., Vahid Dastjerdi, A., Ghosh, S.K., Buyya, R.: iFogSim: a toolkit for modeling and simulation of resource management techniques in the Internet of Things, edge, and fog computing environments. Softw. - Pract. Exp. **47**(9), 1275–1296 (2017)
3. Brauer, K.: Authentication and Security aspects in an international multi-user network, pp. 3–5 (2011)
4. Hansen, E.: Analysis of design for implementing confidentiality, integrity, authentication, and non - repudiation solutions. SANS Inst. 2003, no. Security 401, pp. 1–39 (2003)
5. Zhou, Z., Huang, D.: Efficient and secure data storage operations for mobile cloud computing. In: 8th International Conference Network Service Management (CNSM), pp. 37–45, (2012)
6. Sharma, M., Sharma, V.: A hybrid cryptosystem approach for file security by using merging mechanism. In: Proceedings of 2016 2nd International Conference Application Theoretical Computing Communication Technology iCATccT 2016, pp. 713–717 (2017)
7. Stojmenovic, I., Wen, S.: The fog computing paradigm: scenarios and security issues. In: Proceedings of 2014 Federated Conference on Computer Science and Information Systems, vol. 2, pp. 1–8 (2014)
8. Alrawais, A., Alhothaily, A., Hu, C., Cheng, X.: Fog computing for the Internet of Things: security and privacy issues. IEEE Internet Comput. **21**(2), 34–42 (2017)
9. Vishwanath, A., Peruri, R.: Security in fog computing through encryption. Int. J. Inf. Technol. Comput. Sci. **8**(5), 28–36 (2016)
10. Chen, M., Qian, Y., Chen, J., Hwang, K., Mao, S., Hu, L.: Privacy protection and intrusion avoidance for cloudlet-based medical data sharing. IEEE Trans. Cloud Comput. **XX**(c), 1 (2016)
11. Chidiebere, U., Agbasonu Valerian, C., Ndunagu J.N.: Design and simulation of cloud computing security for data at rest and data on transit. vol. 4, no. 2, pp. 138–156 (2017)
12. Liang, C., Ye, N., Malekian, R., Wang, R.: The hybrid encryption algorithm of lightweight data in cloud storage. In: 2nd International Symposium Agent, Multi-Agent Systems Robotics ISAMSR, 2016, no. August, pp. 160–166 (2017)
13. Roman, R., Lopez, J., Mambo, M., et al.: Mobile edge computing, Fog a survey and analysis of security threats and challenges. Futur. Gener. Comput. Syst. **78**, 680–698 (2018)
14. Mahmud, R., Buyya, R.: Modeling and Simulation of Fog and Edge Computing Environments Using iFogSim Toolkit. Fog Edge Computing, pp. 433–465 (2019)
15. Nxumalo, Z.C., Tarwireyi, P., Adigun, M.O.: Towards privacy with tokenization as a service. In: 2014 IEEE 6th International Conference on Adaptive Science & Technology (ICAST), Ota, 2014, pp. 1–6

Gotcha-I: A Multiview Human Videos Dataset

Paola Barra[1], Carmen Bisogni[1]([✉]), Michele Nappi[1], David Freire-Obregón[2], and Modesto Castrillón-Santana[2]

[1] Università degli Studi di Salerno, 84084 Salerno, Italy
{pbarra,cbisogni,mnappi}@unisa.it
[2] Universidad de Las Palmas de Gran Canaria (ULPGC), 35017 Gran Canaria, Spain
{david.freire,modesto.castrillon}@ulpgc.es

Abstract. The growing need of security in large open spaces led to the need to use video capture of people in different context and illumination and with multiple biometric traits as head pose, body gait, eyes, nose, mouth, and further more. All these traits are useful for a multibiometric identification or a person re-identification in a video surveillance context. Body Worn Cameras (BWCs) are used by the police of different countries all around the word and their use is growing significantly. This raises the need to develop new recognition methods that consider multi-biometric traits on person re-identification. The purpose of this work is to present a new video dataset called Gotcha-I. This dataset has been obtained using more mobile cameras to adhere to the data of BWCs. The dataset includes videos from 62 subjects in indoor and outdoor environments to address both security and surveillance problem. During these videos, subjects may have a different behavior in videos such as freely, path, upstairs, avoid the camera. The dataset is composed by 493 videos including a set of 180° videos for each face of the subjects in the dataset. Furthermore, there are already processed data, such as: the 3D model of the face of each subject with all the poses of the head in pitch, yaw and roll; and the body keypoint coordinates of the gait for each video frame. It's also shown an application of gender recognition performed on Gotcha-I, confirming the usefulness and innovativeness of the proposed dataset.

Keywords: Dataset · Biometric · Face · Gait · Head pose estimation · Mobile device · Body worn cameras

1 Introduction

For security purposes, there are various types of videos to examine with different devices, from different perspectives and in different environments. This type of data increasingly comes from mobile devices such as cameras worn by the body by UK police officers. Body worn cameras are evolving the information consumed by the different security agencies. In addition to providing important information on the health of the agents, the main use of these cameras is to

© Springer Nature Singapore Pte Ltd. 2020
S. M. Thampi et al. (Eds.): SSCC 2019, CCIS 1208, pp. 213–224, 2020.
https://doi.org/10.1007/978-981-15-4825-3_17

record videos useful in dangerous situations to perform subject and action recognition. To test algorithms suitable for data like these, we created Gotcha-I. Our proposal contains videos with different modes. The subjects in the videos are both cooperative and non-cooperative, in order to simulate the user's attempts to avoid the camera. They move along a path or freely and have been captured in different lighting environments. One of the innovations made by Gotcha-I is the possibility of working on videos captured by a moving camera. During the acquisition process, the camera speed is adjusted to the subject pace.

1.1 Related Work

As new needs arise in the world of video surveillance and security, new datasets are created to test recognition methods. In this section we will show an overview of dataset comparable with the one proposed.

COMPACT [2] is a biometric dataset focused on less-cooperative face recognition. Images are in high resolution but acquired in a fully automated manner. This allow to have real-world degradation like expressions, occlusion, blur etc.

Differently form COMPACT, UBEAR [3] is focused on ear images. Subjects in UBEAR are in movements and under varying lighting conditions. The subject can move the head freely and acquired images are in gray scale. In the outdoor environment we can found datasets as QUIS-CAMPI [4]. In QUIS-CAMPI, subjects are on the move and at about 50 m of distance. For the enroll of data, the same subjects were acquired also in indoor scenario and a 3D model of each subject is also available. There are full body images and, from them, a PTZ camera extracted face images.

In previous example images were captured by a camera, but in the surveillance purpose there are also dataset obtained by drones. In DRONEFACE [5], the authors focused on face tracking. This task became difficult to approach due to the distance between the drone and the subjects. For this reason, they built DRONEFACE, composed of facial images taken from various combinations of distances and heights for evaluating how a face recognition technique works in recognizing designated faces from the air.

Another dataset focused on faces on distance is SALSA [7]. Differently from the previous, in salsa we have a fixed camera network that record subjects in two different modalities, both in indoor environment. The first modality simulate a poster presentation, in which there is a presenter and an audience. The second modality simulate a cocktail party in which subjects are freely to move and interact.

All previous datasets are focused on one, or at most two biometric traits. However, recently, also multibiometric dataset were created.

As an example, MUBIDIUS-I [6] is a multibiometric and multienvironment dataset, acquired by drones and cameras. There are many biometric traits in this dataset as ear, face, iris and full body. Most of the modality are at less distance and with fully cooperative subjects, but there are still videos with less-cooperative subjects at distance in a outdoor environment.

Completely different from the previous ones are then the dataset captured with pose estimation purpose. In order to obtain an accurate ground truth, the most used dataset in this field are like BIWI [8]. BIWI is a face dataset captured by a kinect, that allows faces and 3D models of the subject captured in an indoor environment and in a cooperative mode. There are only 20 subjects in the dataset and only with face informations.

The proposed dataset Gotcha-I brings together all the features of the previous ones. This dataset provide a 3D model of each subjects, despite not having any image captured by depth camera. This make us able to perform pose estimation on real faces with a very precise ground truth as BIWI. As MUBIDIUS-I, our dataset can be used for multiple biometric traits due to the different distances and modalities. As in SALSA, our subjects can move freely in different modalities and as DRONEFACE we are able to perform the tracking of a subjects through different videos. We have also outdoor environments as in QUIS-CAMPI and a 180° videos of the subjects that allows us to perform ear recognition as in UBEAR. Finally our modality is more than less-cooperative than COMPACT because our subjects deliberately try to avoid being filmed.

In Table 1, a list of overall specification of each presented dataset is available, compared with Gotcha-I.

In Table 2 a list of annotation furnished from each compared dataset is present. Very few dataset has 3D models of the subjects and Landmark annotation, by which we mean coordinates of keypoint on the faces or bodies of the subjects.

Table 1. Reference datasets with overall specifications. C./N.C. means Cooperative/Non Cooperative Mode

Dataset	Subjects	Biometrics	Environment	Device	C./N.C.
COMPACT	108	Face	Indoor	Camera	No
UBEAR	126	Ear	Indoor	Camera	No
QUIS-CAMPI	320	Full body	Outdoor	Camera	Yes/No
DRONEFACE	11	Face	Outdoor	Camera	Yes/Yes
MUBIDIUS-I	80	Multi	Multi	Multi	Yes/No
SALSA	18	Full body	Multi	Multi	No/Yes
BIWI HEADPOSE	20	Face	Indoor	Camera	Yes/No
Gotcha-I	62	Full body/face	Multi	Camera	Yes/Yes

1.2 Security Purpose Applications

Videos captured by mobile camera with different environments are representative of surveillance data. In the last ten years, more and more countries provided their police officers with body worn cameras [9]. Differently from fixed cameras, mobile cameras has the ability to move around big spaces and cover big areas. However,

Table 2. Reference datasets with type of annotations

Dataset	3D Models	Landmark annotation
COMPACT	No	No
UBEAR	No	No
QUIS-CAMPI	Yes	No
DRONEFACE	No	No
MUBIDIUS-I	No	No
SALSA	No	Yes
BIWI HEADPOSE	Yes	No
Gotcha-I	Yes	Yes

data as images and videos from mobile cameras are quite different from fixed cameras due to the different point of view during recording [10]. Our dataset is proposed as a starting point to test algorithms operating on that topic and we will introduce some algorithms that could benefit from it.

Identity Recognition. A hot topic in surveillance is identity recognition. One of the most used biometric traits for this purpose is the face. In this sense, there are a lot of algorithms in last years that use faces to recognize a subject, both using neural networks [11,12] or mixed methods [13]. In order to do that, on this type of data may be useful use previously a head pose estimation method to select the most frontal frame. This aim can be reached with various algorithm in literature that works in real time, both with Neural Networks and without [14–16]. The proposed dataset also allows to detect a subject from other biometric traits like ear or iris, as algorithms in [17,18] performs. This is possible due to the different distance of the subject from the camera during recording. Thanks to the fact that this happens in the same video sequence, we are also able to fuse biometric traits in order to perform multibiometric recognition using different frames for different biometric trait [19–21].

Traits Classification. Not only the identity of the subject can be useful in security purpose, often we are interested in some physical traits like the gender, the age or facial characteristics in order to classify many subjects in few time. Regarding the gender recognition, it is often performed using face [22,23]. However, it is also possible to use videos in which subjects can move freely, also far from camera, using the gait as biometric traits [24,25] or data collected by mobile devices [26]. It is also interesting how different results are if we consider the cooperativeness or the non cooperativeness of the subjects, labeled in this dataset, as the work in [27]. Using the face or the movement of the subject we can also extract information about their age, as in [29,30]. This problem is often performed together with the previous one, gender recognition, to extract the most intuitive and general information about the subjects [31]. Once some characteristics are captured we may be able to follow the subjects along different paths and cameras, as our dataset allow us. This is called tracking [32, 33] and it is a very hot topic in security due to the ability to find the same people in different environments, in real time, without the need to know the exact identity of the subject [34]. For this purpose, if we focus our attention on face, there are various characteristics we can use to discriminate subjects, as in [28]. At the same times various classification and clustering algorithms were built in this sense [35–37].

In conclusion, taking a look at identification and classification of subjects in security purpose, our dataset allow users to train, test and perform very different algorithms at the state of the art.

2   Gotcha-I

Our proposed dataset stems from the growing need to extract biometrics from video surveillance data and from the need to understand who the user is, where he is and what he is doing. Gotcha-I dataset allows to extract different biometrics: the face, the nose, the mouth, the eyes, the ears and the periocular area. Given the nature of the videos it is also possible to extract behavioral biometrics from gait. Gotcha-I dataset simulates the acquisition of the body worn camera in which a moving subject is acquired by a moving camera. It is available for download at [1].

2.1   Content of the Dataset

To simulate real-world conditions, no accessories (clothes, hats or glasses) were controlled, they were left participant dependent. About the procedure followed by each participant, there were two recording procedures: (I) a cooperative mode with the camera where the subject walks and collaborates with the camera watching it during the walk, see Fig. 1 (top-left), and (II) a non cooperative mode where the same subject walks trying to avoid the camera, see Fig. 1 (top-right). The dataset contains a total of 493 videos with an average duration of 4 min, including 62 subjects, 15 women and 47 men in an average age between 18 and 20 years.

In order to be able to create robust systems, several possible scenarios were considered for the previous described procedures. The dataset is composed of 11 different video modes in different environmental and behavioral contexts.

The contents of the dataset are listed below:

- (EC1) indoor with artificial light - cooperative mode;
- (EC2) indoor with artificial light - non cooperative mode;
- (EC3) indoor without any lights but the camera flash - cooperative mode;
- (EC4) indoor without any lights but the camera flash - non cooperative mode;
- (EC5) outdoor with sunlight - cooperative mode;
- (EC6) outdoor with sunlight - non cooperative mode;
- (EC7) 180° head video;
- (EC8) stairs outdoor - cooperative mode;

Fig. 1. Some Gotcha-I dataset samples: outdoor sunlight in cooperative mode (top left), indoor with artificial light in non cooperative mode (top right) and indoor with the camera flash in cooperative mode (down).

- (EC9) stairs outdoor - non cooperative mode;
- (EC10) path outdoor - cooperative mode;
- (EC11) path outdoor - non cooperative mode;
- (EC12) derived files attached, detailed in Sect. 2.2.

All the videos have been acquired with the camera of the Samsung S9+ mobile phone; the modes (EC8-EC9-EC10-EC11) have also been acquired with an iPhone 10 and a Samsung Galaxy A5.

Illumination Differences. Some real world problems can occur regarding the selected illumination settings. Videos in (EC5-EC6-EC8-EC9-EC10-EC11) were captured outdoors with natural sunlight, Fig. 1 (top-left). Videos in (EC1-EC2-EC7) have been acquired in a room with a white background with the artificial lights on, see Fig. 1 (top-right). Videos in (EC3–EC4) have been acquired in the same room with the lights off and the flash camera on. In these video the use of camera flash can generate blur frames in some sequences Fig. 1 (down); as we can see, in this mode some frames could be blurred increasing the dataset complexity.

Cooperative and Non-cooperative Mode. In cooperative video sequences, the subjects look at the camera during the acquisition and follow the camera lens during the motion. In non-cooperative video sequences, the subjects try to avoid the camera during the motion, can be appreciated in Fig. 1 (top-right). This modality is clearly most competitive.

Figure 2-a shows the distance from the neck to the nose in a cooperative video and Fig. 2-b shows this distance in a non-cooperative video of the same subject. We can observe that the cooperative mode exhibits a linear behaviour, while the non cooperative mode behaves irregular. The differences in the regularity of the subjects pose in cooperative and non-cooperative videos have led us to carry out experiments on different methods to further analyze these differences.

Path and Stairs Outdoor. In these two modes the videos were acquired from different points of view simultaneously between three different cameras: Samsung S9 +, iPhone 10 and a Samsung Galaxy A5. Furthermore not all subjects are present. These videos have been created specifically to perform re-identification and action recognition algorithms. Our aim is that these sequences simulate a video surveillance camera acquisition, so once the face (or the gait) is acquired it is possible to re-identify it and trace it for the whole journey. Furthermore, the action of "going up the stairs" allows to perform algorithms of action recognition in order to predict if a subject is going up the stairs or walking. Example of different frames extracted from these videos are shown in Fig. 3 .

180° Head Video. The facial video sequences were acquired with the most favorable lighting conditions: indoor with lights on. There are 62 sequences, one for each subject, close to less than a meter from the face by rotating the camera around the head 180°: from the left ear to the right ear. The subjects were asked

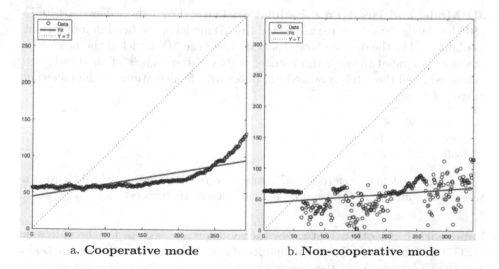

a. **Cooperative mode**   b. **Non-cooperative mode**

Fig. 2. Head-pose variation sequence for each mode.

to sit on a chair placed in a room with a white panel behind them, the operator then made the video by turning around the subject. This mode has the purpose of acquiring the facial details and consequently, can be used to analyze facial traits that require a high resolution of the image, such as iris, ear, profile, nose, mouth, and periocular area (Fig. 3).

Fig. 3. Different outdoor sequences.

2.2 Additional Metadata

Additional related information such as 3D-data extracted from videos is included in our dataset. It was possible to extract from each 3D model the pitch yaw and roll rotation of the face for the Head Pose Estimation.

3D Model and Head Pose Estimation Data. From the videos in "(EC7) 180° head video" we have reconstructed the 3D model of the head in .obj format available within the derived files attached. From the 3D model of the head adequately elaborated through the Blender software, the images of the head were extracted in all the pitch, yaw and roll poses with 5° deviations in the following ranges of values:

– Pitch $(-30°; +30°)$;
– Yaw $(-40°; +40°)$;
– Roll $(-20°; +20°)$.

For 62 subjects therefore 137.826 images were extracted. In Fig. 4 there is a subset of 25 images of the head pose estimation of the subject 62.

Landmark Extraction Data. For each video frame, except for the videos in "(EC7) 180° head video", the landmarks of the 2D pose estimation of the body and the 68 landmarks of the face were extracted using the OpenPose software [38]. This data is useful for gait analysis and performance action recognition.

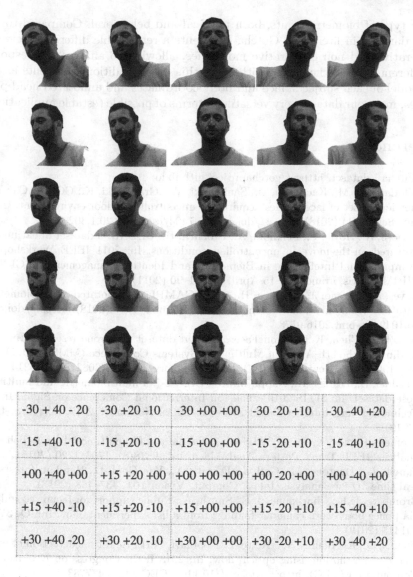

-30 + 40 - 20	-30 +20 -10	-30 +00 +00	-30 -20 +10	-30 -40 +20
-15 +40 -10	-15 +20 -10	-15 +00 +00	-15 -20 +10	-15 -40 +10
+00 +40 +00	+15 +20 +00	+00 +00 +00	+00 -20 +00	+00 -40 +00
+15 +40 -10	+15 +20 -10	+15 +00 +00	+15 -20 +10	+15 -40 +10
+30 +40 -20	+30 +20 -10	+30 +00 +00	+30 -20 +10	+30 -40 +20

Fig. 4. Above some examples of image extracted from 3D model of the subject 62. At the bottom the degrees in pitch, yaw and roll of the head pose estimation corresponding to the position in the table.

3   Conclusion

Gotcha-I is a multiview dataset built to meet the needs of surveillance data from Body Worn Cameras. With a total of 62 subjects in 11 different modalities, Gotcha-I results particularly suitable for tasks such as people tracking and recognition. The high definition and full bodies in video allow to perform different type of biometric traits, both physical and behavioral. Compared to the other datasets in literature, Gotcha-I presents a remarkable difference between cooperative and non cooperative modalities, allowing to analyze the response of different state-of-the-art algorithms on this data. Additional contents as the 3D model of each subjects, face and body coordinates and annotated head pose images, make our dataset very versatile in terms of possible testable applications.

References

1. Gotcha-I dataset. https://gotchaproject.github.io/
2. Włodarczyk, M., Kacperski, D., Sankowski, W., Grabowski, K.: COMPACT: biometric dataset of face images acquired in uncontrolled indoor environment. Comput. Sci. **20**(1) (2018). https://doi.org/10.7494/csci.2019.20.1.3020
3. Raposo, R., Hoyle, E., Peixinho, A., Proença, H.: UBEAR: a dataset of ear images captured on-the-move in uncontrolled conditions. In: 2011 IEEE Workshop on Computational Intelligence in Biometrics and Identity Management (SSCI 2011 CIBIM), Paris, France, 11–15 April, pp. 84–90 (2011)
4. Neves, J., Moreno, J., Proença, H.: QUIS-CAMPI: an annotated multi-biometrics data feed from surveillance scenarios. IET Biom. **7**(4), 7 (2018). https://doi.org/10.1049/iet-bmt.2016.0178
5. Hsu, H.J., Chen, K.T.: DroneFace: an open dataset for drone research. In: Proceedings of the 8th ACM on Multimedia Systems Conference (MMSys 2017), pp. 187–192. ACM, New York (2017). https://doi.org/10.1145/3083187.3083214
6. Di Maio, L., Distasi, R., Nappi, M.: MUBIDUS-I: a multibiometric and multipurpose dataset. In: SITIS 2019 - The 15h International Conference on Signal Image Technology and Internet Based Systems, 26–29 November 2019, Sorrento, Italy (2019)
7. Alameda-Pineda, X., et al.: SALSA: a novel dataset for multimodal group behavior analysis. IEEE Trans. Pattern Anal. Mach. Intell. **38**(8), 1707–1720 (2015)
8. Fanelli, G., Dantone, M., Gall, J., Fossati, A., Van Gool, L.: Random forests for real time 3D face analysis. Int. J. Comput. Vision **101**, 437–458 (2013)
9. Bromberg, D.E., Charbonneau, É., Smith, A.: Public support for facial recognition via police body-worn cameras: findings from a list experiment. Gov. Inf. Q. **37**(1), 101415 (2019)
10. Younis, O., Al-Nuaimy, W., Rowe, F., Alomari, M.H.: Real-time detection of wearable camera motion using optical flow. In: 2018 IEEE Congress on Evolutionary Computation (CEC). https://doi.org/10.1109/CEC.2018.8477783
11. Ding, C., Tao, D.: Trunk-branch ensemble convolutional neural networks for video-based face recognition. IEEE Trans. Pattern Anal. Mach. Intell. **40**(4), 1002–1014 (2018). https://doi.org/10.1109/TPAMI.2017.2700390
12. Guo, G., Zhang, N.: A survey on deep learning based face recognition. Comput. Vis. Image Underst. **189**, 102805 (2019)
13. Yue, G., Lu, L.: Face recognition based on histogram equalization and convolution neural network. IEEE Trans. Pattern Anal. Mach. Intell. **40**(4), 1002–1014 (2018). https://doi.org/10.1109/TPAMI.2017.2700390
14. Ranjan, R., Patel, V.M., Chellappa, R.: Hyperface: a deep multi-task learning framework for face detection, landmark localization, pose estimation, and gender recognition. IEEE Trans. Pattern Anal. Mach. Intell. **41**, 121–135 (2019)

15. Barra, P., Bisogni, C., Nappi, M., Ricciardi, S.: A survey on deep learning based face recognition. Computer Vis. Image Underst. **189**, 102805 (2019)

16. Abate, A.F., Barra, P., Bisogni, C., Nappi, M., Ricciardi, S.: Near real-time three axis head pose estimation without training. IEEE Access **7**, 64256–64265 (2019)

17. Chowdhury, D.P., Bakshi, S., Sa, P.K., Majhi, B.: Wavelet energy feature based source camera identification for ear biometric images. Pattern Recogn. Lett. **130**, 139–147 (2018)

18. Llano, E.G., Vázquez, M.S.G., Vargas, J.M.C., Fuentes, L.M.Z., Acosta, A.A.R.: Optimized robust multi-sensor scheme for simultaneous video and image iris recognition. Pattern Recogn. Lett. **101**, 44–51 (2018)

19. Sonal, Singh, A.: Review on multibiometrics: classifications, normalization and fusion levels. In: 2018 International Conference on Advances in Computing and Communication Engineering (ICACCE), 22–23 June 2018. IEEE (2018). https://doi.org/10.1109/ICACCE.2018.8441727

20. Bisogni, C., Nappi, M.: Multibiometric score-level fusion through optimization and training. In: 2019 3rd International Conference on Bio-engineering for Smart Technologies (BioSMART). 24–26 April 2019. IEEE (2019). https://doi.org/10.1109/BIOSMART.2019.8734162

21. Abate, A.F., Bisogni, C., Castiglione, A., Distasi, R., Petrosino, A.: Optimization of score-level biometric data fusion by constraint construction training. In: Wang, G., El Saddik, A., Lai, X., Martinez Perez, G., Choo, K.-K.R. (eds.) iSCI 2019. CCIS, vol. 1122, pp. 167–179. Springer, Singapore (2019). https://doi.org/10.1007/978-981-15-1301-5_14

22. Dhomne, A., Kumar, R., Bhan, V.: Gender recognition through face using deep learning. Proc. Comput. Sci. **132**, 2–10 (2018)

23. Cerkezi, L., Topal, C.: Gender recognition with uniform local binary patterns. In: 2018 26th Signal Processing and Communications Applications Conference (SIU) (2018). https://doi.org/10.1109/SIU.2018.8404587

24. Isaac, E.R., Elias, S., Rajagopalan, S., Easwarakumar, K.S.: Multiview gait-based gender classification through pose-based voting. Pattern Recogn. Lett. **126**, 41–50 (2019)

25. Barra, P., Bisogni, C., Nappi, M., Freire Obregon, D., Castrillon-Santana, M.: Gender classification on 2D human skeleton. In: 3rd International Conference on Bio-Engineering for Smart Technologies (BioSMART 2019) (2019). https://doi.org/10.1109/BIOSMART.2019.8734198

26. Jain, A., Kanhangad, V.: Gender classification in smartphones using gait information. Exp. Syst. Appl. **93**(1), 257–266 (2018)

27. Barra, P., Bisogni, C., Nappi, M., Freire-Obregón, D., Castrillón-Santana, M.: Gait analysis for gender classification in forensics. In: Wang, G., Bhuiyan, M.Z.A., De Capitani di Vimercati, S., Ren, Y. (eds.) DependSys 2019. CCIS, vol. 1123, pp. 180–190. Springer, Singapore (2019). https://doi.org/10.1007/978-981-15-1304-6_15

28. Liu, Z., Luo, P., Wang, X., Tang, X.: Large-scale celebfaces attributes (CelebA) dataset. The Chinese University of Hong Kong, Multimedia Laboratory (2015)

29. Pakulich, D.V., Yakimov, S.A., Alyamkin, S.A.: Age recognition from facial images using convolutional neural networks. Optoelectron. Instrument. Data Process. **55**(3), 255–262 (2019). https://doi.org/10.3103/S8756699019030075

30. Iqbal, M.T.B., Shoyaib, M., Ryu, B., Abdullah-Al-Wadud, M., Chae, O.: Directional age-primitive pattern (DAPP) for human age group recognition and age estimation. IEEE Trans. Inf. Forensics Secur. **12**(11), 2505–2517 (2017)

31. Rodríguez, P., Cucurull, G., Gonfaus, J.M., Roca, F.X., Gonzalez, J.: Age and gender recognition in the wild with deep attention. Pattern Recogn. **72**, 563–571 (2017)

32. Wen, S.-Y., Yen, Y., Chen, A.Y.: Human tracking for facility surveillance. In: Arai, K., Kapoor, S. (eds.) CVC 2019. AISC, vol. 944, pp. 329–338. Springer, Cham (2020). https://doi.org/10.1007/978-3-030-17798-0_27

33. Dadi, H.S., Pillutla, G.K.M., Makkena, M.L.: Face recognition and human tracking using GMM, HOG and SVM in surveillance videos. Ann. Data Sci. **5**(2), 157–179 (2017). https://doi.org/10.1007/s40745-017-0123-2

34. Lee, Y.G., Chen, S.C., Hwang, J.N., Hung, Y.P.: An ensemble of invariant features for person reidentification. IEEE Trans. Circ. Syst. Video Technol. **27**(3), 470–483 (2017)

35. Anzalone, L., Barra, P., Barra, S., Narducci, F., Nappi, M.: Transfer learning for facial attributes prediction and clustering. In: Wang, G., El Saddik, A., Lai, X., Martinez Perez, G., Choo, K.-K.R. (eds.) iSCI 2019. CCIS, vol. 1122, pp. 105–117. Springer, Singapore (2019). https://doi.org/10.1007/978-981-15-1301-5_9

36. Wang, P., Su, F., Zhao, Z.: Joint multi-feature fusion and attribute relationships for facial attribute prediction. 2017 IEEE Visual Communications and Image Processing (VCIP) (2017). https://doi.org/10.1109/VCIP.2017.8305036

37. Zhuang, N., Yan, Y., Chen, S., Wang, H., Shen, C.: Multi-label learning based deep transfer neural network for facial attribute classification. Pattern Recogn. **80**, 225–240 (2018)

38. Cao, Z., Simon, T., Wei, S.E., Sheikh, Y.: OpenPose: Realtime Multi-Person 2D Pose Estimation using Part Affinity Fields (2018)

Enhancing Enterprise IT Security with a Visualization-Based Process Framework

Tanja Hanauer[1]($\boxtimes$) and Wolfgang Hommel[2]

[1] Leibniz Supercomputing Centre, Boltzmannstr. 1,
Garching n. Munich, Germany
tanja.hanauer@lrz.de
[2] Bundeswehr University Munich, Werner-Heisenberg-Weg 39,
Neubiberg, Germany
wolfgang.hommel@unibw.de

Abstract. This work presents a process framework for security visualization that supports organizational knowledge generation, improves the usability of IT operative tasks, and improves the manageability of data and devices. The framework, as it was built, and how it can be used is described. The framework provides detailed instructions, makes the current status of the environment visible, and demands participation from stakeholders. With this concept, the quality of the used data is improved systematically, and also the overall IT security level of the organization. It consists of a visualization process (ask, manage data, visualize, interact) and a data management process (define data, acquire data, analyze data, ensure data quality, dispose or reuse data). This is illustrated with a proof of concept process run on vulnerability management. Besides, an implementation guide is provided in order to support the adaption of the process framework.

1 Motivation

This work presents an approach on how stakeholder groups responsible for IT operations, IT security, and IT management can improve the security of their organization. This means, for example, how to administer a heterogeneous environment with various systems. Also, how to operate, maintain and dispose systems, and how to configure and manage them according to security standards. A process framework, which takes into account that none of the stakeholders has sufficient concepts and tools at their disposal, has been designed. This framework also takes into account that management often does not understand how IT operations works in detail, and vice versa. Visualization is introduced in order to provide the management with an easy to grasp overview, and also to motivate IT operations to manage systems well and provide them securely.

It is important that IT operations personnel value, implement, and enforce security and also teach the end user accordingly. Otherwise, security will not be implemented properly. It will be circumvented during setup or deployment by the system administrator (sysadmin), or it will be forgotten as soon as the

S. M. Thampi et al. (Eds.): SSCC 2019, CCIS 1208, pp. 225–236, 2020.
https://doi.org/10.1007/978-981-15-4825-3_18

system is in operation, where only keeping it up and running seems important. Many sysadmins look at security matters just as regular users do. Quite often they think that they have more demanding work to do than fulfilling the "additional" security tasks. Implementing, maintaining, and managing systems securely increases the workload, complexity, and interdependence. Complying with security requirements, performing tasks securely, and implementing security specific systems and tasks, is time intensive and requires security knowledge. It is an integral part of their job to handle IT security. Sysadmins not only have to provide properly working systems, but they are also the most tech-savvy people, the ones who deal with the technology, and the ones who have access to and the knowledge about the devices. IT security has to be implemented by IT operations. This becomes clearer when some exemplary tasks are named. Server security not only depends on keeping track of the servers, but also on a secure installation of the operating system, which includes minimizing the attack surface. In order to minimize the attack surface, unnecessary packages must get removed, unneeded services must be disabled, the software has to be kept up to date, and access to the servers and their disposal have to be managed.

The visualization process framework supports implementing security policies to benefit the stakeholders. Existing approaches and frameworks handle information security, some even down to procedures, but they often do not take IT operations personnel into account, who has to implement them. The framework is a new approach, especially with its focus on the operational view and on usability. With this approach, security data can be visualized for the organization as a whole, including the initial configuration, monitoring, and maintenance tasks of IT operations to assist them and the security personnel. Our work introduces a highly accurate data basis embedded into an organization-wide process that generates stakeholder-specific reports and visualizations.

It is very important that the generated visualizations and reports are highly customizable, action-oriented, and that they display as few false positives as possible to minimize the burden of the system administrators who act upon the reports. The process guides the security practitioners from the initiation, where the environment is analyzed, stakeholder requirements are stated, and actions are planned, over the definition of the question and the complete data management to the generation of the visualization. It concludes by interacting with the involved stakeholders and the evaluation. The process character ensures continuous improvement and its organizational integration is supported by each topic-specific process run of Vis4Sec.

This paper introduces Vis4Sec and is structured as follows: Sect. 2 outlines related visualization processes. Section 3 introduces the Vis4Sec process as the basis for its following application. Section 4 shows the implementation guideline. Afterwards, Sect. 5 provides an example process run for Vulnerability Management. Finally, Sect. 6 summarizes the key results and gives an outlook on our ongoing work.

Vis4Sec	Ware	Fry	Marty	Balakrishnan	Burkhard
Initiate					Mental Model Sender
Ask			Define Problem	Visualization Goals	
	Data Collection & Storage	Acquire	Asses Available Data	Data Preparation	
Manage Data	Preprocessing	Parse, Filter	Process Information	Explore	
	Display and Graphics	Mine		Visualize	Attention
Visualize		Represent	Visual Transformation		Context, Overview, Options to Act
Interact	Perception	Interact	View Transformation	Feedback	Details
			Interpret and Decide		Mental Model Recipient
Iterations		Refine			

Fig. 1. Vis4Sec process framework compared to existing visualization processes

2 State of the Art

In this section, literature about visualization processes and a visualization framework is introduced and the requirements are described. It builds the foundation for the new process framework Vis4Sec, which is introduced afterwards. The visualization processes describe how to visualize data, taking into account the knowledge we have about the human brain and the recipient. We closely analyzed existing processes related to data, visualization, and security and compared our newly developed process framework to them. Ware's (2004), Fry's (2004), Marty's (2008), and Balakrishnan's (2015) visualization processes are summarized and compared to Burkhard's knowledge visualization model (Burkhard 2005). A comparison of their phases with the newly designed Vis4Sec is shown in Fig. 1. They all share the process character, but each of them has its own focus. Ware focuses on the visual perception, Fry on data processing, Marty on security together with the problem definition he introduces, Balakrishnan also focuses on security, and Burkhard focuses on the knowledge transportation from the sender to the recipient.

When realizing that it is necessary to develop a new process, a scenario analysis was done to state requirements. Two scenarios, IT operations and IT security management, with three use cases, were analyzed to put IT security into practice. Furthermore, the use cases were chosen from different sections: the highly technical and typical system administration topics in the IT operations scenario and the more (security) management oriented topics in the second scenario with a strong focus on compliance and vulnerability management. The analyzed environments, stemming from the scientific sector with scientific freedom and from the commercial sector with the pressure to be profitable and compliant, also made a holistic approach to the requirements and current practice possible.

3 Process

The security visualization framework Vis4Sec consists of the Visualization Process and the Data Management Process, whereby the latter is either an extensive Data Management Phase or a separate subprocess. This is shown in Fig. 2. The phases resemble the Deming Cycle Plan-Do-Study-Act and bring the IT Service Management orientation of this work to mind.

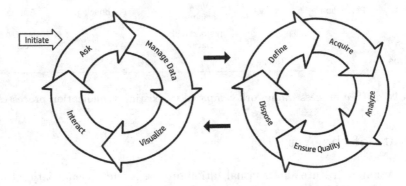

Fig. 2. Vis4Sec process framework

The phases of the visualization process are described in detail below.

3.1 The Initiation

The initiation takes place once for each process run and develops an understanding of the environment, the stakeholders, and the requirements to embed the visualization in the proper context. During the initiation, a team is put together that manages the visualization process by carrying out interviews, coordinating data management, generating the visualizations of the results, guiding the interaction among stakeholders, and triggering iterations.

Environment. The description of the environment is done with semistructured interviews, participatory observation, and the analysis of existing documentation. It results in a description of process properties on the topic in question, which is summed up in Fig. 3 as classification of the environment.

The stakeholders are named and described in detail in a separate section. The management process allows to map the tasks to recommendations and guidelines and those to an appropriate management process. Examples for guidelines are the ITIL Core books, the System Development Life Cycle (SDLC), or the

National Institute of Standards and Technology (NIST) publications. This makes it possible to develop an understanding of the relevant tasks, control gates, and goals. The protection goals – accountability, auditability, authenticity, availability, confidentiality, integrity, non-repudiation, privacy – relevant for the process run are stated. The security control is stated afterwards in order to define the main goal the process run should fulfill. It stems mostly from the Center for Internet Security Critical Security Controls (CSC) or ISO/IEC 27001 controls. The actual maturity level of the management process in question is named in accordance to the Capability Maturity Model Integration (CMMI). The actual usage of visualization in the current setup is also described.

Criterion	Manifestation
Stakeholders	IT operations ... IT management
Management process	SDLC phase ... ITSM process
Protection goal	availability ... integrity
Security control	CSC ... ISO/IEC 270001
Maturity	managed defined quantitatively managed
UsageVis	no partial yes

Fig. 3. Environment classification scheme

Stakeholders. The stakeholder definition specifies for whom the use case is relevant and for whom the visualization is generated. Their differing mental models and points of view have to be considered. There are various stakeholder roles such as executive management, business unit representatives, user community, human resources, information and communications technology specialists, and security specialists. To keep it simple, it is started with a group as small as possible.

Requirements. The requirements that the tool, the process or the visualization has to fulfill, are grouped into the following categories:

- *functional,* for example, Monitoring, Reporting, or KnowledgeGeneration
- *security,* for example, ProtectionGoals, Compliance, or VisualSecurity
- *quality,* for example, Documentation, DataQuality, or MonitoringQuality
- *nonfunctional,* for example, Specification, Usability, or Utility

They are weighted (necessary, important, nice to have) according to the use case. The requirements section describes the deficits in the existing solution and defines the purpose of the process run. It also provides the level of required data quality and the evaluation criteria.

Planned Actions. Actions are planned to meet the requirements. They are categorized into *planned* to be handled in the following process run and its iterations, *manageable* in further process runs, and actions that are *not manageable* in process runs or out of scope. They are environment-specific, goal-specific, or common for all process runs. Common actions are the following:

Fixing major security deficits that came to light during the analysis of the environment, *generating and distributing reports* and visualizations on the defined topic, *defining metrics* that measure the security objective and the process improvement itself (key performance indicators, KPIs), and *developing proactive measures.*

3.2 The Question Phase

The Question Phase 'Ask' checks the functional, security, and non-functional requirements to specify the area of the process run. It defines the question to be asked and answered by the visualization. It defines the specific topic about which knowledge needs to be gained. The problem to solve makes the resulting visualization useful and prevents it from being just a "pretty" picture without a message to transport. Also, basic criteria are stated in this phase to allow to evaluate the utility of the process run and to check whether it fulfills its aim.

3.3 The Data Management Phase

The Data Management Phase 'Manage Data' – or the separate Data Management Process (DMP)– ensures that the data is handled in its entirety. It contains the following phases: Define Data Model, Acquire Data, Process and Analyze It, Ensure Data Quality, Dispose or Reuse It.

It starts with one data source and is complemented with additional sources. In addition, a tool to manage the data collection is chosen. The result is a sum of data source imports – if carefully automated – that ensure data quality, topicality and as a side benefit the data quality of the data sources is verified or improved, which may be useful for other applications in the organization. For each data source a data model, naming conventions, and criteria of data quality are defined and the data is acquired to be processed and analyzed afterwards.

The relevant dimensions of data quality – validity, accuracy, completeness, uniqueness, timeliness, or consistency – are defined and ensured and the overall management of the data, like its disposal or reuse and possible automation, is defined.

3.4 The Visualization Phase

The Visualization Phase 'Visualize' puts into practice the requirements with a visual representation or report. It presents and visualizes the result from the Data Management Phase – managed data and information – for interactive exploration. The generated visualization has the aim to gain actionable knowledge for the single stakeholder and for the organization. This is supported by making best use of existing knowledge about visualization. The resulting visualization is used to generate visibility and attention for security-relevant topics. In consequence, the visualization creates awareness and discussion about a topic and contributes to enhancing the achieved level of security. The type of visualization depends on the question to answer, on the kind of data that needs to be represented, and on the features that need to be clarified. It also depends on the mental model of the stakeholders and their viewing and working customs. Guidelines for visualization generation are used to receive a good result, especially in the sense of a visualization that is designed in a consistent and simple way. Visualizations are also generated to present an overview, monitor defined parameters, report on them, alert, and to improve auditing.

3.5   The Interaction Phase

The Interaction Phase 'Interact' checks and improves the nonfunctional requirements. It delivers the results and ensures that the results are useful, usable, and the expected ones by the stakeholders. This is done with defined interaction points, communication amongst stakeholders, and the established feedback culture. The defined interaction points always distribute data, reports, or visualization to the stakeholders. They consist of the question or task given to them earlier, a few generic questions that need to be answered, and their required reaction. Furthermore, the feedback of the recipients is collected and added as knowledge and experience from within the domain to enhance the results and to transform individual knowledge into organizational knowledge. In further iterations, the feedback and requests from the recipients are used to refine the starting question and to start the next process run.

3.6   The Iterations

The Iterations 'Iterate' take place after each process run. They are additional process runs with the aim to refine or redefine its topic and to broaden its coverage to ensure stepwise refinement. They start with a conclusion summing up the completed process run, the actions taken, the results, and the added value. The utility of the process run and its results are evaluated in relation to the stated question, the consistency and simplicity of its design, and the quality of the results.

4 Implementation Guideline

The Initiation requires the environment, the objective from the security framework, and the area or phase as input and generates the stakeholders, the requirements, and the planned actions as output. It consists of these steps:

- The environment is analyzed and deficits are named.
- The stakeholders are defined.
- The requirements are stated.
- The actions are planned.

The Question Phase requires the objective as input and generates a simplified question, the definition of metrics, and questions for iterations as output.

- The question is deduced from a security objective or control.
- The question is simplified and reduced to its core.
- Metrics are defined to measure progress and to manage its development.
- The simplified question triggers the first iteration.

The Data Management Phase requires the simplified question, the key stakeholders and data quality requirements as input, and generates managed data as well as information and improvement for iterations as output.

- A data model is defined and a common format is chosen.
- The data is acquired from organization-specific repositories.
- The data is processed and analyzed and statistical properties are raised.
- The necessary level of data quality is ensured.
- Reuse or disposal of the data is defined and implemented.

The Visualization Phase requires data or information, the stakeholders, and evaluation criteria as input and generates an overview of data quality, tracking of metrics interactive information, visualizations and ideas for iterations as output. The visualizations are generated by deciding upon a type of visualization, optimizing it by using guidelines and by evaluating its usefulness.

The Interaction Phase requires visualizations, stakeholders, security deficits as input and generates communication points and intervals, required reactions, and feedback as output.

- Defined communication intervals.
- An organization-wide feedback system.
- Distribution of stakeholder-specific reports and visualizations.

The Iterations One iteration requires the conclusion, ideas, and feedback as input. It generates the need for further iteration, refinement and automation as output. An iteration follows this pattern:

- Conclusion summing up the actions taken, results, and added value.
- Refining or redefining the question for the next process iteration.
- The data sources, the reports and visualizations, and the interaction are considering their quality ensured, refined, enhanced, and automated in each iteration.

5   Proof of Concept Vulnerability Management

This section describes a visualization example for vulnerability management. To do so, the first iteration of the Linux server vulnerability management of a higher education institution's data center is described.

5.1   The Initiation

The Environment is a data center, which operates more than 2,500 servers. The servers are managed by more than 70 operating system administrators. It is an overall complex and continuously changing setup. It becomes apparent, when security-relevant questions are asked, that usually little knowledge about the concerned servers and their probable patch state exists.

The Stakeholders are the security practitioners and the IT management. The process run takes place during the operations phase of the System Development Life Cycle. The main protection goals are availability, confidentiality, and integrity. The security control to implement is the Critical Security Control 'Continuous Vulnerability Assessment and Remediation'. The maturity level of the vulnerability process is managed and there is no current use of visualization.

The Requirements are knowing the vulnerability state of the systems, prioritization of the results based on risk and timely mitigation of high risks.

The Actions Planned are generating stakeholder-specific vulnerability reports of the systems in production and their development over time.

The goal of this process iteration is to reduce the results to verified and actionable ones by checking if a vulnerable software package is installed on a server with that port externally reachable.

5.2   The Question Phase

'Continuous Vulnerability Management' (CSC 3) requires a constant acquisition, assessment, and taking measures on new information to identify, remediate, and minimize the window of opportunity for attackers.

This control also reminds us that "defenders face particular challenges in scaling remediation across an entire enterprise, and prioritizing actions with conflicting priorities, and sometimes-uncertain side effects." This leads to the question: *"What are the servers installed with (externally reachable) vulnerable software?"* The related security metric is: *"What percentage of the organization's servers has installed (externally reachable) vulnerable software?"*

5.3   The Data Management Phase

Daily port scans, organizational data, update scan and vulnerability data are the acquired data sources.

Port Scans are set up based on Nmap as the scanning tool, scanners placed both internally and externally, a scanning scope of almost fifty subnets, and scan intervals of 12 h. The resulting data requires organizational information to filter and distribute the results to the stakeholders.

Organizational Data is almost static, e.g., basic information about a device like its IP address, the system administrator's name, and the organizational unit operating it. This information is extracted from an organization-wide Configuration Management Database.

Update Scan Data from an update management system is prepared and imported on a daily basis.

Vulnerability Data is refreshed and imported from (a) the National Vulnerability Databases CVE[1] feed (b) the security advisories from common Linux distributions on a daily basis and (c) results from regular Nessus scans.

It quickly became obvious that the data quality of the sources is often unreliable, whereas high data quality is crucial to provide useful results. The data quality is assured regarding its uniqueness, timeliness, validity, and consistency by comparing the data sources and automating checks.

5.4   The Visualization Phase

For the security practitioners, interactive visualizations, that support identification of exposed servers and highlight newly disclosed vulnerabilities, are generated. The visualization is generated with real data from more than 190 externally reachable productive Linux servers. It informs on a per-server basis about vulnerabilities that should be mitigated in a timely manner as (a) they are externally reachable, (b) the server has the exact software package, and (c) version installed, the CVE describes. The 'CVEs per server' dashboard in Fig. 4 provides an overview and offers additional details about servers with vulnerabilities. It clusters them by severity (according to CVSS[2] score) and the number of CVEs and exploits that are publicly available. It depicts each vulnerable server as a bubble, whereby the most vulnerable servers are in the upper right. The highest scores are on the right and the number of vulnerabilities increases the position of the bubble. The size of the bubble depends on the number of exploits found, so the bigger the bubble, the more exploits have been found. The three dimensions represent the severity of the highest CVSS score (x-axis) found, the number of CVEs (y-axis), and the number of detected exploits (bubble size). Its design follows the Visual Information Seeking Mantra proposed by Ben Shneiderman in 1996.

5.5   The Interaction Phase

Reports with detailed information about the systems are generated and distributed among the security practitioners and the IT management. Continuous interaction initiated by the reports led, for example, to updating responsible contacts, changing firewall settings, and the disposal of devices. To increase the

---

[1] Common Vulnerabilities and Exposures (CVE).
[2] Common Vulnerability Scoring System (CVSS).

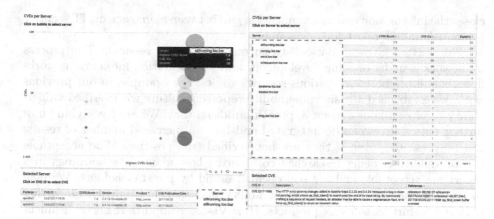

Fig. 4. Interactive display of the server vulnerabilities grouped by their CVSS score

significance of the reports, only true positive vulnerabilities are reported as the results are verified. In addition, feedback is demanded and the vulnerabilities and their mitigation is tracked over time.

5.6 Iterations

The process initially acquires the data sources necessary to identify servers with vulnerable software and provides an overview of the vulnerable systems. The results are prioritized by restricting them to the externally reachable servers. The verified results are distributed amongst the stakeholders and a feedback system is implemented. It also minimizes the workload of the stakeholders by providing the opportunity to act upon verified alerts rather than manually dismissing false positives. Further iterations are planned to automate the data import, to enhance the data quality and to provide results covering a wider area.

6 Conclusion and Future Research

The introduced visualization process framework Vis4Sec supports the generation of stakeholder-specific vulnerability management visualizations. Existing processes do not offer the required details and have made the development of a new process framework necessary. Hence scenarios and use cases were selected and a detailed process description for the visualization and the data management processes, including an implementation guide, was generated. The process framework was put into practice and has shown its usefulness as previous work has pointed out Hanauer (2018a), Hanauer (2018b), Hanauer (2019). Improving the security of an organization is a challenging task and, together with generating organizational knowledge, it requires the integration of various stakeholders. Vis4Sec supports mastering this challenge. Using stakeholder-specific interactive visualization and the process around it when generating the visualization, it closes the information and communication gap between management, IT security personnel, and IT operations personnel.

This section gives an outlook to current and future research. The process framework is under ongoing development and its integration into current workflows is still promoted for various security topics. For example, in our previous work, we established a basic vulnerability reporting culture with verified vulnerability results and our current approach builds on that. We are researching how further data sources can be integrated and how an increased number of results can be presented, even if they are not verified true positives. The acceptable loss of validity is being researched considering how many false warnings in a report are acceptable and are still deemed useful by the stakeholders. We plan to improve the coverage of our vulnerability management approach on further devices and further software products. How Vis4Sec supports the establishment of a vulnerability management culture and how stakeholders can be addressed best, is also part of the research. Therefore, the feedback of the stakeholders and their reactions to the reports is highly relevant.

Another area of research is evaluating if and how using Vis4Sec supports ensuring data quality. Currently, this is evaluated for the data management process as it is used to integrate data sources into a newly developed organizational Configuration Management Database and to ensure their quality. In addition, we plan to further improve the visualization process, especially the interaction phase, where we plan to conduct a long-term observation on how it can be integrated into the organization and how to accompany a change in security culture.

References

Fry, B.J.: Computational Information Design. Massachusetts Institute of Technology (2004)

Ware, C.: Information Visualization: Perception for Design. Morgan Kaufmann Publishers Inc., San Francisco (2004)

Burkhard, R.A.: Knowledge Visualization: The Use of Complementary Visual Representations for the Transfer of Knowledge. ETH Zürich, Zürich (2005)

Marty, R.: Applied Security Visualization. Addison-Wesley Professional, Boston (2008)

Balakrishnan, B.: Security Data Visualization. SANS Institute InfoSec Reading Room, October 2015

Hanauer, T., Metzger, S.: Stakeholder Specific Visualization and Automated Reporting of Network Scanning Results applying Vis4Sec. 11. DFN-Forum Kommunikationstechnologien, Günzburg, Germany (2018a)

Hanauer, T., Hommel, W., Metzger, S., Pöhn, D.: A process framework for stakeholder-specific visualization of security metrics. In: Proceedings of the 13th International Conference on Availability, Reliability and Security (ARES 2018), Hamburg, Germany, August 2018b

Hanauer, T., Hommel, W., Wüstner, Ch.: VESPER – a tool for managing Vulnerabilities and Exploits in Software with Portscan-Endorsed Results. Sicherheit in vernetzten Systemen: 26. DFN-Konferenz (2019)

Pipelined Implementation of Millar-Rabin Primality Tester Using Altera FPGA Kit

Qasem Abu Al-Haija[1,2(✉)], Ibrahim Marouf[1], Mohammad M. Asad[1], and Pankaj Mishra[2]

[1] Department of Electrical Engineering, King Faisal University, Hufof, Eastern Region, Saudi Arabia
qabualha@my.tnstate.edu

[2] Department of Computer Information and Systems Engineering, Tennessee State University, Nashville, TN, USA

Abstract. Due to the demand for large prime numbers to be used by many public key cryptographic systems such as RSA and SSC (Schmidt-Samoa cryptosystem), this led for the development of fast and reliable methods for primality testing to determine whether a given integer is prime or composite. Many algorithms were proposed by to address the efficient method of testing the primality of the integer number. In this paper, we propose a pipelined reconfigurable FPGA implementation for the primality testing coprocessor using Millar-Rabin method by employing the maximum possible parallelism of the internal operations. The proposed design targeted the ALTERA Cyclone IV FPGA (EP4CGX22CF19C7) along with Quartus II simulation package. The proposed design was evaluated in terms of the maximum operational frequency, the total path delay, the total design area and the total thermal power dissipation. The synthesized results revealed that the proposed parallel architecture implementation has recorded: critical path delay of 22.65 ns, maximum operational frequency of 51.11 MHz, hardware design area (number of logic elements) of 6184 LEs, and total thermal power dissipation estimated as 151.30 mW. Consequently, the proposed PT architecture can be efficiently employed by many public key cryptographic mechanisms.

Keywords: Cryptography · Number theory · FPGA design · Hardware synthesis · Primality testing · Millar-Rabin algorithm

1 Introduction

In recent years, we are witness that how communication technologies has been changed rapidly. This brings our attentions in the area of communication technologies and its security. Securing our data as well as transferring our data to the authorized user is very crucial task and securing is the key problems now days due to the intensity and complexity of the data. As the size and complexity of data increases, it leads to acquaint with the technology of Big Data and Internet-Of-Things (IoT) [1]. In addition, it increases the needs of secure communication to provide the user's privacy and prevent the availability

© Springer Nature Singapore Pte Ltd. 2020
S. M. Thampi et al. (Eds.): SSCC 2019, CCIS 1208, pp. 237–246, 2020.
https://doi.org/10.1007/978-981-15-4825-3_19

of information to the unauthorized users. As an outcome, several security techniques are used to deliver the reliable, secure, assurance of data as a group known as Cryptography.

The basic terminology of cryptography is a procedure where user's information (messages) coded into another form of text called Cipher-text. Three major practices are involved in the art of cryptography, including: converting message from simple text to ciphertext, the number of keys used to create the ciphertext which can be symmetric key (single key) or asymmetric key (two different keys for encryption and decryption), and finally, the method used to process the plaintext (i.e. the algorithmic process of plaintext-to-ciphertext change).

Accordingly, the symmetric key encryption (SKE) uses one key to do both encrypting (E_k) the plaintext to ciphertext and to decrypting (D_k) the message back from ciphertext to plaintext (i.e. $E_k = D_k$). Indeed, the most problematic issue of such kind of symmetric encryption is that all users involved in the communication process must interchange their encryption/decryption keys over the non-secure communication network prior to start exchanging a secure message. In other hand, the asymmetric key encryption is also known as public key cryptography (PKC) [2] uses two different keys to secure the communication process between the participants, that is, one for encrypting the plaintext (E_k) that is made public and another different key for decrypting the ciphertext (D_k) and made private for the authorized receiver only.

In other words, $E_k \neq D_k$, which means that the private key must be secured to safeguards that malicious persons do not misuses the private key while the public key is available to all senders who wants to send messages. Indeed, public key cryptography plays a key role to resolve many problems associated with symmetric-key cryptography especially at stages of key creation, identification, and encryption. There are several public key cryptographic algorithms that are in-use, such RSA [3] and SSC [4]. However, public key cryptography requires substantial computational power [5], since, its computation-in general-based on the use of number theory and modular arithmetic which are intense and time consuming thus it requires substantial computational. Thus, several fast number theory and digital arithmetic algorithms and implementations contributes to the overall performance of the coprocessors, such as the greatest common devisor [6], fast parallel adders [7], fast multipliers [8], and many other operations can be comprehended from [9].

Indeed, most public key algorithms requires the use of large key sizes comprising the use of large prime numbers with to guarantee the security of the system. Selecting significant large prime number is not an easy task even if we come up with a large number how to find the selected number is prime or composite (i.e. not prime). Therefore, we need to have unique approach to test whether the selected numbers are prime number or not. Such approaches are known as testing prime numbers or primality testing [5]. Testing prime number is a pure mathematics problem to find if the given integer is prime or not. There are several primality testing algorithms were proposed to address the prime testing problem.

Table 1. Primality testing algorithms

Primality tester	No. of arithmetic operations
Miller-Rabin	$O(\log n)$
Solovay-Strassen test	$O(\log n)$
Fermat Primality testing	$O(m \log n)$
AKS test	$O(\log^5 n)$
Baillie-PSW Primality test	$O((\log n)^3)$

Table 1 shows the most appropriate algorithms for prime testing [10]. The table provides the performance complexity of each approach in terms of *Big O* notation. Accordingly, only two approaches are nowadays competed to perform the primality testing of different applications, Miller-Rabin algorithm and Solovay-Strassen algorithm. However, Solovay-Strassen algorithm [11] is still under theoretical development and is not yet practicable. Miller-Rabin is one of the widely used algorithm for the primality testing as it recorded the highest throughput with minimized execution time especially when they implemented in hardware such as the FPGA kits used in [12].

In this paper, we propose a pipelined FPGA implementation of 64-bit Miller-Rabin Prime Tester that exploits the maximum parallelization of the algorithm partial operations. We are reporting on the performance of Miller-Rabin algorithm using ALTERA Cyclone IV FPGA (EP4CGX22CF19C7) device in terms of total design delay, maximum operational frequency, the area of the design as number of required logic elements, and the total FPGA thermal power dissipation. The rest of this paper is organized as follows: Sect. 2, discusses the system modeling and the implementation architecture to be applied to the FPGA, Sect. 3, presents the developed system and the evaluation metrics as well as evaluate the hardware synthesize results in terms of the cost factors of FPGA design, including: the total design delay from input toward getting the result, the maximum operation frequency in MHz, the total design area in terms of the number of hardware utilization of logic gates, and the total FPGA thermal power dissipated by the implemented coprocessor. Finally, Sect. 4, concludes and summarize the paper.

2 Implementation Environment

Generating prime numbers is a very essential part in any cryptosystem since they depend heavily on prime's properties. There are two main methods to generate a prime number. The first method is called Prime Sieve where primes in a specified range are generated. However, this method is useful if the need is only for an individual prime. The second method is the use of primality testers which are more convenient since the first method is very slow comparing to the second as well as generating many unneeded primes [13]. Primality testers are a group of algorithms used to check if the selected number is whether a prime or composite. Unlike integer factorization, primality testers do not generate a prime, but they state whether the input is prime or not. Some of the Primality testers are used to prove a number is prime where some are used to prove a compositeness. Thus, the prime number generation module consists of two stages of computations: generating the random number [14, 15] and then test its primality.

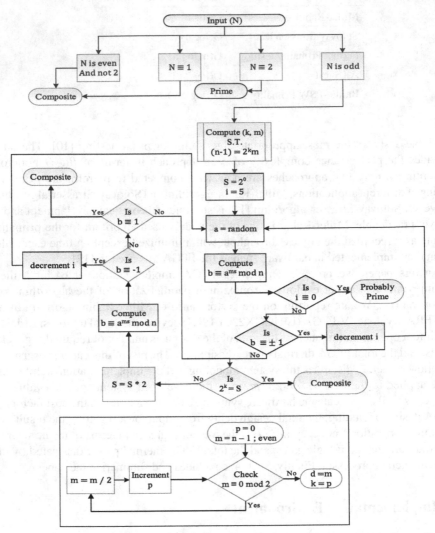

Fig. 1. Logic diagram architecture of Miller-Rabin algorithm exploiting the Maximum Parallelism

In order to generate a prime number, the random number generating stage should be followed by primality testing [8] phase to check whether the generated number is prime or not. The basic principal of PT is: Let n be an integer and suppose there exist integers x *and* y with $x^2 \equiv y^2 mod\, n$, but $x \neq \pm y\, mod\, n$, then n is composite. Moreover, $gcd(x - y, n)$ gives a nontrivial factor of n. Also, in number theory , a Carmichael number (also called pseudo-prime) is a composite number n which satisfies the modular arithmetic congruence relation for primes:

$$\alpha^{p-1} \equiv 1 \, mod \, p$$

Where: α is a random base used for testing and p is the prime number, for all $1 < \alpha < p$ which are relatively prime to p. However, this number is not prime!

Therefore, more sophisticated primality testers were developed and reviewed in senior design I report. As a result, one possible efficient algorithm is commonly in use for prime testing is Miller-Rabin algorithm [8]. Miller-Rabin algorithm is a probabilistic test used to check whether an input number is prime, or composite based on the basic principle discussed previously. Since it is probabilistic, Miller-Rabin test guarantees the compositeness of a number only and declare a primality with high accuracy. Accordingly, Carmichael numbers (i.e. pseudo-primes) are categorized into two groups: strong and weak. If a composite number n passed Miller-Rabi test with base a, then it is a strong pseudo-prime, otherwise it is a weak pseudo-prime. For example, n = 561 for base = 2. It turns out 261 is not a strong pseudo-prime since it could not pass Miller-Rabin test.

The complete internal architecture for the implemented PT is shown in Fig. 1. The unit encompasses two main phases as follows:

- Initial number test phase: if the number is '1' or even it will be composite. If it's '2' then it's a prime. If it's odd, then go to next test.
- Odd number test phase: it tests the number with random base α based on basic prosperity of primes. If the test fail, then it will generate "composite", else it properly "prime".

To reduce the probability of Carmichael numbers, the odd test is repeated five times with different base. After the fifth round if the number success the test it will be prime mostly.

3 Performance Evaluation

Prime number generators are vastly used in many branches of science, especially in network security protocols, simulation and cryptology (public encryption). If the generated numbers are insufficient or faulty, this could lead to the failure of the application. In this work, we have implemented a primality tester unit based Miller-Rabin algorithm utilizing Altera Cyclone IV (EP4CGX-22CF19C7) FPGA device as a target device to implement the afore PT coprocessor using structural VHDL coding as hardware description language along with Altera Quartus II and Modelism-Altera 10.1d for simulation and synthesizing purposes. An illustration of the target FPGA kit is provided in Fig. 2 below. To achieve the best performance, we have pipelined the partial operations of Miller-Rabin algorithm to exploit the maximum possible parallelism between the internal units to gain in speed and enhance the design performance.

Fig. 2. Target FPGA Kit: Altera Cyclone IV (EP4CGX-22CF19C7) device

Indeed, to verify the correctness and efficiency of the proposed PT architecture (provided in Fig. 1), we have implemented a 64-bit Primality Testing (PT) module-based Millar Rabin Algorithm. The top view of the implemented PT unit is given in Fig. 3. It's clearly seen that PT based Millar_Rabin unit is triggered by CLK signal along with enable line. The generated number can be obtained from the output portliness "test" which indicates if the results of the PT testing which give one for prime and zero for

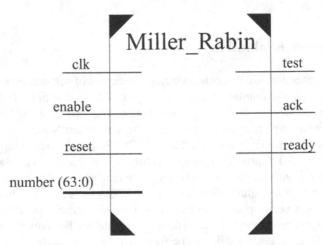

Fig. 3. Top level block diagram of the implemented PT unit (64-bit)

composite number. Besides the unit composed of three control input signals (enable, reset, clk) and two control output signals (Ack and Ready).

To illustrate the synchronized phases of the implemented PT unit, Fig. 4 shows the finite state machine (FSM) diagram for the implemented PT unit which is generated using Quartus II package for Altera FPGA devices. The FSM of implemented PT unit passes through eight synchronized modes before revealing the results for the test, this induces: set mode that is triggered by clk control input, initial values for the algorithm, set mode for initial number test phase: if the number is '1' or even it will be composite (mod_2 phase). If it's '2' then it's a prime. If it's odd, then go to next test (mod1__2 phase), the shift mode which started when number to be tested is odd (it tests the number with random base α based on basic prosperity of primes. If the test fail, then it will generate "composite", else it properly "prime"), and finally the clk is rested (reset_1_2 mode) to trigger the output (output mode) and initiate any new testing operation.

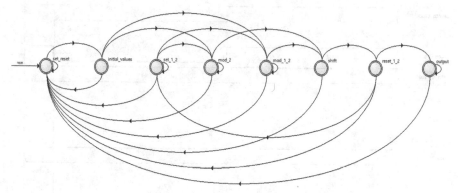

Fig. 4. FSM diagram for the implemented PT unit (64-bit)

Moreover, Fig. 5 illustrates a sample wave form numerical example of the proposed PT that is generated from implementing our VHDL code using Quartus II simulation tool. As can be depicted from the figure, we have performed the test for $4294967279_{(10)}$, and the unit has successfully provided the results as "prime" for this number. Indeed, we have performed many tests for almost 50 different numbers, where we tested all of them using our implemented PT unit, and the unit responded successfully for all them (we have verified our results using many pre-established number theory website such as the web-based application for prime numbers hosted by the University of Tennessee-Martin (UTM) [16].

Furthermore, we evaluated the performance of the implemented PT module in terms of area, delay, and the maximum operational frequency for different data path sizes. Timing analysis of the critical clock cycle for the implemented PT is illustrated in Fig. 6. The figure shows that the critical path delay is listed as 22.646 ns in which 3.081 ns for the clock delay and 19.565 ns for the data delay giving a maximum frequency for the circuit of 51.11 MHz.

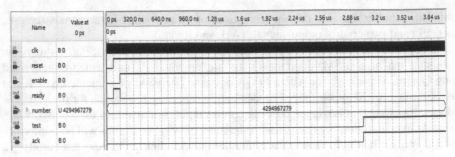

Fig. 5. Example of prime number test process for $4294967279_{(10)}$.

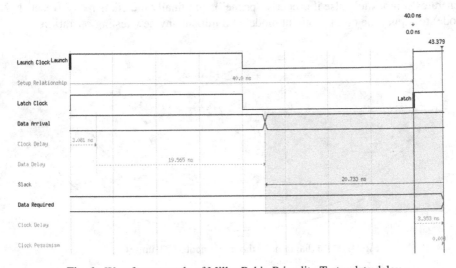

Fig. 6. Waveform sample of Miller Rabin Primality Tester data delay

In addition, the area of the design has recorded a constant number of logic elements (i.e. 6184 LEs). Each LE has comprises four-input look-up table (LUT), which can implement any function of four variables, in addition to many others registers and functionalities. Thus, the proposed implementation encompasses about $4 \times 6184 = 24736$ LUTs. Finally, the total thermal power dissipation is this design is estimated by using PowerPlay Power analyzer tool which is estimated as 151.29 mW.

4 Conclusions and Remarks

Prime testing operation is one of the most important operations for many public key cryptographic algorithms such as RSA (Rivest–Shamir–Adleman) and SSC (Schmidt-Samoa cryptosystem). In this paper, we have implemented, synthesized and discussed the FPGA design for Millar Rabin primality test module using enhanced parallel architecture. The proposed design was evaluated in terms of many aspects including maximum frequency and critical path delay, design area, and the total FPGA power consumption.

Also, the proposed hardware design targeted the Altera Cyclone FPGA chip technology using Quartus II and Modelsim 10.1 for Altera kits. To sum up, we have successfully implemented and synthesized the pipelined primality test (PT) module via the target FPGA technology for 64-bits and the synthesizer results showed an attractive result in terms of several design factors that can improve the computation performance for many primality testing-based applications.

References

1. Gubbi, J., Buyya, R., Marusic, S., Palaniswami, M.: Internet of Things (IoT): a vision, architectural elements, and future directions. Future Gener. Comput. Syst. **29**(7), 1645–1660 (2013)
2. Trappe, W., Washington, L.C.: Introduction to Cryptography with Coding Theory, vol. 1. Prentice Hall, Upper Saddle River (2002). Chapters 1, 4, 5, 7, and 7
3. Al-Haija, Q.A., Smadi, M., Al-Ja'fari, M., Al-Shua'ibi, A.: Efficient FPGA implementation of RSA coprocessor using scalable modules. In: Proceedings of the International Symposium on Emerging Internetworks, Communication and Mobility (EICM 2014), pp. 647–654. Elsevier, Amsterdam (2014)
4. Al-Haija, Q.A., Asad, M.M., Marouf, I.: A systematic expository review of Schmidt-Samoa cryptosystem. Int. J. Math. Sci. Comput. (IJMSC) **4**(2), 12–21 (2018). Modern Education and Computer Science Press (MECS)
5. Menezes, A.J., Van Oorschot, P.C., Vanstone, S.A.: Handbook of Applied Cryptography. CRC Press, Boca Raton (1996)
6. Al-Haija, Q.A., Al-Ja'fari, M., Smadi, M.A.: A comparative study up to 1024-bit Euclid's GCD algorithm FPGA implementation and synthesizing. In: IEEE 5th International Conference on Electronic Devices, Systems and Applications (ICEDSA) (2016)
7. Marouf, I., Asad, M.M., Bakhuraibah, A., Al-Haija, Q.A.: Cost analysis study of variable parallel prefix adders using Altera Cyclone IV FPGA kit. In: International Conference on Electrical and Computing Technologies and Applications (ICECTA) (2017). https://doi.org/10.1109/icecta.2017.8252011
8. Asad, M.M., Marouf, I., Al-Haija, Q.A.: Radix-8 design alternatives of fast two operands interleaved multiplication with enhanced architecture. Int. J. Adv. Netw. Monit. Controls **4**(2), 15–24 (2019). Exeley publication
9. Ercegrovac, M.D., Lang, T.: Digital Arithmetic. vol. 1, Chapters (1, 5), Morgan Kaufmann Publishers, an Imprint of Elsevier Science (2004)
10. Asad, M.M., Marouf, I., Al-Haija, Q.A.: Investigation study of feasible prime number testing algorithms. Acta Technica Napocensis Electron. Telecommun. **58**(3), 11–15 (2017). Users. Utcluj.Ro/~Atn/Papers/Atn_3_2017_3.Pdf
11. Agrawal, M.: Primality tests based on Fermat's little theorem. In: Chaudhuri, S., Das, S.R., Paul, H.S., Tirthapura, S. (eds.) ICDCN 2006. LNCS, vol. 4308, pp. 288–293. Springer, Heidelberg (2006). https://doi.org/10.1007/11947950_32
12. Al-Haija, Q.A., AlShuaibi, A., Al Badaw, A.: Frequency analysis of 32-bit modular divider based on extended GCD algorithm for different FPGA chips. Int. J. Comput. Technol. **17**, 7133–7139 (2018). https://doi.org/10.24297/ijct.v17i1.6992
13. Ishmukhametov, S., Mubarakov, B.: On practical aspects of the Miller-Rabin Primality Test. Lobachevskii J. Math. **34**(4), 304–312 (2013)
14. Al-Haija, Q.A., Asad, M.M., Marouf, I.: A double stage implementation for 1-K pseudo RNG using LFSR and TRIVIUM. J. Comput. Sci. Control Syst. (JCSCS) **10**(1), 1–6 (2018). University of Oradea Publisher

15. Al-Haija, Q.A., Jebril, N.A., AlShua'ibi, A.: Implementing variable length pseudo random number generator (PRNG) with fixed high frequency (1.44 GHZ) via Vertix-7 FPGA family. In: Network Security and Communication Engineering, pp. 105 –108. CRC Press (2015)
16. University of Tennessee –Martin (UTM). Prime number testing or Prime curios. primes.utm. edu/curios/includes/primetest.php

Realization of Re-configurable True Random Number Generator on FPGA

M. Priyatharishini[✉] and M. Nirmala Devi

Department of Electronics and Communication Engineering, Amrita School of Engineering,
Amrita Vishwa Vidyapeetham, Coimbatore, India
{m_priyatharishini,m_nirmala}@cb.amrita.edu

Abstract. True random number generation (TRNG) is one of the prominent research areas in present scenario of cryptography and security. It has been reported in the recent past that even TRNG encounters security threats. In order to ensure the security of the random numbers, entropy of random numbers being generated should be high. There are different approaches to generate the random numbers from the physical processes, ranging from jitter to chaos. Various schemes employing the jitter as entropy source have been reported. The usage of jitter in ring oscillator aids in obtaining a high speed real-time random number generation (RNG). On the other hand, the asynchronous architecture ensures high security, which has been implemented in the work. Re-configuring these two architectures develops a RNG with high-speed and security. The statistical tests along with internal tests are conducted to ensure security in the architecture. National Institute of Standards and Technology (NIST) tests validated the unpredictability and randomness of the true random number (TRN) generated.

Keywords: Hardware Trojan · TRNG · Security · Jitter · NIST test · Entropy source

1 Introduction

With the advent of Internet of Things (IoT), security has become a major concern for every physical entity. There are a number of attacks on hardware which becomes a threat to the usage of chips in secured applications. Different approaches to detect and diagnose hardware Trojan is another field of research [1, 2]. It is highly alarming that even the hardware modules like TRNG which are designed to ensure security in financial applications are subjected to malicious modifications [7]. True random numbers (TRNs) are pure random numbers, which does not show any pseudo random property at any long run [5]. These random numbers are generated from physical variations like thermal noise, chaos, jitter or meta-stability [6] as shown in Fig. 1.

In the classification, noise and chaos are implemented in analog component based phenomena. Analog circuits are more prone to malicious attacks than digital circuits [3, 7]. Thus, noise and chaos architectures are not considered in this work. The meta-stability is the uncertain state between zero and one in a circuit. This uncertain state can be sampled for generating the random bits. The Jitter based concept is the most

S. M. Thampi et al. (Eds.): SSCC 2019, CCIS 1208, pp. 247–256, 2020.
https://doi.org/10.1007/978-981-15-4825-3_20

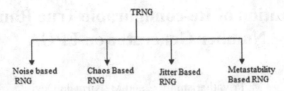

Fig. 1. Classification of TRNG

preferred architecture to generate the bit streams with true randomness because of the easiness to capture the jitter. Two different architectures confined in this work using jitter concept are Free Running Oscillator (FRO) based and Self Timed Rings (STRs) based. The inverter ring oscillator (IRO) based provides a simple implementation [4], while STR provides highly secured random bits [8]. Till now no attacks has been reported to the STR based TRNG, which uses jitter as entropy source. These two architectures have commonality while implementation, in terms of type of noise source used and method of digitization. Reconfiguring these two provides an advantage of providing security with less complex circuit realization.

This paper shows how re-configuring the architecture provides an advantage in- terms of randomness and hence security with effective resource utilization. Section 2 briefs the research methods that have been adopted in conventional TRNG architecture. Section 3 presents the proposed methodology. Simulation results and analysis of the implemented design is presented in Sect. 4. Section 5 concludes the scheme with suggestions for future scope.

2 Related Works

Conventionally, the concept of true random number generation had been attempted using Phase Locked Loops (PLLs) [5]. The analog PLL noise is the source of randomness in the circuit. The jitter is identified by using a correlated signal (clock) generated by PLL to sample the reference signal (clock). The ideal performance is limited between hundreds to several thousand bits and the capability of FPGAs.

The Free Running oscillators (FROs) Based TRNG design [9] is the modified architecture of that shown in [4]. This is designed such that, the post processing stage is not needed for raw bits to ensure the correctness of bits. Every ring is provided with an extra DFF to improve the performance. This is tested by DIEHARD and NIST tests. It provides a fast TRNG with less number of rings. The Chaos based architecture [10] uses well defined switching capacitor. Optimization is done to reduce the influence of supply voltage to provide enough randomness. The sequential circuits consist of memory elements, which may go to unstable state if not properly synchronized. This unstable condition is used to generate the true random bits in several systems [11]. Due to delay variation in clock and data path, setup and hold violations can occur. Sampling is done during this time give rise to random bit sequences. Another method of generation is by using Thermal Noises and are generated using ring oscillators to maximize the throughput and maintain the quality of random bits [12]. In paper [15], various trojan models are explained, in which triggering an analog trojan varies the temperature during the silicon nitrite layering process and it affects the IC life time. Analog processing increases the vulnerability to attacks and limits the performance. By replacing inverter oscillator rings with self-timing rings, a more secure random number generator is developed [10]. The properties of various types of TRNGs fir the two architectures are shown in Table 1.

Table 1. Various types of TRNG

TRNG	Type	Noise source	Implementation details	Limitations/advantages
PLL TRNG [4]	Based	Jitter	Altera FPGA	Restricted only to FPGA with analogue components
FRO TRNG [10]	Based	Jitter	Altera Cyclone II FPGA	Simple design to implement
Chaos TRNG [11]	Based	Chaos	Mixed-Signal PSoC	Does not provide high randomness
Metastability TRNG [12]	Based	Metastability	Xilinx Virtex 5	Delay variations in the system is checked to generate random bits
Noise TRNG [13]	Based	Thermal Noise	CMOS process of TSMC	Noisy Analogue Behaviors limits performance
Self-timed rings TRNG [9]	Timed based	Jitter	Xilinx Virtex 6	More Secure TRNG

In [4], basic inverter ring oscillators are developed to generate the true randomness in bits. It involves random switching at the XOR tree before registering the raw data. It is modified [9] such that combinational gate switching is considerably reduced. The PLL [5] is used to generate the random bits streams but it is dependent on the FPGA vendors. Analog component based generators also provide true randomness [10–12], but these circuits have high sensitivity to attacks [3, 7]. The meta-stability of bi-stable circuits are the commonly existing phenomenon, that can be used for generating the bits [11], by sampling the uncertainty caused due to the violation of setup and hold window.

Device independence with improved security and unpredictability are the most important traits of a good random number generator. From the comparisons made, Phase Locked Loops (PLL) based is more devices dependent and the aim is to generate a random number which shows true randomness and need to be implemented on FPGA. The Free Running Oscillators oscillates due to the delay variations in the gates. Those can be sampled such that the frequency deviation is almost same. Since the most secured one among these is STR based, it is used in the proposed implementation along with FRO. The challenging task is to generate high speed architecture with more se- cured random bits in a single chip. This can be accomplished by using reconfigurable architecture of both inverter ring oscillator and self-timed rings.

3 Methodology

The method used for the development of the architecture is shown in Fig. 2. Each TRNG consists of noise sources. The noise source generates the true random bits from number of oscillations in each architecture. The noise source can be IRO or STR. The ring oscillators are produced by connecting the odd number of inverters [13]. The feedback loop causes the inverter to oscillate and hence produces the unpredictable random numbers. The delay of all the components causes the period as 2X, that is X is the delay of all the components. The phenomenon of any electronic circuit involving a switching digital signal is represented as Jitter. The ring oscillator uses clock jitter to sample the data signal. The several equal length ring oscillators produce the jitter signals, which are sampled using DFF and then combined together using a XOR tree. Self-timed rings are basically the asynchronous ripple FIFO (First in First Out) memories, connected in the form of a ring [14]. The data transfer is accomplished using asynchronous handshake protocol. The protocol assures the even distribution of events through the different stages in the ring. The operation is such that upon request the data is sent with an acknowledgment. There is a forward input F and a reverse input R to a stage. If both the forward and reverse inputs are same, the output takes same value of forward input F. Else the previous value is maintained.

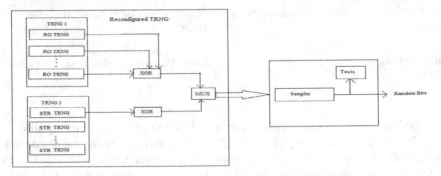

Fig. 2. Block diagram of the reconfigured architecture

The, raw random numbers obtained from noise sources are thus evaluated. The mode selection is done at this phase based on the requirement of the bits. The coherent sampling (CS) is the sampling procedure done for both modes, where CS is a technique, which allows a fixed number of samples to confine to the sampling interval. The sampling interval can be predefined, which makes it advantages without any loss in bits. Mathematically [9], it can be represented as

$$\frac{f\text{in}}{f\text{s}} = \frac{N\text{c}}{N\text{s}} \tag{1}$$

where fin is the frequency of sampled signal, fs is the frequency of sampling signal, Nc is the number of sampled signal cycles and Ns is the samples strength. The design should ensure that Nc and Ns are high and should be co-prime to obtain a high resolution of sampled signal. The random data is selected as per need and statistical tests are conducted for those bit sequences. The procedure followed is as shown in pseudo code.

PSEUDO CODE

Step 1: Generation of raw random bits by two architectures.
Step 2: Calculation for entropy of the raw bits.
Step 3: Digitizing the generated raw noise data.
Step 4: Selecting the mode of operation of TRNG.
Step 5: Securing true random bits.
Step 6: Applying Statistical Tests.

The reconfigurable architecture is as shown in Fig. 3. These two architectures provide two important aspects of the true random number generators; speed and security. The IRO oscillator involving number of rings connected together with the same ring structure is used to sample the data bits.

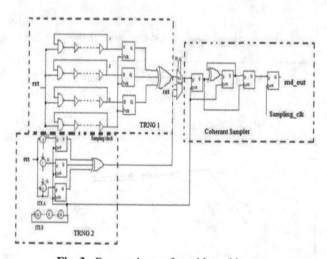

Fig. 3. Proposed reconfigurable architecture

If the inverter rings are replaced by self-timed rings (STR) are included, then the structure becomes more complex but provides an added advantage of security. These two architectures used on a single system helps the bits to be more secured with shared resource utilization. The several statistical test are performed to ensure the quality of each random numbers. The general statistical test suites employed to test the random sequence are from NIST (National Institute of standards and technology). The security level is evaluated and enhanced statistical analysis is done using these tests.

4 Simulation Results and Analysis

Reconfigured architecture is implemented and the results are validated using the standard random number tests. After the accumulation of the jitter, the jitter is sampled. The standard deviation of the bits obtained is shown in Fig. 4 for frequency measured (MHz) and in Fig. 5 for period measured (ns). The average count is shown in X-axis with respect to STR and RO based architectures. The jitter variation in RO is more in between the limits as shown in Fig. 5. The standard deviation of the bits varies more from zero indicating the randomness property of the sequences. The ring oscillator and self-timed rings are used as noise source when considering the jitter based sampling. Each Ring oscillators is connected to a DFF to form single TRNG unit.

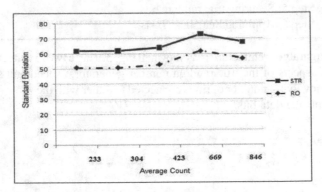

Fig. 4. Standard deviation in frequency

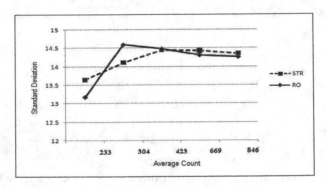

Fig. 5. Standard deviation in period

The standard deviation in frequency in each count is uniform and alike. At each count, the deviation is high for STR based TRNG compared to RO Based architecture as shown in Fig. 5. The average counting is done till 846 to determine the frequency deviation. Standard deviation is high for both when the count reached 699 indicating more variation in frequency from zero indicates true randomness.

Figure 5 shows the standard deviation in period for both the architectures. When the count is 304, the ring oscillator based deviates more than self-timed rings. This average count gives a high jitter accumulation since the deviation is high.

The number of TRNG units are connected together using XOR tree to increase the randomness. By replacing ROs in the above with self-timed rings (STRs), FIFO architecture is obtained. The power calculations for both structures implemented using Synopsys Design compiler are as shown Table 2. The power calculations are made in Watts (W). The ring oscillator TRNG consumes more than half internal power compared to STR TRNG. The STR architecture power consumption is more pronounced in terms of leakage and internal power. The area calculations of corresponding individual implementation are as shown in Table 3.

Table 2. Power calculations

Power (W)	RO TRNG	STR TRNG
Cell internal power	18.325	37.3103
Net switching power	186.27	0.1619835
Total dynamic power	204.595	37.4723
Cell leakage power	1.471	6.8288

Table 3. Area calculations

Area (nm square)	RO TRNG	STR TRNG
Combinational area	18.465	479.231
Non combinational area	593.043	1032.19
Net interconnect area	34.619	43.0398
Total cell area	611.508	1511.424
Total area	646.127	1554.46

The evaluation of the random bit's sequence is done using the NIST tests suite and the results are shown in Table 4. The p-value is the probability value which sets a standard limit for determining the quality of random bits. The p-value range should be more than 0.01 (>0.01) to say the numbers as random. The highlighted value is the values that are complimentary to the values of the corresponding tests of whole block. Since the architecture has increased its complexity, more resources are being used.

The resource utilization of different TRNG along with the proposed method is shown in Table 5, along with the entropy value per bit. The area is measured based on LUT count for the realization. The power and area are obtained after implementing in Xilinx ISE design suite. The aggregate of all the hardware modules utilized as per the exposed results in [16] are 71.25% of area utilization.

The implementation in FPGA indicates the proof of the concept being stated. The hardware implementation of the TRNG is done in SPARTAN-6 XC6SLX45-2-CSG484 An-vyl boards as shown in Fig. 6. The visualization of the output is done Mixed Signal Oscilloscope (MSO) of 100 MHz 4GSa/s. The Agilent 54620-61601. Logic analyzer

Table 4. P-values of proposed and simple ring oscillator TRNG architecture

Tests	Simple RO TRNG	Multiple RO TRNG	Multiple STR TRNG
Frequency test	0.1718	0.2495	0.4251
Block frequency	0.3504	0.3846	0.3258
Runs	0.1521	0.1864	0.6975
Longest run of ones	0.7048	0.8476	0.1758
Non-overlapping matching	0.2475	0.1446	0.3214
Overlapping template matching	0.4792	0.5224	0.1514
Cumulative Sums	0.2314	0.3148	0.2434

Table 5. Resource utilization's

TRNG type	AREA(LUT)	Power (mW)	Entropy
Simple RO TRNG	67	2.16	0.98
Multiple RO TRNG	523	54.72	0.999
STR TRNG	346	68.9	0.998
Reconfigurable TRNG	602	115.7	0.999

probe cable is used as the interface for connecting the oscilloscope with FPGA board. The coding is done in the Xilinx ISE design suite 14.7.

Fig. 6. Hardware implementation of the TRNG

The re-configurable random number scheme is essential in today's embedded system. The ring oscillator based TRNG are less complex compared to STR based TRNG with coherent sampling scheme. Both are combined together making the system more reliable by including the advantages of both the architectures. The power value obtained shows the usage, which is less than when both the architectures are combined without providing any reconfiguration.

5 Conclusion and Discussion

In this work, a modified TRNG architecture is proposed by re-configuring the architectures such that a RNG can be used for highly random and secured as well as high speed architecture. The security of the random numbers is ensured by validating the true random properties of the bits being generated. The inverter ring oscillators generate the bits so fast indicating the decrease in delay of the inverters in the structure. Even though the STR is more complex than IRO, it provides more secured bits for long run. The proof of the architecture being implemented is done in Xilinx FPGA upon validating the results using NIST tests.

In future, the chip can include the online temperature tracking system to evaluate the robustness conditions and ensure the protection against the hardware Trojan attacks. Metastable architecture can be incorporated with this by evaluating the delay variations of the system. Whenever system is encountering any delay variations and fluctuations in signals such that it may violate the setup and hold time, then automatically the system can be made to operate in metastable mode and hence generate random bits.

References

1. Sree Ranjani, R., Nirmala Devi, M.: Golden-chip free power metric based Hardware Trojan detection and diagnosis. Far East J. Electron. Commun. 17(3), 517–530 (2017)
2. Karunakaran, D.K., Mohankumar, N.: Malicious combinational Hardware Trojan detection by gate level characterization in 90nm technology. In: Fifth International Conference on Computing, Communications and Networking Technologies (ICCCNT), Hefei, pp. 1–7 (2014)
3. Bayon, P., et al.: Contactless electromagnetic active attack on ring oscillator based true random number generator. In: Schindler, W., Huss, S.A. (eds.) COSADE 2012. LNCS, vol. 7275, pp. 151–166. Springer, Heidelberg (2012). https://doi.org/10.1007/978-3-642-29912-4_12
4. Sunar, B., Martin, W.J., Stinson, D.R.: A provably secure true random number generator with built-in tolerance to active attacks. IEEE Trans. Comput. 56(1), 109–119 (2007)
5. Fischer, V., Drutarovský, M.: True random number generator embedded in reconfigurable hardware. In: Kaliski, B.S., Koç, ç.K., Paar, C. (eds.) CHES 2002. LNCS, vol. 2523, pp. 415–430. Springer, Heidelberg (2003). https://doi.org/10.1007/3-540-36400-5_30
6. Stipčević, M., Koç, Ç.K.: True random number generators. In: Koç, Ç.K. (ed.) Open Problems in Mathematics and Computational Science, pp. 275–315. Springer, Cham (2014). https://doi.org/10.1007/978-3-319-10683-0_12
7. Markettos, A.T., Moore, S.W.: The frequency injection attack on ring-oscillator-based true random number generators. In: Clavier, C., Gaj, K. (eds.) CHES 2009. LNCS, vol. 5747, pp. 317–331. Springer, Heidelberg (2009). https://doi.org/10.1007/978-3-642-04138-9_23
8. Martin, H.: A new TRNG based on coherent sampling with self-timed rings. IEEE Trans. Industr. Inf. 12(1), 91–100 (2016)
9. Wold, K., Tan, C.H.: Analysis and enhancement of random number generator in FPGA based on oscillator rings. Int. J. Reconfig. Comput. 2009, 4 (2009)

10. Drutarovsky, M., Galajda, P.: A robust chaos-based true random number generator embedded in reconfigurable switched-capacitor hardware. In: 2007 17th International Conference on Radioelektronika. IEEE (2007)

11. Majzoobi, M., Koushanfar, F., Devadas, S.: FPGA-based true random number generation using circuit metastability with adaptive feedback control. In: Preneel, B., Takagi, T. (eds.) CHES 2011. LNCS, vol. 6917, pp. 17–32. Springer, Heidelberg (2011). https://doi.org/10.1007/978-3-642-23951-9_2

12. Bucci, M., et al.: A high-speed oscillator-based truly random number source for cryptographic applications on a smart card IC. IEEE Trans. Comput. 52(4), 403–409 (2003)

13. Ma, Y., Lin, J., Chen, T., Xu, C., Liu, Z., Jing, J.: Entropy evaluation for oscillator-based true random number generators. In: Batina, L., Robshaw, M. (eds.) CHES 2014. LNCS, vol. 8731, pp. 544–561. Springer, Heidelberg (2014). https://doi.org/10.1007/978-3-662-44709-3_30

14. Cherkaoui, A., et al.: A self-timed ring based true random number generator. In: 2013 IEEE 19th International Symposium on Asynchronous Circuits and Systems (ASYNC). IEEE (2013)

15. Chakraborty, R.S., et al.: Hardware Trojan: threats and emerging solutions. In 2009 IEEE International High Level Design Validation and Test Workshop, HLDVT 2009, pp. 166–171 (2009)

16. Sklavos, N., Kitsos, P., Papadomanolakis, K., Koufopavlou, O.: Random number generator architecture and VLSI implementation. In: Proceedings of IEEE International Symposium on Circuits & Systems (IEEE ISCAS 2002), USA, 26–29 May 2002, vol. IV, pp. 854–857 (2002)

Secret Image Sharing Scheme for Gray-Level Images Using Toeplitz Matrix Based Stream Cipher

Shailendra Kumar Tripathi[1](✉), Bhupendra Gupta[1], K. K. Soundra Pandian[2], and Yumnam Jayanta Singh[3]

[1] PDPM-Indian Institute of Information Technology, Design and Manufacturing, Jabalpur 482005, India
shailendratripathi26@gmail.com, gupta.bhupendra@gmail.com
[2] Ministry of Electronics and Information Technology, New Delhi, India
soundra.pandiankk@gmail.com
[3] National Institute of Electronics and Information Technology & Kolkata, Kolkata, India
yjayanta@nielit.gov.in

Abstract. The need of providing secret image sharing allows us protecting the information in terms of data integrity, confidentiality and authenticity, which has become obvious in the past few years. However, in the construction of secret image sharing schemes the disadvantages; image size extension and loss of contrast are necessary to be addressed. In this paper, an efficient gray-level image sharing scheme using Toeplitz Matrix-based Stream Cipher is proposed to addresses these problems. The Toeplitz one-way function based key is engendered using the sequence generated by the register with nonlinear update function (NLUF) and the public-key. Further, it is utilized in generating the secured dynamic keystream. The proposed scheme helps to achieve single-fold image sharing, unlike the existing Chen's scheme. Also, the secret image is restored without any size extension and loss in contrast as well. The experiments such as entropy, correlation, differential, and the histogram of plaintext and ciphertext images are performed for analyzing the security performance of the proposed scheme. Further, the generated dynamic binary keystream sequence is analyzed for randomness using NIST statistical tests.

Keywords: Secret image sharing · Image size extension · Nonlinear update function · Toeplitz matrix · Contrast · Stream cipher

1 Introduction

In the openness of the Internet, numerous adventurers can easily plagiarize the useful information. Subsequently, how to adequately ensure the security of the information has turned into an essential issue these days. To resolve the problem of information security, image sharing schemes have been pulled in many

© Springer Nature Singapore Pte Ltd. 2020
S. M. Thampi et al. (Eds.): SSCC 2019, CCIS 1208, pp. 257–271, 2020.
https://doi.org/10.1007/978-981-15-4825-3_21

researcher's consideration because of the feature of imperceptibility, security, and not to devour much time in unscrambling. Image sharing is used to scramble the undisclosed information in visual form by splitting it into n shares and distributed among participants securely via any communication channel, and the undisclosed information can only be disclosed when a pre-fixed number of shares combined together. Then, many other techniques evolved in this direction with some limitations. In 1979, Shamir [1] and Blakley [2] postulated the method of undisclosed information sharing (k, n). It refers to scramble an undisclosed information into n shares and can only be reconstructed when they (at least $k \leq n$) combined together, less than k shares cannot extract any secret information. Also, the advantages of secret sharing schemes are; (a) no-key management, (b) loss-tolerance characteristics, and (c) ease of access control.

Meanwhile, in 1994, Shamir *et al.* [3] proposed a visual secret sharing scheme (VSS). In this scheme, to share the black and white pixels basic matrices are constructed, and digital image is scrambled into image shares by using these matrices. To clearly understand this scheme, Lena image is scrambled into shares for Shamir *et al.* [3] $(2, 2)$ VSS. Results are shown in Fig. 1. The disadvantage of this scheme is pixel expansion. Due to this, there is a size extension in shares and the restored image, and also lesser contrast in the restored image. Later, in 2018 Tripathi *et al.* [4] designed Hybrid Image Sharing Scheme (HISS) for binary images to solve the problem of size extension in shares and restored image, and loss of contrast in the restored image.

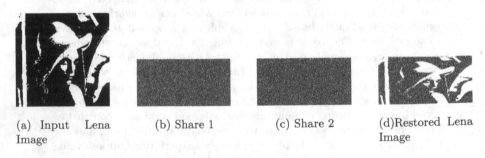

(a) Input   Lena   (b) Share 1   (c) Share 2   (d)Restored Lena
Image   Image

Fig. 1. Results for Shamir scheme

Considering, the problem of size extension and loss of contrast due to pixel expansion, in 2003 Thein and Lin [5] proposed the concept of secret image sharing (SIS) using GF(251). In this scheme, the undisclosed image is scrambled using the Shamir secret sharing scheme [1]. This scheme uses modular operation of GF(251) and the pixel intensities range 251–255 are truncated. Due to the truncation in the pixel intensities, the restored image gets distorted. Also, this scheme does not follow the definition of VSS because decryption cannot be legitimately seen by the Human Visual System. In 2007, Yang *et al.* [6] designed SIS using $GF(2^8)$ and solved the problem of size extension and loss of contrast as well. Later using the concept of simple modular arithmetic method few of the schemes [7,8] were designed, and solved the problem of size extension. However, in these schemes, the problem of loss of contrast remains unsolved.

In 2012, Lukac [9] designed sharing scheme for gray-level images using bit-plane methods. Then few probabilistic methods [10,11] were designed for improving the contrast and solving the problem of size extension. Also, following the Kafri [12] work, many other methods [13–16] were designed using the concept of random grids, and user friendly shadow constructions [17,18], goal-programming associated visual cryptography method without any size extension in image shares [19], progressive secret sharing [20] for binary, grayscale, and color images. Later, in 2012, Chen [21] motivated to improve the quality and designed a secret image sharing scheme based on Hill-scrambling [22] and random grid. This scheme solved the problem of size extension in the restored image and restores the image without any loss of contrast. The drawbacks of Chen's Scheme are; (a) needs key management (i.e., it requires to share the key to each participant, and random grid), (b) two-fold secret image sharing scheme (i.e. first hill encryption then XORing with random grid), (c) this schemes reveals undisclosed information after hill encryption (i.e., at restoration stage a single user can recover the partial information because of having the random grid). Although Chen claimed that his scheme is secure and restores the image without any distortion that reduces the storage. Later, Bunker *et al.* [23] observed the flaws in Chen's scheme and claimed that Hill-scrambling keys can be easily guessed and made the scheme vulnerable. The Hill scrambling remains no longer be effective in unscrambling since XOR operation is performed between scrambled grids and random grid, the results are already shown in Chen's paper [21]. However, to construct an efficient SIS scheme for gray-level images sharing is still a challenging issue. Keeping this in mind that to restore an undisclosed image without any loss of contrast in the restored image and reducing the size in shares, a scheme is proposed.

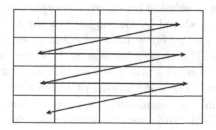

Fig. 2. The method of raster-scanning process

In the proposed scheme, the Toeplitz one-way function value is utilized in generating the dynamic keystream of the size of the input undisclosed image. Therefore, the undisclosed input image is divided into shares, where pixels would be scanned in raster scanning order (as shown in Fig. 2). In the proposed scheme, the key generated by using Toeplitz one-way function is considered to be cryptographically secure and works like a pseudorandom binary sequence that's why it is used in generating the secure dynamic keystream. Also, the proposed image sharing scheme is highly sensitive about the initial binary sequence used as input to register with non-linear update function (NLUF) called seed value. The various measures are used and performed to check the efficiency of the scheme discussed in the experiment as subsequent sections.

The rest of the paper is organized as follows. Section 2 briefly presents preliminaries techniques utilized to design the new scheme. Section 3 presents the algorithm to generate dynamic keystream. Then, Sect. 4 introduces the proposed scheme in detail using the generated dynamic keystream. Section 5 covers the experimental part of the work and compares the performance of the proposed scheme with the other schemes using some statistical measures. Finally, the paper is concluded in Sect. 6.

2   Preliminaries

This section presents the various techniques to be used in the proposed image sharing scheme.

2.1   Nonlinear Update Function

The register with nonlinear update function (NLUF) is used to generate the pseudorandom binary sequence. In NLUF, there are binary storage bit elements called as register are represented as $u_0, u_1, ... u_{n-1}$. The value of register from u_0 to u_{n-2} are updated by the value of its previous register such that $u_0 = u_1, \cdots, u_{n-2} = u_{n-1}$, and u_{n-1} is updated by nonlinear function $f(u_0, u_1, \cdots, u_{n-1})$. The update function may be either of the form $f = u_0 \oplus u_1 \oplus u_2 \oplus u_3$ or $f = u_0 \oplus u_1 \oplus u_2 \oplus u_1 \cdot u_2$ with representation 0, 1, 2, (1,2) for 4 bit register with NLUF. The initial value input to register with NLUF termed as a seed value. The register operates in a deterministic way. The stream of output produced by the register at the current state completely depends on its previous state. For n-bit seed value input to register with NLUF has a finite number of $2^n - 1$ possible states. However, an NLUF by using a well-chosen update function can produce a sequence of bits having a long cycle that appears at random. The applications of register with NLUF are generating pseudorandom numbers, pseudo-noise sequences, fast digital counters, and whitening sequences. Both hardware and software implementations for register with NLUFs are common.

In cryptography, LFSRs are the most popular device to generate the sequence of a long period with less hardware circuit-complexity. However, the sequence generated through LFSRs are susceptible due to its linearity property. Hence, the register with NLUF is utilized to produce the succession of a nonlinear sort with significant higher hardware circuit-complexity and randomness. However, in the construction of NLUF (i.e., the generalization of NLFSRs) it is not known how to construct them with a guaranteed long period [24]. Existing algorithms cover special cases only [25]. Further, with the security perspective, the output sequence of NLUF is utilized in the construction of the Toeplitz matrix one-way function to generate the key. The construction of Toeplitz matrix is addressed in the following subsection.

2.2 Toeplitz Matrix

The t-dimensional Toeplitz matrix is represented as $l_{p,q} = l_{p-1,q-1}$, $2 \leq p,q \leq t$. In Toeplitz matrix, same binary value is used along the diagonal. The t-dimensional matrix is shown below.

$$
\begin{bmatrix}
l_0 & l_1 & l_2 & \cdots\cdots & l_{t-1} \\
l_{-1} & l_0 & l_1 & & \vdots \\
l_{-2} & l_{-1} & \ddots & \ddots & \vdots \\
\vdots & & \ddots & \ddots & \ddots & \vdots \\
\vdots & & \ddots & \ddots & l_1 & l_0 & l_1 \\
l_{-(t-1)} & \cdots & \cdots\cdots\cdots & l_0
\end{bmatrix}
$$

In Toeplitz matrix, the initial row and column is determined by the output sequence of register with NLUF $t + P_k - 1$ bits pseudorandom sequence. The t states degree of non-recursive hash represented as H_v and k states the length of the public-key. The input to register with NLUF called seed value is $n = (u_0, u_1, \ldots u_{n-1})$, where n is determined as satisfying relation $t + P_k - 1 \leq 2^n - 1$.

The Toeplitz matrix has the trademark property, by which the value of the matrix column is achieved by the computation of function to the underlying column of the and shifting the value down to the previous column [26]. It shows that the value of each column in the Toeplitz matrix is the feedback for the next stages in NLUF. Further, the algorithm for generating the dynamic keystream using Toeplitz one-way function is discussed in detail in the following subsection.

3   Toeplitz One-Way Function Based Dynamic KeyStream

In 2016, Pandian *et al.* [26] proposed a methodology based on real-time dynamic non-recursive pseudorandom keystream using Toeplitz one-way function based stream cipher to transmit the ECG signal. The one-way property of this function is considered as the cryptographically secure pseudorandom binary sequence. The used stream cipher was byte-oriented in which keystream; the size of the key is 8 bits. Thus, the degree of hash H_v is $t = 8$-bit (order of Toeplitz matrix is 8×8) and the length of the public-key PK is $P_k = 8$-bit. Hence, initially Toeplitz matrix requires $p + k - 1 = 8 + 8 - 1 = 15$ bits, *i.e* is generated by $n = 4$ bit register with NLUF binary sequence [26].

This paper presents a generalized secret image sharing scheme using Toeplitz one-way function based stream cipher. In proposed image sharing scheme, the n-bit seed $u = (u_0, u_1, \ldots, u_{n-1})$ is used as input to NLUF with update function $f(u_0, u_1, \ldots u_{n-1})$. The output of register with NLUF is represented as

---

Algorithm 1. Toeplitz one-way function based dynamic keystream

---

Input: Public-key $PK = (P_{k_0}, P_{k_1}, \ldots, P_{k_{t-1}})$:, where $t = 1, 2, \ldots$:. Sequence
$u = (u_0, u_1, \ldots, u_{n-1})$, where $n = 0, 1, \ldots$; is used for initial seed in
NLUF with update function $f(u_0, u_1, \ldots u_{n-1})$. The output sequence
$l = l_{-(t-1)}, \ldots, l_{-1}, l_0, l_1, \ldots l_{t-1}$ with $|l| = 2^n - 1$:

Output: Dynamic KeyStream $(K_{S_0}, K_{S_1}, \ldots)$.

/* key $N_{Rk}[i]$ computation using Toeplitz matrix multiplication output H_v */
1: Assume $count \leftarrow 0$
2: The t dimensional Toeplitz Matrix T is constructed (as described in subsection [2.2]).
3: $for\ a = 0 : t - 1$
4:     $H_a = \oplus_{a=0}^{t-1} T : l_a \cdot P_{k_a}$ $where\ a = 0, 1, 2, \ldots$
5: end
6:     $for\ v = 0 : t - 1$
7:         $kt[v] \leftarrow H_a';$ // $'$ denotes the matrix transpose.
8:     end
9:     $for\ v = 0 : count + 7$
10:         $ke[v] \leftarrow kt;$
11:     end
12:     $count \leftarrow count + 8\ mod\ t.$
13:     $N_{Rk}[i] \leftarrow decimal\ value\ ke.$
14:     Further $T[(t-1),:]$ is used base for matrix with function $f(u_0, u_1, \ldots u_{n-1})$ (as described in subsection [2.2] will be used at step 2).
    /* State Initialization */
15: $for\ p = 0 : 255$
16:     $S[p] \leftarrow p$
17: end
    /* Psuedorandom Key Generation using key $N_{Rk}[i]$ */
18: $p \leftarrow 0;\ q \leftarrow 0;$ //Initialization.
19: $while(for\ size\ of\ the\ input\ image)$
20: $p \leftarrow (p + N_{Rk}[i])\ mod\ 256$
    for $i = 0$ go to step 1 and for $i = 1, \ldots$ go to step 2
21:     $q \leftarrow (q + S[p] + N_{Rk}[i])\ mod\ 256$
22:     $swap\ (S[p],\ S[q])$
23:     $K_{S_i} \leftarrow S[(S[p] + S[q])\ mod\ 256]$
24:     $i \leftarrow i + 1$
25: end

$l = l_{-(t-1)}, \ldots, l_{-1}, l_0, l_1, \ldots l_{t-1}$ with $|l| = 2^n - 1$--bit. Then, this sequence
l is used to construct the first row and column of the Toeplitz matrix. Thus,
required t-bit public-key $P_{k_0}, \cdots, P_{k_{t-1}}$ is available to all. The Toepliiz matrix
multiplication output H_v is t-bit. Thus, the first Toeplitz one-way function
based 8-bit key $N_{Rk}[i]$ is considered as $H_{(0\ mod\ t)}, \cdots, H_{(7\ mod\ t)}$, and next is
$H_{(8\ mod\ t)}, \cdots, H_{(15\ mod\ t)}$. The Toeplitz matrix for each $N_{Rk}[i]$ is constructed
using the last row of the matrix used in the $N_{Rk}[i-1]$ key. For each $N_{Rk}[i]$, the
same procedure is followed. The algorithmic steps are elucidated below.

4 Proposed Image Sharing Scheme

This section presents (2, 2) secret image sharing scheme. The proposed image sharing scheme is having two stages; dividing and restoration stage.

4.1 Proposed Dividing Stage

The steps to divide the undisclosed image are given below.

Step 1. An input gray-level undisclosed image I of size $U \times V$ is selected. Then, Key matrix K_S of the same size generated from the Algorithm 1 for a secretly chosen seed value. Also, seed value is divided into shares using one degree of the polynomial.

Step 2. Convert from decimal value to binary value to undisclosed image and key matrix as well.

Step 3. Select one gray-level pixel (8 binary bits) from both matrices and perform XOR operation between them. Find two scrambled grid 1 and 2 by using methodology (Sect. 4.2), where gray-level pixels are scanned in raster-scanning order.

Step 4. Convert from binary value to decimal value and distribute two scrambled grid 1 and 2 with the size $M \times N/2$ in different participants along with shared seed value.

4.2 Proposed Restoration Stage

The steps to restore the undisclosed image are given below.

Step 1. Receive scrambled grid 1 and 2 with the shared seed values. Then, by constructing the Vandermonde matrix system of linear equations is solved to recover the seed value.

Step 2. Convert scrambled grid 1 and 2 from decimal to a binary value.

Step 3. Successively take one gray-level pixel (8 bits), first from scrambled grid 1, then 2 (in alternate order, the methodology (Sect. 4.2) is given below) and generate dynamic keystream by the Algorithm (1 using received seed value and also convert it from decimal to a binary value). Then, perform XOR operation between them and restore the original undisclosed image I.

Step 4. Convert from binary value to decimal and recover the original undisclosed image without any distortion.

Here, I is an input image, and K_S is the dynamic keystream. The methodology for performing the XOR operation at step 3 for both dividing and restoring stage is given below.

Methodology for Performing XOR Operation in Step 3 for Both Proposed and Diving Stage

Proposed dividing stage	Proposed restoration stage
Assume $jj_1, jj_2 \leftarrow 1$	Assume $jj_1, jj_2 \leftarrow 1$
for $i = 1 : U$	for $i = 1 : U$
for $j = 1 : V$	for $j = 1 : V$
if j is odd	if j is odd
$Sg1(i, jj_1) = I(i,j) \oplus K_S(i,j)$	$I(i,j) = Sg1(i, jj_1) \oplus K_S(i,j)$
$jj_1 \leftarrow jj_1 + 1$	$jj_1 \leftarrow jj_1 + 1$
else	else
$Sg2(i, jj_2) = I(i,j) \oplus K_S(i,j)$	$I(i,jj) = Sg2(i, jj_2) \oplus K_S(i,j)$
$jj_2 \leftarrow jj_2 + 1$	$jj_2 \leftarrow jj_2 + 1$
end	end
end	end
$jj_1 \leftarrow 1$	$jj_1 \leftarrow 1$
$jj_2 \leftarrow 1$	$jj_2 \leftarrow 1$
end	end

The detailed methodology of the dividing and sharing stage is shown in Fig. 3.

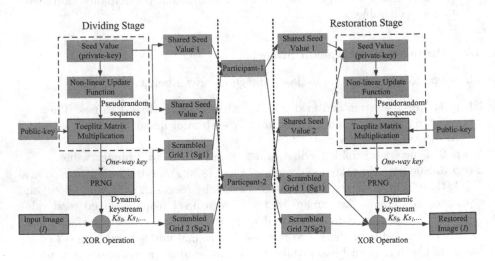

Fig. 3. Methodology: proposed scheme for diving and sharing stage

5   Experimental Results and Analyses

This section briefs the experimental results for the gray-level Lena image of size 512×512. In experiment, 10-bit register with nonlinear update function (NLUF) is used to generate the Toeplitz one-way function based stream cipher by using the update function $f = 0, 1, 2, (8, 9)$. The experiment is performed by using 10-bit; 0, 1, 1, 0, 0, 1, 0, 0, 0, 1 seed value input to NLUF. NLUF using $f = 0, 1, 2, (8, 9)$ generates 1023-bit (i.e., equal to $2^{10} - 1$) pseudorandom sequence. By utilizing this sequence Toeplitz matrix is constructed of size 512×512. Then, the 512-bit key $N_{Rk}[i]$ is generated through multiplication of Toeplitz matrix with 512-bit public-key $P_k = 0, 0, \ldots, 1, 1, 0, 1$ (i. e., publically announced). For the next $N_{Rk}[i+1]$ the Toeplitz matrix is constructed using the last row of Toeplitz matrix used in the computation of $N_{Rk}[i]$, and same procedure is followed in the computation of all keys. Then, these keys are used in generating the secure and dynamic keystream $K_{S_0}, K_{S_1}, \ldots$. These steps are explained in Algorithm 1. Next, by following the steps of the dividing stage of proposed image sharing scheme, scrambled grid 1 and 2 are generated and distributed in two different participants along with the seed value. Thus, both participants are combined together and generating the keystream by using the shard seed value through Algorithm 1. Then, by following the steps of the restoration stage of the proposed image sharing scheme, restore the shared undisclosed image from two scrambled grid 1 and 2. Results for Lena image are shown in Fig. 4. Also, the experiment is performed by one bit altering the seed (i.e., **1**, 1, 1, 0, 0, 1, 0, 0, 0, 1) with the same algorithm at restoration stage of the proposed image sharing scheme. It is seen in Fig. 4(e) that how the result is unavailing the undisclosed information for Lena image.

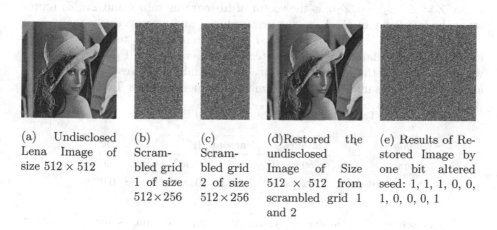

(a) Undisclosed Lena Image of size 512×512

(b) Scrambled grid 1 of size 512×256

(c) Scrambled grid 2 of size 512×256

(d)Restored the undisclosed Image of Size 512×512 from scrambled grid 1 and 2

(e) Results of Restored Image by one bit altered seed: 1, 1, 1, 0, 0, 1, 0, 0, 0, 1

Fig. 4. Results for proposed scheme using Lena image

5.1 Histogram of the Plaintext and Ciphered Images

The histogram of an image gives information about the distribution of its pixel values that have been calculated for the undisclosed Lena image and shown in Fig. 5. In histogram plots, pixel distributions are fairly uniform for scrambled images and significantly different from the undisclosed test images. However, the histogram is used for visual inspection, and variance of the histograms is another useful metric (see ref. [27]). The formula is defined as follows:

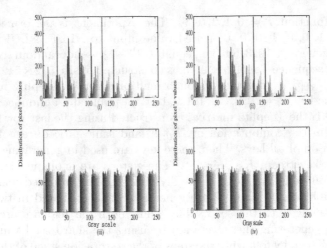

Fig. 5. (i) Histogram of the undisclosed Lena image, (ii) Histogram of the restored Lena image, (iii) Histogram of scrambled Lena image, (iv) Histogram of scrambled Lena image by one bit seed

$$\mathrm{Var}(Z) = \frac{1}{n^2} \sum_{i=1}^{n} \sum_{j=1}^{n} \frac{1}{2}(Z_i - Z_j)^2 \tag{1}$$

where $Z = Z_1, Z_2, \cdots, Z_{256}$ is the vector of histograms values and Z_i, Z_j represents the frequency of pixels having gray values i and j respectively.

The variance is calculated by Eq. 1 for the undisclosed test and scramble images (also calculated by one-bit altered seed), shown in Table 1. The lower variance indicates the higher uniformity and scrambled images have fewer variances compared to undisclosed Lena image and mentioned in Table 1.

Table 1. Performance measure of Lena image

Image	Variance	Entropy	HC	VC	DC
Lena	4.5694×10^4	7.5983	0.962	0.988	0.0992
Scrambled Lena	1.2026×10^5	7.9581	0.0015	0.0008	0.0005

The closeness of variances for different scrambled images for given input undisclosed test image indicates that both images have higher uniformity in distribution when the seed value used for scrambling varies.

5.2   Entropy Analysis

Entropy is the measurement of randomness or disorderedness of the system, that has been calculated by the following equation (see ref. [27]).

$$H = \sum_{i=1}^{2^k} p(m_i) \, log_2(p(m_i)). \tag{2}$$

The entropy is calculated for the Lena and scrambled Lena image with seed value $(0, 1, 1, 0, 0, 1, 0, 0, 0, 1)$. The calculated values are shown in Table 1. It is very clear from the calculated values that the entropy value of the scrambled image is greater than the undisclosed test image causes more randomness in scrambled image.

5.3 Correlation Analysis

For correlation analysis, the randomly chosen pairs of two adjacent pixels i.e., $R = 80$ from an input undisclosed image are selected. Then, correlation coefficients for these selected pairs of two adjacent pixels are calculated in horizontal, vertical and in diagonal directions by following formula (see ref. [27]).

$$Coef_{pq} = \frac{cov(p, q)}{\sqrt{var(p)}\sqrt{var(q)}}, \tag{3}$$

where

$$cov(p, q) = \frac{1}{R}\sum_{i=1}^{R}(p_i - E(p))(q_i - E(q)) \tag{4}$$

with $E(p) = \frac{1}{R}\sum_{i=1}^{R}(p_i)$ and $var(p) = \frac{1}{R}\sum_{i=1}^{R}(p_i - E(p))^2$.

The calculated correlation coefficients in vertical, horizontal and in diagonal directions for undisclosed Lena image mentioned in Table 1. It is noted that the adjacent pixels exhibit a very high correlation for undisclosed Lena and very low correlation for scrambled images. This is expected for a good scrambled image.

5.4 Pixel Similarity Analysis

The Number of Pixel Change Rate (NPCR) and UACI (Unified Average Changing Intensity) are two important measures to compute the pixel similarity between two random-like images. These are calculated by the following mathematical expression.

$$NPCR = \frac{1}{UV}\sum_{x=1}^{U}\sum_{y=1}^{V}D(x, y), \tag{5}$$

where

$$D(x, y) = \begin{cases} 0, & \text{if Im } S_1(x, y) = \text{Im } S_2(x, y). \\ 1, & \text{if Im } S_1(x, y) \neq \text{Im } S_2(x, y). \end{cases} \tag{6}$$

$$UACI = \frac{100}{UV}\sum_{x=1}^{U}\sum_{y=1}^{V}\frac{|\text{Im } S_1(x, y) - \text{Im } S_2(x, y)|}{255}. \tag{7}$$

The calculated values of NPCR and UACI for undisclosed Lena image is mentioned in Table 2 for two scrambled image (i.e., one is the for altered seed).

Table 2. NPCR and UACI

Image pair	NPCR	UACI
Scrambled Lena 1 and 2	99.61	33.42

From Table 2, it is observed that the NPCR value is 99.6121 which leads to the conclusion that the dissimilarity is good between scrambled images. The average value of UACI (32.30%), indicates that altering one bit in the seed is enough to find the dissimilarity between scrambled images. Further, the randomness test is performed for the generated dynamic keystream in the following subsection.

5.5 Randomness Tests

The randomness test is evaluated using the NIST statistical test suit [28] to measure the robustness of the generated dynamic keystream using Toeplitz one-way function. Also, the statistical test is used to distinguish the deviance of dynamic keystream sequence from a pseudorandom sequence. The statistical test is performed by using few number of random bits stream sequence of 2^{15}-$bits$ generated by the 10-bit register with NLUF (by using the function $f = 0, 1, 2, (8, 9)$) with different initial seeds.

Table 3. Key sequences randomness test $(\beta = 0.01)$ $^*p$-value **(Trail probability)**

NIST statistical test suites [28]	Proposed dynamic keystream
Serial Test$^\sharp$	0.187832
Lempel-Ziv Compression Test	1.000000
Approximate Entropy Test	0.024334
Linear Complexity	0.481201
Overlapping Template of All Ones Test	0.148912
FFT Test	0.821922
Block Frequency Test	0.987992
Frequency Test	0.963449
Runs Test	0.0922871
Non periodic Templates Test$^\sharp$	0.822550
Rank Test	0.1798002
Longest Runs of Ones Test	0.215332
Random Excursion (variant) Test	0.671135
Universal Statistical Test	0.621058
Cumulative Sums (Forward) Test	0.932146
Cumulative Sums (Reverse) Test	0.946802

* Result passes for value $(p \geq \beta)$, $\sharp$ represents multiples tests

Table 4. Comparison of proposed scheme with few existing image sharing schemes

Image sharing scheme	Undisclosed image size	Image share size	Loss of contrast
Yang's [10] Image sharing scheme	Binary $(U \times V)$	$(U \times V)$	Yes
Shyu's [14] Image sharing	Binary, Gray-level, color $(U \times V)$	$(U \times V)$	Yes
Chen's *et al.* [16] Image sharing	Binary $(U \times V)$	$(U \times V)$	Yes
Chen's [21] Image sharing	Gray-level $(U \times V)$	$(MU \times V/2)$	No, Two-fold sharing scheme
Proposed scheme	Gray-level $(U \times V)$	$(U \times V/2)$	No, Single-fold sharing scheme

In the statistical randomness test for a pseudorandom sequence [28] of the generated dynamic keystream is evaluated by p-value $\geq \beta$ where p represents the trail probability. The calculated trail probability would postulate the confidence of 99%. Here, β of 0.01 states except for 1 sequence of 100 sequences to be rejected. By using the method specified in statistical NIST [28], the randomness test is performed and results are shown in Table 3, where $\sharp$ represents multiples tests. Two serial tests are performed and one of the values mentioned and the same for Non-periodic templates test passes 143 tests out of 147 tests. From the results, it permits the randomness statistical test suit properties with the calculated p-value is greater than 0.01, as pass the test binary dynamic keystream sequence to be random. This is helpful to protect from adversary threat.

Further, a comparison Table 4 is made with some existing schemes. In the proposed scheme, there is no size extension in images shares as well as in restored image. Also, there is no loss of contrast in the restored image.

6   Conclusion

In this paper, the proposed image sharing scheme is used to scramble the undisclosed image into shares by using the Toeplitz one-way function based stream cipher. The multiplication of Toeplitz matrix and public-key provides the diffusion in the keystream. The proposed image sharing scheme is a single-fold sharing scheme, which does not suffer the problem of size extension and restores the image without any loss of contrast. The NPCR value (99.61%) and UACI (33.42%) state that the proposed image sharing scheme yields good security performance. Further, the experiment results and analysis such as entropy, correlation, differential, and the histogram of plaintext and ciphertext images are performed to prove to be secure and random.

References

1. Shamir, A.: How to share a secret. Commun. ACM **22**(11), 612–613 (1979)
2. Blakley, G.R.: Safeguarding cryptographic keys. In: Proceedings of the National Computer Conference 1979, vol. 48, pp. 313–317 (1979)
3. Naor, M., Shamir, A.: Visual cryptography. In: De Santis, A. (ed.) EUROCRYPT 1994. LNCS, vol. 950, pp. 1–12. Springer, Heidelberg (1995). https://doi.org/10.1007/BFb0053419
4. Tripathi, S.K., Gupta, B., Pandian, K.K.S.: Hybrid image sharing scheme using non-recursive hash key based stream cipher. Multimed. Tools Appl. **78**(8), 10837–10863 (2018). https://doi.org/10.1007/s11042-018-6663-4
5. Thien, C.C., Lin, J.C.: Secret image sharing. Comput. Graph. **26**(5), 765–770 (2002)
6. Yang, C.N., Chen, T.S., Yu, K.H., Wang, C.C.: Improvements of image sharing with steganography and authentication. J. Syst. Softw. **80**(7), 1070–1076 (2007)
7. Ghebleh, M., Kanso, A.: A novel secret image sharing scheme using large primes. Multimed. Tools Appl. **77**(10), 11903–11923 (2017). https://doi.org/10.1007/s11042-017-4841-4
8. Wu, X., Yang, C.N., Zhuang, Y.T., Hsu, S.C.: Improving recovered image quality in secret image sharing by simple modular arithmetic. Sig. Process.: Image Commun. **66**, 42–49 (2018)
9. Lukac, R., Plataniotis, K.N.: Bit-level based secret sharing for image encryption. Pattern Recogn. **38**(5), 767–772 (2005)
10. Yang, C.N.: New visual secret sharing schemes using probabilistic method. Pattern Recogn. Lett. **25**(4), 481–494 (2004)
11. Ryo, I., Kuwakado, H., Tanaka, H.: Image size invariant visual cryptography. IEICE Trans. Fundam. Electron. Commun. Comput. Sci. **82**(10), 2172–2177 (1999)
12. Kafri, O., Keren, E.: Encryption of pictures and shapes by random grids. Opt. Lett. **12**(6), 377–379 (1987)
13. Shyu, S.J.: Image encryption by random grids. Pattern Recogn. **40**(3), 1014–1031 (2007)
14. Shyu, S.J.: Image encryption by multiple random grids. Pattern Recogn. **42**(7), 1582–1596 (2009)
15. Chen, T.H., Tsao, K.H.: Visual secret sharing by random grids revisited. Pattern Recogn. **42**(9), 2203–2217 (2009)
16. Chen, T.H., Tsao, K.H.: Threshold visual secret sharing by random grids. J. Syst. Softw. **84**(7), 1197–1208 (2011)
17. Fang, W.P.: Friendly progressive visual secret sharing. Pattern Recogn. **41**(4), 1410–1414 (2008)
18. Thien, C.C., Lin, J.C.: An image-sharing method with user-friendly shadow images. IEEE Trans. Circuits Syst. Video Technol. **13**(12), 1161–1169 (2003)
19. Hsu, C.S., Hou, Y.C.: Goal-programming-assisted visual cryptography method with unexpanded shadow images for general access structures. Opt. Eng. **45**(9), 097001 (2006)
20. Prasetyo, H., Hsia, C.-H.: Lossless progressive secret sharing for grayscale and color images. Multimed. Tools Appl. **78**(17), 24837–24862 (2019). https://doi.org/10.1007/s11042-019-7710-5
21. Chen, W.K.: Image sharing method for gray-level images. J. Syst. Softw. **86**(2), 581–585 (2013)

22. Hill, L.S.: Cryptography in an algebraic alphabet. Am. Math. Mon. **36**(6), 306–312 (1929)
23. Bunker, S.C., Barasa, M., Ojha, A.: Linear equation based visual secret sharing scheme. In: 2014 IEEE International Advance Computing Conference (IACC), pp. 406–410. IEEE (2014)
24. Dubrova E.: On constructing secure and hardware-efficient invertible mappings. In: 2016 IEEE 46th International Symposium on Multiple-Valued Logic (ISMVL), 18 May, pp. 211–216 (2016)
25. Dubrova E.: A list of maximum-period NLFSRs. Cryptography ePrint Archive, Report. http://eprint.iacr.org/2012/166 (2012)
26. Pandian, K., Ray, K.C.: Dynamic hash key-based stream cipher for secure transmission of real time ECG signal. Secur. Commun. Netw. **9**(17), 4391–4402 (2016)
27. Abanda, Y., Tiedeu, A.: Image encryption by chaos mixing. IET Image Process. **10**(10), 742–50 (2016)
28. Rukhin, A., et al.: Statistical test suite for random and pseudorandom number generators for cryptographic applications. NIST Special Publication (2010)

On the Hardware Implementation Performance, of Face Recognition Techniques, for Digital Forensics

Maria Pantopoulou[1], Nicolas Sklavos[1(✉)], and Ivana Ognjanovic[2]

[1] SCYTALE Group, Computer Engineering and Informatics Department, University of Patras,
Patras, Hellas
nsklavos@upatras.gr
[2] University of Donja Gorica, Podgorica, Montenegro

Abstract. As face recognition systems constitute a very useful tool in the sector of Digital Forensics, they should provide accurate and fast results. Although several software implementations for face recognition exist, they are unable to achieve high recognition rate in reasonable time, due to the complex and numerous needed calculations. As a result, there is an on-going research in low-cost hardware implementations, especially based on Field Programmable Gate Arrays (FPGAs), in order to reduce the processing time and the false alarm identification rate. In this work, we introduce the fundamental of algorithms, for face recognition, such as Principal Components Analysis (PCA), and its modified methods, as well as the Local Binary Pattern (LBP). These approaches are applied in different architectures, and alternative FPGA implementations are introduced. We also present implementation synthesis results, based on the recognition time and the allocated hardware resources.

Keywords: Digital forensics · Face recognition · FPGA · Hardware security · Cyber security

1 Introduction

Nowadays, with criminality rate increasing day by day, the digital forensics sector is growing rapidly [1]. Digital forensics is the process of identifying, preserving, analyzing and finally presenting digital evidence. Digital data are now everywhere and should be extensively examined in every investigation. Not only they are able to sometimes reveal whether a person is a suspect of a crime, or when and how the crime was committed, but they can also be used to verify or reject someone's statement in court. One of the most important digital evidence might be an image, captured by a video-camera, indicating someone's presence in a place at the time a crime occurred [2]. This kind of snapshots is very powerful evidence, due to the fact that nobody can change their context and thus they are trustworthy [3]. Images can now lead us to image recognition and subsequently to face recognition, which is the main subject of our work. Computer vision includes methods that gather, process and analyze real world data, so it also contains image recognition, which refers to technologies that detect and identify objects and people in digital images or video [2, 4, 5].

Face recognition describes the situation where the main issue is to detect faces and match them to a person's face in a database. It is proven very popular in forensics science, and it is widely used in this field, as investigators can detect a suspect easier and faster, in a not manual way. However, it is more challenging to be implemented and more difficult in giving satisfying results than simple face recognition. This applies mainly because of the different conditions that may have to be dealt with, such as angle or not forward pose, change of illumination and facial expressions. The resolution of the camera and its distance, are several additional obstacles that make it sometimes even impossible to identify the right person or the original face.

Due to the fact that these conditions will always exist, thus making face recognition hard to be implemented, new systems are being constructed to increase the Identification Rate (IR). Some other terms similar to IR are False Positive Identification Rate (FPIR) and Failure to Acquire (FTA), which are included in [6]. The first one, FPIR, refers to the test samples that, although being false, they end up being true after the process is completed and lead to the reduction of the system's IR. On the other hand, the term FTA is about the unsuccessful attempt to create face templates from a given dataset. There are many software facial recognition systems that provide a satisfactory IR; however, they have speed problems mainly because of the big number of calculations during the process. The idea of using hardware architectures to speed up the system is nowadays very popular and under the major interest of the research community.

In this paper, a comparison between different implementations on FPGAs is presented, and their implementation synthesis results –after using different face databases– are reported. Some of these implementations do not use the same algorithms for feature extraction and classification, and each of them is implemented on different FPGA devices. Design costs and clock frequencies are shown. There are many algorithms for identification and recognition. Therefore, they should be used wisely, combined with the best architecture in order to achieve the best integration results, and consequently the desirable identification rate.

The rest of this paper is organized as follows: in Sect. 2, some commonly used in face recognition algorithms are presented and briefly explained. Section 3 presents three different architectures for face recognition, which are implemented on FPGAs, while in Sect. 4 some popular face databases with their characteristics are discussed. Section 5 illustrates the experiment results of the above architectures when they are combined with specific algorithms. Detailed comparisons of the implementations, are given in the next Sect. 6, in terms of hardware resources. Finally, conclusions and outlook are discussed in Sect. 7.

2   Fundamental Algorithms in Face Recognition

In this section a brief analysis of some basic algorithms used in face recognition will be presented. PCA, MPCA, WMPCA, Wavelet based techniques and Local Binary Pattern methods will be explained below.

2.1 Principal Component Analysis (PCA)

PCA is considered to be a very successful method among other face recognition algorithms, as it achieves high rates of recognition when used in different systems. However, when using this algorithm, testing databases must not be large, due to the fact that computations and memory requirements for the process increase enormously. The main goal of PCA is to remove the correlations among the different input dimensions and significantly reduce the data dimensions. This algorithm is used to extract features of face images and construct the eigenface space. The basic steps of the PCA algorithm are shown below:

1. Create a training set of M images I1, I2, ..., IM.
2. Each image in the training set is converted into a vector form, as PCA does not work with images directly. These vectors are in the face vector space, have N^2 values each and are called Γi.
3. Normalize these face vectors and calculate the average face vector ψ. Normalization is the process of removing all the common features that these faces share together. When these features are removed from each face, only the unique features will remain. The average face is computed by the next equation:

$$\psi = \frac{1}{M} \sum_{i=0}^{M} \Gamma_i \tag{1}$$

4. Subtract average face from each face vector:

$$\Phi_i = \Gamma_i - \psi \tag{2}$$

These are the normalized vectors.

5. To calculate the eigenvectors, the covariance matrix is first computed

$$C = AA^T \tag{3}$$

where $A = [\Phi 1, \Phi 2, ..., \Phi M]$ with each column being each normalized face vector. The C matrix has N^2 × N^2 values, which is a huge number. The solution to this problem is dimensionality reduction, in order to reduce the calculations and the effect of noise on the needed eigenvectors and calculate them from a much smaller covariance matrix. A lower dimensional space of the vector space will be used with the C matrix now computed as:

$$C = A^T A \tag{4}$$

which has M × M values. This matrix will return M eigenvectors.

6. Select the K best eigenfaces, where $K \leq M$, to represent the whole training set. The selected K eigenfaces must be in the original dimensionality, of the face vector space.
7. Convert lower dimensional K eigenvectors to original face dimensionality:

$$u_i = Av_i \tag{5}$$

where u_i is the vector in higher dimensional space, and v_i is the vector in lower dimensional space.

8. Each image in the training set will be represented as a linear combination of these K eigenfaces plus the mean image. K weights are associated with the respective K eigenfaces. These weights show the percentage that each eigenface contributes to the face image.
9. When it comes to recognizing a face, project normalized test face vector on the eigenspace and get the weight vector of this input image. Calculate the "distance" between the input weight vector and all the weight vectors of the training images.

2.2   Alternative PCA Methods

Although PCA algorithm achieves satisfactory results, it should not be used in cases where local variations of the face images are taken into account. Illumination, facial expressions and head pose affect the accuracy of the recognition, as the algorithm considers the global information of each face image. Modular PCA method seems to be the solution to this problem. The original image is divided into L sub-images, each of N^2/L size, and the feature extraction is now computed for each of these sub-images. The process for each sub-image is the same with this on PCA. Now the average face image is given by the Eq. (6).

$$\psi = \frac{1}{M \cdot L} \sum_{i=1}^{M} \sum_{j=1}^{L} \Gamma_{ij} \tag{6}$$

The images' division into smaller regions renders the algorithm much more efficient as the local projection will now be more representative for each region. However, these regions must not be too small, in order to maintain valuable information. The weight vectors are computed for each region, but only some of them will vary, whereas rest of them will remain the same.

Another algorithm similar to PCA, but more efficient, is the Weighted MPCA (WMPCA) Method. Using this method, the face image is split into n horizontal sub-regions, each one of which is analyzed and processed as in PCA. There are n − tasks of recognition, all of which may be done in parallel. The forehead, the eye, the nose and the chin region are some of the regions that the original image is divided into. For each sub-region, the average sub-region is computed and then the calculation of the covariance matrix, the eigenvectors and the weight vectors follow as in PCA. The difference of this algorithm is that it computes the weighted sum of errors in each sub-region, where these weights are acquired based on the variations of features in different conditions, such as different face expressions and illuminations.

In some cases, before applying the PCA method, some other feature extraction techniques could be performed, in order to increase the Identification Rate. WT is a method that can be used to extract valuable information from the image. The signal to be analyzed is passed through filters with different cut-off frequencies at different scales. This method transforms the spatial domain pixels of an image into frequency domain information that are represented in multiple subbands. These subbands are LL, HL, LH and HH. The LL subband is wavelet approximation of the signal and HL, LH and HH are the horizontal, vertical and diagonal coefficients.

2.3 Local Binary Pattern Method

Local Binary Pattern Method (LBP) is an effective texture descriptor for images, which is not affected by illumination changes, as will be shown below. This algorithm processes a little block of three by three pixels at a time, and it is particularly interested at the central pixel. The steps of this algorithm, as presented in [7] are:

- LBP value calculation,
- region division,
- histogram statistic,
- prediction.

For the calculation of the LBP value the LBP operator is used, which considers a neighborhood of a circle with radius r. Every pixel in the neighborhood is compared with the central pixel. If the value of the neighboring pixel is smaller than the central pixel value, then a '0' is assigned to this pixel; if it is greater or equal to the central pixel value, then a '1' is assigned. If the light is changed, all the pixel values will increase, but the relative difference between the pixels will remain the same, and the LBP code will be the same. For each central pixel, one can generate a binary 8-bit number which is produced by concatenating the neighbors' bits in a clockwise manner, starting from the top-left neighbor. The decimal number generated from the binary 8-bit number replaces the central pixel's value. This process is indicated in following Fig. 1.

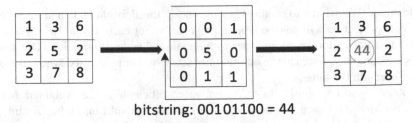

bitstring: 00101100 = 44

Fig. 1. Calculation of an LBP pixel value.

The LBP picture is divided into blocks with the same size. After encoding every point in the block as a pattern, gathering the statistics of LBP occurrence in a histogram form is the next step for every region. The result of this step is a characteristic vector for each region. The combination of the different regions' vectors produces the characteristic vector for the entire image. For the process of prediction, the minimum "distance" between the input vector and the test images' characteristic vectors is found.

3 Architectures and FPGA Devices

3.1 Multi-pipeline Architecture

A multi-pipeline architecture is used in [8] to implement a face recognition system with a high recognition rate using the PCA algorithm and its alternative approaches. This architecture is implemented on a Xilinx FPGA Device (xc3s4000-4fg900). One of the advantages of this architecture, which uses four units to achieve the face recognition, is that it reduces the time needed for the process, because of the pipelining technique. Moreover, the hardware resources that are used are limited, as basic modules are reused. The proposed architecture will be explained below.

On the WMPCA algorithm, which was described in detail above, there is a weighted sum of errors from the sub-images and the "distance" on the final stage is given by the equation:

$$e = \min_{1 \leq i \leq M} \left[\sum_{j=1}^{n_r} \left| Weight_{i,j}[w_{trainset} - \{eigenface \times (\Gamma_{test} - \psi)\}] \right| \right] \quad (7)$$

where $Weight_{i,j}$ is the weight that corresponds to image i from each sub-image.

The proposed architecture consists of four different units and tries to compute this "distance" in an efficient multi-pipeline way. Each of these units contributes in a different way to the whole process. The four parts are: Multi-Pipeline Control Unit (MPCU), Process Element Unit (PEU), Region Summing Unit (RSU) and finally Recognition Indexing Unit (RIU), as it is shown in the next Fig. 2.

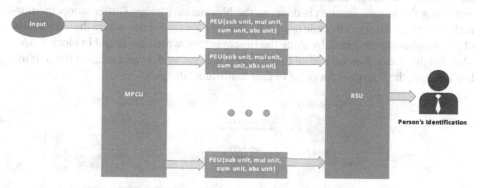

Fig. 2. The multi-pipeline proposed architecture.

The input vectors (test image, mean face image, eigenface image, project image) are fed to the MPCU, before transferred to the PEU units for the needed calculations. The MPC Unit manages the input vectors in a pipelining way. Then, the data are transferred to the PEUs. The number of the PEUs is equal to the number of regions that the image will be divided into. Each of the PEUs deals with a single sub-region and includes a subtraction unit, a multiplication unit, a sum unit and an absolute unit. Each of these operation units will be used in all the stages until finding the minimum "distance".

In order to extract the similar features and leave each image with its unique characteristics, the subtraction unit is used and the result of this computation is the centering result of the image. Both the test and mean image vectors have size N^2. The centering image is multiplied with the K eigenfaces (using the multiplication and the sum unit), so as to get the project test image, which will be subtracted from the projection coefficients of the training images. The next step in the PEU is to get the absolute value of the previous difference (for each region) and multiply it with the $Weight_{j,i}$ term to find the weighted projection image. As was mentioned before, this process is done for each sub-region of the image in each PEU.

In the next unit, RSU, the results from the PEUs are added together in order to find the final weighted difference vector, from all sub-regions and will be sent to the RIU, for the recognition result. The RIU generates the result, after finding the minimum "distance" among the M-project images. As, it was mentioned before, this architecture achieves better processing time, due to the fact that it is designed in multi-pipelining manner, and the hardware resources are reduced as modules are reused.

3.2 5-Unit Architecture

Another similar architecture, combined with the PCA algorithm is used in [9] and is implemented on a Xilinx FPGA Device (Virtex-5). It is similar to the previous architecture, as it consists of 5 different modules; Image Reader, Normalized Image Calculator, Weight Vector Finder, Weight Vector Reader and Classifier (Fig. 3). The Image Reader module takes as an input the test image and saves the pixels of the image into the Image Frame Buffer. If a previous image's pixels are in this module, they are transferred to the Normalized Image Calculator. In the Normalized Image calculator, the process of extracting the unique features is done, as the Normalized Image Buffer stores the normalized image. The next module used is the Weight Vector Finder, where the calculation of the weights is performed, by using the Eigenvectors, which are stored in block RAM. The Weight Vector Reader is used to read the weighted vectors and transfer them to the last module, the Classifier, in order to find minimum "distance".

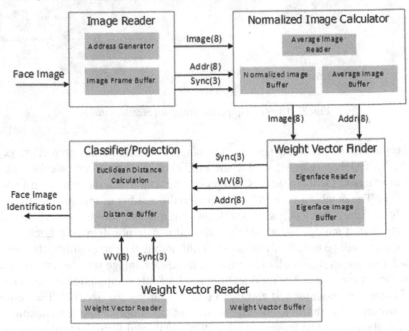

Fig. 3. The 5-unit proposed architecture.

On the stage of Normalization during the face recognition process, the average image buffer is stored in a block RAM. The subtraction operations that are done between the test image's pixels and the average image's pixels can be performed in parallel as they are totally independent operations. After storing the normalized image into a register, the calculation of the weight vectors can be also performed in a parallel manner, due to the fact that the eigenvectors stored in the block RAM are independent of each other. Finally, even the computation of the Euclidean distances can be performed in parallel.

3.3 3-Unit Architecture

Another proposed architecture [7] is the following one, shown in Fig. 4. This architecture is implemented on a Xilinx FPGA Device (Virtex7). It uses the Local Binary Pattern (LBP) algorithm. This architecture seems efficient as when it calculates the LBP values, it also does operations on the histogram statistic and when it comes to find the Chi-square distances it increases the parallelism. As shown in Fig. 3, it consists of 3 units; the LBP Calculation Unit, the Histogram Statistic Unit and finally the Prediction Unit. In this approach, after significant tests so as to find how to increase the IR, 5 images per individual are used and the data bit-width is 32-bit. The data bit-width of prediction module is 256. In order to avoid the long recognition time, five characteristic vectors are produced on the LBP Calculation Unit. Moreover, in the Prediction Unit the comparison of five test images with the trainset is done in parallel.

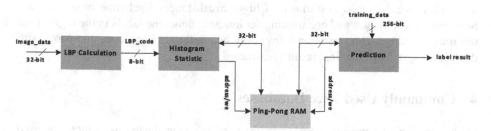

Fig. 4. The 3-unit proposed architecture.

The LBP calculation module consists of a line buffer with three lines, whose register number is equal to the horizontal pixels of the image. As was mentioned before, in the section where LBP algorithm was explained, in order to find a LBP value of a pixel, a central pixel in a region 3×3 is chosen. This central pixel is compared with its neighboring 8 pixels, so as to calculate the bit-string which corresponds to this pixel. In this module, the register R5 is compared with registers R1-R9. Every time data is fed as input in this module, the calculation moves to the next pixel. This way, the LBP codes for each pixel are generated.

The Histogram Statistic module uses a Ping-Pong RAM like the following one of Fig. 5.

When a calculated LBP value is entered from the LBP calculation module, according to the value and its location on the image, the related statistic data are extracted from the Ping-Pong RAM, in order to be added with "1" and then stored back into the RAM. The

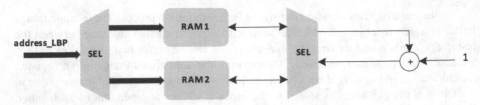

Fig. 5. The Ping-Pong RAM architecture.

Ping-Pong RAM is comprised of two RAMs, each of them used for different process every time. As the Ping-Pong RAM is addressed according to the entering value, the one of the two RAMs is used for the histogram statistic, while the other one for storing the statistical data of the test pictures.

The Prediction Module is responsible for the final decision and the labels matching. There are two inputs in this module; the characteristic vector of the test images from the Ping-Pong RAM, and the training data. Due to the fact that the bit-width of these data must be the same in order to do the calculations, the bit-width of the data coming from RAM must expand to 256-bit. Eight registers share 32-bit each (eight registers for the test images and eight registers for the training data) and then, the calculation of the Chi-square distance between the test images and the training images with summing units is done. The Prediction Module architecture also has a set of registers, which store the identity labels of the trainset images and another set of registers with the test image label. There are also registers storing the Chi-square distances. Each time the comparison between the test images and one training set image is done, the labels in the register for test images change. This operation is over only when all train images are compared with the test images. Then the final result is extracted.

4   Commonly Used Face Databases

In this section, we present a brief overview of the face databases, which are used commonly. ORL, Yale and AR databases are introduced and analyzed in the next sections.

4.1   ORL Face Database

This face database is commonly used in different face recognition systems, because of the variety of images it consists of. ORL database consists of 400 facial images, each of them in a 112×92 resolution [10]. There are 40 different persons and 10 images per individual. The light conditions, facial expressions, such as smiling/not smiling, open eyes/closed eyes, facial details, such as wearing glasses/not wearing glasses, and scale are different among the images. Faces are in an upright position in frontal view, with a slight left/right rotation. For some of the individuals, the pictures were captured at different times.

4.2 Yale Face Database

This database is constructed by Yale University. Yale database includes 165 grayscale images, each of them in a 320 × 243 resolution, in GIF format, of 15 different persons. There are 11 images per person, and each one of them displays the following features or configurations: center-light, w/glasses, happy, left-light, w/no glasses, normal, right-light, sad, sleepy, surprised, and wink [11].

4.3 AR Face Database

This database consists of 4000 images of 126 different persons (70 male and 56 female) [12]. The images are colored and their resolution is 768 × 576. There are frontal-view face images and quarter-profile images with 4 facial expressions: anger, smile, scream and neutral. The illumination conditions differ as the database includes images where the faces are lit from left, from right, or from all sides. Persons on the images wear accessories like scarfs and glasses.

4.4 Outlook

All of the above three databases consist of different images captured in several conditions, so they can be used for finding a face recognition system's accuracy. However, the ORL database is one of the most widely used databases, as it consists of enough images to use for testing and these images have a resolution of 112 × 92 pixels [10]. These images need less storage resources than AR and Yale databases' images need [11, 12].

5 Implementation Synthesis Results

5.1 Multi-pipeline Architecture with PCA and Modified PCA Algorithms

In the case of the Multi-pipeline architecture presented above, the FPGA used is the Xilinx FPGA Device (xc354000-4fg900) [8]. The algorithms used for examination in this experiment are PCA, MPCA_3 (with 3 horizontal partitions), MPCA_sym4 (with 4 symmetrical partitions), WMPCA3, WMPCA_sym4 and the wavelet-based techniques of the previous algorithms. The testing input images come from the Yale and ORL databases and their resolution for this experiment is 32 × 32 pixels.

The wavelet based techniques that are implemented are W1MPCA3, W1MPCA_sym4, W3MPCA3 and W3MPCA_sym4, which correspond to the wavelet decompositions at level 1 and level 3 with 3 horizontal and 4 symmetrical partitions. The hardware resources used differ depending on the algorithm used. When using the PCA method and its modified wavelet-based techniques with decomposition at level 1 and level 3, only the 20% of Slices and LUTs are used and almost 5% of the BRAMs and Mult18x18. For the MPCA_3 algorithm, as well as for the WMPCA3, W1MPCA3, W1WMPCA3, W3MPCA3, W3WMPCA3 the hardware cost is equal to almost 55% of the Slices, 53% of the LUTs and almost 15% of the Mult18x18. Finally, the MPCA_sym4, WMPCA_sym4, w1MPCA_sym4, w1WMPCA_sym4, w3MPCA_sym4 and w3WMPCA_sym4 methods use 80% of the Slices, 77% of the LUTs and 18% of the Mult18x18 and the BRAMs.

As for the recognition time achieved, the PCA methods with decomposition at level 1 and level 3 complete the recognition process in almost 27 ms. The next six methods finish the process in approximately 10 ms and the last six methods complete the whole operation in under 10 ms.

According to these results, it can be deduced that when the recognition time is the minimum, the hardware cost is the maximum. Another fact that can be concluded from the above information is that when the number of the sub-regions increases, the hardware cost is also increased. A compromising solution would be to use the W1MPCA3 technique with the level1 decomposition and the 3 horizontal partitions. Finally, the processing time is 8.84 ms and the clock rate is 13.38 MHz.

5.2 5-Unit Architecture with PCA Algorithm

The second architecture is implemented on a Xilinx FPGA Device (Virtex-5) and examines the performance of the PCA algorithm [9]. It is assumed that the detection face part is ready and there is no need to be implemented now. The resolution of the images here is 20×20 pixels after a down sampling method to reduce the image of the face that is detected. The used face databases are in the ORL database and another one which consists of 60 images from 6 individuals. The face recognition system runs at 45 frames per second and when it is compared with an equivalent software implementation on Core2 Duo CPU, it is found that it achieves a 15x speed-up.

With this implementation the hardware resources are: 77% of the Slices is used, 72% of the number of LUTs is used, 56% of the number of BRAMs is used and only the 8% of the number of DSP48s is used.

5.3 3-Unit Architecture with LBP Algorithm

The last architecture is implemented on a VC707 development board that contains a Xilinx FPGA Device (XC7VX485T-2FFG1761C). This approach, examines the performance of the Local Binary Pattern (LBP) algorithm, on a face recognition system [7]. The test images used here come from the ORL database in a resolution of 60×60 pixels.

In this implementation, the recognition speed is examined as the number of images is increased. As it is mentioned in [7], the FPGA's speed is reduced from 174 to 1.74 faces per second as the number of images is increased from 1000 to 100000. The system operates at up to 233 MHz. If this system is compared with a CPU for the same number of images, the FPGA is 74 times faster.

The FPGA resources are enough, as this implementation uses only 1.96% of the FPGA's LUTs, 0.372% of the existed registers, 0.857% of the DSPs and 12.4% of the BRAMs.

6 Comparisons: Advantages and Trade Offs

The specified parameters and values, for each one of the compared implementations, are summarized in the following Table 1, in detail.

As it is reported in Fig. 6, although PCA methods, which use four symmetrical partitions of the images' regions, achieve the lowest recognition time, they use much more of the FPGA's resources than the other techniques, as it is analyzed in the previous Sect. 5. On the other hand, PCA methods with decomposition at level 1 and level 3, use small percentage of the resources, but the system completes the process much slower. So it turns out, that a compromising solution for the Multi-pipeline architecture, is the Wavelet based Modular PCA algorithm with decomposition, at level 1 and three horizontally partitions. This method provides the lowest False Positive Identification Rate (FPIR) in a reasonable time.

Table 1. Alternative approaches & implementations.

Architectures parameters	Multi-pipeline	5-Unit	3-Unit
FPGA Device	Xilinx (xc354000-4fg900)	Xilinx (Virtex-5)	Xilinx (XC7VX485T-2FFG1761C)
Algorithm(s)	PCA, MPCA, WMPCA, Wavelet Techniques	PCA	LBP
Frequency (MHz)	13,38	–	Up to 233,37
Processing Time	8,84 ms (Best)	–	–
Resolution (Pixels)	32 × 32	20 × 20	60 × 60

If this implementation is compared with the other two, as it is illustrated in the following Fig. 7, the FPGA's resources which are used, are much more in the 5-Unit Architecture, than in any of the other two implementations. Although we can't make an accurate comparison between the used hardware resources of these implementations, due to the fact that the implementation of the 5-Unit Architecture also implemented face

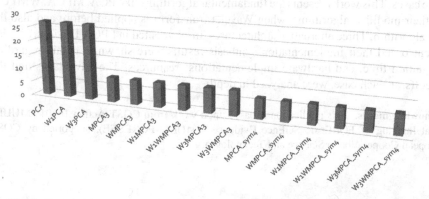

Fig. 6. Recognition times for PCA and modified methods: multi-pipeline architecture.

detection, it is clear that the 3-Unit architecture, when combined with the LBP algorithm uses a very small percentage of the used FPGA.

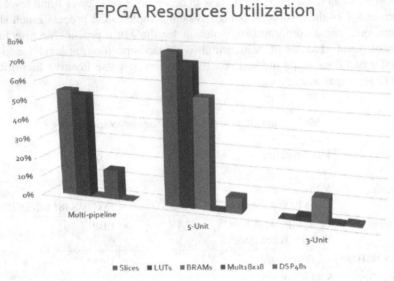

Fig. 7. Hardware implementation cost.

7 Conclusions

Face recognition is a very active research area and systems which are implemented for this reason, are widely used in different sectors and applications in the real world [13]. Systems like these are used for authentication, access control and information security.

Digital Forensics sector needs accurate and fast face recognition systems, so as to help investigators complete their work faster, when for example they have to do with crime cases. This work presents the fundamental algorithms like PCA, MPCA, WMPCA and their modified algorithms, when Wavelet transform is applied before and also the LBP algorithm. Three alternative architectures, implemented in FPGA Devices, are also presented and their implementation synthesis results were shown in detail, regarding recognition time, and hardware implementations' resources. The advantages and the tradeoffs, in each case, were analyzed in depth.

Acknowledgments. This publication is based upon work from COST Action 16101 "MULTI-modal Imaging of FOREnsic SciEnce Evidence" (MULTI-FORESEE), supported by COST (European Cooperation in Science and Technology).

References

1. Casey, E.: Digital Evidence and Computer Crime, 3rd edn, p. 840. Elsevier, Amsterdam (2011). ISBN 9780123742681
2. Ioannidou, I., Sklavos, N.: Digital forensics: video manipulation detection techniques and security systems. In: Proceedings of 3rd MULTI-modal Imaging of FOREnsic SciEnce Evidence Tools for Forensic Science 2019, Catania, Italy, 16–18 September 2019
3. Casey, E.: Handbook of Digital Forensics and Investigations, p. 600. Elsevier, Amsterdam (2010). ISBN 9780123742674
4. Amato, G., et al.: Face verification and recognition for digital forensics and information security. In: Proceedings of 7th International Symposium on Digital Forensics and Security 2019 (ISDFS 2009), Barcelos, Portugal, 10–12 June 2019
5. Ognjanovic, I., Sklavos, N., Sendelj, R.: Multi criteria, for decision making systems, in face recognition process. In: Proceedings of 3rd MULTI-modal Imaging of FOREnsic SciEnce Evidence Tools for Forensic Science 2019, Catania, Italy, 16–18 September 2019
6. Alkawaz, H., Clarke, N.L., Furnell, S., Li, F., Alruban, A.: Advanced facial recognition for digital forensics. In: Proceedings of 17th European Conference on Cyber Warfare and Security 2019, Oslo, Norway, June 2018
7. Zhang, Y., Cao, W., Wang, L.: Implementation of high performance hardware architecture of face recognition algorithm based on local binary pattern on FPGA. In: Proceedings of IEEE 11th International Conference on ASIC 2015 (ASICON 2015), Chengdu, China, 3–6 November 2015
8. Visakhasart, S., Chitsobhuk, O.: Multi-pipeline architecture for face recognition on FPGA. In: Proceedings of International Conference on Digital Image Processing 2009, Bangkok, Thailand, 7–9 May 2009
9. Matai, J., Irturk, A., Kastner, R.: Design and implementation of an FPGA-based real-time face recognition system. In: Proceedings of IEEE International Symposium on Field-Programmable Custom Computing Machines 2011, Salt Lake City, UT, USA, 1–3 May 2011
10. The ORL Face Database, Cambridge University, Computer Laboratory (2019). http://www.cl.cam.ac.uk/research/dtg/attarchive
11. Yale Face Database, Yale University (2019). http://vision.ucsd.edu/content/yale-face-database
12. Martinez, A.M., Benavente, R.: The AR face database. CVC Technical report #24, June 1998
13. Sklavos, N.: Design and implementation of integrated circuits in trusted environments. In: Design Test Verification and EDA (DTVEDA 2017) Workshop, Volos, Hellas, 6–7 July 2017

Detecting the Zeus Banking Malware Using the Random Forest Binary Classification Algorithm and a Manual Feature Selection Process

Mohamed Ali Kazi[✉], Steve Woodhead, and Diane Gan

Old Royal Naval College, The University of Greenwich, Park Row, London SE10 9LS, UK
mk0889h@gre.ac.uk

Abstract. The Zeus malware is one of the most prolific banking malware variants ever to be discovered and this paper examines how the Zeus malware network traffic can be detected using the Random Forest machine learning algorithm. The key to this paper is that the features used for the experimentation and detection of Zeus are manually selected, providing the researcher more control over which features that can and should be selected. This also helps the researcher understand the features and the impact they have on the accuracy of the Random Forest binary classification algorithm when used to detect the Zeus banking malware.

Keywords: Zeus banking malware · Machine learning · Random Forest · Manual feature selection

1 Introduction

1.1 The Growth of Malware and Paper Contribution

It has been reported by [1] that cybercrime is the most prevalent and widespread threat to cyber-security and according to IBM's CEO '…is the greatest threat to every company in the world'. [2] also reported that cyber-attacks resulted in losses of around £11bn to the UK in 2016 rising to £30bn of losses in 2017. Banking malware is also on the increase and a report by [3] states that as of May 2017, the threat from banking malware was 2.5 times greater than that of ransomware. Banking malware is also costing industry large amounts of money for example, [4] estimate that some of the highest "earning" banking malware campaigns in 2018 could potentially earn a banking malware operator around US$1M–2M in revenue which is a significant increase from what could typically be "earned" in 2010 (estimated to be around US$100k–$300k). Finally, [5] states that Ramnit, Bebloh and Zeus (all banking malware), accounted for 86% of all the financial attacks conducted in 2017. For these reasons, it is important to detect and block banking malware. This paper proposes a methodology and approach, using machine learning, to analyze and detect the Zeus banking malware.

Researchers have developed various methodologies to detect malware and the majority of these are either signature based or anomaly-based. Researchers have also used

© Springer Nature Singapore Pte Ltd. 2020
S. M. Thampi et al. (Eds.): SSCC 2019, CCIS 1208, pp. 286–297, 2020.
https://doi.org/10.1007/978-981-15-4825-3_23

machine learning (ML) algorithms to detect malware and some of these are discussed in Sect. 2. This paper expands on this work with a view to enhance and improve the detection accuracy of banking malware (focusing on Zeus) and to also propose a methodology that can be used by ML algorithms to detect Zeus. This paper uses the Random Forest ML algorithm to detect, classify and differentiate between the Zeus banking malware and benign (non-malicious) traffic. An important differentiation between this research and the research discussed in Sect. 2 is that this research proposes selecting the features manually allowing the authors to have a better understanding of the features and how they can impact the accuracy and detection results. It also provides the authors with more control over which features that are and should be selected by the ML algorithm. Furthermore, this research proposes a methodology that can be used by ML algorithms to detect Zeus and compares the accuracy between selecting the features manually and the automated feature selection methods discussed in Sect. 2.

1.2   Introduction to the Zeus Banking Malware

According to [6], Zeus has become the leading banking malware and is the most advanced credential stealing malware ever discovered and in 2015, Zeus accounted for around 90% of global banking fraud. Another report by [7] shows that in the first quarter of 2017, Zeus had already accounted for 28% of all infections, the highest amongst the banking malware infections. In 2011, the source code for Zeus was leaked, allowing malware authors to develop new variants of Zeus [8] resulting in a customizable malware that allows malware authors to develop new modules which can be traded in underground forums [6].

As discussed by [9], Zeus propagates like a virus and targets Windows systems and is usually delivered via spam email and targets sensitive information such as credentials and banking passwords. Zeus steals credentials using two methods. The first is by using automatic actions hardcoded in the binary itself which allow Zeus to capture passwords and the second is to steal information stored in the Windows PSTORE (protected storage) [10]. An important aspect of the Zeus malware is the command and control (C&C) channel used for communication purposes. As discussed by [9], the communication architecture is either centralized or peer to peer (P2P). Some versions of Zeus use the P2P architecture and other variants of Zeus, such as IceIX and Citadel, use the centralized architecture [7]. An issue with the centralized C&C architecture is that the IP address of the C&C server is hard coded within the Zeus binary itself [7]. If the C&C server becomes unreachable or is taken down, the Zeus bots will not be able to communicate with the C&C server preventing them from receiving commands, updating themselves and downloading new configuration files [7]. Newer variants of the Zeus bots use the P2P C&C architecture and are much harder to track and block and are also more resistant to takedown efforts as the configuration file does not point to a static C&C server [11]. Instead, the C&C server information is obtained from other bots (proxy bots) and these proxy bots have the potential to act as a C&C server and configuration files and executables can also be downloaded from these C&C capable bots [12]. Stolen data is also routed through these proxy bots to the malware authors' C&C server [12] and when the stolen data reaches the C&C server it is decrypted and saved to a database [6]. The botnet uses two C&C channels for communication purposes. The first, referred to as 'log', communicates the status information of the bot. The second, referred to as 'report', is used for operational activities such as updating the configuration file [13]. Furthermore, if the Zeus bot becomes disconnected from the botnet it can use a Domain Generation Algorithm to generate unique domain names which can be used for establishing a new communication channel [14]. The Zeus malwares' operational characteristics are described by [9] and 2 important characteristics are that the C&C data is transmitted using the HTTP/HTTPS protocol and Zeus targets Windows by exploiting Windows vulnerabilities.

2   Related Work

2.1   Detecting Malware Infections Through IDS Driven Dialog Correlation

[15] proposed a passive monitoring system called Bothunter which consists of a correlation engine and three malware sensors. The first sensor uses SNORT and the other two sensors, SLADE and SCADE, were custom developed. SCADE is a Snort pre-processor which consists of two scan engines that scan inbound and outbound traffic. SCADE scans traffic based on the following criteria: Local hosts that conduct high-rate scans to external IP addresses; Outbound connection failures; A uniformly distributed scan pattern (a pattern which is likely to be malware). SLADE is a payload analysis engine which alerts the administrator if the byte distribution of the packets deviates from an established profile. SLADE is based on PAYL which examines the distribution of the payload i.e. it extracts 256 features from the payload and represents each feature based on the frequency of its occurrence [15].

Bothunter was developed as a perimeter scanning solution which attempts to detect botnet activities and attempts to detect network activity that occurs between an infected host and an external entity. The alerts that are generated are fed into a dialogue correlation tool which tracks activities over a temporal window and attempts to identify malware infections. Bothunter can also enhance the prediction of the malware activity by correlating some of the outbound flows to inbound flows and the correlation engine attempts to determine if the traffic patterns are malicious or benign. However, the limitation with Bothunter is that it is not able to scan local network traffic i.e. local DNS resolution traffic or the traffic generated by malware when it scans a local network for vulnerable hosts. Malware can also evade Bothunter by encrypting its payload as Bothunter is unable to inspect encrypted traffic.

2.2   Detecting Bots Using the C4.5 and CFS Feature Selection Algorithm

[16] proposed a machine learning (ML) software tool called CONIFA which was used to detect network traffic generated by Zeus. CONIFA uses the C4.5 classification algorithm along with the correlation-Based feature selection (CFS) algorithm (automated feature selection) to train and classify the ML algorithm to identify specific application traffic and the Zeus Malware. The authors developed a cost-Sensitive version of the C4.5 classification algorithm which used both a lenient and strict classifier to enhance CONIFA's classification and detection capabilities. CONIFA was actually developed to detect and

classify application traffic generated by Skype however, CONIFA was also evaluated against the Zeus banking malware.

The author in [16] also discussed a 'standard framework' which used the cost-Insensitive version of C4.5 to classify network traffic and identify Zeus. The authors then compared CONIFA's recall results with the 'standard framework' and the results showed that CONIFA was more effective than the standard framework at detecting Zeus network activity. The standard framework's detection rate was good when evaluating the training dataset, however, when evaluating the test data, the recall rate dropped to 56% resulting in around half of the Zeus network flows not being detected. CONIFA's results demonstrated an improvement in the detection accuracy with the recall rate increasing to 67%.

2.3 Detection of Randomized Bot Command and Control Traffic on an End-Point Host

[17] proposed a software tool called RCC Detector (RCC) which analyzed network traffic, generated by a host, to identify and classify bot generated and benign traffic. RCC aimed to identify bots in the early phases of infection and also aimed to detect bots that attempt to hide by randomizing their communication activities. RCC uses a Multi-Layer Perceptron (MLP) classifier and a Temporal Persistence (TP) classifier to identify botnet communication activities generated by a host. The MLP classifier has an input layer, an output layer and one hidden layer consisting of four neurons. The following criteria were used for the classification: Flow count - Flows that are counted over a period of time; Session length - Non-botnet HTTP traffic is bursty occurring over a short period of time whereas bot traffic is generally low profile persisting over a longer period of time; Uniformity score - This is based on packet count values. Bots portray regularity in packet counts while the benign traffic's packet count is typically more varied; Kolmogorov–Smirnov Test - Which is used to compute the distance between flows as benign traffic is bursty and generates traffic at very close time intervals whilst bots generate traffic at larger time intervals. These criteria were used to calculate a 'temporal persistence' value which is then used by the classifier to identify botnet activities. The classifier was evaluated against a sample of bots and [17] reported that 99.8% of the bots were identified from the sample however, the False Positive (FP) rate was 48%. Although the results were promising, the FP rate was quite high and more importantly, the tool is a host-based detection tool making it difficult to implement.

3 Research and Methodology

3.1 Introduction

ML algorithms have been used by researchers to detect banking malware and some of these were discussed in Sect. 2. The research discussed in Sect. 2 used automated feature selection algorithms to train and test the ML algorithms. There is no evidence of any research being conducted that proposes selecting the features manually for the ML algorithms, particularly for the binary classification algorithms when used to detect

Zeus. This research paper proposes a methodology to select the features manually and then uses these features to understand the impact that these features have on the detection accuracy. Once the appropriate and best features have been identified, these will be used by the Random Forest (RF) classification algorithm for the final training, testing and validation activities. The manual feature selection process allows greater flexibility and more control over which features that can be used by RF and which features produce the best results. Precision, Recall and F-score will be used to determine the accuracy of the ML algorithm. A confusion matrix will also be generated, as shown in Table 1, and will measure the performance and detection accuracy of the RF algorithm when tested against the unseen dataset.

Table 1. Confusion matrix used to measure the detection accuracy.

	Predicted Zeus	Predicted benign
Actual Zeus	(TP)	(FN)
Actual benign	(FP)	(TN)

The following variables will be used to quantify the accuracy of the ML algorithm, and are defined as set out below:

$$\text{Recall} = TP / (TP + FN). \tag{1}$$

$$\text{Precision} = TP/(TP + FP). \tag{2}$$

The F-score is the calculated mean of the Recall and Precision scores. If the value is 1 then the accuracy of RF is 100%, if the value is 0 then the accuracy is 0%.

3.2 Research Methodology

Zeus can obfuscate its payload by encrypting the network datagrams however, this research will not attempt to decrypt the network communication traffic during the detection of the Zeus malware. This research will use the Random Forest (RF) algorithm and will aim to predict and classify the communication traffic as either Zeus (Malware) or benign. This research will focus on the general statistical features of the network packet and the following steps were followed: Extract the statistical features from the datagrams and prepare the data for the RF algorithm; Manually select the features and through experimentation, determine which features produce the best prediction results. The framework for this research follows the approach described by [18] and includes: Obtain the Zeus and benign traffic samples and then split the data into a training and evaluation dataset; Use the Random Forest algorithm to train the ML algorithm to make accurate prediction; Evaluating the ML algorithm with an unseen dataset.

3.3 Data Collection and Preparation

The Zeus samples for this research were obtained from Zeustracker [19], a website which monitors Zeus C&C activities, and were downloaded as pcap files in February 2019. The benign traffic samples were collected manually from a new installation of Windows 10, version 10.0.17763.615, and were also collected during the same time. To ensure that both the Zeus and benign samples were comparable, 524 samples of each were used during this research (total of 1048). From each sample, 44 statistical features were extracted and a description of all the statistical features can be found at [20]. The statistical features were extracted using Netmate-flowcalc (NF), a tool developed by [21], and then exported into a CSV file. NF was used because it is an open source tool and has been used by other researchers such as [16]. Although NF extracts 44 statistical features from the pcap files, for this research, not all the features were used. The features that were used are discussed in Sect. 3.5 and these were determined and identified, through experimentation, to provide the best detection results. The statistical features of both the Zeus and benign traffic were then imported into a Pandas' data frame and an additional column called 'is_botnet' was created and was used as the label which is what the RF algorithm is trained against. The label is set to 1 to identify Zeus and 0 to identify benign traffic. Finally, the Zeus and benign statistical feature outputs were combined and randomized into a final Panda's data frame and a subset of this dataset can be seen in Table 2.

3.4 Feature Selection and Training Using the RF Algorithm

One of the main issues in ML is selecting the appropriate features from the dataset. [22] states that a dataset could have many features and selecting the best features has many benefits and these include: Variance (overfitting) is reduced, as this can produce incorrect results; Computational cost and the time for running the algorithm is reduced; Enables the ML algorithm to learn faster. [23] discusses several techniques that can be used for feature selection and these predominately include:

- Filter method - Feature selection is independent of the ML algorithm.
- Wrapper method - A subset of the features are selected and used to train the ML algorithm. Based on the results, features are either removed or added. The test is then repeated and the results are compared.

The analysis conducted for this research used the wrapper method, allowing the features to be manually selected. The number of features were increased and decreased manually which had an impact on the detection accuracy and a subset of the experimental results can be seen in Table 3. K-Fold (10-Fold) cross validation was used during the training stage and for this research, 70% of the dataset was used for training and validation and 30% was used for testing. The experimental results are discussed in Sect. 3.5 and 3.6.

Table 2. Combined Zeus and benign staistics in a single Pandas' frame.

sflow_bbytes	fpsh_cnt	bpsh_cnt	total_fhlen	total_bhlen	is_botnet
0	0	0	28	0	1
4207	4	4	412	412	0
4012	4	3	412	372	0
393	1	1	292	172	0
0	0	0	28	0	1
2594	0	0	48	120	1
0	0	0	48	0	1
130	0	0	28	20	0
0	0	0	498	0	1
2579	0	0	48	120	1

3.5 Training the Dataset Using the Random Forest Algorithm

According to [24], the RF algorithm is a supervised ML algorithm which works by building and combining multiple Decision Trees and can reduce overfitting and variance and provides better results compared to other binary classification algorithms. Various feature combinations were trained and testing during this research and a subset of the feature combinations tested during this research can be seen in Table 3. It was determined that the best detection results were obtained when using the following 13 features: total_fpackets, total_fvolume, total_bpackets, total_bvolume, min_fpktl, mean_fpktl, max_fpktl, std_fpktl, min_bpktl, mean_bpktl, max_bpktl, std_bkptl, min_fiat. The lowest detection results were obtained when using the following feature combination: duration, max_active, max_biat, max_bpktl. It is important to note that the best detection accuracy is defined as the feature combination which detected the most Zeus samples correctly. The 13 features used during this research are described below and a description of all the features can be found at [20].

total_fpackets - Total packets in the forward direction; total_fvolume - Total bytes in the forward direction; total_bpackets - Total packets in the backward direction; total_bvolume - Total bytes in the backward direction; min_fpktl - The size of the smallest packet sent in the forward direction (in bytes); mean_fpktl - The mean size of packets sent in the forward direction (in bytes); max_fpktl - The size of the largest packet sent in the forward direction (in bytes); std_fpktl - The standard deviation from the mean of the packets sent in the forward direction (in bytes); min_bpktl - The size of the smallest packet sent in the backward direction (in bytes), mean_bpktl - The mean size of packets sent in the backward direction (in bytes), max_bpktl - The size of the largest packet sent in the backward direction (in bytes), std_bkptl - The standard deviation from the mean of the packets sent in the backward direction (in bytes), min_fiat - The minimum amount of time between two packets sent in the forward direction (in microseconds).

The prediction results of both the Zeus and benign traffic and the weighted average of these, when using the 13 best features, are shown below:

Table 3. Random Forest accuracy results for various feature combinations

Features selected	Precision for Benign traffic	Recall for Benign traffic	F-score for Benign traffic	Precision for Zeus Traffic	Recall for Zeus Traffic	F-Score for Zeus Traffic	TP	FP	FN	TN
total_fpackets	0.89	0.47	0.61	0.61	0.93	0.74	78	89	10	138
total_fpackets total_fvolume	0.87	0.94	0.9	0.93	0.85	0.89	153	10	23	129
total_fpackets total_fvolume total_bpackets total_bvolume	0.91	0.97	0.94	0.97	0.92	0.94	145	4	14	152
duration, max_active max_biat, max_bpktl	0.89	0.64	0.74	0.71	0.92	0.80	102	58	12	143
total_fpackets total_fvolume total_bpackets total_bvolume min_fpktl, mean_fpktl max_fpktl, std_fpktl	0.80	0.97	0.88	0.97	0.78	0.86	144	4	37	130
total_fpackets total_fvolume total_bpackets total_bvolume min_fpktl, mean_fpktl max_fpktl, std_fpktl min_bpktl, mean_bpktl	0.85	0.99	0.91	0.99	0.83	0.90	154	2	27	132
duration, max_active max_biat, max_bpktl	0.89	0.66	0.75	0.70	0.91	0.79	109	57	14	135
duration, max_active max_biat, max_bpktl max_fiat	0.92	0.93	0.93	0.93	0.92	0.92	149	11	13	142
total_fpackets total_fvolume total_bpackets total_bvolume min_fpktl, mean_fpktl max_fpktl, std_fpktl min_bpktl, mean_bpktl, max_bpktl, std_bkptl, min_fiat'	100	0.84	0.92	0.89	100	0.93	158	0	25	132

- Prediction results for detecting benign traffic during training

  - Recall = 100%
  - Precision = 84%
  - F Score = 92%

- Prediction results for detecting Zeus traffic during training

  - Recall = 89%
  - Precision = 100%
  - F Score = 93%

- The weighted average of these are as follows:

  - Recall = 95%
  - Precision = 92%
  - F Score = 93%

3.6 Evaluation of the Random Forest Machine Learning Algorithm (Testing)

Testing, using the 13 best features, was performed on 30% of the unknown and untrained version of the dataset and the results of this can be seen in Table 4. Table 4 shows that out of 163 Zeus cases only 3 of these were incorrectly classified (FN) and out of the 152 benign cases 37 of these was incorrectly classified (FP). Testing was also performed using the 4 features that had the lowest detection accuracy, and the results of this can be seen in Table 5. Table 5 shows that out of 160 Zeus cases 58 Zeus cases were undetected and out of 155 benign cases 12 were undetected.

Table 4. Confusion matrix for the RF algorithm using the 13 best features

	Predicted Zeus	Predicted Benign
Actual Zeus	160	3
Actual benign	37	115

Table 5. Confusion matrix for the RF algorithm using the 4 lowest performing features

	Predicted Zeus	Predicted Benign
Actual Zeus	102	58
Actual benign	12	143

Figure 1 compares the best and worst detection results for both the Zeus and benign traffic and shows that when using only 4 features almost half of the Zeus samples are undetected but when using the 13 best features only 3 Zeus samples are missed resulting in a high detection accuracy.

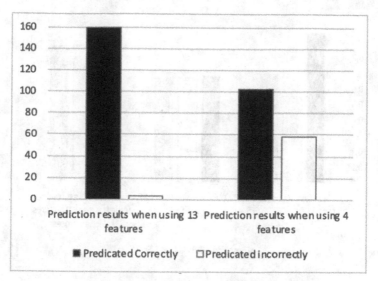

Fig. 1. Comparison of the detection results of both the Zeus and benign network samples.

3.7 Conclusion

Selecting the features manually for the RF algorithm has produced good results when compared with the automated feature selection methods discussed in Sect. 2. The results for the standard framework show that more than half of the Zeus flows were undetected with an F-score value of .56. The detection results of the CONIFA framework did show an improvement and produced an F-score value of .67. The manual feature selection methodology does show an improvement when detecting Zeus and Fig. 2 compares the results of the automated feature selection process with the manual feature selection process as discussed in this paper.

3.8 Further Work

The preliminary results of this research are promising and the manual feature selection process can be leverage by other machine learning algorithms to detect banking malware. It is acknowledged that further testing should be conducted on newer variant of Zeus and there is a need to test against other banking malware variants such as Neverquest. There is also a need to test against a larger dataset to enhance the detection results. Additionally, the manual feature selection methodology can be expanded to other binary classification algorithms and then further expanded and tested on other machines learning approaches such as unsupervised machine learning algorithms.

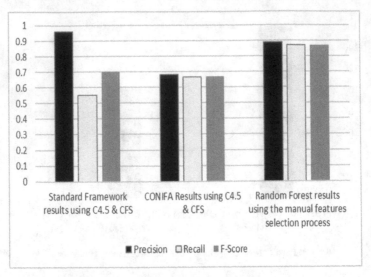

Fig. 2. Comparison of the accuracy results.

References

1. Morgan, S.: IBM's CEO On Hackers: 'Cyber Crime Is The Greatest Threat To Every Company In The World' (2015). https://www.forbes.com/sites/stevemorgan/2015/11/24/ibms-ceo-on-hackers-cyber-crime-is-the-greatest-threat-to-every-company-in-the-world/#1b1914e173f0. Accessed 5 Nov 2019
2. Clarke, J.: Cybercrime cost UK residents £210 each in the last year. http://www.independent.co.uk/news/uk/crime/cyber-crime-hacking-fraud-213-a-year-a7365816.html. Accessed 5 Nov 2019
3. Wueest, C.: Financial Threats Review 2017 (2017). https://www.symantec.com/content/dam/symantec/docs/security-center/white-papers/istr-financial-threats-review-2017-en.pdf. Accessed 5 Nov 2019
4. Macafee: Mobile Threat Report (2018). https://www.mcafee.com/enterprise/en-us/assets/reports/rp-mobile-threat-report-2018.pdf. Accessed 5 Nov 2019
5. InTELL: Gameover Zeus Background on the Badguys and the Backends (2015). https://www.blackhat.com/docs/us-15/materials/us-15-Peterson-GameOver-Zeus-Badguys-And-Backends-wp.pdf. Accessed 5 Nov 2019
6. Ibrahim, L.M., Thanon, K.H.: Analysis and detection of the Zeus botnet crimeware. Int. J. Comput. Sci. Inf. Secur. **13**(9), 121 (2018)
7. Crowe, J.: Top 10 Banking Trojans for 2017: What You Need to Know (2017). https://blog.barkly.com/top-banking-trojans-2017. Accessed 5 Dec 2018
8. Etaher, N., Weir, G.R., Alazab, M.: From zeus to zitmo: trends in banking malware. In: 2015 IEEE Trustcom/BigDataSE/ISPA, vol. 1, pp. 1386–1391. IEEE, August 2015
9. Kazi, M., Woodhead, S., Gan, D.: A contempory taxonomy of banking malware In: First International Conference on Secure Cyber Computing and Communications. IEEE Xplore Digital library (2018)
10. Falliere, N., Chien, E.: Zeus King of the bots (2014). https://www.symantec.com/content/dam/symantec/docs/security-center/white-papers/security-response-zeus-king-of-bots-09-en.pdf. Accessed 5 Nov 2019

11. Researcher, L.: Gameover: ZeuS with P 2P Functionality Disrupted (2014). https://blog. trendmicro.com/trendlabs-security-intelligence/gameover-zeus-with-p2p-functionality-disrupted/. Accessed 5 Nov 2019
12. Lelli, A.: Zeusbot/Spyeye P 2P Updated, Fortifying the Botnet (2012). https://www.symantec. com/connect/blogs/zeusbotspyeye-p2p-updated-fortifying-botnet. Accessed 5 Nov 2019
13. Riccardi, M., Di Pietro, R., Palanques, M., Vila, J.: Titans' revenge: detecting Zeus via its own flaws. Comput. Netw. **57**(2), 422–435 (2013)
14. Andriesse, D., Bos, H.: An Analysis of the Zeus Peer-to-Peer Protocol (2014). https://syssec. mistakenot.net/papers/zeus-tech-report-2013.pdf. Accessed 6 Nov 2019
15. Gu, G., Porras, P., Yegneswaran, V., Fong, M., Lee, W.: Detecting objective-C malware through memory forensics. Digit. Investig. **18**, S3–S10 (2007)
16. Azab, A., Alazab, M., Aiash, M.: Machine learning based botnet identification traffic. In: 2016 IEEE Trustcom/BigDataSE/ISPA. IEEE, Tianjin (2016)
17. Soniya, B., Wilscy, M.: Detection of randomized bot command and control traffic on an end-point host. Alex. Eng. J. **55**(3), 2771–2781 (2016)
18. Mayo, M.: Frameworks for Approaching the Machine Learning Process (2018). https://www. kdnuggets.com/2018/05/general-approaches-machine-learning-process.html. Accessed 6 Nov 2019
19. Hüssy, R.: Zeustracker.abuse.ch (2014). https://zeustracker.abuse.ch/. Accessed 15 Feb 2019
20. Code.google.com. Google Code Archive - Long-term storage for Google Code Project Hosting (2014). https://code.google.com/archive/p/netmate-flowcalc/wikis/Features. Accessed 15 Nov 2019
21. Arndt, D.: DanielArndt/netmate-flowcalc (2011). https://github.com/DanielArndt/netmate-flowcalc. Accessed 6 Nov 2019
22. Albon, C.: Feature Selection Using Random Forest (2017). https://chrisalbon.com/machine_learning/trees_and_forests/feature_selection_using_random_forest/. Accessed 6 Nov 2019
23. Kaushik, S.: Feature selection methods with example (Variable selection methods) (2016). https://www.analyticsvidhya.com/blog/2016/12/introduction-to-feature-selection-methods-with-an-example-or-how-to-select-the-right-variables/. Accessed 6 Nov 2019
24. Liberman, N.: Decision Trees and Random Forests (2017). Available at: https://towardsdatascience.com/decision-trees-and-random-forests-df0c3123f991. Accessed 6 Nov 2019

Exploitation of HTTP/2 Proxies for Cryptojacking

Meenakshi Suresh[1]([✉]), V. Anil Kumar[2], M. Sethumadhavan[1], and P. P. Amritha[1]

[1] TIFAC-CORE in Cyber Security, Amrita School of Engineering, Coimbatore,
Amrita Vishwa Vidyapeetham, Coimbatore, India
msthacheri@gamil.com
[2] CSIR Fourth Paradigm Institute, NAL Belur Campus, Bangalore, India

Abstract. In this paper we explore the feasibility of exploiting HTTP/2 proxies to facilitate cryptojacking, an adversary scenario in which compute resources are used for mining crypto currency without the consent of the owner of the resources. In particular, we intercept the encrypted traffic passing through the proxy and inject malicious cryptojacking script, used for mining Monero cryptocurrency, into the traffic. Here, we show the security implications that are possible even in an encrypted network, while using a middle-box like proxy. We conclude by proposing some radical and neoteric approach(s) that can be used to contain the effects of cryptomining in secure HTTP/2 networks. To the best of our knowledge, this paper is one of the initial studies that demonstrate the feasibility of intercepting HTTP/2 traffic at proxy level and injecting malicious code for performing cryptojacking. Our results are important as the Internet has several open Proxies, which could perform such activities.

Keywords: HTTP/2 · Cryptojacking · Crypto currency · Open proxy

1 Introduction

June 2017 saw 51% [1] of the world's population using the Internet. The web users know that some of their important personal information is available online and these growing categories of people are worried about the safety of these data available freely. It is very crucial for the people to have an authority over their information, like in many cases, who can be given access to their personal data or whether it can be shared without their permission. Users always strive to ensure that their Internet handling procedure is always safe and secure, as now everything from buying groceries to paying bills are done via the Internet. Out of the 51% of the Internet users, 74.6% [2] of the top 1,000 widely used sites are accessed through a secure web. Secure webs are implemented with Hyper Text Transfer Protocol Secure (HTTPS). HTTP is the protocol with which the whole Internet is administered. HTTPS is the secure version of HTTP.

Newer versions of the protocol with different updates and upgrades are introduced for enhancing a secure Internet experience. The latest upgrade for the HTTP protocol was the HTTP/2 version of it.

© Springer Nature Singapore Pte Ltd. 2020
S. M. Thampi et al. (Eds.): SSCC 2019, CCIS 1208, pp. 298–308, 2020.
https://doi.org/10.1007/978-981-15-4825-3_24

Most of the web clients would like to be anonymous online; however, many think it is inconceivable to be totally unknown on the web. 86% [3] of the Internet users online have begun to eliminate or cover up their digital impressions - going from clearing cookies to encrypting their email, abstain from using their names to utilizing virtual networks or middle boxes that veil their Internet protocol (IP) address. Anonymity online can be brought about by using middle boxes like open proxies. Proxies once installed act as a machine that is present between the client and the rest of the Internet. Every page that is requested goes through the proxy server. The downside of anonymous proxies is the malicious activities that can be performed online unbeknown.

This work demonstrates one such malicious activity, called cryptojacking. Cryptojacking is a method of mining cryptocurrency like Bitcoin, Monero, and Ethereum without the consent of the user. This is a stealthy attack which when performed utilizes the victims CPU resource for the purpose of mining the cryptocurrency. This paper shows the cryptojacking procedure for mining Monero (XMR) cryptocurrency. We have specifically chosen Monero because it is more secretive and anonymous when compared to any other cryptocurrency [16]. Monero maintains utmost secrecy during the complete transaction, to the extent that, the transaction history of both the sender and the receiver is kept confidential and untraceable. In this paper we ask an important question whether HTTP/2 proxies can be exploited for cryptojacking. To the best of our knowledge, we are not aware of any prior work focusing on cryptojacking through HTTP/2 proxies. The following are our main contribution in this paper: We explore the feasibility of cryptojacking in the context of HTTP/2 proxies.

We implement and systematically demonstrate the feasibility of conducting the cryptojacking attack in a real world scenario. Our experimental results show that it is not only possible to conduct cryptojacking through HTTP/2 proxies, but also a high level of control can be achieved, by carefully manipulating code, in terms of the percentage of CPU usage and thereby maintaining the covert nature of the attack.

We discuss possible mitigation strategies as well as the probable threats and consequences that may arise, if this attack prevails. The remainder of the paper is organized as follows. Section 2 explains the background knowledge on the key terms mentioned in the paper like HTTP/2, proxies and cryptojacking. Section 3 introduces the experimental setup followed by the implementation details in Sect. 4. The results obtained are explained in Sect. 5. After providing the related works in Sect. 6, we conclude the paper by discussing the future works in Sect. 6.

2   Background

Hyper Text Transfer Protocol version 1.1 (HTTP/1.1) is a protean convention. It is an elemental protocol that administers the complete World Wide Web (WWW). The application of this protocol has been with the end goal that conjoining services and augmentations over it is less demanding than building anything fresh from the start. Nevertheless, extensive use of all the features of this protocol has not been done. Certain extensions of HTTP/1.1 which were implemented led to contradictions in the operational structures of the client and server using them.

For more than 10 years, HTTP/1.1 remained as the de-facto protocol version which prevailed as the basis of WWW until the development of the SPDY [5] protocol. SPDY was developed by Google as an experimental protocol for a faster web [4]. This protocol was devised to surmount the drawbacks encountered by the HTTP/1.1 protocol, mainly the latency of web pages. Even though SPDY was a better protocol when in comparison with HTTP/1.1, it never replaced the latter completely. The modified property of the former was appended along with HTTP/1.1.

As SPDY provided compatibility with HTTP/1.1, applications could easily adapt to the changes during the transition of the protocol. The final draft of the protocol, SPDY3, was taken as the basis of the upgrade to the HTTP/2 protocol. The salient features required for the upgrade of the HTTP protocol, from version 1.1 to version 2, was initially tried out with SPDY3. HTTP/2 [6] was deployed in 2015 with all the major enhancements from HTTP/1.1. It also includes a diminished approach of latency by adding compression to the header fields and allows numerous concurrent transactions on the same connection. Security and anonymity are two features that users of web are anxious about. The advent of Internet has escalated the need for anonymity in cyber communications. Security of the data provided by the users is handled by the SSL/TLS encryption feature provided in the HTTP/2 protocol. Anonymity is achieved by using middle boxes like proxies, VPN etc. These types of servers send data to the end server through itself rather than from the client directly. Proxy servers are publicly available in the Internet, which can be used by prospective users. In recent years, open proxies are the seat of malicious attackers. Malicious proxies are mainly used for man-in-the-middle (MITM) attacks. One such attack is Cryptojacking, which is done by injecting unwanted mining scripts into the users request which passes through the proxy.

2.1 HTTP/2 Protocol Overview

The elemental principle of HTTP/2 [20] is to elevate the efficiency of the transport layer and furthermore include higher threshold with reduced latency. HTTP/2 along with its new and improved characteristics like binary property, multiplexing, server push, header compression, flow control, priorities and stream dependencies etc., promises to provide a better web experience.

Multiplexing - In order to solve the issues created by the Head-of-the-line blocking in HTTP/1.1, a single TCP connection is multiplexed to handle multiple request in the same connection as shown in Fig. 1. This connection remains open till the communication channel is closed. Prioritization of the requests send is also done to mitigate the same issue. Header Compression - Sending of the headers along with each message caused overheads and performance deterioration. This concern was solved by compressing the headers with the help of HPACK compression technique [7].

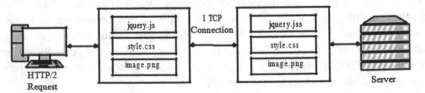

Fig. 1. HTTP/2 Protocol

Server Push - This feature pushes additional responses other than the ones requested by the user. The responses are proactively pushed, in such a manner, by predicting the requirements of the users, apart from the ones mentioned in the request. Server push is an optional feature and can be disabled if not required.

TLS - Transport Layer Security (TLS) is responsible for maintaining the authentication and privacy between the communicating parties. TLS is not a mandatory feature in the HTTP/2 protocol, but the browsers support HTTP/2 only if TLS is enforced. Owing to the browsers decision, encryption is now an obligatory factor for HTTP/2 protocol.

2.2 Proxy

Proxy servers act as an intermediary between a client and server. The end server processes the request send by the client only after passing through the proxy. Figure 2 shows a forward proxy which is commonly used to retrieve data from the Internet. There are hundreds of open anonymous proxies available in the Internet [8] that allows the users to conceal their identity by changing their IP addresses. An anonymous proxy is a special type of proxy lade with software that erases our IP address from any page requests and substitute it with its (proxy) own IP. When the page is sent back by the Web server, the proxy server then forwards it back to making it free of any additional software scripts that might weaken the identity.

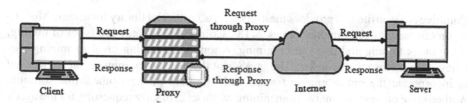

Fig. 2. Forward proxy

2.3 Cryptojacking

Imperceptible use of vulnerable user's computational resources for mining cryptocurrency is known as cryptojacking or coinjacking. The mining of the user's computational power shall lead to a noticeable reduction in the performance of the users system. In this paper we demonstrate the cryptojacking for mining Monero cryptocurrency. Monero cryptocurrency was introduced on April, 2014 as a substitute for Bitcoin. The main feature of Monero is its egalitarian mining nature, thereby distributing the mining efforts to all the people. It is said to be more secure, private, untraceable and synonymous with respect to other cryptocurrency like Bitcoin, Ethereum etc. [9]. Monero holds its position for being the number one cryptocurrency in terms of privacy, by using ring signature that can scramble the users address, making it undetectable. By virtue of these features Monero banking can be done without leaving any footprints in its wake. Unlike many other cryptocurrency which are clones of Bitcoin, Monero is devised using the CryptoNight algorithm which comes from the CryptoNote protocol [10–12]. Figure 3 shows the basic structure of cryptojacking, Fig. 1. shows the attacker compromising a website with the cryptojacking code. Figure 2 show the end users using this infected website for their needs. Figure 3 illustrates the users unknowingly mining cryptocurrency on behalf of the attacker and Fig. 4 implies the attacker getting rewards for successfully completing another block in the cryptomining procedure.

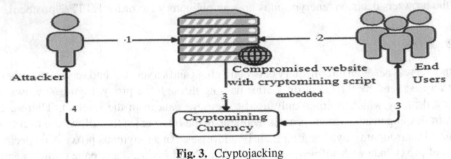

Fig. 3. Cryptojacking

2.4 Coinhive

Coinhive is a website that provides the users with a JavaScript library for mining Monero cryptocurrency directly in their browser [13]. Coinhive facilitates two types of mining, anonymous mining and user opt-in mining. Anonymous mining involves mining currency, without the user's consent. The JavaScript that is used for mining can be tweaked to incorporate the opt-in mining feature with the help of the AuthedMine solution. AuthedMine prevents Coinhive from mining, without explicitly requesting for the user's permission before initiating the mining procedure.

3   Experimental Setup

The experimental setup used for our work is shown in Fig. 4. It consists of 3 major components. A client machine that acts as a base user, an anonymous open proxy server through which all the client communications passes and an HTTP/2 web server that provides HTTP/2 service to the client machine.

3.1   HTTP/2 Server Setup

HTTP/2 re-uses the same application connotation of HTTP/1.1, such as, the HTTP methods, status codes, header fields, etc., but modifies the aspect on how the requests and responses are formulated, conducted, and handled. In this experimental structure we setup the web server using NGINX server of version 1.12.1. It is configured on a base machine which works on UBUNTU 16.04 LTS. During the onset of the server creation, it is by default set to listen to port 80 which is the standard HTTP port. The server is configured to handle HTTP/2 request and response. As most of the browsers support HTTP/2 only with encryption, we configure the server to handle HTTPS requests by facilitating TLS. This is accomplished by changing the listening port of the server from 80 to 443. Along with that we also enable the HTTP/2 module in the server configuration. Next we configure our server to use the SSL certificates.

The server framework is concluded by routing all the unencrypted server requests via port 443 [14]. In Fig. 4 the web server is the component where the HTTP/2 server is used.

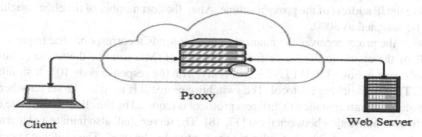

Fig. 4. Experimental set up

3.2 Anonymous Open Proxy

An anonymous proxy is setup on a base machine which is installed with Ubuntu 16.04 LTS operating system. The proxy that we are using here is the mitmproxy [15]. It is a free and open source interactive proxy. It acts as a man-in-the-middle, as the name says, and is used to interrupt network traffic. It can intercept and modify the HTTP and HTTPS website traffic adaptively while using them. It can also save and replay previous HTTPS responses that were encountered. Mitmproxy can also be used to modify the HTML content by adding python scripts to the server pages. We mainly concentrate on secure HTTP sites, thereby dealing with HTTP/2 websites. In this case we make use of our HTTP/2 server to serve our purpose. We have deliberately chosen this protocol because of its versatile nature. It not only supports command line and web interface but also enables the use of a python programming interface.

In the aforementioned experiment we use the open proxy to intercept and modify the HTTP/2 response of the web server by inserting a JavaScript into the html <head> tag of the web page. The script that we are injecting from the proxy is acquired from coinhive's website and is used for mining Monero cryptocurrency.

3.3 Client Machine

The client machine or the base user as shown in Fig. 4 is set up with Ubuntu 16.04 LTS operating system. The client machine is prepared by equipping it with a necessary web browser.

4 Attack Methodology

We implemented the attack using the in-browser mining technique as shown in Fig. 5. The middle box used here, mitmproxy; act as the gateway for the attack. This attack uses the proxy server to act as a man-in-the-middle, which injects cryptojacking JavaScript into the webpage being accessed by the user.

Initially, the client requests to connect to the HTTP/2 configured web server, www. example.com, through the proxy. For establishing a connection through the proxy, the client's network proxy configuration should be altered. The network proxy address must be set to the IP address of the proxy machine. Also, the port number of the client machine must be assigned as 8080.

Once the proxy receives the connect request it sends a correspondence request, on behalf of the client, to the server for fetching the HTML page of the website. Since the web page is hosted in HTTP/2 it will reply with the response code 101. It signifies the HTTP/1.1 Switching Protocol. The switching protocol is used by the server when it understands that an upgrade to a different protocol is required by the client to facilitate the smooth communication between them [17, 18]. The server shall also initiate an Upgrade request, as given, with which it indicates the protocol to be used. The switching occurs only if the server feels that it is advantageous to proceed in that direction, for example, using a higher version of the same protocol as mentioned here.

HTTP/1.1 101 Switching Protocols Connection Upgrade: h2c

Once the switching of the protocol is complete, the HTTP/2 protocol is initiated by sending a connection preface [6]. The connection preface is send by both the end-points to confirm the protocol in use. Along with the connection preface HTTP/2 settings are also exchanged by the proxy, which is in-turn confirmed by the server. Once the confirmation is transmitted, the server will send the HTTP/2 response with the index.html file of www. example.com. Since HTTP/2 protocol implements the server push feature all the server contents required for the loading of the web page is send along with the index.html page [6]. Till the beginning of the connection Preface, the communication is still occurring in terms of HTTP/1.1, even though the request was made in HTTP/2. Once the connection preface starts, it is an HTTP/2 communication. The connection preface needs to be send only once, the consecutive request response from the client to that server will automatically come in the HTTP/2 format. As soon as the proxy receives the HTTP/2 response, i.e., the html page, it will inject the miner code into the web page. As we have mentioned earlier, the mining procedure that we do is in correspondence with the website www.coinhive.com. Coinhive has a JavaScript miner code which can be used for mining cryptocurrency. The mining procedure is done by injecting the JavaScript which contains the public key assigned to the user. It will have its private key pair, which will be mapped to the user, thereby mapping the mining procedure to the corresponding miner. The mining code will be injected into the html <head> tag of the web page. The cryptojacking procedure can be done in 2 ways, either manually or in an automated manner using Python Script. In the manual procedure the proxy is being monitored live and the miner code is injected manually each time the proxy is used. This procedure can be done using the mitmproxy interface or using the mitmweb console. The Java Script when used along with a python code automates the cryptojacking procedure from the time the proxy is turned on. The python script is initiated along with the proxy using the following code:

.\mitmproxy -s miner.py –anticache

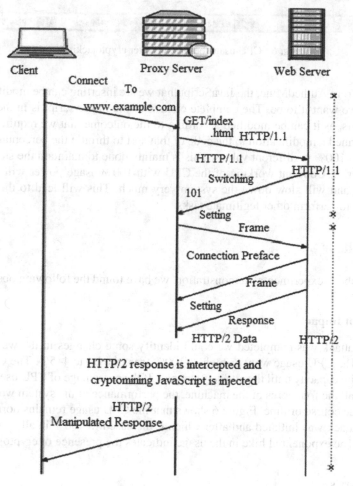

Client   Proxy Server   Web Server

Connect To www.example.com

GET/index .html HTTP/1.1

HTTP/1.1

HTTP/1.1

HTTP/1.1 Switching 101

Setting Frame

Connection Preface Frame

Setting Response

HTTP/2 Data   HTTP/2

HTTP/2 response is intercepted and cryptomining JavaScript is injected

HTTP/2 Manipulated Response

Fig. 5. Attack sequence

Anticache is used for disabling the cache mechanism. and miner.py is the python code that does the cryptojacking. So if a person is using the proxy for malicious purpose like in our attack structure, then they can easily insert the cryptomining code and perform cryptojacking.

Another method of performing cryptojacking is using the opt-in method. This is done using the AuthedMine [19] concept. The base JavaScript is tweaked in such a manner that the users are asked for their permission to perform cryptomining in their browsers. So this makes the mining a legitimate procedure rather than jacking the CPU power without their permission.

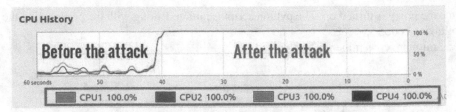

Fig. 6. CPU usage before and after cryptojacking.

Apart from AuthedMine, the JavaScript that we are inserting can be modified to any extent as we want it to be. The complete control of the miner script is in the hands of the attackers, as it can be modified according to the outcome that we require. We have also performed a modification to the code of that sort to throttle the percentage of CPU usage from 100% to different values. This is mainly done to maintain the stealthiest of the JavaScript. Constant working of the CPU with 100% usage power will tend to be noticeable and will slow down the system very much. This will lead to the users not being able to perform other legitimate tasks.

5 Results

From the above experimental demonstration, we have found the following observations:

5.1 Client Impact

Once the attack was completed we could identify some changes in the way the CPU behaves. The CPU usage went as high as 100% from the basic 4–5%. The CPU would use its entire capacity until the attack is stopped. If the percentage of CPU used becomes 100% for all the four cores of the machine, the performance of the system would deteriorate in due course of time. Figure 6 shows that the CPU usage remains normal till the time the attack was initiated and after which it increased to 100% in all 4 cores of the machine. The exponential hike in the usage indicates the presence of cryptojacking.

5.2 Analysis

After the open anonymous proxy is infected with the cryptojacking script, the proxy can insert the malicious JavaScript into any website using the proxy for its purpose. Figure 7 shows the infected miner-JavaScript on the target website. The miner scripts are very anonymous and stealthy thereby leaving the user getting caught off-guard by the attack.

5.3 Modifications

The covertness of this attack can be maintained very easily by the attacker. The malicious JavaScript is extremely flexible and can be modified according to our requirements. This reduces the continued usage of CPU in its complete 100%. The throttling of the CPU

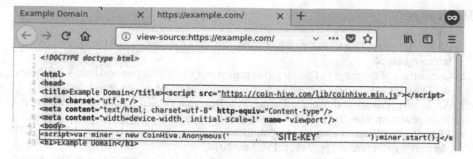

Fig. 7. Coinhive Javascript injected on the web site through proxy machine

usage maintains the covertness of the attack. Figure 8 shows a modified JavaScript with which the percentage of Cryptojacking can be throttled to our requirements. It shows the CPU usage to be initially at around 40% and later being increased to a value between 70% to 80% and finally dropping to around 50%. In this way the malicious JavaScript can be completely controlled by attacker to maintain a pattern and thereby avoid early detections.

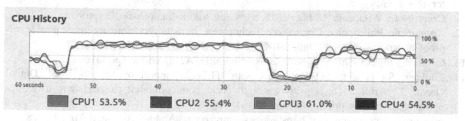

Fig. 8. Throttled CPU usage

6 Conclusion

The cryptojacking involves making money illegally by hijacking victim's computer resources like CPU processing power and memory to mine cryptocurrency like Monero. The rate of such attacks drastically increases day by day as there is no effective and proper defense mechanism to prevent this attack. This paper explains how Internet middle boxes play a crucial role in implementing this attack on a larger scale environment. We conducted an extensive analysis to implement this attack on an open anonymous proxy and exploiting this attack through open anonymous proxy cause greater damage to the CPU resources of the users who are connected to it.

The defense mechanisms available to prevent cryptojacking are AdBlockers and also blocking external scripts (miner or not) from being executed in the machine with the help of NoScripts. But these mechanisms are now being easily overpowered by a new technique of mining called Coinhive Stratum mining which fetches the scripts from another mining server instead of, coinhive directly. Because of this procedure, the AdBlockers will not be able to block the mining script as it is not from coinhive.com.

References

1. Global Internet usage, Wikipedia, 1 May 2018. https://en.wikipedia.org/wiki/Global_ Internet_usage4
2. Comparison of the usage of Default sub domain www vs. Default protocol https for websites, W^3Techs, 21 May 2018. https://w3techs.com/technologies/details/ce-httpsdefault
3. Anonymity, Privacy and Security Online, Pew Research Center, 5 September 2013. http:// www.pewinternet.org/2013/09/05/anonymity-privacy-and-security-online/
4. Elkhatib, Y., Tyson, G., Welzl, M.: Can SPDY really make the web faster? In: 2014 IFIP Networking Conference, pp. 1–9. IEEE, June 2014
5. Belshe, M., Peon, R.: SPDY Protocol., draft-mbelshe-httpbis spdy-00, February 2012. https:// tools.ietf.org/html/draft-mbelshe-httpbis-spdy-00
6. Belshe, M., Peon, R., Thomson, M.: Hypertext Transfer Protocol Version 2 (HTTP/2), RFC 7540, May 2015. https://tools.ietf.org/html/rfc7540
7. Peon, R., Ruellan, H.: HPACK: Header Compression for HTTP/2, RFC 7541, May 2015. https://tools.ietf.org/html/rfc7541
8. Lyon, G.F.: Nmap network scanning: The official Nmap project guide to network discovery and security scanning. Insecure (2009)
9. MONERO private digital currency, Monero (2014). https://getmonero.org/. Accessed 4 June
10. Monero (cryptocurrency), Wikipedia, 6 June 2018. https://en.wikipedia.org/wiki/Monero_ (cryptocurrency)
11. CryptoNote, Wikipedia, 18 May 2018. https://en.wikipedia.org/wiki/CryptoNote
12. CryptoNote Philosophy, CryptoNote Technology. https://cryptonote.org/inside.php#equal-proof-of-work. Accessed 7 June 2018
13. Coinhive blog, Coinhive. https://coinhive.com/blog. Accessed 12 Apr 2018
14. Zhukaev, S.: How to Set Up Nginx with HTTP/2 Support on Ubuntu 16.04, Digital Ocean, 12 April 2016. https://www.digitalocean.com/community/tutorials/how-to-set-up-nginx-with-http-2-support-on-ubuntu-16-04
15. mitmproxydocs, mitmproxy. https://docs.mitmproxy.org/stable/. Accessed Apr 24 2018
16. Qamar, A.: Why Monero (XMR) should be Preferred over Bitcoin (BTC), Globcoin Report, 15 April 2018. https://globalcoinreport.com/why-monero-xmr-should-be-preferred-over-bitcoin-btc/
17. Switching Protocols, MDN web docs moz://a. https://developer.mozilla.org/enUS/docs/Web/ HTTP/Status/101. Accessed 21 Sep 2017
18. Fielding, R., Reschke, J.: Hypertext Transfer Protocol (HTTP/1.1): Semantics and Content, RFC 7231, June 2014. https://tools.ietf.org/html/rfc7231#section-6.2.2
19. Coinhive - Monero JavaScript Mining, CoinHive (2018). https://coinhive.com/
20. Suresh, M., Amritha, P.P., Mohan, A.K., Kumar, V.A.: An investigation on HTTP/2 security. J. Cyber Secur. Mobil. 7(1), 161–189 (2018)

Android Malware Detector Based on Sequences of System Calls and Bidirectional Recurrent Networks

Khaled Al-Thelaya and El-Sayed M. El-Alfy(✉)

King Fahd University of Petroleum and Minerals, Dhahran, Saudi Arabia
alfy@kfupm.edu.sa

Abstract. With the increasing popularity and wide-spread use of Android systems to empower a variety of devices including smart phones, tablets, watches, televisions, and cars, security becomes a more crucial issue, especially with the increasing level of attacks targeting vulnerabilities in these systems. Subsequently, new approaches need to be explored to detect more sophisticated malware designed to evade detection by installed anti-malware software. This paper presents a new methodology for behavioral analysis of sequences of system calls incurred by various applications to distinguish Android malware from benign applications. We model these sequences using two variants of bidirectional deep recurrent neural networks: Long Short Term Memory (LSTM) and Gated Recurrent Unit (GRU). The performance is evaluated and compared with other systems employing support vector machines and decision trees with traditional feature extraction methods.

1 Introduction

The many benefits and advantages of the inevitable integration of advanced technology into human life are put to risk due to the rise of several challenging problems related to safety and security aspects. For instance, mobile phones are one of the most heavily used devices to conveniently accomplish most of our daily tasks including communication and exchange of different highly sensitive private information. However, with the increasing connectivity to the Internet of these smart gadgets, protection and privacy become of greater concern than ever before. The revealed security breaches are excessively rising in volume, complexity and severity. Therefore, several security researchers have been attracted to identify and develop novel solutions and control measures to detect and prevent more sophisticated attacks on confidentiality/privacy, integrity, and availability of data and services [8].

An important strategy in security is Defense-in-Depth (DiD), where multiple defensive mechanisms are put in layers such that if one fails, another can thwart the attack. A common step under this strategy is vulnerability analysis and deployment of suitable protection methods to mitigate the attack consequences. Another major direction in security is malware analysis and detection. This

© Springer Nature Singapore Pte Ltd. 2020
S. M. Thampi et al. (Eds.): SSCC 2019, CCIS 1208, pp. 309–321, 2020.
https://doi.org/10.1007/978-981-15-4825-3_25

problem has been studied for long time but is still recurrent due to the continuous evolution of new methods to evade detection mechanisms. As mentioned in a recent security report by McAfee, "If 2018 was the year of mobile malware, 2019 is the year of everywhere malware"[1]. Besides static or signature-based analysis, behavioral analysis of malware plays an important role to detect more illusive malware and prepare suitable defensive strategies to stop them and eliminate threats [16].

Though static analysis methods are also commonly used to efficiently perform detection, new malware obfuscation methods are adopted by new variants of malware to evade static analysis detection methods. Therefore, a new generation of robust detection and mitigation methods should be developed to respond to the evolving challenges. Besides static analysis, dynamic behavioral analysis is a vital tool for advanced malware analysis. It depends on observing the malicious intent of the malware through recording and monitoring system calls and data exchange during the execution time. Based on the analysis process, the malware can be detected using different types of modeling approaches. Most of the operations conducted by mobile applications need to be served by the operating system through system calls. Monitoring, tracing, and modeling system calls is one of the effective methods used to infer the application type and identify whether it is a malware or not [1,2,12].

During the past decade, deep learning emerged as one of the most advanced machine learning techniques. It was developed based on the artificial neural networks (ANN) methodology in which a set of weights is spread over many layers and adjusted to perform modeling based on given data. ANNs can only model certain amount of data using a limited number of layers. Processing huge amount of data requires a larger processing mechanism to achieve higher performance. In contrast, a deep learning architecture is more complex than ANNs. It consists of several learning layers and a larger number of neurons which can be trained to model more sophisticated and huge data. Many deep modeling techniques were proposed in the literature to construct detection models. Since system calls invoked by applications exhibit sequential patterns, deep Recurrent Neural Network (RNN) can be used to train more efficient models for malware detection [10,18].

In this paper, we review some related works, which use behavioral dynamic analysis based on sequences of system calls to detect and identify malware [13–15,17,18]. We then propose a dynamic analysis method for Android-based devices based on Deep Recurrent Neural Network using bidirectional Long Short Term Memory (LSTM) and Gated Recurrent Unit (GRU) networks. Several models were trained to detect whether the underlying software is malware or not based on sequences of system calls. Experiments were conducted to evaluate the proposed detection methodology. We also conducted a number of experiments to investigate unigrams and bigrams of system call sequences as inputs to detection models developed using decision tree and SVM. The experimental results of the

---

[1] https://www.mcafee.com/enterprise/en-us/assets/reports/rp-mobile-threat-report-2019.pdf.

proposed methodology are evaluated and compared with traditional methods on the same benchmark dataset.

The paper is organized as follows. Section 2 reviews most related works. The proposed methodology is discussed in Sect. 3. The conducted experiments are discussed in Sect. 4. Conclusion remarks are presented in Sect. 5.

2   Related Work

A popular method to detect malware is static program analysis. Some studies performed static analysis over the Android Package (APK) application format to obtain an analytical description representing its functionalities. Modeling the set of system API calls may help to detect the behavior of the application and identify whether it is malicious or benign. Nix and Zhang [11] conducted static analysis over the APK code by tracing the code without execution. The proposed detection method depended on program flow analysis. A sequence of system API calls were captured during each analyzer tracking run. The study employed convolutional neural network (CNN) and LSTM to perform learning and classification.

Aafer et al. [1] developed a methodology to detect malware for Android. They aimed to avoid the drawbacks of the permission-based detection method and trained an efficient and lightweight classifier for Android malware detection. In order to define and use a set of features which distinguish between benign and malicious apps, they depended on API level calls within the bytecode because it reflects important indication semantics about the apps' malicious behavior. Therefore, they built the model based on the critical API calls, their parameters, and package level information. They performed the feature extraction based on API level and data flow analysis and developed a tool to perform reverse engineering of apps. They used four different classifiers and the best results obtained using KNN on a large corpus of different malware families.

Many studies suggested that some malware showed the ability to avoid static analysis detection methods. Therefore, they advocated the use of behavioral analysis methods to detect and identify malware. Canali et al. [3] conducted several experiments to test and compare different behavioral models based on several input structures using system calls. The study investigated the impact of using different input structure and parameters of the system calls. The collected dataset consists of several malware execution traces recorded and monitored in real-world machines, in a synthetic environment, and under normal operating circumstances. The study concluded that the detection accuracy depends on a limited constructed shape of system calls with their arguments. They suggested that changing the shape of input that system call constructs has a significant impact on the accuracy.

Moreover, Dahl et al. [6] used tri-gram representation to construct the features form sequences of system calls. They built their classification model based on huge collected data and used logistic regression and Multi-Layer Perceptron (MLP). They compared several models to perform multi-class malware classification. The study extracted several types of features such as tri-grams of system

API calls, null-terminated patterns observed in the process memory, and distinct combinations of a single API system call and one input parameter. The study used feature selection to reduce the dimensionality of the data and improve the accuracy.

Malware designed specially to attack mobile platforms grew exponentially during 2012 and 2013 as stated by Dimjašević et al. [7]. The study indicated that around 92% of mobile malware targets Android platform. Therefore, they developed a dynamic malware detection approach based on monitoring and analyzing system calls. The proposed methodology is composed of three phases. The first phase aimed at collecting and recording malware behavior during real time execution. They developed and used a special tool called MALINE designed to monitor malware applications. The second phase performed feature extraction and representation, they used frequency and dependency methods to represent system calls. Data modeling and learning is conducted in the third phase. The experiments included several types of machine learning classification methods such as support vector machine and random forest to perform data classification. The collected dataset is composed of several parts based on number of events injected to applications during the run time. The evaluation experiments conducted by our study used a part of the dataset collected by this study. We used log files produced by single event execution of applications and malware as described by Dimjašević et al. [7].

Due to the efficient modeling performance shown by deep learning techniques, different types of deep learning modeling techniques were also exploited by many studies in the literature. LSTM was used by Xiao et al. to identify malware [18]. They analyzed sequences of system calls as sequences of words forming sentences. They adopted the same methodology used for natural language processing where in semantic information is considered as sequential elements. The proposed methodology mainly developed based on probabilistic similarity measures which are used to determine the malware applications. Canfora et al. [4] proposed a feature extraction methodology based on tracing system calls of malware to perform the detection. The study conducted several experiments using different length of system calls traces and sequences. They used support vector machine (SVM) to perform the training on different configurations of features extracted from the system calls dataset.

Kolosnjaji et al. [10] suggested that the best way to recognize malware behavior is by tracing its invoked system calls. They developed two methodologies using neural networks to model sequences of system calls. They used recurrent and convolutional layers. The input of the convolutional network represented by system calls sequences as a set of n-grams. This kind of modeling does not explicitly depend on the position of system calls, but uses the frequency of presence of system calls as n-grams in a behavioral trace. Despite the simplicity of this approach, it causes loss of fidelity of information patterns. The proposed mode designed using one convolutional neural network layer followed by another LSTM layer. To evaluate the proposed approach, they monitored and observed the API system calls of group of malware and non-malware software executed in a sandboxed environment.

Our study conducts several experiments to compare a proposed architecture developed using bidirectional GRU and LSTM with other types of methodologies proposed in the literature. The evaluation process depends on a publicly available dataset collected by processing sequences of system call traces generated at the run time by set of applications. We compare different models developed by bidirectional and simple architectures of LSTM and GRU, in addition to traditional models developed by SVM and decision tree using unigrams and bigrams as input features.

3   Methodology

The availability of huge labeled data and power of high-processing computing were two of the many reasons that led to the development of deep learning methodology. Moreover, employing a different type of activation functions such as ReLU with gated units has alleviated the vanishing gradient problem which was one of the problems associated with simple ANNs. Several types of deep learning networks were proposed in the literature to model different types of input data collected from different application domains.

Deep Recurrent Neural Network (RNN) is one of the deep architectures proposed to model sequential data. It can be used to solve several kinds of prediction and classification problems. It is commonly used for natural language processing, time series forecasting, text mining, etc. Several variants of deep RNNs have been proposed in the literature such as Long Short Term Memory (LSTM) and GRU. They have been developed to overcome the vanishing gradient problem associated with simple RNNs. LSTM has been developed by Hochreiter and Schmidhuber [9] to process longer sequences of data and capture deeper dependency between data elements. It uses four gated units representing the hidden states of the network. GRU is an extension to LSTM introduced in 2014 by Kyunghyun Cho et al. [5]. It uses fewer gated units and needs less number of parameters compared to the LSTM. The LSTM transition equations are as follows [9]:

$$i_t = \sigma(W_i x_t + U_i h_{t-1} + V_i c_{t-1}) \tag{1}$$
$$f_t = \sigma(W_f x_t + U_f h_{t-1} + V_f c_{t-1}) \tag{2}$$
$$o_t = \sigma(W_o x_t + U_o h_{t-1} + V_o c_t) \tag{3}$$
$$\tilde{c}_t = \tanh(W_c x_t + U_c h_{t-1}) \tag{4}$$
$$c_t = f_t^i \odot c_{t-1} + i_t \odot \tilde{c}_t \tag{5}$$
$$h_t = o_t \odot \tanh(c_t) \tag{6}$$

The transition equation in hidden units of GRU are given as follows [5]:

$$h_t = (1 - z_t) \odot h_{t-1} + z_t \odot \tilde{h}_t \tag{7}$$
$$\tilde{h}_t = g(W_h x_t + U_h(r_t \odot h_{t-1}) + b_h) \tag{8}$$
$$z_t = \sigma(W_z x_t + U_z h_{t-1} + b_z) \tag{9}$$
$$r_t = \sigma(W_r x_t + U_r h_{t-1} + b_r) \tag{10}$$

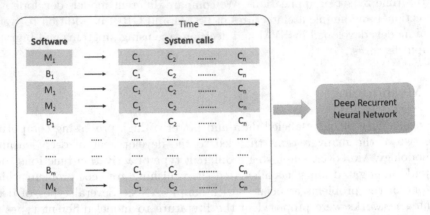

Fig. 1. Methodology used to form the dataset and feed it to the network.

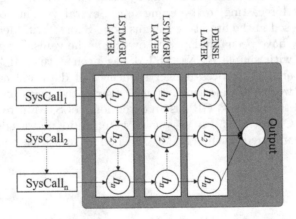

Fig. 2. The generic multilayer architecture of the trained bidirectional recurrent networks for both LSTM and GRU.

One of the most useful dynamic traceable information to distinguish malware behavior is system calls. For the malware to execute payload malicious actions or propagation code, it needs the services offered by the operating system. These services are necessary for any software to execute. Based on this assumption, we use sequences of system calls generated by malware or non-malware software to train a classification model. Although malware can change its behavioral actions, it has to execute its payload and perform propagation and hiding mechanism. These kinds of actions require services provided by the operating systems through system calls. Analyzing system call patterns observed in the execution timeline of applications helps to identify whether a piece of code is trying to conduct a malicious action. Based on sequences of system calls captured during the run time, detection models can be trained to identify and learn dynamic behavior of malware and legitimate (benign) applications. Evidently, patterns exhibited by sequences of system calls invoked by malware are different from those invoked by legitimate applications. Therefore, we use GRU and LSTM to model system call sequences and perform the malware detection process. The proposed model processes the input as streams of sequential system calls based on different executions of several malware and legitimate applications. We train the model on different system calls for multiple executions of different malware based on a specific timing window. It is also trained on different system calls of several executions of benign apps to enable the model to distinguish between malware and benign software. Figure 1 shows a diagram to illustrate the formation of the input sequences, where C denotes system calls, M denotes malware process of certain malware type, and B denotes benign software process.

The proposed model developed using two layers of LSTM or GRU. Each of the two layers processes data sequences following opposite direction. One layer processes system calls sequences forward, whereas the other layer performs the learning backward. It enables the network to process and learn from data in both directions. This kind of processing improves the ability of the network to extract contextual information from system calls sequences. We compare performance of two types of the proposed architectures. The recurrent activation units of LSTM and GRU layers use the hard sigmoid transfer function, whereas the output units use tanh transfer function. The final output (malware or non-malware) is computed by a dense layer using the sigmoid activation function. Figure 2 illustrates the architecture of the trained network for both bidirectional LSTM and GRU.

Generally, applications produce different lengths of system call execution sequences. Sequences which have length less than the slide window size are padded with zeros, whereas sequences which have length greater than slide window size are split into many subsequence samples. Therefore, some applications have only one sample sequence whereas others have many execution samples. Therefore, we use two evaluation methods based on split method of sequence samples into training and testing. The first method randomly splits sequence samples into training and testing regardless of applications which have more than one sequence sample. This methodology was developed based on the assumption that if an execution sequence sample shows an abnormal behavior or performs a malicious action, the execution sequence sample is identified as a malware. This methodology treats execution sequences instead of the whole application execution which can be used to identify which part of the application execution sequence generates malicious code.

The second split method is employed to solve the problem of having many execution sequence samples which belong to the same applications. This methodology is applied by dividing the data into training and testing based on applications, not based on samples of system call sequences. We first split applications randomly into training and testing, then perform the training on system calls sequences produced by training applications. Since each application can have many sequence samples, the classification model, during the test phase, may give different prediction labels to the same application based on how many sequence samples generated by the application. To solve this problem, we use majority of votes of all sequence samples which belong to the same application. If most of the execution sequence samples indicate that the application's execution shows an abnormal behavior or a malicious action, it is identified as a malware. Otherwise, the application is considered benign.

4   Experiments

Several experiments were conducted in this study to evaluate the proposed modeling approach. We adopted the dataset collected by [7], where sequences of applications' system calls were recorded in a sandbox environment in a chronological order. Different types of log files were generated according to number of events inserted to applications. We used single event log files in our experiments to evaluate the proposed methodology. We parsed the set of log files generated for each malicious and benign application. Log files include system calls, time stamps, input and return values. The chronological ordering of system calls is the main analysis focus of our study. Our proposed methodology is based on capturing behavioral patterns of application executions at the run time to detect malicious actions and identify whether a certain application is a malware or not. We trained several models using different types of feature extraction methods. We represented system calls by assigning unique consecutive numbers for each system call name. Some of the system calls were triggered several consecutive times. We considered each sequence of the same system call as a single call.

The encoded system calls were fed as input to two training models developed using the proposed bidirectional LSTM and GRU models. We trained the models for up to 30 and 50 epochs using 100 memory cells. Execution of applications usually generates different length of system calls sequences, therefore we used a slide window to reshape the sequences into the same length sample sequences. Execution system calls of applications divided into several input samples. We reshaped the data using 500 and 1000 system calls sequences slide window. Execution samples which have length less than 500 or 1000 were padded with zeros. We used a masking layer before we fed the data into the network to alleviate the impact of the padding operation on the training performance.

Results were estimated using three different measures in order to assess the effectiveness of the proposed methodology. The results were calculated based on the test data by performing binary classification into benign or malware. Several performance metrics were used to evaluate the trained models including

Accuracy, Precision, Recall, and F_1 score. The employed metrics were calculated based on the values of true positive (tp), which denotes the number of correctly labeled malware samples; true negative (tn) denotes the number of samples classified correctly as benign; false negative (fn) represents the number of malware samples labeled incorrectly as benign, whereas the false positives (fp) is the number of benign samples incorrectly labeled as malware. The respective equations for the performance metrics are:

$$Accuracy = \frac{tp + tn}{tp + tn + fp + fn} \tag{11}$$

$$Precision = \frac{tp}{tp + fp} \tag{12}$$

$$Recall = \frac{tp}{tp + fn} \tag{13}$$

$$F_1 = 2 * \frac{Precision * Recall}{Precision + Recall} \tag{14}$$

Table 1. Percentage results for both bidirectional LSTM and GRU models trained using 500 and 1000 slide windows of system call sequences samples (approx. to 3 decimal digits)

Model	Window	Accuracy	Precision	Recall	F_1
Bidirectional LSTM	500	91.505	77.004	54.380	63.744
	1000	89.347	70.053	59.356	64.262
Bidirectional GRU	500	91.056	75.788	50.646	60.717
	1000	90.014	77.692	51.775	62.139

The dataset consists of samples of system calls sequences generated by a single execution of each of the 13,561 applications. Executions have one or more sequence samples depending on the slide window used to form data samples. All sequence sample executions were randomly split into 80% for training and 20% for testing. Also, 20% of the training sequences was allocated for validation of performance during training of the model to avoid overfitting. The results of the conducted experiments for the developed models using bidirectional LSTM and GRU are shown in Table 1. The ROC curves and areas under the curve for both models using 500 slide window size are shown in Figs. 3 and 4, respectively. Table 1 shows the results of using sequence samples as input to train the models. These results demonstrate high level of detection rate, especially for the bidirectional model based based on GRU.

The developed models were able to identify newly unseen malware executions successfully. Most of the malware samples were identified by analyzing and learning sequences of system calls runtime execution patterns. According

Table 2. Percentage results of both bidirectional LSTM and GRU models trained using 500 and 1000 slide windows based on majority of votes of samples belong to same application system call sequence (approx. to 3 decimal digits)

Model	Window	Accuracy	Precision	Recall	F_1
LSTM	500	76.710	70.858	53.042	60.669
	1000	77.760	67.862	52.591	59.259
GRU	500	81.687	79.380	60.235	68.495
	1000	80.638	75.451	62.890	68.600
Bidirectional LSTM	500	80.171	82.897	49.223	61.769
	1000	83.356	79.119	77.187	78.141
Bidirectional GRU	500	82.076	80.000	59.544	68.273
	1000	86.858	80.317	78.776	79.539

Table 3. Percentage results of both bidirectional LSTM and GRU models trained using 500 and 1000 slide windows based on majority of votes of samples belong to same application system call sequence (approx. to 3 decimal digits)

Model	Features	Accuracy	Precision	Recall	F_1
SVM	Unigram	75.995	82.061	41.372	41.372
	Bigram	77.028	77.467	41.069	41.069
Decision Tree	Unigram	81.710	70.544	75.028	75.028
	Bigram	81.670	70.851	73.833	73.834

to the detection rate results, malware code shows different behavioral pattern than benign applications. Malware usually follows certain patterns of execution which can be exploited effectively to develop a detection mechanism using sequence analysis methods.

However, the same application can have many execution sequence samples. Therefore, we performed experiments by randomly separating the data into 20% for testing and 80% for training such that all execution sequences which belong to one application are either used for the training or testing. Thus, no application would have sequence samples in both training and testing data. We used majority voting to combine decisions of many sequence samples belong to same application to determine whether the application is malware or not. Table 2 shows the evaluation results in this case. The results show that the developed bidirectional architecture using LSTM and GRU attains higher accuracy compared to models developed using simple LSTM and GRU layers. The bidirectional architecture succeeds to extract more useful patterns from the data. Moreover, the bidirectional GRU model shows a higher level of accuracy compared to the other three types of models as shown in Table 2.

We also conducted experiments to compare the performance of the modeling architecture proposed by this study with that of two of the common methods in

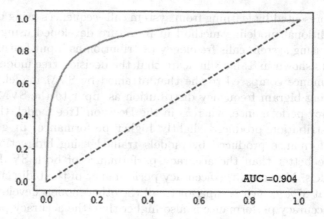

Fig. 3. ROC curve and area under the curve (AUC) for the Bidirectional GRU model trained using data formed by slide window of size 500.

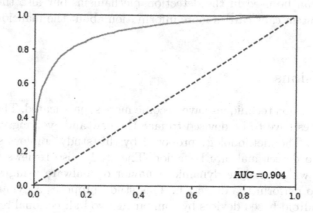

Fig. 4. ROC curve and area under the curve (AUC) for the Bidirectional LSTM model trained using data formed by slide window of size 500.

literature used to perform malware detection based on sequences of system calls. The first traditional method depends on frequency of the system calls (unigram). This kind of analysis is developed based on the assumption that the frequencies of the system calls may represent an indication of a malicious behavior. Thus, new malware should be recognized when that fingerprint is found. Another common approach usually employed to learn from execution patterns of malware is extracting frequency of each two consecutive system calls which is usually called bigram. A bigram or digram refers every sequence of two adjacent system calls in a sequence of execution. The system calls frequency distribution of bigrams is used to extract useful patterns and identify abnormal behavior of an application. We developed detection models using SVM and decision tree based on different input features designed using frequency distribution of system calls unigrams and bigrams. We compared the performance of the methodology proposed by this study represented by learning from system calls sequences using deep RNNs with the traditional modeling method in literature developed using SVM and decision tree using system calls frequency distribution as input features.

The results shown in Table 3 indicate that the decision tree model produced better performance compared to the that attained by SVM model. They also show that using bigram frequency distribution as input to the SVM produced higher accuracy performance, whereas in the Decision Tree model, the unigram frequency distribution produced slightly higher performance. In general, the accuracy performance produced by models trained using bidirectional LSTM and GRU are better than the accuracy performance of both SVM and decision tree models. Moreover, the accuracy performance of the bidirectional GRU model is about 87% which is superior to all the other models developed by this study. This accuracy performance is also higher than the accuracy performance reported in some of the related work [7] which reaches to about 83%. It is clear from the attained results that not only the type of system calls triggered by the malware can be used in the detection mechanism, but also the order and sequence of system calls carries more information about the malicious code and intent.

5   Conclusions

Malware obfuscation techniques have become more sophisticated. Therefore, new countermeasures have to be devised to face the new and evolving malware hiding techniques. The methodology proposed by this study employs sequences of system calls to detect malware behavior. The study also reviews some of the related works which analyze dynamic behavior of malware using sequences of system calls to perform the detection. This study proposes a dynamic analysis method for android-based devices by comparing two bidirectional recurrent networks. Several models based on LSTM and GRU were trained to detect whether the underlying software is a malware or not based on different sequences of system calls. We also conducted several experiments to investigate unigrams and bigrams of system calls sequences used as input to detection models developed using decision tree and SVM. The proposed methodology was evaluated against the two other detection models. The results of the experiments show that the proposed methodology has attained a higher level of accuracy.

Acknowledgements. The authors would like to thank King Fahd University of Petroleum and Minerals (KFUPM), Saudi Arabia, for the support during this work.

References

1. Aafer, Y., Du, W., Yin, H.: DroidAPIMiner: mining API-level features for robust malware detection in android. In: Zia, T., Zomaya, A., Varadharajan, V., Mao, M. (eds.) SecureComm 2013. LNICST, vol. 127, pp. 86–103. Springer, Cham (2013). https://doi.org/10.1007/978-3-319-04283-1_6

2. Burguera, I., Zurutuza, U., Nadjm-Tehrani, S.: Crowdroid: behavior-based malware detection system for android. In: Proceedings of the 1st ACM Workshop on Security and Privacy in Smartphones and Mobile Devices, pp. 15–26 (2011)
3. Canali, D., Lanzi, A., Balzarotti, D., Kruegel, C., Christodorescu, M., Kirda, E.: A quantitative study of accuracy in system call-based malware detection. In: Proceedings of the 2012 International Symposium on Software Testing and Analysis, pp. 122–132. ACM (2012)
4. Canfora, G., Medvet, E., Mercaldo, F., Visaggio, C.A.: Detecting android malware using sequences of system calls. In: Proceedings of the 3rd International Workshop on Software Development Lifecycle for Mobile, pp. 13–20. ACM (2015)
5. Cho, K., et al.: Learning phrase representations using RNN encoder-decoder for statistical machine translation. arXiv preprint arXiv:1406.1078 (2014)
6. Dahl, G.E., Stokes, J.W., Deng, L., Yu, D.: Large-scale malware classification using random projections and neural networks. In: 2013 IEEE International Conference on Acoustics, Speech and Signal Processing, pp. 3422–3426. IEEE (2013)
7. Dimjašević, M., Atzeni, S., Ugrina, I., Rakamaric, Z.: Evaluation of android malware detection based on system calls. In: Proceedings of the 2016 ACM on International Workshop on Security And Privacy Analytics, pp. 1–8. ACM (2016)
8. Faruki, P., et al.: Android security: a survey of issues, malware penetration, and defenses. IEEE Commun. Surv. Tutor. $17(2)$, 998–1022 (2014)
9. Hochreiter, S., Schmidhuber, J.: Long short-term memory. Neural Comput. $9(8)$, 1735–1780 (1997)
10. Kolosnjaji, B., Zarras, A., Webster, G., Eckert, C.: Deep learning for classification of malware system call sequences. In: Kang, B.H., Bai, Q. (eds.) AI 2016. LNCS (LNAI), vol. 9992, pp. 137–149. Springer, Cham (2016). https://doi.org/10.1007/978-3-319-50127-7_11
11. Nix, R., Zhang, J.: Classification of android apps and malware using deep neural networks. In: 2017 International Joint Conference on Neural Networks (IJCNN), pp. 1871–1878. IEEE (2017)
12. Peiravian, N., Zhu, X.: Machine learning for android malware detection using permission and API calls. In: Proceedings of IEEE 25th International Conference on Tools with Artificial Intelligence, pp. 300–305 (2013)
13. Rosenberg, I., Shabtai, A., Rokach, L., Elovici, Y.: Generic black-box end-to-end attack against RNNs and other API calls based malware classifiers. arXiv preprint arXiv:1707.05970 (2017)
14. Rosenberg, I., Shabtai, A., Rokach, L., Elovici, Y.: Generic black-box end-to-end attack against state of the art API call based malware classifiers. In: Bailey, M., Holz, T., Stamatogiannakis, M., Ioannidis, S. (eds.) RAID 2018. LNCS, vol. 11050, pp. 490–510. Springer, Cham (2018). https://doi.org/10.1007/978-3-030-00470-5_23
15. Sewak, M., Sahay, S.K., Rathore, H.: An investigation of a deep learning based malware detection system. In: Proceedings of the 13th International Conference on Availability, Reliability and Security, p. 26. ACM (2018)
16. Stamp, M.: Introduction to Machine Learning with Applications in Information Security. Chapman and Hall/CRC, Boca Raton (2017)
17. Wang, X., Yiu, S.M.: A multi-task learning model for malware classification with useful file access pattern from API call sequence. arXiv preprint arXiv:1610.05945 (2016)
18. Xiao, X., Zhang, S., Mercaldo, F., Hu, G., Sangaiah, A.K.: Android malware detection based on system call sequences and LSTM. Multimed. Tools Appl. $78(4)$, 3979–3999 (2017). https://doi.org/10.1007/s11042-017-5104-0

Efficient Ciphertext Policy Attribute Based Encryption (ECP-ABE) for Data Deduplication in Cloud Storage

Abhishek Kumar[1]([✉]) and P. Syam Kumar[2]

[1] School of Computer and Information Sciences,
University of Hyderabad, Hyderabad, India
ak101singh@gmail.com

[2] Institute for Development and Research in Banking Technology, Hyderabad, India
psyamkumar@idrbt.ac.in

Abstract. The cloud is the most suitable platform for storing and processing of data. Users are outsourcing data to the cloud to reduce the storage and maintenance cost locally. However, there are challenges to both cloud users as well as to the cloud service provider. The challenge for cloud service providers is to optimize the associated cost for the management and maintenance of uploaded data. The challenge for users is data privacy. To address these issues, encrypted data deduplication schemes proposed, but existing schemes suffer from security weakness and do not support data access control. In this paper, we propose an efficient ciphertext policy attribute-based encryption scheme for deduplication over encrypted data (ECP-ABE) in the cloud storage. Our scheme achieves privacy,deduplication along with access controls. The security and performance analysis demonstrates that our scheme is secure and efficient.

Keywords: Attribute based Encryption · Cloud computing · Data deduplication · Access controls · Privacy

1   Introduction

Cloud computing is emerging day by day due to its ability to provide cost effective solution and working on pay-per-use model. It offers a new way for IT services by rearranging various resources such as storage, computation, etc. The most important and popular cloud service is data storage. The expansion of digitization also stores huge data even in petabytes or exabytes in size. It amounts huge data storage in the cloud and requires optimum storage of resources. Cloud users outsource their personal and confidential data to the cloud service provider (CSP) and allow it to maintain these data. CSP can not be fully trusted because of intrusion and various attacks on the sensitive data in the cloud. Encrypting the data before uploading in the cloud becomes an important technique for protecting the confidentiality of data. Data encryption provides the guarantee for

© Springer Nature Singapore Pte Ltd. 2020
S. M. Thampi et al. (Eds.): SSCC 2019, CCIS 1208, pp. 322–334, 2020.
https://doi.org/10.1007/978-981-15-4825-3_26

confidentiality but the different users may upload same encrypted data to cloud, especially when data is shared among multiple users. Although cloud storage space is huge, data duplication greatly wastes network resources, consumes a lot of energy, and complicates data management. According to the International Data Corporation (IDC) analysis, the amount of data stored in the cloud is expected to reach 40 TB in 2020. Data deduplication is critical for data storage and processing in the cloud. Hence, there are the two issues to be handled in the cloud environment: maintain the confidentiality of the outsourced data and minimize the storage cost.

1.1   Related Works

Data deduplication is a technique in cloud storage to eliminate matching data and store only a unique copy of the file. Douceur et al. [1] proposed a data deduplication scheme over encrypted data that addressed both issues- privacy and optimum utilization of storage. They introduced the convergent encryption scheme to eliminate redundant data. The limitation of this scheme is that the keys for encryption and decryption are produced straight from the message. Bellare et al. [2] proposed message locked encryption (MLE) scheme for data deduplication. Moreover this scheme does not satisfied the semantic confidentiality. Abadi et al. [3] overcome the security of previous scheme and proposed MLE with lock-dependent messages. In this scheme, message length is not solely responsible for the length of the ciphertext. Bellare et al. [4] introduced a new server-aided encryption scheme for data deduplication, called DupLESS.

In this scheme, an independent key server generates the key, but this scheme suffered from large computation time. Later, there have been different efforts taken to improve key management [5–7]. Li et al. [8] proposed a reliable key management concept in the data deduplication scheme. In their further work, Li et al. [9] achieved the deduplication in the distributed environment. The main theme of this scheme is to disperse the chunks of data across multiple cloud servers. Liu et al. [10] proposed a password-authenticated key exchange protocol in cross user client side deduplication scheme. Recently there have been various schemes in the literature to improve the data deduplication efficiency and security. Yan et al. [11] proposed the data deduplication scheme along with access control among data owners using proof of ownership and proxy re-encryption. Liu et al. [10] proposed a randomized MLE scheme that enhances the efficiency. Wang et al. [12] enhanced security by pre-authenticate the user before sharing of the data in deduplication scheme. Yang et al. [13] proposed a scheme that restricts the brute force attack in data deduplication scheme. This scheme is also addressed the data availability. Yang et al. [14] proposed an "efficient and privacy-preserving deduplication" scheme by generating a random tag and a constant number of random ciphertext for each data. Youn et al. [15] proposed scheme that provides client-side deduplication with support of confidentiality to prevent users' sensitive data on untrusted cloud servers.

1.2   Contributions

In this paper, we propose an efficient ciphertext policy attribute-based encryption (CP-ABE) scheme to achieve data privacy and data deduplication. The major contributions of our scheme as follows:

  i. Our scheme employs CP-ABE to achieve data privacy and access control.
 ii. We employ the data deduplication technique to remove the duplicate data by storing only a single copy of the file that saves the storage cost and network bandwidth.
iii. Security analysis proves that our scheme provides confidentiality, protected from chosen-plaintext attack (CPA), and user collusion attack.
 iv. Performance analysis certifies that this scheme reduces the computation and communication overhead.

2   Preliminaries

Here, we describe the mathematical backgrounds, basic definitions, and concepts that are required to design the proposed scheme.

2.1   Bilinear Pairing

Let p be the large prime number. Let $\mathcal{G}_0$ and $\mathcal{G}_1$ be the additive and multiplicative cyclic group of prime order p respectively. The generator of group $\mathcal{G}_0$ is denoted by g and x, y are the random numbers from Z_p. A bilinear pairing function is denoted by $\mathcal{P}$ and it is defined as $\mathcal{P} : \mathcal{G}_0 * \mathcal{G}_0 \rightarrow \mathcal{G}_1$, which must satisfy the following properties [16–18]:

  i. Bilinearity: For $g \in \mathcal{G}_0$; $x, y \in Z_p$, $\epsilon(g^x; g^y) = \epsilon(g, g)^{xy}$.
 ii. Non-degeneracy: $\epsilon(g, g) \neq 1$, where $g \in \mathcal{G}_0$.
iii. Computability: The bilinear pairing function $\epsilon(g, g)$ can be efficiently computable by polynomial time algorithm.

2.2   Access Structure

Let us consider $\rho = \{\rho_1, \rho_2, ..., \rho_n\}$ is a collection of parties. A collection $\Gamma \subseteq 2^\rho$ is defined as monotonic if $\forall R, S$: if $R \subseteq S$, then $S \in \Gamma$. An access structure [19] is defined as Γ, in which subsets of ρ should not be empty. In mathematical terms, $\Gamma = 2^\rho \setminus \{\emptyset\}$. Authorized sets are defined as the sets present in Γ, or else are termed as the unauthorized sets.

2.3   Access Tree

Access tree [17,18,20] is the access structure which is used to provide the data access only for the authorized users. The access tree is denoted by τ and r_0 denotes root node. Each node in the access node τ is denoted by x. Let $\mathcal{U}$ be a set of attributes. The leaf nodes consist of attributes and non-leaf nodes consists of AND, OR gates. Assign an integer number to the child node of x from 1 to N for each node x. Further, each node is assigned with threshold value th. The threshold value of all leaf nodes are 1 and for the non-leaf node is between 1 and N. The threshold value of OR gate is 1 and AND gate is N. The function parent(x) returns the parent node of x. The function att(x) outputs the attribute stored in x. The function index(x) outputs the integer value associated with x. Figure 1 shows the example of access tree.

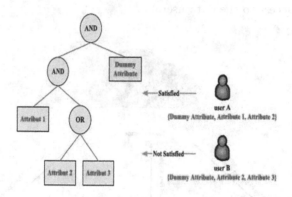

Fig. 1. Access tree

3   ECP-ABE Scheme System Outline

Here, we describe the proposed scheme system architecture, design goals, security threats, and security model.

3.1   System Architecture

The system architecture of the proposed ECP-ABE scheme consists of five entities such as trusted authority (TA), Group manager (GM), data owner (DO), data user (DU) and cloud as depicted in Fig. 2.

- i. Trusted Authority (TA): The main function of trusted authority is to generate public parameter $pub.Key$, master secret key $M_{sec.Key}$, and secret key $sec.Key_{curr}$ for the decryption cryptographic operation.

ii. Group Manager (GM): The group manager is a trusted entity in our proposed scheme. The main function of GM is to create group master key GMK_{curr}, and generates certificate χ_{curr} for each user belonging to a particular group. This certificate helps the users to prove their membership in the group.

iii. Data Owner (DO): In our ECP-ABE scheme, the data owner is a trusted entity who wants to outsource their data to the cloud. Before uploading data into the cloud, DO creates the tag $\mathscr{T}$ with the help of some random hash functions.

iv. Data User (DU): Data user can download the ciphertext from the cloud and decrypts it. Only those users can obtain the plaintext whose attributes set entertains the access policy defined in the ciphertext.

v. Cloud: Cloud is a semi-trusted entity. It provides unlimited storage to the data owners to upload their data based on the pay-per-use model and provides data access to the data user.

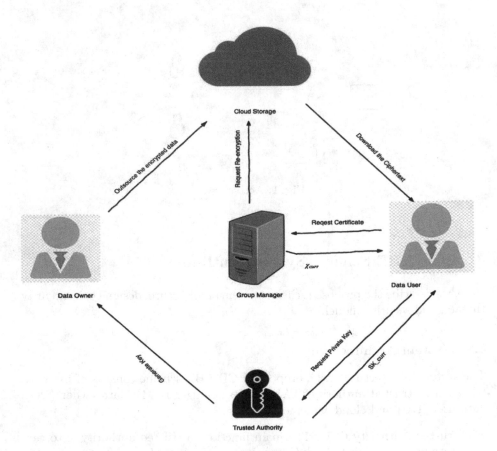

Fig. 2. System architecture

3.2   Design Goals

The proposed ECP-ABE scheme for data deduplication is designed with four design goals such as privacy, fine-grained access control, efficient data deduplication and efficiency.

i. Privacy: The data stored in the cloud storage should not be disclosed to anyone.
ii. Fine-grained access control: Allowing only those users who satisfies the access policy defined by data owner to decrypt the outsourced data.
iii. Efficient data deduplication: Store only a single copy of the redundant data and saves both the disk space and network bandwidth.
iv. Efficiency: Reduce the storage overhead, communication overhead and computational overhead.

3.3   Security Threats

The following are the possible threats that can breach the security of our proposed scheme.

a. User Collusion Attack: The goal of user collusion attack is to reduce the security of outsourced data by unauthorized access. The unauthorized users who denied the permission to access the uploaded data (void user) may collude their private key with other users private key in the same group to access the outsourced data.
b. Chosen Plaintext Attack (CPA): The main goal of this attack is to violate the confidentiality of the outsourced data. An attacker receives the ciphertext for the given arbitrary plaintext and tries to obtain the information.

3.4   Security Model

To demonstrate that the ECP-ABE scheme is secure against chosen plaintext attack, we introduced the following security game. In this game, there are two players defined as challenger ϑ and adversary φ. Adversary chooses two equal size messages $\mathcal{M}$ and $\mathcal{M}^*$ and is given to the challenger ϑ. Concerning this, ϑ forwards the $\mathcal{C}^*$, the ciphertext for a plaintext $\mathcal{M}_\mu$, where $\mu \in \{0,1\}$ to the adversary φ. Now, φ randomly estimates the precise μ value. If the estimation of the adversary is true, then he/she wins the game and the security of the proposed scheme is compromised. The advantage for the adversary winning this game is defined as $Adv_\varphi = |Pr[\mu = \mu'] - \frac{1}{2}|$.

4   Detailed Construction

Here, we construct the proposed scheme. In this scheme, there are eight algorithms named as System Setup, Group Setup, CertGen, TagGen, Duplicate-Check, KeyGen, Data Encryption, and Data Decryption. The detailed construction of various algorithms are given below.

4.1   System Setup

This algorithm is performed by trusted authority (TA). It takes security parameter st, attribute universe $\mathcal{U}$ as inputs and outputs its master secret key $M_{sec.Key}$ and public parameter $pub.Key$. Generate $\mathcal{G}_0$ and $\mathcal{G}_1$ as additive and multiplicative group of order p with a bilinear pairing $\mathcal{P} : \mathcal{G}_0 * \mathcal{G}_0 \rightarrow \mathcal{G}_1$. TA randomly chooses $\alpha, \beta \in Z_p^*$. Compute g^α, g^β, and $f = \epsilon(g,g)^\alpha$. For each attribute $a_j \in \mathcal{U}$, randomly choose $t_{j1}, t_{j2} \in Z_p^*$ and Compute $T_j = g^{t_{j1}t_{j2}/(t_{j1}+t_{j2})}$. Return public parameter $pub.Key = (\epsilon,\ g,\ f,\ \forall a_j \in \mathcal{U} : T_j)$, and master secret key $M_{sec.Key} = (\beta,\ \forall a_j \in \mathcal{U} : (t_{j1}, t_{j2}),\ g^\alpha)$.

4.2   Group Setup

This algorithm is performed by group manager GM. It takes public parameter $pub.Key$ as input and outputs the group master key GMK_{curr}, group public key GPK_{curr} and dictionary Dic_{curr} which is initially empty. GM choose a random exponent $x_0 \in Z_p^*$ as group master key $GMK_{curr} = \{x_0\}$. Computes g^{x_0} and $\epsilon(g,g)^{x_0}$. Group public key $GPK_{curr} = \{\mathcal{G}_{id}, g^{x_0}, \epsilon(g,g)^{x_0}\}$, where $\mathcal{G}_{id}$ is denoted as group identifier. Dic_{curr} is a dictionary which is initially empty.

4.3   CertGen

This algorithm is performed by group manager GM. It takes inputs as public parameter $pub.Key$, user's identity $\mathcal{U}_{id}$, group master key GMK_{curr} and output a certificate χ_{curr}.

4.4   KeyGen

This algorithm is performed by trusted authority TA. It takes public parameter $pub.Key$, master secret key $M_{sec.Key}$, group public key GPK_{curr}, attribute set $\mathcal{S}$, user identity $\mathcal{U}_{id}$, certificate χ_{curr} as inputs and output as secret key $sec.Key_{curr}$. TA verifies $\epsilon(g^{\chi_{curr}}) = \epsilon(g^{\beta * \mathcal{H}(\mathcal{U}_{id})}, g^{\chi_{curr}})$ to check whether the user is a member of the group or not. If user is the member of group, then return secret key $sec.Key_{curr}$ to the user. Else, TA chooses $r_k \in Z_p^*$ for each attribute $k \in \mathcal{S}$, $r_g \in Z_p^*$ for the group identity $\mathcal{G}_{id}$, and random numbers $q, s_1, s_2 \in Z_p^*$. TA also computes $\mathcal{H}(\mathcal{U}_{id})^{\chi_{curr}} = \chi_{curr}/(g^{\chi_{curr}})^\beta$. Compute the private keys: $sec.Key_{\mathcal{S}} = \{\mathcal{D}_1 = g^{t_1(\alpha+r)/\beta}, \forall k \in \mathcal{S} : \mathcal{D}_k = \mathcal{H}(\mathcal{U}_{id})^{\chi_{curr}} * \mathcal{H}(k)^{s_1 * q_k}\}$, and $sec.Key_{\mathcal{G}_{id}} = \{(g * \mathcal{H}(\mathcal{U}_{id}))^{\chi_{curr}.t_2/\beta}, \mathcal{D}_g = g^{t_{2r}} * \mathcal{H}(\mathcal{G}_{id})^{t_{2r_g}}\}$.

4.5   TagGen

TagGen algorithm is used to generate tag for the data which the data owner DO wants to outsource. The tag is mainly used to check whether the newly uploaded data is already available in the cloud or not. The inputs for this algorithm are message $\mathcal{M}$, public parameter $pub.Key$ and output is tag $\mathcal{T}$.

4.6 DuplicateCheck

After tag generation, the cloud will perform the DuplicateCheck operation. The inputs for this algorithm are message $\mathcal{M}^*$, secret value β and outputs either 0 or 1. Initially, the cloud stores the tag of the current node $(g^\beta, g^{\beta.\mathcal{H}(\mathcal{M})})$ in the tag list. Cloud verifies $g^{\beta.\mathcal{H}(\mathcal{M})} \stackrel{?}{=} g^{\beta.\mathcal{H}(\mathcal{M}^*)}$. If $g^{\beta.\mathcal{H}(\mathcal{M})} = g^{\beta.\mathcal{H}(\mathcal{M}^*)}$, then cloud sends 1 as the output, i.e., duplication is there and cloud send tag, id to GM. Else, data owner encrypts the data and outsource the data in the cloud.

4.7 Data Encryption

This algorithm is performed by data owner DO. It takes public parameter $pub.Key$, message $\mathcal{M}$, access tree τ over attribute universe $\mathcal{U}$ and output the ciphertext $\mathcal{C}$. Randomly choose a secret value $\beta \in Z_p^*$. Compute $\mathcal{C}_1 = g^\beta$, $\mathcal{C}_2 = \mathcal{M}.f^\beta = \mathcal{M}.\epsilon(g,g)^{\alpha\beta}$. Let r_0 denote the root node of τ and th_x denote the threshold value of node x. Calculate the share value of each child node ch using Shamir's sharing scheme. The share value $Val_{ch} = Q_{r0}(index(ch))$. Compute $\mathcal{C}_j = \mathcal{T}_j^{Q_x(0)} = g^{Q_x(0)t_{j1}t_{j2}/(t_{j1}+t_{j2})}$. Return ciphertext $\mathcal{C} = (\tau, \mathcal{C}_1, \mathcal{C}_2, \forall l \in \mathcal{L}: \mathcal{C}_j)$.

4.8 Data Decryption

This algorithm is performed by data user DU. DU downloads and decrypts the ciphertext stored in CSP by his/her virtue of holding the required attributes and belonging to the specified group. The inputs for this algorithm are ciphertext $\mathcal{C}$ and secret key $sec.Key_{curr}$. It outputs either the plaintext $\mathcal{M}$ or $\perp$. For each leaf node $l \in \mathcal{L}$, if $a_j \in \mathcal{U}$, $\eta_x = \epsilon(g_x^Q(0)t_{j1}t_{j2}/(t_{j1}+t_{j2}), g^{r/t_{j1}}g^{r/t_{j2}}) = \epsilon(g^{Q_x(0)t_{j1}t_{j2}/(t_{j1}+t_{j2})}, g^{r(t_{j1}+t_{j2})/t_{j1}t_{j2}}) = \epsilon(g,g)^{r.Q_x(0)}$, else $\eta_x = \perp$. For each non-leaf node $x \in \tau$, find the share value of all child nodes ch and compute the share value of node x using Lagrange Interpolation formula. Let r_0 denote the root node of τ. If $\eta_{r0} = \perp$, τ is not satisfied by attribute universe $\mathcal{U}$ and return $\perp$. Else, compute $A = \dfrac{\epsilon(\mathcal{U}_1, \mathcal{C}_2)}{Sv_{r0}} = \dfrac{\epsilon(g^{r+\alpha}, g^\beta)}{\epsilon(g,g)^{r.\beta}} = \dfrac{\epsilon(g,g)^{\alpha\beta}.\epsilon(g,g)^{r.\beta}}{\epsilon(g,g)^{r.\beta}} = \epsilon(g,g)^{\alpha\beta}$. Compute $\mathcal{M} = \dfrac{\mathcal{C}_1}{A} = \dfrac{\mathcal{M}.\epsilon(g,g)^{\alpha\beta}}{\epsilon(g,g)^{\alpha\beta}}$. Return $\mathcal{M}$.

5 Security Analysis

Here, we demonstrated that the proposed ECP-ABE scheme is secure from chosen plaintext attack and the user collusion attack.

Theorem 1: Our ECP-ABE scheme is secured against the user collusion attack.

Proof: In the proposed scheme, along with user's private keys, we are embedding user's certificate for each user with identification $\mathcal{U}_{id}$. The certificate for a particular user is generated as $\chi_{curr} = g^{\beta.x_{curr}} * \mathcal{H}(\mathcal{U}_{id})^{x_{curr}}$. In this scenario, user's private keys can be modified but each user will generate different certificate by the group manager.

Theorem 2: If Decisional Bilinear Diffie-Hellman (DCDH) assumption holds, then the probabilistic polynomial time adversary φ have a trivial advantage in selectively breaching the data in our proposed ECP-ABE data deduplication scheme.

Proof: We defined the security game between adversary φ and challenger ϑ. Let p be the large prime number. $\mathcal{G}_0$ and $\mathcal{G}_1$ be described as the additive and multiplicative cyclic group of prime order p respectively. g signifies the generator of cyclic group $\mathcal{G}_1$. The challenger randomly selects $x, y \in Z_p^*$ and submits $(A, B) = (g^x, g^y)$ to simulator ψ.

Initialisation: The adversary φ picks the challenger τ^*, $\mathcal{G}_{id}^*$, and $curr^*$ and forwards the same to simulator ψ.

Setup: Simulator ψ performs the following steps to produce public parameter $pub.Key$ and group public key GPK_{curr}.

i. Randomly choose $\alpha, \beta \in Z_p^*$ and compute g^α, g^β, and $f = \epsilon(g, g)^\alpha$. The public parameter and the corresponding master secret key is interpreted as $pub.Key = \{\epsilon, g, f\}$, and $M_{sec.Key} = \{\beta, g^\alpha\}$ respectively.

ii. Choose a random exponent $x_0 \in Z_p^*$. Compute g^{x_0} and $\epsilon(g, g)^{x_0}$ to originate group public key $GPK_{curr} = \{\mathcal{G}_{id}, g^{x_0}, \epsilon(g, g)^{x_0}\}$, where $\mathcal{G}_{id}$ is denoted as group identifier and $GMK_{curr} = \{x_0\}$.

Simulator ψ sends public parameter $pub.Key$ and group public key GPK_{curr} to the adversary.

Query 1: Adversary requests the certificate and secret key from the challenger. The challenger ϑ executes the CertGen $(pub.Key, \mathcal{U}_{id}, GMK_{curr})$ algorithm to generate the certificate as $\chi_{curr} = g^{\beta.x_{curr}} * \mathcal{H}(\mathcal{U}_{id})^{x_{curr}}$ and also ψ returns χ_{curr} to the adversary. Simulator φ run KeyGen $(pub.Key, M_{sec.Key}, GPK_{curr}, \mathcal{S})$ algorithm to generate the private keys. ϑ chooses $r_k \in Z_p^*$ for each attribute $k \in \mathcal{S}$, $r_g \in Z_p^*$ for $\mathcal{G}_{id}$, and random numbers $q, s_1, s_2 \in Z_p^*$. Private keys is computed as $sec.Key_{\mathcal{S}} = \{\mathcal{D}_1 = g^{s_1(\alpha+q)/\beta}, \forall k \in \mathcal{S} : \mathcal{D}_k = \mathcal{H}(\mathcal{U}_{id})^{\chi_{curr}} * \mathcal{H}(k)^{s_1*q_k}\}$, and $sec.Key_{\mathcal{G}_{id}} = \{(g * \mathcal{H}(\mathcal{U}_{id}))^{\chi_{curr}.s_2/\beta}, \mathcal{D}_g = g^{s_2q} * \mathcal{H}(\mathcal{G}_{id})^{s_2q_g}\}$. The certificate and private key are send to the adversary .

Challenge: Adversary φ outputs a pair of equal length messages $\mathcal{M}$ and $\mathcal{M}^*$ to the simulator. ψ randomly selects $\mu \in \{0,1\}$ and apply the encryption algorithm with inputs public parameter $pub.Key$, message $\mathcal{M}$, access tree τ over attribute universe $\mathcal{U}$ to construct the ciphertext.

i. Let's define a secret value $\beta \in Z_p^*$ randomly.
ii. Figure out $\mathscr{C}_1 = g^\beta$, $\mathscr{C}_2 = \mathcal{M}.f^\beta = \mathcal{M}.\epsilon(g,g)^{\alpha\beta}$.

ψ sends ciphertext $\mathscr{C}^* = (\tau, \mathscr{C}_1, \mathscr{C}_2, \forall l \in \mathscr{L}: \mathscr{C}_j)$ to the adversary φ.

Query 2: Adversary φ proceeds with similar steps described in query 1 with same limitations.

Guess: Finally, adversary φ presents the guess μ' for μ. If ϑ does not return $\perp$, then adversary guess is identical to the original scenario, i.e, $\mu' = \mu = 0$. Otherwise, ϑ will return zero. The advantage for the adversary succeeding this game is specified as $Adv_\varphi = |Pr[\mu = \mu'] - \frac{1}{2}|$.

6 Performance Analysis

Here, we describe the implementation details and the results that we obtain after the successful execution of the algorithms. In experimental analysis, we compute the computation time of key generation, encryption and decryption operations and plotted the graph on SS512 and MNT224 elliptic curve and shows the comparative study.

6.1 Experimental Analysis

We implement the key generation, data encryption, and data decryption cryptographic operations on Windows 8.1 Pro operating system with hardware configuration of Intel core $i7$ processor @ 2.50 GHz, 16 GB RAM. During this process, JetBrains PyCharm with Charm crypto-0.42 library [21] with SS512 and MNT224 elliptic curve is also used.

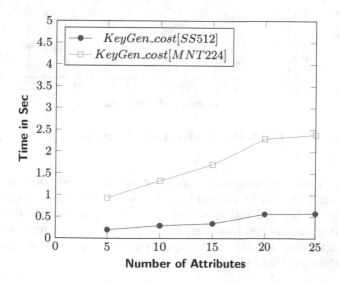

Fig. 3. Computation time of KeyGen

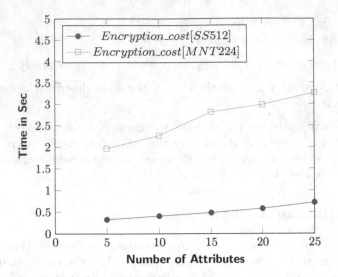

Fig. 4. Computation time of encryption

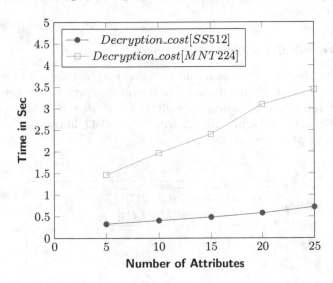

Fig. 5. Computation time of decryption

Figure 3 shows the computation time of the key generation algorithm on SS512 and MNT224 elliptic curve library. It is perceived from Fig. 3, that the time required for key generation is directly proportional to the number of user attributes. It is also noticed from Fig. 3 that key generation time concerning the number of attributes for MNT224 elliptic curve is always more than the key generation time for SS512 elliptic curve cryptography.

Figure 4 shows the computational complexity of encryption operation regarding the number of attributes. As shown in Fig. 4, our ECP-ABE scheme requires less computation time for the encryption process on SS512 elliptic curve than the MNT224 elliptic curve cryptography. It is observed from Fig. 4 that for both the elliptic curve, i.e., SS512 and MNT224, the nature of the encryption computation graph is linear in nature.

Figure 5 shows that the computational complexity of the decryption process on the elliptic curve SS512 and MNT224 concerning the number of attributes. From Fig. 5, it is observed that the SS512 elliptic curve cryptography scheme has the least decryption computation cost. The average computation time of decryption operations in the SS512 and MNT224 elliptic curve cryptography schemes ranges between 0.4 s to 3.5 s.

7 Conclusion

Data deduplication in cloud computing finds several applications such as cloud storage for backup, reduce the computation cost of virtual server, etc. CP-ABE scheme is also widely used in the applications where data owner would like to make their sensitive or private data only accessible to the authorized people whose attributes satisfies the access policy defined by the owner. In this scheme, our main goal is to simultaneously fulfill both aspects of cloud storage. It means to eliminate the redundant data so that the storage cost and the network bandwidth utilization would be more and fine-grained access policy should also be possible. To fulfill our above-defined goal, we proposed algorithms based on the idea of data deduplication and CP-ABE schemes called as ECP-ABE scheme for deduplication over encrypted data in cloud. To demonstrate that our scheme is secure against chosen plaintext attack and user collusion attack, we designed the security model. With the help of the mathematical framework, we describe the security analysis and it shows that our scheme is protected from the CPA and the user collusion attack. Performance analysis also demonstrates that our scheme is efficient concerning to storage overhead, computation cost, and communication overhead.

References

1. Douceur, J.R., Adya, A., Bolosky, W.J., Simon, P., Theimer, M.: Reclaiming space from duplicate files in a serverless distributed file system. In: 22nd International Conference on Distributed Computing Systems, 2002. Proceedings, pp. 617–624. IEEE (2002)
2. Bellare, M., Keelveedhi, S., Ristenpart, T.: Message-locked encryption and secure deduplication. In: Johansson, T., Nguyen, P.Q. (eds.) EUROCRYPT 2013. LNCS, vol. 7881, pp. 296–312. Springer, Heidelberg (2013). https://doi.org/10.1007/978-3-642-38348-9_18
3. Abadi, M., Boneh, D., Mironov, I., Raghunathan, A., Segev, G.: Message-locked encryption for lock-dependent messages. In: Canetti, R., Garay, J.A. (eds.) CRYPTO 2013. LNCS, vol. 8042, pp. 374–391. Springer, Heidelberg (2013). https://doi.org/10.1007/978-3-642-40041-4_21

4. Bellare, M., Keelveedhi, S., Ristenpart, T.. DupLess: server-aided encryption for deduplicated storage. In: Proceedings of the 22nd USENIX Conference on Security, pp. 179–194. USENIX Association (2013)

5. Rezai, A., Keshavarzi, P., Moravej, Z.: Key management issue in SCADA networks: a review. Eng. Sci. Technol. Int. J. **20**(1), 354–363 (2017)

6. Rezai, A., Keshavarzi, P., Moravej, Z.: Advance hybrid key management architecture for SCADA network security. Secur. Commun. Netw. **9**(17), 4358–4368 (2016)

7. Rezai, A., Keshavarzi, P., Moravej, Z.: Secure SCADA communication by using a modified key management scheme. ISA Trans. **52**(4), 517–524 (2013)

8. Li, J., Chen, X., Li, M., Li, J., Lee, P.P., Lou, W.: Secure deduplication with efficient and reliable convergent key management. IEEE Trans. Parallel Distrib. Syst. **25**(6), 1615–1625 (2013)

9. Li, J., et al.: Secure distributed deduplication systems with improved reliability. IEEE Trans. Comput. **64**(12), 3569–3579 (2015)

10. Liu, J., Asokan, N., Pinkas, B.: Secure deduplication of encrypted data without additional independent servers. In: Proceedings of the 22nd ACM SIGSAC Conference on Computer and Communications Security, pp. 874–885. ACM (2015)

11. Yan, Z., Ding, W., Yu, X., Zhu, H., Deng, R.H.: Deduplication on encrypted big data in cloud. IEEE Trans. Big Data **2**(2), 138–150 (2016)

12. Wang, K., Yu, J., Liu, X., Guo, S.: A pre-authentication approach to proxy re-encryption in big data context. IEEE Trans. Big Data (2017)

13. Yang, X., Lu, R., Shao, J., Tang, X., Ghorbani, A.: Achieving efficient and privacy-preserving multi-domain big data deduplication in cloud. IEEE Trans. Serv. Comput. (2018)

14. Yang, C., Ren, J., Ma, J.: Provable ownership of files in deduplication cloud storage. Secur. Commun. Netw. **8**(14), 2457–2468 (2015)

15. Youn, T.Y., Jho, N.S., Rhee, K.H., Shin, S.U.: Authorized client-side deduplication using CP-ABE in cloud storage. Wirel. Commun. Mobile Comput. **2019** (2019)

16. Boneh, D., Franklin, M.: Identity-based encryption from the weil pairing. In: Kilian, J. (ed.) CRYPTO 2001. LNCS, vol. 2139, pp. 213–229. Springer, Heidelberg (2001). https://doi.org/10.1007/3-540-44647-8_13

17. Premkamal, P.K., Pasupuleti, S.K., Alphonse, P.J.A.: A new verifiable outsourced ciphertext-policy attribute based encryption for big data privacy and access control in cloud. J. Ambient Intell. Hum. Comput. **10**(7), 2693–2707 (2018). https://doi.org/10.1007/s12652-018-0967-0

18. Premkamal, P.K., Pasupuleti, S.K., Alphonse, P.J.A.: Efficient revocable cp-abe for big data access control in cloud computing. Int. J. Secur. Netw. **14**(3), 119–132 (2019)

19. Li, J., Yao, W., Zhang, Y., Qian, H., Han, J.: Flexible and fine-grained attribute-based data storage in cloud computing. IEEE Trans. Serv. Comput. **10**(5), 785–796 (2016)

20. Goyal, V., Pandey, O., Sahai, A., Waters, B. Attribute-based encryption for fine-grained access control of encrypted data. In: Proceedings of the 13th ACM Conference on Computer and Communications Security, pp. 89–98. ACM (2006)

21. Akinyele, J.A.: Charm: a framework for rapidly prototyping cryptosystems. J. Cryptogr. Eng. **3**(2), 111–128 (2013)

Controlling Uncertainty with Proactive Cyber Defense: A Clausewitzian Perspective

Sampsa Rauti[✉]

University of Turku, 20014 Turku, Finland
sjprau@utu.fi

Abstract. This study argues that the fundamental tenets Carl von Clausewitz presented about warfare in his influential book *On War* can be applied to defensive cyberwar. This will help in forming a new multidisciplinary perspective on the topic, which can benefit policy makers, political and military scientists and cyber security specialists alike. Moreover, by applying Clausewitz's principles of defensive warfare and his concepts of uncertainty and friction to cyberdefense, we outline a conceptual framework for resilient and proactive cyberdefense.

1 Introduction

With the ongoing digitalization of society, cyberwar is being discussed everywhere. The term has gained popularity after the cyberattacks in Estonia in 2007 [22]. In the academic literature, political scientists, military-academic scholars, and technical cyber security experts have studied the topic actively. The debate has often circled around how to define cyberwar or whether cyberwar exists in the first place.

Carl von Clausewitz's extensive work *On war* is commonly seen as the most essential book on warfare in the Western world [15]. Therefore, it is not that surprising several scholars have applied Clausewitz's principles to cyberwar, although the book was written back in 1832 [6,13,18,32]. Many argue that cyberwar is coming [7,30], while other academics are skeptical or deny the whole existence of cyberwar [14,32]. This discussion seems to mainly derive from the lack of a commonly agreed definition for cyberwar and cyberattack [26].

Regardless of the exact definition of cyberwar, cyberconflict and cyberattacks do exist and they have real implications for society and the physical world. We argue that Clausewitz can provide a useful framework for analyzing the incidents in cyberspace, cyberconflicts and cyberattacks. It is an interesting theoretical lens through which cyberwar can be discussed and understood from a new perspective. Using Clausewitz's principles, we can also bridge the conceptual gap between disciplines of cyber security and political science and give both sides a new conceptual tool to examine cyber attacks and cyber defense.

As the title suggests, this study concentrates on defensive cyberwar. It is well known that Clausewitz sees defense as the stronger form of waging war compared

© Springer Nature Singapore Pte Ltd. 2020
S. M. Thampi et al. (Eds.): SSCC 2019, CCIS 1208, pp. 335–347, 2020.
https://doi.org/10.1007/978-981-15-4825-3_27

to offense [8, p. 358]. On the other hand, in the cyberspace the attacking side is usually thought to be stronger. While it may be true that the attacker has an upper hand in cyberspace in several situations, it is interesting to see how Clausewitz's principles can be used to analyze and strengthen cyber defenses.

The primary contribution of this study is to link Clausewitz's conceptual description of defensive war to the technical concepts and means of realizing cyber defenses. Specifically, we argue Clausewitz's framework can be linked to many proactive cyberdefenses that increase uncertainty for the attacker and employ deception technology to protect computer systems. It could be interesting for policy makers, political scientists, technical cyber security experts alike to learn what Clausewitz can teach us about the subject. Military scientists can also benefit from understanding both political and technical side of cyberwar.

The rest of the paper is organized as follows. Section 2 discusses the main principles presented by Clausewitz and the applicability of *On War* in cyberspace. Section 3 analyzes how Clausewitz's principles can be applied to implement proactive cyber defenses and how these ideas can be translated into technical concepts in order to better thwart cyberattacks. Section 4 contains the discussion and Sect. 5 presents some concluding remarks.

2   Background

2.1   The Main Ideas of the Clausewitzian Framework

Clausewitz's most well-known aphorism is probably the famous statement that war is "a continuation of political intercourse, carried on with other means" [8, p. 87]. It is worth noting, however, that the German word *Politik* Clausewitz originally used is not only restricted to state affairs [18]. In *On War*, the word is not only used to refer to politics but also to *policy*. A policy can be briefly defined as a set ideas and decisions by a state or group to pursue an objective. An important thing to note in the context of cyberspace is that as Clausewitz is not a state-centrist (although he is often mistakenly interpreted as one). Therefore, the Clausewitzian framework also allows the actors other than states, such as hacktivist groups, to participate in cyber war. For the same reason it is not a problem for the framework that the states cannot fully control what happens in cyberspace.

Clausewitz also states that the war is an act where the enemy is rendered powerless and forced to comply with the attacker's will [8, p. 75]. However, in reality, war does not always lead to the destruction of the enemy. Forcing the enemy the do one's will can take many forms, and warfare can also include methods such as cyber attacks.

For success in war, Clausewitz stresses the importance of a clear objective (defined by a policy or politics). Creative and talented army that can counter the enemy and handle the unpredictability of the war is also a necessity. Moreover, passion of the people is also a vital component of success. It is easy to see these elements are also important in cyberwar. A cyber operation cannot even begin without a clear objective, and creativity and talent are necessary in order to implement and use cyberweapons or defense mechanisms. Passion of the people is also an interesting point in the context of cyberwar – in modern digitalized society the cyberspace is open for any passionate individual to participate in cyber operations.

A very important concept in cyberspace is *friction*. It refers to the unpredictability and unforeseen occurrences in war, which inexorably make the real war different from a plan on paper [8, p. 119]. In cyberspace, friction might include bad network connections, unexpected collateral effects and programming mistakes made by humans. However, what makes friction especially interesting in cyberspace in our opinion is the constantly changing structure of and the complexity of cyberspace. Also, what Clausewitz says about friction and unpredictability in form of unreliable information [8, p. 117] is especially true in cyberspace. This is because unlike the physical world, one does not really have anything tangible as a proof of the authenticity of information. Instead, one only receives network messages and information in digital form, the contents of which can often be forged quite easily.

It follows from the significance of friction that it is very important for a good general to understand the uncertainty that friction causes, and to be able to see through this "fog of war" as well as possible. An essential ability when aiming to disperse the fog of uncertainty is something Clausewitz calls *coup d'oeil*. He describes this as "an intellect that, even in the darkest hours, retains some glimmerings of the inner light which leads to truth" [8, p. 102]. In other words, the commander's coup d'oeil is intuition, the ability to recognize truth quickly. In more modern terms, the commander is quickly able to reach a state of accurate *situational awareness*, a conception that "the mind would ordinarily miss or would perceive only after long study and reflection" [8, p. 102]. Naturally, a good situational awareness and the ability to make quick decisions without hesitation (determination) are essential in fast-paced cyberwar. Therefore, in our view, coup d'oeil and determination should also be taken into account when applying *On War* in cyberspace. Unfortunately, nearly all writings discussing how to apply Clausewitz's framework in the age of cyberwar have failed to do so [18, 32].

Finally, Clausewitz divides warfare into offensive and defensive forms. One of the main arguments Clausewitz makes is that defense is an inherently stronger form of war [8, p. 102]. Many theorists such as Farwell [12] have claimed this principle can not be applied to cyberwar, because in cyberspace, the attacker has an advantage over the defender. As we will discuss later, and as also noted by [18], this assumption is not necessarily true. Clausewitz goes on to explain how the familiar *terrain* usually gives the benefit to the defender.

We strongly believe these concepts, summarized in Table 1, can also be applied in cyberspace and used to bridge the conceptual gap between practitioners of political and military sciences and cyber security specialists. Defensive warfare and applying Clausewitz's framework to cyber defense is the topic we will turn to next.

Table 1. Clausewitzian concepts and their counterparts in cyberspace.

Concept	Meaning in cyberspace
Friction	Intrinsic uncertainty of cyberspace and potential countermeasures introduced by the defender
Terrain	Cyberterrain – structure of a targeted network or a computer system and its interfaces, can be modified to increase friction
Coup d'oeil	Situational awareness based on the gathered data
Creative army	Creatively devising defense mechanisms
Passionate people	Anyone with an access to cyberspace may take part in cyberconflicts

2.2   Can Clausewitzian Principles Be Applied to Cyberspace?

It may be seem weird or even absurd to apply principles devised in 1800s to modern cyberattacks. However, as we will see, many high level principles and maxims presented in *On War* still remain valid today. Regardless, it is worth taking a brief look at why we agree with several other authors (such as [30] and [18]) that most Clausewitzian principles have retained their validity, and can be used as a useful lens through which cyberwarfare can be analyzed and understood.

In the debate on cyberwar, Thomas [32] has been one of the most vocal advocates of the view that "cyberwar is not coming". Rid argues that according to Clausewitzian principles, lethal violence is a necessary element in warfare, and cyberwar completely lacks this important characteristic. While violence undeniably does play a role in the Clausewitzian framework, we also have to take into account how the concepts change over time [19]. In fact, Clausewitz himself repeatedly notes that war is a true chameleon that changes its nature regularly [8, p. 89].

The nature of war has indeed changed – technology plays a bigger role in war than before and information is becoming a more and more important resource in today's digitalized world. Violence may not be such an essential element in all areas of warfare anymore, or at the very least, violence does not need to be lethal or physical in cyber warfare. If one only constrains violence to the physical world, its manifestations in cyberspace, used to achieve the same objectives, will be disregarded [4]. That having been said, some cyberattacks, such as the Stuxnet worm targeting a uranium enrichment facility in Iran, do have the ability to cause physical harm. This threat will only grow more prominent as cyberspace continues to become increasingly intertwined with the physical world. Clausewitz also notes that war is an act to compel our enemy to do our will [8, p. 75]. Physical violence, however, is only an instrument to achieve this objective. The goal can often be accomplished by using alternative methods in cyberspace. Clausewitz states: "When we speak of destroying the enemy's forces we must emphasize that nothing obliges us to limit this idea to physical forces: the moral element must also be considered." [8, p. 97].

Thomas Rid and many other authors who rebut cyberwar also seem to discuss "pure" cyberwar that would be fought only, or at least primarily, in cyberspace. This kind of cyberwar is indeed unlikely to take place in the foreseeable future. The possible dangers of cyberwar are often greatly exaggerated and cyberwar is currently not a "one strike and you are out" type of threat like some doomsday scenarios seem to imply. However, cyber warfare can still be seen as one dimension of war [5]. There does not need to be pure cyberwar without traditional dimensions of warfare and for now, this would be an unrealistic assumption.

Of course, it would probably be correct to argue that the four first dimensions of warfare – land, sea, air and space – can often be used much more effectively to quickly achieve strategic objectives compared to the fifth dimension, cyberspace. However, not all parts of warfare are about using extreme force and Clausewitz was well aware of this fact when introducing the concept of *limited war* [8, p. 612]. In fact, Clausewitz only uses "total war" as a theoretical, ideal type of war that does not occur in practice. Indeed, in today's world, there are many conflicts where the political objective is not to conquer enemy territory or overthrow government, but the end goal can be something much smaller, and therefore, the applied methods to achieve the objective also do not need to be lethal or physically destructive. Modern hybrid warfare [1, 27] takes place in a grey zone between war and peace, and also employs many unconventional means to reach the desired objective. In the Clausewitzian framework, the political objective explains the war, and the means used to achieve it are less important.

Moreover, while the discussion about the concept of cyberwar is still definitely necessary, the semantic rigor and pedantry associated with many theories about cyberwar can sometimes prevent us from concentrating on what is really happening in reality [4, 21]. The term cyberwar is already widely used and acknowledged as the fifth dimension of warfare, and most importantly, it is treated as a hostile act that can be countered with the use of military force. For instance, in the "International Strategy for Cyberspace", published in 2011, the White House states that military force can be used in response to a cyberattack [34].

Finally, Clausewitz intended the write a book that would resist the effects of time. The reason the Clausewitzian framework still remains valid to a great extent today is that Clausewitz's main principles are not dependent on the current technology that is employed in waging war. Therefore, the timeless framework is useful also in cyberspace. Nevertheless, it is worth noting that it would be an anachronism to directly claim Clausewitz had something to say about cyberwar. Although Clausewitz did not predict the age of cyberwar, he created a framework that can be successfully connected to the concepts of modern cyber warfare.

3   A Clausewitzian Perspective to Cyberdefense

3.1   Is Defense Weaker Than Offense in Cyberspace?

Considering the nature of interconnected cyberspace, one can easily think that offense is inherently stronger than defense. In cyberspace, where data can travel from the other side of the world instantly and all the connected devices can connect to other devices immediately, it is easy to think launching successful cyberattacks is easy and lightning fast. However, in order to launch a cyberattack and infiltrate an enemy system successfully, one has to know what kind system the enemy possesses and what are the potential vulnerabilities the system has. Gathering intelligence on the enemy's system, discovering previously unknown vulnerabilities and possibly creating new cyber weapons – that is, writing custom malware – takes resources, time and money.

If we assume that systems are regularly updated and patched – like they should be in any critical infrastructure that is likely to be at the receiving end of cyber attacks – the same vulnerabilities can not be continuously exploited over a long period of time. Finding new vulnerabilities again takes more time. Although a hundreds of thousands of unique pieces of malware are manufactured every day [3] and many of them only consist of few hundred lines of code, finding exploitable vulnerabilities still remains a challenge for the attacker. The oft-repeated argument that cyber attacks consume no resources is therefore not completely correct.

Moreover, even when the attacker has succeeded to infiltrate the system, this can still be detected and the system can be defended, by using intrusion detection systems or proactive cyber defense mechanisms, for instance. It is important to note that cyber defenses are often multilayered, which also strengthens defense. Also, when an attacker has infiltrated our system, we can get lots of useful information about enemy's technologies and objectives if we have an appropriate intrusion detection system in place. Attackers are always in the danger of revealing critical information about themselves.

Many existing and well-known exploits also demonstrate that a successful attack often either takes a lot of work or is dependent on infecting systems with very poor cyber security. Take the Stuxnet worm we mentioned before, for example. The Stuxnet source code made use of four previously unknown zero-day vulnerabilities [11]. It is quite clear the malware was created by professionals who had a good understanding of how cyber defenses such as anti-virus technologies work, as well as information about yet unknown vulnerabilities. While Stuxnet is an extreme example, it demonstrates that an advanced attack requires lots of work and carefully gathered knowledge about the target system.

Another interesting example is the Mirai malware from 2016. Mirai turns infected network devices running the Linux operating system into remotely controlled bots [17]. These bots then form a botnet that can be used to launch large-scale distributed denial of service (DDoS) attacks, which can cause disturbances in web services or even cause services to go offline. Mirai infected tens of thousands of Internet of Things (IoT) devices easily, but only because their security was so poor that the default passwords had not been changed. In this case, cyber defense was just poor, not really intrinsically weaker than offense. Unfortunately, large numbers of IoT devices still have poor security [10], which gives advantage to cyber attackers in many cases.

Of course, sometimes cyber attacks do overpower defenses. For instance, large DDoS attacks are often difficult to counter immediately. Also, in the cases where the adversary has planted a backdoor[1] or a logical bomb[2] in the system beforehand, the attacker has the initial advantage. Even in these cases, however, the attacker has done some work beforehand, by gathering information and infecting vulnerable machines. Also, Clausewitz actually states that the attacker often has an initial advantage, but the defender becomes stronger when the battle drags on [8, p. 624].

It is difficult to conclusively evaluate whether defense is stronger form of warfare in cyberspace. However, because in many cases only successful cyberattacks are noticed and get media coverage, and failed attacks are not always even detected or they are kept secret, it would seem the strength of cyberattacks is often overestimated compared to defenses. As Jacobsen states, this stance can then easily become a self-fulfilling prophecy [18]. Clausewitz's framework can help us to see things differently and provide interesting insights on how to better take defensive warfare into account.

3.2   Taking Control of Uncertainty and Friction

Based on the discussion above, it seems Clausewitz's framework can be applied to cyber defense, but how exactly can we derive benefit from it? As we have seen before, Clausewitz maintains that uncertainty is a central component in war: "War is the realm of uncertainty; three quarters of the factors on which action in war is based are wrapped in a fog of greater or lesser uncertainty." [8, p. 101]. Strongly associated with this uncertainty is the concept of friction. Friction causes a difference between how things are expected happen on paper and the actual way they happen due to unexpected distractions [8, p. 119]. Unexpected events cause friction that sets the initial plan off course. In cyberspace, too, there are many things that are beyond our control, such as mistakes made by humans and unexpected collateral effects of cyber attacks, for instance. However, it is interesting to note that in cyberspace we can also effectively attempt to use the friction to our advantage by causing asymmetry between the friction we encounter and the friction the enemy experiences. Clausewitz notes that the defender has the advantage of familiar terrain in the battle [8, pp. 269, 361]. This home-field advantage is even greater in cyberspace because the "cyberterrain" can be shaped according to the defenders needs much more easily than in the physical world. This is definitely something the defender can proactively take

---

[1] A backdoor is a method that allows a system security mechanism to be bypassed secretly to access computer system and its data.

[2] A logic bomb is a piece of harmful code, inserted in a computer system. When certain conditions are met, the code will execute predefined malicious functionality.

advantage of even before a cyberattack takes place. As Clausewitz observes, the terrain can act "as an obstacle to the approach, as an impediment to visibility, and as cover from fire", making the attackers job more difficult [8, p. 348].

In what follows, we will discuss methods to take control of uncertainty and friction, both by making the enemy encounter more uncertainty and by attempting to provide our own cyber army with the necessary tools to see through the thick fog. Here, we will mainly limit our discussion to technical methods.

Make the Cyber Terrain Unpredictable by Diversity. Friction can be introduced and cyberterrain the adversary has to navigate can be made more uncertain by introducing software diversity in the target system under attack. Malicious attackers and programs benefit from the fact that computers use a relatively small group of different operating system versions. In other words, software monoculture prevails and an attacker can plan cyber attacks that use well-known facts about the target system. For instance, a malicious program can use a well-know operating system interface in the system to reach its goals (for example, to open and edit files with sensitive information). However, if the interfaces malware wants to use and interact with were uniquely diversified in each system, the malware would have much more trouble attempting to reach its goals [9]. It would no longer know the "language" of the system under attack. This would probably render the piece of malware useless for quite some time. This way, asymmetric friction can be created through increased resilience, and the system can be defended effectively without disturbances in its operation. There are methods to create diverse software systems automatically without human intervention [20,24].

Dynamically Changing Cyberterrain. As new attacks are launched, the advantage between attackers and defenders seems to continuously keep shifting. To use the friction to defenders advantage in an attempt to stop this never-ending cycle, the paradigm of moving target defense (MTD) can be employed [16]. This defense mechanism creates a dynamic and constantly changing attack surface implemented across several system dimensions. As stated by Clausewitz, in the fast-paced war, one reason the gathered intelligence is unreliable is because it is so transient [8, p. 117]. When a report arrives, the situation has already changed.

MTD makes the shape of cyber terrain transient, which increases uncertainty for malicious adversaries and makes attacking the target much more difficult. After all, it is quite a challenge to attack something you cannot understand and see clearly. MTD can be applied to wide range of attacks surfaces in computer networks and systems. One example is to have a set of constantly evolving interfaces in the system. Unknown interfaces that constantly change are difficult targets for a malicious program or attacker. MTD can also be implemented on network level for example by constantly changing the IP addresses of certain targets.

Cyber Deception. Deception is one obvious way to expose the attacker to more friction and uncertainty. While Clausewitz does not seem to believe in deception and surprise on strategical level, he does suggest deceiving the enemy can be a very useful tactical maneuver when conditions are favorable [8, p. 198]. Even though surprise is not the key element in success of the war, it can be a useful tactical device. In cyberspace, deception is easier than in the real battlefield, because cyberspace is made of bits and bytes that can be changed and forged quite easily, at least in our own territory we are defending. Moreover, because the enemy often appears in the form of a malicious program rather than a living human, it is often easy to introduce uncertainty and friction. An intelligent hacker is naturally more difficult to fool for long periods of time.

How can an enemy be deceived in cyberspace? Different deception technologies can be used to provide an attacker with fake targets that look valuable [2,9]. In terms of technical solutions, this can be anything from network with several honeypots machines (computers with data that appears to be valuable and interesting) to planting simple fake files in a system. Also the important system interfaces we mentioned previously could be forged in this manner. When someone interacts with these fake resources, we immediately know there is an attacker in the system, because no legitimate process or user should access these resources [35]. This is especially convenient for detecting previously unknown malware. Several fake targets will considerably slow down the attacker and the enemy is more likely to gather false intelligence.

Gathering Intelligence. Honeypots and other fake resources are there not only for deception. They are also great at gathering intelligence about the enemy and their potential objectives [29]. With monitoring software, such as intrusion detection systems and honeypots, we can record information on what is going on in the network and in a specific system. For example, network packets arriving to and leaving from our local network and system calls issued in our systems can be recorded for further analysis [23]. According to Clausewitz, intelligence gathered in war is mostly untrustworthy and false, because fear has an effect of multiplying lies and inaccuracies [8, p. 117]. Automatically collected information does not have this weakness.

However, on a high level it is necessary to combine conflicting information from many sources, check credible external sources for worldwide cyber threat information, and also put together intelligence from other disciplines (human intelligence, geospatial intelligence) to get a comprehensive grasp of the current situation. The difficulty of recognizing the important pieces of information that should be prioritized constitutes one of the most serious sources of friction in war, because things often appear entirely different from what one has expected. Therefore, we need mechanisms to dig out the truth from the data we have gathered.

Coup D'oeil in Cyberspace. Coup d'oeil, as we discussed previously, is a great general's intuitive grasp of what is going on in the battlefield. The process of quickly perceiving what is happening in the strategically significant locations in cyberspace and making a rapid and accurate decision can be made easier by making use of artificial intelligence (AI) that is able to provide the commander

Table 2. Summary of proactive defenses.

Proactive defense	Example
Increase uncertainty by diversity	Diversifying system interfaces
Changing cyberterrain	Moving target defense
Cyber deception	Planting honeypots in a network
Gathering intelligence	Logging the adversary's activities
Coup d'oeil in cyberspace	Using AI to form situational awareness from the gathered data
Offensive defense	Giving fake data to the attacker

with appropriate situational awareness. This kind of tool could help the commanders to do better and improve the ability to use their coup d'oeil.

The process would still be human-centered – after all, with Clausewitz's principles, it is difficult to imagine an AI waging war independently – it would only provide a device to see through the fog and avoid the friction more effectively by providing necessary information for fast decisions. An advanced AI system can also have the ability to learn, and ultimately use an extensive corpus of battle experience and knowledge to augment the commander's capability to weight different options and make decisions based on solid evidence and the underlying political objective.

Offensive Defense. Clausewitz maintains that even when war is defensive, it still often contains offensive components [8, p. 357]. Indeed, above we have already discussed methods that can be used to annoy the attacker and disrupt enemy operations. We can also annoy the attackers by feeding them false replies and information [31], while at the same monitoring how they react to this. This can also help us to get even more information on attacker's methods and objectives. Attribution – the process of tracking and identifying the perpetrator behind the attack – is also an important part of offensive cyber defense [25]. After all, if we do not know who the attacker is, we cannot strike back.

The proactive defenses are summarized in Table 2.

4   Discussion

In this study, we have suggested Carl von Clausewitz's principles of defensive warfare can be useful in conceptualizing and designing resilient methods for cyberdefense. Software diversification and moving target defense increase resilience of the defender's systems and at the same time, create uncertainty and friction for the enemy. Cyberterrain can further be modified with fake targets that annoy and stall the enemy, while also gathering intelligence. Finally, with an AI-enhanced coup d'oeil, talented commanders can assess the collected information and make the correct and quick decisions under stress and continuous information overload.

When the defender succeeds in adding enough uncertainty for the enemy, the situation can also be compared to the difficulties of executing a night attack described by Clausewitz. The attacker should effectively attack in the darkness and know the complete layout of enemy's defenses, while keeping its own disposition secret from the enemy for as long as possible [8, p. 273]. At the same time, the defender can see the familiar cyber terrain clearly and keep learning more about the enemy, while also preparing for a potential counterattack.

As cyberspace keeps getting increasingly intertwined with the physical world and critical infrastructure of society, significance of defending systems from cyber threats also keeps growing [28,36]. Billions of networked IoT devices with poor security are a reminder of the fact that cyber security has not yet been taken as seriously as it should. This paper has presented a conceptual framework inspired by Clausewitz's ideas of defensive warfare and taking advantage of emerging proactive cyber defense mechanisms. Naturally, this is not to say we should not keep using more traditional security measures such as anti-virus software, encryption, whitelisting and strong authentication mechanisms. In the face of advanced persistent threats and zero-day exploits, however, we also need novel defenses that change the cyber terrain to our advantage and take control of uncertainty. Therefore, these defenses are not mutually exclusive. Indeed, a multilayered approach to defense fits well to today's complex cyber security landscape, where no single countermeasure is totally effective against every threat or exploit. Clausewitz writes about how important it is for a defender to have several fortresses that attract the attention of the enemy but are resilient enough to withstand attacks [8, p. 372].

It is also interesting to note that while our discussion of cyber defenses has mainly focused on technical considerations, Clausewitz also emphasizes a creative army and passion of the people as important factors in successful warfare. When defending cyber infrastructure, a creative army is needed to keep the defense mechanisms up to date and to innovate novel resilient defenses to counter constantly developing threats. Passionate people are also needed to defend cyberspace. Max Weber's notion of the state claiming a monopoly of use of force [33] is becoming obsolete, and one reason for this is that in cyberspace anyone can pick up weapons and become involved in warfare. It is also increasingly important for all sectors of society to be passionate about positive cyber security culture. In an interconnected cyberspace coupled with the physical world, it is essential for all stakeholders to cooperate in improving security.

Finally, there are a couple of limitations in the approach we have proposed in this paper. Clausewitz's work does not mark end of history and cannot explain all characteristics of modern cyber war in detail. Although Clausewitz does note that the nature of war is continuously changing, it is only one lens through which cyberwar can be observed. Moreover, On War contains many outdated sections that are not applicable to modern warfare. Still, at least for the technical aspects of cyberdefense we have focused on, the Clausewitzian principles of warfare provide a useful framework for further discussion between different fields of science.

5   Conclusion

This paper has argued that most of the fundamental tenets Carl von Clausewitz presented about warfare in his influential book *On War* can be applied to cyberwar to get a new multidisciplinary perspective on the topic. We have further shown how Clausewitz's theory on uncertainty and friction in the war and his ideas of defense as a stronger form of warfare can be used to build a conceptual framework for proactive cyberdefense. In this approach, we combined Clausewitz's theoretical ideas with technical cyber defense solutions, which can help policy makers, political and military scientists as well as cyber security specialists to reach a common understanding of defensive cyber security.

References

1. Almäng, J.: War, vagueness and hybrid war. Def. Stud. **19**(2), 189–204 (2019)
2. Almeshekah, M., Spafford, E.: Planning and integrating deception into computer security defenses. In: Proceedings of the 2014 Workshop on New Security Paradigms Workshop, pp. 127–138. ACM (2014)
3. AVTest: Malware statistics. https://www.av-test.org/en/statistics/malware/. Accessed 20 Aug 2019
4. Brantly, A.: The violence of hacking: state violence and cyberspace. Cyber Def. Rev. **2**(1), 73–92 (2017)
5. Bunker, R.: Five-dimensional (cyber) warfighting: can the army after next be defeated through complex concepts and technologies? Report. Strategic Studies Institute (1998)
6. Canabarro, D.R., Borne, T.: Reflections on the fog of (cyber) war (2013)
7. Clarke, R., Knake, R.: Cyber War: The Next Threat to National Security and What to Do About It. Ecco (2011)
8. Clausewitz, C.V.: On War. Princeton University Press, Princeton (1989)
9. Cohen, F.: Operating system protection through program evolution. Comput. Secur. **12**(6), 565–584 (1993)
10. Hewlett Packard Enterprise: Internet of things research study (2015)
11. Falliere, N., Murchu, L., Chien, E.: W32. Stuxnet dossier. White paper, Symantec Corporation Security Response, vol. 5, no. 6, p. 29 (2011)
12. Farwell, J., Rohozinski, R.: Stuxnet and the future of cyber war. Survival **53**(1), 23–40 (2011)
13. Garard, O.A., Friedman, B.: Clausewitzian alchemy and the modern character of war. Orbis **63**, 362–375 (2019)
14. Gartzke, E.: The myth of cyberwar: bringing war in cyberspace back down to earth. Int. Secur. **38**(2), 41–73 (2013)
15. Heuser, B.: Reading Clausewitz. Pimlico, London (2002)

16. Huang, Y., Ghosh, A.K.: Introducing diversity and uncertainty to create moving attack surfaces for web services. In: Jajodia, S., Ghosh, A., Swarup, V., Wang, C., Wang, X. (eds.) Moving Target Defense: Creating Asymmetric Uncertainty for Cyber Threats. Advances in Information Security, vol. 54, pp. 131–151. Springer, New York (2011). https://doi.org/10.1007/978-1-4614-0977-9_8
17. Imperva: Breaking Down Mirai: An IoT DDoS Botnet Analysis. https://www.imperva.com/blog/malware-analysis-mirai-ddos-botnet/. Accessed 20 Aug 2019
18. Jacobsen, J.: The cyberwar mirage and the utility of cyberattacks in war: how to make real use of Clausewitz in the age of cyberspace. Report. Danish Institute for International Studies (2014)
19. Koselleck, R., Presner, T.: The Practice of Conceptual History: Timing History, Spacing Concepts. Stanford University Press, Palo Alto (2002)
20. Larsen, P., Homescu, A., Brunthaler, S., Franz, M.: SoK: automated software diversity. In: IEEE Symposium on Security and Privacy (SP), pp. 276–291 (2014)
21. Lawson, S.: Putting the "war" in cyberwar: metaphor, analogy, and cybersecurity discourse in the united states. First Monday **17**(7) (2012)
22. Lesk, M.: The new front line: Estonia under cyberassault. IEEE Secur. Priv. **5**(4), 76–79 (2007)
23. Rauti, S., Leppänen, V.: A survey on fake entities as a method to detect and monitor malicious activity. In: 2017 25th Euromicro International Conference on Parallel, Distributed and Network-based Processing (PDP), pp. 386–390 (2017)
24. Rauti, S., Laurén, S., Hosseinzadeh, S., Mäkelä, J.-M., Hyrynsalmi, S., Leppänen, V.: Diversification of system calls in Linux binaries. In: Yung, M., Zhu, L., Yang, Y. (eds.) INTRUST 2014. LNCS, vol. 9473, pp. 15–35. Springer, Cham (2015). https://doi.org/10.1007/978-3-319-27998-5_2
25. Rid, T., Buchanan, B.: Attributing cyber attacks. J. Strateg. Stud. **38**(1–2), 4–37 (2015)
26. Robinson, M., Jones, K., Janicke, H.: Cyber warfare: issues and challenges. Comput. Secur. **49**, 70–94 (2015)
27. Rõigas, H.: Cyber war in perspective: lessons from the conflict in Ukraine. In: Cusumano, E., Corbe, M. (eds.) A Civil-Military Response to Hybrid Threats, pp. 233–257. Springer, Cham (2018). https://doi.org/10.1007/978-3-319-60798-6_11
28. Satchidanandan, B., Kumar, P.R.: Dynamic watermarking: active defense of networked cyber-physical systems. Proc. IEEE **105**(2), 219–240 (2016)
29. Spitzner, L.: Honeypots: Tracking Hackers. Addison-Wesley Longman Publishing Co., Inc., Boston (2002)
30. Stone, J.: Cyber war will take place! J. Strateg. Stud. **36**(1), 101–108 (2013)
31. Strand, J., Asadoorian, P., Robish, E., Donelly, B.: Offensive Countermeasures: The Art of Active Defense. CreateSpace Independent Publishing Platform, North Charleston (2013)
32. Thomas, R.: Cyber war will not take place. J. Strateg. Stud. **35**(1), 5–32 (2012)
33. Weber, M.: Politics as a Vocation. Fortress Press, Philadelphia (1965)
34. White House: International Strategy for Cyberspace (2011)
35. Yuill, J., Zappe, M., Denning, D., Feer, F.: Honeyfiles: deceptive files for intrusion detection. In: 2004 Proceedings from the Fifth Annual IEEE SMC Information Assurance Workshop, pp. 116–122 (2004)
36. Zheng, Z., Reddy, A.: Towards improving data validity of cyber-physical systems through path redundancy. In: Proceedings of the 3rd ACM Workshop on Cyber-Physical System Security, pp. 91–102. ACM (2017)

Protecting Computer Systems from Cyber Attacks with Internal Interface Diversification

Sampsa Rauti[✉]

University of Turku, 20014 Turku, Finland
sjprau@utu.fi

Abstract. Internal interface diversification is a proactive technique that protects software and devices from malicious cyber attacks by making interfaces unique in every separate system. As malware cannot use the knowledge about internal interfaces in the system to its advantage anymore, it is rendered useless. The current study gauges the effectiveness of internal interface diversification by analyzing three cyber attacks as case studies and showing why internal interface diversification is an effective countermeasure against them. The study will further serve to demonstrate that internal interface diversification is a feasible and widely applicable security measure against numerous common cyber attacks.

1 Introduction

Malware is a huge threat in today's interconnected computer systems. New malicious programs keep appearing at a staggering pace. Hundreds of thousands of new malicious programs are being discovered daily [3]. After a vulnerability is found in a piece of software, adversaries can usually take advantage of it much faster than patches are created and delivered by software vendors. At the same time, anti-virus programs are struggling to keep up with this development, and what is more, they cannot even be run on many resource constrained environments, such as IoT. Therefore, novel proactive methods to mitigate malware attacks are needed [2,10,29].

To successfully carry out its objectives, a piece of malware has to know the target system's internal interfaces. For example, a piece of malware knows the system call number it should use or the library function to invoke in order to take use the services provided by the operating system. Therefore, instead of trying to detect each specific type of exploit and render it useless, an apparent solution to the malware problem is to make the well-known internal interfaces secret by obfuscating them. In other words, it is possible to uniquely diversify the internal interfaces in each system to render harmful programs useless and prevent adversaries from reaching their goals.

Trusted binaries and scripts in the system are then altered accordingly so that they conform to the new diversified "language" and can still operate normally. Malicious programs, however, do not know the diversification secret (e.g.

© Springer Nature Singapore Pte Ltd. 2020
S. M. Thampi et al. (Eds.): SSCC 2019, CCIS 1208, pp. 348–359, 2020.
https://doi.org/10.1007/978-981-15-4825-3_28

a secret unique diversification function used to diversify the interfaces). They are prevented from operating correctly and cannot do harm in the system. Moreover, even if the diversification secret of one system should somehow be compromised, other systems cannot be attacked with this knowledge because they have different unique diversification. The idea of diversifying the critical parts of a system is not new, and schemes following this general idea have been published in the academic literature [9,22]. However, steps still need to be taken in the direction of applying diversification in practice and analyzing its effectiveness against different threat scenarios.

While there are papers presenting obfuscation frameworks and gauging the practical applicability of this technique in real-world systems [4,13,23], less attention has been paid on analyzing the practical cyber attacks and demonstrating that diversification renders the exploits useless. Previously, Rauti et al. [25] showed that diversification could potentially mitigate or prevent over 80% of the analyzed exploits. The current study continues this earlier work, but takes a different approach by analyzing three cyber attacks more profoundly as case studies and showing why internal interface diversification is an effective countermeasure against them. This will hopefully further serve to demonstrate that interface diversification is a feasible and widely applicable security measure against many common cyber attacks.

The rest of the paper is structured as follows. Section 2 presents the general idea of interface diversification and covers the interfaces suitable for diversification. Section 3 demonstrates how diversification can be used to defend against different practical cyber attacks. We present examples of real malware and analyze the reasons diversification is an effective countermeasure against these threats. Section 4 discusses the implications of our findings and Sect. 5 concludes the paper.

2   Interface Diversification

2.1   The General Idea

Interface diversification makes interfaces on each specific system unique. In other words, diversification is about making the operating environment unpredictable for the malware [17,18]. Diversifying internal interfaces decreases the number of assumptions an adversary or a piece of malware is able to make about the surrounding system where it is run. In practice, diversification can be implemented using obfuscation transformations [9]. In interface diversification, even quite simple obfuscation transformations such as altering the names of functions and changing the order in which parameters appear in function signatures can be used.

An example of diversification is diversifying the system call interface. For example, in the Linux operating system, the numbers that identify the system calls can be altered according to a secret diversification function. When the interface is altered, we also have to modify the trusted libraries and programs that make calls to this interface accordingly.

In this context, the term *interface* is interpreted quite broadly. By interface, we do not only mean ordinary interfaces provided by software components but also for instance commands of a script language or memory addresses of important services or resources are considered as interfaces to which diversification can be applied. Therefore, in a broad sense, an interface is anything used to gain access to essential services or resources of a device.

2.2   Interfaces Suitable for Diversification

The important internal interfaces include but are not limited to the following ones:

- *The system call interface.* The critical functionality of the device is accessed through the system call interface of the operating system. The system calls usually have numbers that are used to invoke them, and these numbers can be diversified (altered according to a secret diversification function) in order to prevent a harmful program that uses the system calls from working [6,19,23]. The system calls numbers in the trusted library and application binaries are then changed accordingly. This way, the trusted applications remain compatible with the operating system.

  The malware, however, would need to execute system calls in order to interact with its environment (that is, cause any real harm in the targeted system), but because it does not know the diversified system calls it can not do anything with them. For example, the code injection attacks in which the adversary gets the system to run malicious code containing system calls do not have any effect because the system call numbers are wrong in that specific system. Any other attacks where the attacker depends on system call numbers will also fail.

- *Library functions.* Diversifying the system call interface is a good start, but there are other ways to make system calls indirectly that the adversary could make use of. That is why we also have to prevent the malicious attacker from reaching the critical resources using operating system libraries [6,23]. These libraries contain wrapper functions that directly or indirectly lead to invocation of system calls (in other words, this is the transitive closure of system calls in the binary files throughout the system). All these functions are diversified – their names are altered and e.g. order of parameters can be changed.

  Moreover, just like with diversification of system calls, we have to propagate the diversification of library functions. Therefore, all calls to these diversified library functions in binary files are also diversified. This means the symbol strings in trusted binaries are altered so that they still work with the diversified system.

- *The command line interpreter.* The protection of library functions and system calls can be circumvented by using the command line interpreters. A piece of malware could employ interpreted languages like command shell script languages. Similarly to the library functions, the command shell also gives an indirect access to the services provided by the operating system. To prevent this threat, the language interface used by the command line interpreter can be diversified [15,28]. In practice, this means changing the tokens that are recognized by the command line interpreter. In other words, the command interpreter is modified so that it supports running diversified scripts. The trusted scripts in the system are then diversified accordingly.

– *Address space.* The memory space can also be diversified. Address Space Layout Randomization (ASLR) randomly rearranges the address space locations of important parts of processes [1,7,30]. With randomized addresses, it becomes difficult for an attacker to find the memory addresses of a specific piece of code he or she might want to abuse [16]. In other words, the malicious adversary cannot reliably move to a particular position in the memory anymore. ASLR is the only diversification method that is already widely being used; many operating systems such as Linux and Windows implement it. However, not all IoT operating systems are armed with this protection method, for example.

– *SQL query language.* Domain-specific languages such as SQL (Structured Query Language) can also be seen as targets of diversification [5,20,24]. This provides protection against SQL injection attacks in which the adversary injects nefarious SQL commands for instance through a web form and the provided data gets interpreted as executable statements.

It is worth noting our study only targets internal interfaces. That is, the diversification focuses on the internal interfaces used by programs but not usually by users. Therefore, the user experience does not suffer from internal interface diversification. Also, unique versions of diversified software for different systems can be created automatically in many cases. Internal interface diversification works against attacks that depend on the knowledge about internal interfaces. Different injection attacks are a common example. Naturally, many other attacks such as circumventing a broken authentication mechanism cannot be prevented by diversification.

3 A Case Study of Defending Against Three Cyber Attacks with Diversification

In what follows, we will take a close look at three different exploits and demonstrate how diversifying the internal interfaces prevents them from wreaking havoc in the target system.

3.1 The Mirai Malware and OS Library Diversification

Mirai is a piece of malicious software that is used to create a large botnet by connecting number of infected devices called bots [14]. Mirai uses SSH and Telnet protocols for malicious login attempts, trying commonly used default user names and passwords. Then, without the consent of the owners, the infected devices are then used to launch attacks against computers on the Internet. These attacks are usually Distributed Denial of Service (DDoS) attacks, with a huge number (even tens of thousands) of bots sending traffic to a server, consuming resources and preventing the server from responding to requests coming from normal clients. It is interesting to note that the devices Mirai infected are different from the infected devices usually gathered to form botnes. While most botnet attacks have in the past have made use of infected home computers, Mirai infected IoT devices such as security cameras [8].

The source code of Mirai [21] was released in October 2016. Mirai widely scans IP addresses and compromises IoT devices in order to increase the number of devices in the botnet. The malware can participate in different kinds of DDoS attacks, for example GRE IP flood and SYN and ACK floods, according to the instructions received from a remote command and control server. Mirai is also a territorial malware, as it also closes processes that use SSH, Telnet and HTTP ports, thus preventing remote connections to the IoT device [12]. Moreover, it searches and kills some competing malicious programs potentially residing on the infected computer.

```
396                     if (util_stristr(exe, util_strlen(exe), inode) != -1)
397                     {
398     #ifdef DEBUG
399                         printf("[killer] Found pid %d for port %d\n", util_atoi(pid, 10), ntohs(port));
400     #else
401                         kill(util_atoi(pid, 10), 9);
402     #endif
```

Fig. 1. An excerpt from Mirai's source code. The code kills a process that uses a specific port number.

```
157         int pid1, pid2;
158
159         pid1 = fork();
160         if (pid1 == -1 || pid1 > 0)
161             return;
162
163         pid2 = fork();
164         if (pid2 == -1)
165             exit(0);
166         else if (pid2 == 0)
167         {
168             sleep(duration);
169             kill(getppid(), 9);
170             exit(0);
```

Fig. 2. An excerpt from Mirai's `attack_start` function that invokes several system call wrapper functions.

The Mirai source code makes use of the well known wrapper functions in order to indirectly use system calls. For example, we can see in Fig. 1 that a short excerpt of the malicious code that kills a process that uses a specific port number in the system. If the `kill` wrapper function in C standard library was diversified by modifying the symbols in the binaries (the library and the trusted programs using it), Mirai would not be able to invoke it and would be rendered useless. Similarly, Fig. 2 shows an excerpt from Mirai's `attack_start` function that uses several wrapper functions that act as wrappers for system calls, such as `fork` and `exit`. Aside from these examples, interface diversification would naturally also prevent many other actions taken by the malware, such as contacting the command and control server for further instructions.

In Unix-based systems, symbol modification can be done by rewriting executable ELF (Executable and Linkable Format) binaries. The symbols in an ELF file can be found by inspecting the sections with the `DYNSYM`-type. The symbols are then gathered, diversified and rewritten in the file. Changing symbols does not have a large effect on performance. However, if the new diversified symbols are longer than the old ones, the size of the ELF file grows.

It is worth noting that interface diversification is a good fit for resource constrained IoT devices. Unlike security solutions such as anti-virus software or intrusion detection systems, internal interface diversification is a very performance efficient security measure. Although Mirai used simple default passwords to compromise IoT devices and could be defeated by paying closer attention to this simple security issue, interface diversification would have provided another layer of security.

3.2 ShellShock and Command Language Diversification

ShellShock is a vulnerability in Bash (the Unix command shell), first discovered in September 2014. With ShellShock, a malicious adversary can make Bash execute arbitrary commands and gain unauthorized access to public-facing services, for instance web servers that use the Bash shell to handle requests [26]. The vulnerability comes up when a newly created shell instance encounters an environment variable containing code that looks like a function and then evaluates it. The Bash code had a bug where the evaluation did not stop when the function definition ended. The vulnerability can be exploited as follows:

```
env x='() { :;}; echo TEST' bash -c :
```

In the code, the value set to the variable x bears a resemblance to a function definition. Here the function is just a single colon, a simple command that does nothing. After the semi-colon ending the function definition, there is an `echo` command. Although this command is not supposed to be here, nothing prevents the adversary from putting it there. Finally, a new shell instance is started, again with a colon command that does nothing.

However, when the new shell instance starts up and reads the environment we have provided, it also receives the reads the x variable. Because the contents of this variable look like a function, they are evaluated. After the function definition gets loaded, the malicious payload crafted by the adversary is executed as well. Therefore, on a vulnerable system, the code above would print the string TEST. However, it is clear that the attacker could do something much worse than simply printing some innocent messages.

Apart from fixing the bug, a proactive approach to prevent a malicious attack exploiting ShellShock can be put in place. In this solution, a diversified version of the Bash command language is used in the system. When the keywords in the command shell language are diversified and the malware does not know them, it cannot get proper malicious code executed in the system. In the example above, the echo keyword will not work and the malware will not know how to print messages. For example, the diversified version of the command language can use a secret keyword echo7419 instead of echo. What is more, the way function definitions are made and the way statements are ended can be completely different in the diversified version of the command language.

Each script in the system can be diversified differently for additional security but in this case the performance also suffers as each script has to be decoded by the modified Bash interpreter. For example in tests by Uitto et al. [28] the diversified scripts took 2.7 times longer to execute. However, even this is quite performance increase in systems where script execution does not play a large role.

The discovery of the ShellShock vulnerability clearly showed that widely used and trusted older software can still have unknown critical bugs and zero day exploits taking advantage of the vulnerability will appear. As a proactive security measure, interface diversification can protect against this kind of unpredictable and completely novel threats.

3.3   The "Advanced Power" Botnet and Diversifying the SQL Language

One of the significant threats web applications face today is an SQL injection attack. Consider the following example that shows pseudocode run on a web server. It is used when a user authenticates with a user name and a password. The database has table users with columns username and password.

```
// Get the POST variables
user = request.POST['username'];
pass = request.POST['password'];

// Form the (vulnerable!) SQL query
sql = "SELECT id FROM users WHERE username='"
      + user + "' AND password='" + pass + "'";

// Execute the query
database.execute(sql);
```

In the example, an adversary can use malicious SQL commands in the input so that the SQL statement the database server executes is changed. For instance, if the password field is set to

```
password' OR 1=1
```

the server executes the following SQL query:

```
SELECT id FROM users WHERE username='username'
                 AND password='password' OR 1=1'
```

The OR 1=1 statement makes the WHERE clause return the first id of the users table. It does not matter what the values of the username and password are. If the user listed first is an administrator (which is often the case), the attacker also gains administrator privileges.

Of course, inventing and testing malicious SQL inputs can be a tedious and time consuming process. Therefore, SQL injection attacks has been automated in many attacks, such as the "Advanced Power" botnet. This malware disguised itself as a legitimate Firefox add-on and used the infected machines to test several different SQL injection attacks on websites browsed by the user.

Much like in the case of Bash command line interpreter, the solution here is to diversify SQL so that the attacker does not know keywords. For example, in MySQL, this can be done by altering the symbols in the C header file sql/lex.h. This file contains a symbols array defining the keywords and the operators of the language. In the same manner, an array named sql_functions defines the SQL functions.

As a results of the changes, the diversified version of SQL engine excepts something like this as an input (here we have just added numbers after the keywords for clarity, but naturally the keywords could be better obscured):

```
SELECT3892 id FROM6370 users WHERE2081 username='username'
                 AND1187 password='password' OR0385 1=1'
```

The attacker, in the attack described above, has to know how the keyword OR is presented in the diversified language in order to be successful. For additional security, operators can be diversified as well. Also, the expected diversification of a keyword can even vary depending on time or on the location of that specific keyword in the statement. This way, even if the process of searching for SQL injection vulnerabilities is automated with a program like "Advanced Power" chances for success are very slim. Moreover, continuous attempts to guess keywords of the diversified language can be detected and stopped.

The attacks and countermeasures are summarized in Table 1.

4 Discussion

The previously discussed examples have shown that novel proactive solutions are needed in today's complex threat landscape. In this study, we have further

Table 1. Summary of attacks and countermeasures.

Attack	Countermeasure	Performance overhead
Malicious use of library functions	Diversify symbols in binaries	None/negligible
SQL injection	Use diversified SQL	Modest
Shell script injection	Use diversified command shell	Modest/moderate

demonstrated the effectiveness of internal interface diversification by presenting several real-life examples of vulnerabilities and exploits that can be defeated with diversification. Internal interface diversification prevents – or at the very least mitigates – several different exploits and vulnerabilities.

Internal interface diversification as a security measure has several advantages. First, it is a solution that effectively helps to mitigate the threat of large-scale cyber attacks targeting interfaces (e.g. injection attacks). Billions of devices are being distributed with identical publicly known interfaces. By breaking this software monoculture, diversification prevents the attackers from building a single exploit that could easily attack all instances of a specific piece of software.

Second, as we have mentioned, internal interface diversification causes only a negligible overhead in many cases. Many IoT devices, for instance, only have extremely limited resources in terms of computational power and memory. Diversification is a good fit for this environment because it only incurs either very small overheads or no overhead at all. Simply replacing the system call numbers with new ones or altering the keywords of a domain-specific language often has no performance penalties and no unfavorable effect on memory usage. Compared to resource intensive security solutions that scan the system for malware or monitor processes to detect abnormal behavior, interface diversification is much less performance-intensive. This also has positive implications on energy efficiency: in many cases, interface diversification provides a nice trade-off between sufficient security and energy consumption.

Third, many devices are not updated regularly or updates may be absent altogether. There are some embedded devices, for example, that cannot be updated at all. Still, when a vulnerability is found, these devices are left exposed to malicious attacks. Interface diversification does not (always) prevent the malware from entering the system and it most definitely does not fix vulnerabilities, but it makes it much more difficult for a harmful program to operate in the surrounding system. This also makes interface diversification *proactive*: it protects the system against many zero-day exploits that are not publicly known at the time they happen.

Fourth, although interface diversification is not a silver bullet that protects against all attacks, it is *orthogonal* in the sense it can be used in combination with other security measures such as encryption and intrusion detection systems. Moreover, internal interface diversification can act as a safeguard when some other security measure fails (such as weak passwords in Mirai's case). At the same time, diversification also has a wide applicability, as it can be applied practically to any critical internal interface in a computer system.

Finally, interface diversification usually prevents the propagation of malware. When a piece of malware cannot operate on a machine, it cannot spread to the surrounding network. This makes building botnets such as Mirai significantly more difficult.

Of course, there are also some limitations in the presented approach. First, internal interface diversification cannot prevent all attacks. For example, in Return-oriented Programming (ROP) attacks, the attacker executes carefully selected instruction sequences that are already present in the memory. By chaining these sequences together, an adversary can execute arbitrary code on the machine. Because these attacks do not depend on the well-known interfaces the same way many other attacks do, diversification is not in general a very effective measure against these attacks. There are, however, also some positive results on using fine-grained diversification to mitigate ROP attacks [11, 27].

Another limitation is that setting up the diversified system is not completely straightforward, as all trusted programs have to be diversified so that they correspond to the diversified interfaces. There are, however, promising results regarding automatic diversification of binaries [18, 23]. It would seem diversification is a very feasible security approach at especially in smaller environments with restricted set of programs such as IoT operating systems and devices.

5 Conclusion

In the current study, we have discussed internal interface diversification as a method that prevents malware from using the important resources of the target system. We presented analysis of three different real world attacks and demonstrated how diversifying different interfaces can prevent these attacks from working.

While diversification of internal interfaces has been discussed in the academic literature, operating systems and other pieces of software still do not widely employ this solution in practice – address space layout randomization being the only exception. However, although internal interface diversification may not provide the most usable security solution for all systems – such as a system of an average home user – at the moment, we believe it has lots of potential in systems with relatively small number of programs, especially in lightweight IoT operating systems. Therefore, we hope to see practical diversification solutions implemented and used to protect operating systems in the near future.

References

1. Abadi, M., Plotkin, G.: On protection by layout randomization. In: 2010 23rd IEEE Computer Security Foundations Symposium, pp. 337–351 (2010)

2. Albanese, M., Jajodia, S.: Proactive defense through deception. Industrial Control Systems Security and Resiliency. AIS, vol. 75, pp. 169–202. Springer, Cham (2019). https://doi.org/10.1007/978-3-030-18214-4_9

3. AVTest: Malware statictics. https://www.av-test.org/en/statistics/malware/. Accessed 20 Aug 2019

4. Boyd, S., Kc, G., Locasto, M., Keromytis, A.: On the general applicability of instruction-set randomization. IEEE Trans. Dependable Secure Comput. **7**(3), 255–270 (2008)

5. Boyd, S.W., Keromytis, A.D.: SQLrand: preventing SQL injection attacks. In: Jakobsson, M., Yung, M., Zhou, J. (eds.) ACNS 2004. LNCS, vol. 3089, pp. 292–302. Springer, Heidelberg (2004). https://doi.org/10.1007/978-3-540-24852-1_21

6. Chew, M., Song, D.: Mitigating buffer overflows by operating system randomization. Technical report, CMU (2002)

7. Chongkyung, K., Jinsuk, J., Bookholt, C., Xu, J., Peng, N.: Address space layout permutation (ASLP): towards fine-grained randomization of commodity software. In: Computer Security Applications Conference. ACSAC 2006, pp. 339–348 (2006)

8. Cloudflare: Inside the infamous Mirai IoT Botnet: a retrospective analysis. https://blog.cloudflare.com/inside-mirai-the-infamous-iot-botnet-a-retrospective-analysis/. Accessed 20 Aug 2019

9. Cohen, F.: Operating system protection through program evolution. Comput. Secur. **12**(6), 565–584 (1993)

10. Evans, N., Horsthemke, W.: Active defense techniques. In: Kott, A., Linkov, I. (eds.) Cyber Resilience of Systems and Networks. RSD, pp. 221–246. Springer, Cham (2019). https://doi.org/10.1007/978-3-319-77492-3_10

11. Gupta, A., Kerr, S., Kirkpatrick, M.S., Bertino, E.: Marlin: a fine grained randomization approach to defend against ROP attacks. In: Lopez, J., Huang, X., Sandhu, R. (eds.) NSS 2013. LNCS, vol. 7873, pp. 293–306. Springer, Heidelberg (2013). https://doi.org/10.1007/978-3-642-38631-2_22

12. Imperva: Breaking down Mirai: an IoT DDoS botnet analysis. https://www.imperva.com/blog/malware-analysis-mirai-ddos-botnet/. Accessed 20 Aug 2019

13. Jiang, X., Wang, H.J., Xu, D., Wang, Y.: RandSys: thwarting code injection attacks with system service interface randomization. In: 26th IEEE International Symposium on Reliable Distributed Systems. SRDS 2007, pp. 209–218 (2007)

14. Kambourakis, G., Kolias, C., Stavrou, A.: The Mirai botnet and the IoT zombie armies. In: MILCOM 2017–2017 IEEE Military Communications Conference (MILCOM), pp. 267–272 (2017)

15. Kc, G., Keromytis, A., Prevelakis, V.: Countering code-injection attacks with instruction-set randomization. In: Proceedings of the 10th ACM Conference on Computer and Communications Security. CCS 2003, New York, NY, USA, pp. 272–280. (2003)

16. Kim, J., Jang, D., Jeong, Y., Kang, B.B.: Polar: Per-allocation object layout randomization. In: 2019 49th Annual IEEE/IFIP International Conference on Dependable Systems and Networks (DSN), pp. 505–516. IEEE (2019)

17. Larsen, P., Brunthaler, S., Franz, M.: Security through diversity: are we there yet? IEEE Secur. Priv. **12**(2), 28–35 (2014)

18. Larsen, P., Homescu, A., Brunthaler, S., Franz, M.: SoK: automated software diversity. In: 2014 IEEE Symposium on Security and Privacy (SP), pp. 276–291 (2014)

19. Liang, Z., Liang, B., Li, L.: A system call randomization based method for countering code injection attacks. In: International Conference on Networks Security, Wireless Communications and Trusted Computing. NSWCTC 2009, pp. 584–587 (2009)

20. Locasto, M., Keromytis, A.: PachyRand: SQL Randomization for the PostgreSQL JDBC Driver. Technical report CUCS-033-05. Columbia University, Computer Science (2005)

21. Mirai source code: https://github.com/jgamblin/Mirai-Source-Code. Accessed 20 Aug 2019

22. Portokalidis, G., Keromytis, A.D.: Global ISR toward a comprehensive defense against unauthorized code execution. In: Jajodia, S., Ghosh, A., Swarup, V., Wang, C., Wang, X. (eds.) Moving Target Defense. Advances in Information Security, vol. 54, pp. 49–76. Springer, New York (2011). https://doi.org/10.1007/978-1-4614-0977-9_3

23. Rauti, S., Laurén, S., Hosseinzadeh, S., Mäkelä, J.-M., Hyrynsalmi, S., Leppänen, V.: Diversification of system calls in linux binaries. In: Yung, M., Zhu, L., Yang, Y. (eds.) INTRUST 2014. LNCS, vol. 9473, pp. 15–35. Springer, Cham (2015). https://doi.org/10.1007/978-3-319-27998-5_2

24. Rauti, S., Teuhola, J., Leppänen, V.: Diversifying SQL to prevent injection attacks. In: Proceedings of Trustcom/BigDataSE/ISPA, pp. 344–351 (2015)

25. Rauti, S., et al.: A survey on internal interfaces used by exploits and implications on interface diversification. In: Brumley, B.B., Röning, J. (eds.) NordSec 2016. LNCS, vol. 10014, pp. 152–168. Springer, Cham (2016). https://doi.org/10.1007/978-3-319-47560-8_10

26. Shetty, R., Choo, K.-K.R., Kaufman, R.: Shellshock vulnerability exploitation and mitigation: a demonstration. In: Abawajy, J., Choo, K.-K.R., Islam, R. (eds.) ATCI 2017. AISC, vol. 580, pp. 338–350. Springer, Cham (2018). https://doi.org/10.1007/978-3-319-67071-3_40

27. Sinha, K., Kemerlis, V.P., Sethumadhavan, S.: Reviving instruction set randomization. In: 2017 IEEE International Symposium on Hardware Oriented Security and Trust (HOST), pp. 21–28 (2017)

28. Uitto, J., Rauti, S., Mäkelä, J.M., Leppänen, V.: Preventing malicious attacks by diversifying Linux shell commands. In: Proceedings of the 14th Symposium on Programming Languages and Software Tools. SPLST 2015, CEUR Workshop Proceedings, vol. 1525 (2015)

29. Wang, C., Lu, Z.: Cyber deception: overview and the road ahead. IEEE Secur. Priv. 16(2), 80–85 (2018)

30. Xu, H., Chapin, S.: Address-space layout randomization using code islands. J. Comput. Secur. 17(3), 331–362 (2009)

Braille Based Steganography System Using Dynamic Key Exchange

Shreyas Sriram[✉], Susheel Polani Sathishkumar, and J. Bhuvana

Department of Computer Science and Engineering, SSN College of Engineering,
Chennai, Tamilnadu, India
{shreyas16101,susheel16111}@cse.ssn.edu.in, bhuvanaj@ssn.edu.in

Abstract. Cryptography provides a method for obscuring the original data, whereas steganography provides a means for obscuring the mere presence of data. Many different carriers are used such as audio, video, images etc. to hide the data. Images are the most commonly used carriers. Once the data is hidden, the image can then be sent to the receiver. This method is secure because only the sender and receiver are aware of the communication. Many different steganographic techniques have been proposed for secure data communication, but these are highly vulnerable to attacks when the presence of hidden data is exposed. In this paper, an improved image steganography method is proposed. The data is initially encrypted using RSA algorithm. Instead of using the traditional Least Significant Bit encoding, the proposed system uses a method similar to the Braille form of character representation. Using this representation, the encrypted text and the key are encoded into the image. The resultant image is the steganographic image that is used for communication. This proposed method has proven to be more secure than the existing methods. The results and experiments have been explained in detail.

Keywords: Steganography · RSA · Dynamic key · Cryptography · Braille · PSNR · MHC

1 Introduction

The world of technology as we know, is growing rapidly. People's access to technology has risen by large margins in the past decade. The number of social media platforms available is innumerable. This has resulted in mind-boggling figures in terms of data generated every day. Such amounts of data in the wrong hands combined with the right usage, can prove to be disastrous. Hence, there is a high need for protection of data in today's world.

There are several ways to protect data. One way is to encrypt the data. Data encryption is a method where the original data is changed into an intelligible form such that the original data cannot be retrieved without a specific required key [8]. Another way is to hide the fact that the data is present in the first place, this is referred to as steganography. Most steganographic techniques use

© Springer Nature Singapore Pte Ltd. 2020
S. M. Thampi et al. (Eds.): SSCC 2019, CCIS 1208, pp. 360–373, 2020.
https://doi.org/10.1007/978-981-15-4825-3_29

images, videos, audios to perform the hiding. Steganography is based on the ch2aracteristic that a negligible change to the pixel values of the carrier signal will not affect the perceivable quality of the signal. The inability of the human visual system is exploited to perform steganography using images. Thus, data can be hidden in images with a high amount of security [1].

Traditional methods of steganography involve direct sequential manipulation of the Least Significant Bit (LSB) in order to hide data. This paper proposes an enhanced form of data hiding technique that uses a method similar to the Braille form of character representation to hide data. Traditional Braille uses a 6-bit matrix to represent characters. Since RSA algorithm is used in this proposed method, the output encrypted data constitutes only digits [3]. Hence, it was concluded that 4 bits are sufficient to represent each digit. Using a 4-bit matrix representation, instead of a 6-bit representation, also increases the Maximum Hiding Capacity (MHC).

This paper is organized as follows. Section 1 is an introduction. Section 2 introduces the related work done previously to the proposed system. Section 3 introduces proposed method in detailed. Section 4 contains the experimental results pertaining to the proposed system. Section 5 presents the conclusion of the experimental results and also about the scope and expandability of the proposed methodology.

2   Related Works

In [2], the authors encode the secret message into the image using Braille method representation of characters. Each character in Braille is represented using only six dots using the 6 - dots matrix called (Braille Cell). First the secret message is stripped and each character is converted to its equivalent Braille representation. As each character needs 6 bits for Braille representation, the unfilled 6 pixels are taken from the image and LSB is applied on those pixel value. While decryption, 6 pixels are read at a time and based on the pixel values, the Braille Cell is constructed which is later decrypted to its character equivalent to form the message.

In [5], the authors proposed a new LSB method rather than the general LSB-1 of the cover for hiding the message. LSB-3 which is a method in which the third least significant bit of the pixel has been used for encoding the particular message bit and the first and second bits are modified according to the message bit. By changing the first and second bits accordingly, the overall PSNR value is improved.

In [6], the authors proposed a dynamic key cryptography scheme in which the keys for encryption and decryption are used just once. This significantly improves the security of the algorithm. The dynamic key scheme is implemented to enhance the performance and security of the cryptographic algorithms.

In [7], the authors talk about the various attacks on the steganography system and some tools to decrypt the obvious messages. Steganography is just meant to hide data and does not guarantee the confidentiality of the message whereas cryptography focuses mainly on the confidentiality of the message.

In [3], the authors proposed a highly secure encryption method called RSA. It is a public key cryptography method. It requires a pair of prime numbers (p, q) to be chosen by both parties. A public key (e, n) and a private key (d, n) are generated from the pair (p, q). This method is based on the difficulty of factorizing a large prime number.

In [10], the authors have applied various steganalysis techniques on the common LSB based techniques. As steganography is becoming significant day by day, we also need to check whether the data hiding method still serves its purpose on the present standards. Therefore a cryptanalysis is performed on various LSB based steganography methods. This result is used to compare the security aspect of any steganography based encryption method.

In [11], the authors have proposed a LSB based encryption of steganography image which takes the 1st, 2nd, 3rd and last bit of every pixel and performs triple XOR operations among them for encrypting the secret message accordingly. MSE and PSNR parameters are used to compare the results.

In [12], the authors have proposed a method to check whether an image has any secret messages encoded in it also knows as steganalysis. Among the various methods used, one of them includes comparing the PSNR and Chi-Sqaured value of the encrypted image to that of the original clan image. If the parameters have deviations then the image is said to be tampered.

In [13], the authors have proposed a method to compare various image steganography methods. The most frequently used comparison parameter are PSNR, MSE and MHC.

The authors of [14] have added the security analysis along with the parameter comparison which includes testing of pixel difference by brute force and parameter variations compared to the original image.

3   Proposed System

The proposed system uses a combination of cryptography, dynamic keys [6] and steganography to enhance the security of communication between two parties. A diagrammatic representation of the system is shown in Fig. 1. The plain text characters are first mapped to their equivalent ASCII values [9]. Then, these ASCII values are encrypted using RSA cipher to obtain the cipher text. The cipher text and the key are converted to a matrix representation and encoded in the image to obtain the steganographic image. This image is then sent to the receiver. On receiving, the matrix representation of hidden cipher text and the key are read. This representation is converted to a text form using matrix decoding. Then, the plain text is obtained by deciphering the cipher text using the key.

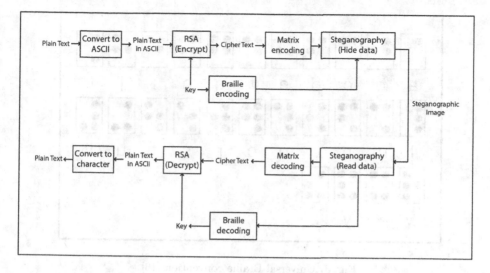

Fig. 1. Overview of the proposed system

A comparison between the cover image and output image of the proposed system has been provided in Fig. 2. There is no visually perceivable difference between the two images.

Fig. 2. Comparision of before and after encoding

The existing method uses Braille encoding [16], a 6-bit matrix representation, to encode data in an image which is shown in Fig. 3. This type of encoding is weak and the hidden data is vulnerable to attacks.

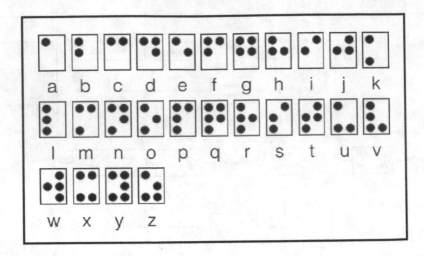

Fig. 3. Universal Braille convention [16]

In the proposed method, a 4-bit matrix is used. With a 4-bit matrix representation, it is possible to represent $2^4 = 16$ characters. Out of the 16 possible representations, 12 have been used. The proposed 4-bit matrix is given in Fig. 4. An empty matrix represents "End of text". An example to represent the number "343" has been given in Fig. 5.

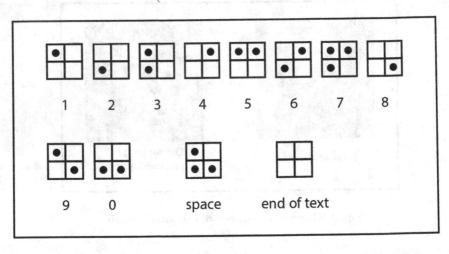

Fig. 4. Proposed 4-bit matrix representation

Each cell in the 4-bit matrix can be thought of as a pixel in an image. This is shown in Fig. 6. To represent a dot in a cell, the LSB value of the corresponding pixel is set to 1. Similarly, to represent a dot-less cell, the LSB value of the corresponding pixel is set to 0. Characters along with their 4-bit matrix cell representation is given in Table 1. The values represent the cells in which the LSB is set to 1.

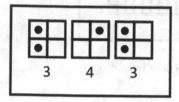

Fig. 5. Sample representation of number 343

Fig. 6. Mapping of 4-bit matrix to image pixels

Table 1. Dot positions for encoding characters

Character	Cells numbers with Black dot
1	1
2	2
3	1, 2
4	3
5	1, 3
6	2, 3
7	1, 2, 3
8	4
9	1, 4
0	2, 4
Space	1, 2, 4
End of text	

By this convention, the entire data can be encoded in an image as shown in Fig. 7.

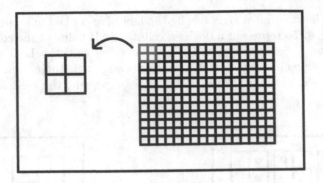

Fig. 7. Expanded view of 4 bit matrices in an Image

Steganographic techniques are safe as long as the fact that a hidden data is present is unknown. Existing techniques like LSB, LSBraille [1,2] are highly susceptible to data exposure once it is known that hidden data is present in an image. To address this issue, the data is encrypted using a dynamic key. A dynamic key is a key that changes every time. This ensures an extra layer of security for communications.

RSA cipher has been used to encrypt and decrypt data in this proposed system. RSA fundamentally requires a pair of prime numbers, p and q. These two are then multiplied to obtain n, which is a basis for choosing a key [3]. This system required the two parties A and B to initially share a common pair (p_0, q_0). During the following communications, party A chooses a new value for p (p_1) and performs RSA encryption using p_1 and q_0. Then the encrypted data is encoded in the image along with n (p_1 x q_0). By this method, only the n value is known to any interceptor of the image. RSA is based on the difficulty of factorizing n, hence it becomes difficult for the interceptor to break the encryption by just knowing n. On the other side of the communication, party B can easily factorize n. Since the previous q (q_0) is known, p_1 can easily be derived from n. The encrypted message can then be decrypted using the pair (p_1, q_0). To reply back to party A, party B can choose a new value for q (q_1). Using p_1 and q_1, n can be calculated. The data is then encrypted using this n and encoded in the image along with the new value of n. Receiver A can then follow the same method for decryption as described before. Further communication can happen by changing p and q successively and sharing the corresponding n along with the data within an image. This system of communication is shown in Fig. 8.

Since the possible values of RSA encryption ranges from *1* to *(n-1)*, the number of bytes to encode for each character varies according to n. For example, if $p = 17$ and $q = 23$, then $n = 391$. In this case, we need 3 bytes to encode each input character. For instance, RSA encryption of the text *"hi"* will produce a 6 (2 × 3) byte output. The same number of bytes will have to be read in order to decrypt the cipher text at the receiver end.

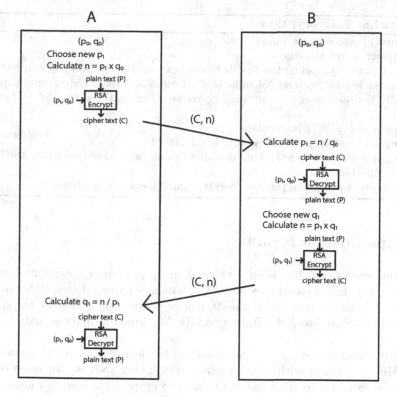

Fig. 8. Data flow between two parties

A detailed encryption and decryption algorithm for the proposed system is given in Algorithms 1 and 2 respectively. The initial step is for the sender and receiver to agree upon two prime numbers p_0, q_0 and e.

Algorithm 1. Encryption

Input: Cover Image I; Secret Message M; Prime Numbers p, q
Output: Steganographic Image S

1 A new prime number p_{i+1} is chosen
2 Using p_{i+1} and q_i, public key (e,n) is calculated
3 M is converted into its ASCII characters with spaces unchanged to get Plain ASCII Text *plainAsciiText*
4 The ASCII bytes of *plainAsciiText* are encrypted using (e,n) to get Cipher ASCII Text *cipherAsciiText*
5 Pad every byte of *cipherAsciiText* to get a constant length that is equal to the size of n
6 Embed bytes of *cipherAsciiText* into I by changing the pixel values according to Braille representation
7 Embed *End Of Text*
8 Embed bytes of n into I by changing the pixel values according to Braille representation
9 Embed *End Of Text*

Algorithm 2. Decryption

Input: Steganographic Image S; Key n
Output: Secret Message M

1 n is obtained by reading the Braille blocks between the two *End Of Text* blocks
2 From the beginning, read N Braille blocks from S at a time, convert into Cipher ASCII Text and store it in an array *cipherAsciiText* until the *End Of Text* is read
3 Using n and q_i, p_{i+1} is calculated
4 Using p_{i+1} and q_i, private key *(d,n)* is calculated
5 The bytes of *cipherAsciiText* are decrypted using *(d,n)* to obtain Plain ASCII Text *plainAsciiText*
6 The bytes of *plainAsciiText* are converted into characters to obtain M

---

4   Experimental Results

The proposed system has been developed using python. Experimental results have been concluded based on standard test images namely Lena, Baboon, Barbara, Lost Lake. To measure the performance of the proposed system, parameters like Peak Signal-to-Noise Ratio (PSNR), Maximum hiding Capacity (MHC) were used.

Table 2 summarizes the results for a fixed key length of 3. As it can be seen, the MHC is constant with a given image size. The PSNR is also more or less within the same range. This indicates that the proposed system is robust.

Table 2. Variation of PSNR and MHC for various images

Image	Image size	MHC (Bytes)	PSNR
Lena	256×256	5459	51.1424
Lena	512×512	21843	51.1314
Baboon	512×512	21843	51.1458
Barbara	512×512	21843	51.1348
Lost Lake	512×512	21843	51.1456

The MHC in the proposed system is fundamentally dependent on the value of the key length (n). This has been tabulated in Tables 3 and 4 for two different image sizes. It is clearly seen that there is an inverse relationship between the key length (n) and MHC. A balance between the two parameters is necessary for an efficient usage of the proposed system.

Table 3. Variation of MHC with key length for image size 256 × 256

Key Length (bytes)	MHC
3	5459
256	62
512	30
1024	14

Table 4. Variation of MHC with key length for image size 512 × 512

Key Length (bytes)	MHC
3	21843
256	254
512	126
1024	62

A comparison between the LSBraille method [2] and the proposed system reveals that the PSNR of the proposed method is slightly lower. This is due to the usage of a 4-bit matrix instead of a 6-bit matrix for character encoding. Using a 4-bit matrix is more efficient and compact, hence the PSNR ratio is slightly lower. The proposed system also provides an extra layer of security by using dynamic keys. The slightly lower PSNR is a trade-off for the better security of the system.

A comparison between SMMWB method [4] and the proposed system has been shown in Table 5. PSNR has been calculated by taking the MHC for both systems respectively. It is evident that the PSNR is better in the proposed system by significant numbers. Table 6 compares the PSNR of the method [11] and the proposed method for message length = MHC. The key length (n) is chosen to be 3 for the proposed method. Although the PSNR of the proposed method is slightly lower, it is an acceptable value and moreover, it provides enhanced security as discussed above.

Table 5. Comparison of PSNR between SMMWB [4] method and Proposed method

Image	Image size	PSNR	
		SMMWB [4]	Proposed method
Lena	256 × 256	45.3325	51.1424
Lena	512 × 512	45.4991	51.1314
Baboon	512 × 512	45.1437	51.1458

Table 6. Comparison of PSNR between method [11] and Proposed method

Image	Method [11]	Proposed method
Cameraman	54.665	51.124
Barbara	54.037	51.143
Lena	54.616	51.116

Steganographic systems are evaluated based on 3 broad categories namely Capacity, Distortion and Secureness [14]. Capacity refers to the maximum amount of data the system is able to hide. Distortion measures the amount of difference between the carrier image and the steganographic image. And finally, secureness evaluates the overall difficulty to break the system and extract the hidden information. As already discussed, MHC and PSNR have been used as a metric to evaluate the capacity and distortion of the system, respectively.

Multiple levels have to be bypassed in order to access the hidden information in an image using this proposed system. The security analysis of the system is done from the standpoint of an interceptor who has access to an image. First and foremost, it must be identified that the image obtained is a steganographic image. If the carrier image is available to the interceptor, this can be done by comparing the carrier image with the steganographic image. The difference in pixel values will reveal that changes have been made to the carrier image. But if the carrier image is not available, it becomes difficult to analyse the steganographic image. Two common attacks to find steganographic images are discussed below.

4.1   Visual Attack - Histogram

Figure 9 compares the histogram of the original image and the steganographic image of Lena and Cameraman obtained using the proposed system. Although, it seems like the histograms are unchanged, a closer look reveals the minor differences in the intensity values.

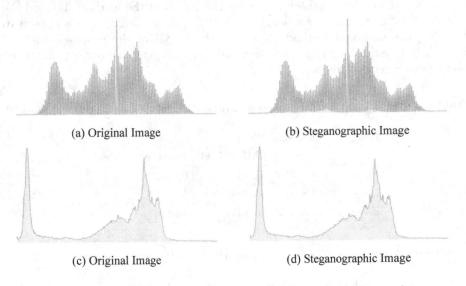

(a) Original Image   (b) Steganographic Image

(c) Original Image   (d) Steganographic Image

Fig. 9. Histogram comparison of Lena (top) and Cameraman (bottom) images

4.2   Statistical Attack - Chi-Square Analysis

In some cases, visual attacks fail to identify steganographic images. In that case, more complex approaches are used. One such approach is Chi-square attack [12].

Figures 10 and 11 show the results of Chi-Square attack on the steganographic images of Lena and Cameraman using the Guillerminto Steganalysis Tool [15]. Steganographic images are identified based on the characteristics of the graphical output of the tool:

1. The spread of the red dots is closer to the value 1
2. The spread of the green dots in closer to the value of 0.50

As seen in Fig. 10(a), the Chi-Square Attack on the original image reveals no presence of hidden data. Whereas in Fig. 10(b), although the red dots are closer to 0, the position of the green dots suggest the presence of hidden data. On the other hand, there is no pattern of green or red dots in Fig. 11(b) that suggests the presence of hidden data. Hence, it can be inferred that the system is robust against common attacks like Chi-Square Attack.

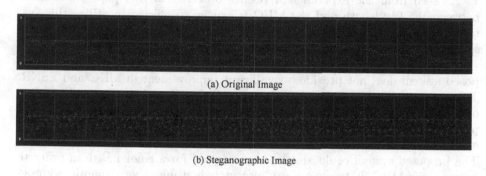

(a) Original Image

(b) Steganographic Image

Fig. 10. Chi-Square Attack on Lena image (Color figure online)

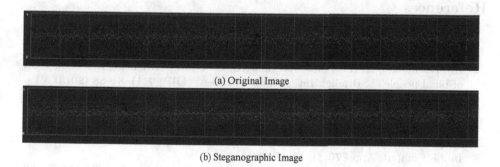

(a) Original Image

(b) Steganographic Image

Fig. 11. Chi-Square Attack on Cameraman image (Color figure online)

The attacks mentioned above suggest that LSB-steganography is used. However there are multiple LSB-steganography techniques and it is difficult to figure out which one is used for a given image. Once the technique used is known, the encrypted message and the n-value can be extracted. The difficulty of decrypting this message depends solely on the value of n(key). The proposed method uses dynamically changing keys based on RSA algorithm along with steganography. Hence, even if the methodology is known to the interceptor, it is extremely difficult to extract meaningful information from the image.

5   Conclusion

The proposed system implements a new methodology for secret message transmission using image steganography and dynamic key exchange. Using dynamic keys, the proposed system provides an additional layer of security. This is in contrast to the existing methods. The evaluating parameters PSNR and MHC are heavily dependent on the key length (n).

As seen from the experimental results observed in this paper, a balance between the key length and the MHC is crucial to efficiently utilize this system. It can also be concluded that the performance of the proposed system is significantly better. This is evident from the results of Table 5.

However, when compared to certain other steganography methods, the proposed system does not provide a significant improvement in MHC and PSNR. This comes at the cost of an overall better secure methodology. Hence depending on various requirements, the methodology can be chosen. A longer key length provides a higher security, but this drastically reduces the MHC. As it was discussed before, there needs to be a balance between the key length and the MHC. The proposed system could also be implemented for a color image in order to improve the MHC. Future work can also include using other dynamic cryptography algorithms in order to make the system even better.

References

1. Johnson, N.F., Jajodia, S.: Exploring steganography: seeing the unseen. Computer **31**, 26–34 (1998)
2. Ali, A.A., Saad, A.-H.S.: Image steganography technique by using Braille method of blind people (LSBraille). Int. J. Image Process. (IJIP) **7**(1), 81–88 (2013)
3. Rivest, R.L., Shamir, A., Adleman, L.: A method for obtaining digital signatures and public-key cryptosystems. Commun. ACM **21**(2), 120–126 (1978)
4. Ali, A.A., et al.: Enhancing SMM image steganography method by using LSBraille image steganography Method (SMMWB; Secret Message Matching With Braille). Int. J. Comput. Appl. **70**(8), 12–17 (2013)
5. Abdul-Sada, A.I.: Hiding data using LSB-3. J. Basrah Res. (Sci.) **33**(4A), 81–88 (2007)
6. Ngo, H.H., Wu, X., Le, P.D., Wilson, C., Srinivasan, B.: Dynamic key cryptography and applications. IJ Network Secur. **10**(3), 161–174 (2010)
7. Westfeld, A., Pfitzmann, A.: Attacks on steganographic systems. In: Pfitzmann, A. (ed.) IH 1999. LNCS, vol. 1768, pp. 61–76. Springer, Heidelberg (2000). https://doi.org/10.1007/10719724_5
8. Gupta, A., Walia, N.K.: Cryptography algorithms: a review. Citeseer (2014)

9. Bhattacharyya, S., Indu, P., Sanyal, G.: Hiding data in text using ASCII mapping technology (AMT). Int. J. Comput. Appl. **70**(18), 29–37 (2013)
10. Rashid, A., Rahim, M.K.: Scrutiny of steganalysis for flipping steganography method. J. Adv. Math. Comput. Sci. **31**(5), 1–18 (2019)
11. Astuti, Y.P., Rachmawanto, E.H., Sari, C.A., et al.: Simple and secure image steganography using LSB and triple XOR operation on MSB. In: 2018 International Conference on Information and Communications Technology (ICOIACT), pp. 191–195 (2018)
12. Mewalal, N., Leung, W.S.: Improving hidden message extraction using LSB steganalysis techniques. In: Kim, K.J., Baek, N. (eds.) ICISA 2018. LNEE, vol. 514, pp. 273–284. Springer, Singapore (2019). https://doi.org/10.1007/978-981-13-1056-0_29
13. Asok, A., Mohan, P.: Implementation and comparison of different data hiding techniques in image steganography. In: 2019 3rd International Conference on Trends in Electronics and Informatics (ICOEI), pp. 1180–1183 (2019)
14. Pradhan, A., Sahu, A.K., Swain, G., Sekhar, K.R.: Performance evaluation parameters of image steganography techniques. In: 2016 International Conference on Research Advances in Integrated Navigation Systems (RAINS), pp. 1–8 (2016)
15. El-Loco G A few tools to discover hidden data. http://www.guillermito2.net/stegano/tools/index.html
16. Braille Facts. https://www.royalblind.org/national-braille-week/about-braille/braille-facts

Author Index

Printed in the United States
By Bookmasters